FAMILIES AND RELIGIONS

FAMILIES AND RELIGIONS

Conflict and Change in Modern Society

edited by

WILLIAM V. D'ANTONIO
JOAN ALDOUS

SAGE PUBLICATIONS
Beverly Hills / London / New Delhi

To Our Parents

Copyright © 1983 by Sage Publications, Inc.

For information address:

SAGE Publications, Inc.
275 South Beverly Drive
Beverly Hills, California 90212

SAGE Publications India Pvt. Ltd.
M-32 Market
Greater Kailash I
New Delhi 110 048 India

SAGE Publications Ltd
28 Banner Street
London EC1Y 8QE
England

Printed in the United States of America

Library of Congress Cataloging in Publication Data

Main entry under title:

Families and religions.

Papers originally presented at a special seminar on families and religions, held at the University of Notre Dame in 1981.
Includes index.
I. Family—United States—Religious life—Congresses.
1. D'Antonio, William V. II. Aldous, Joan.
BV4256.2.A43   1983   291.1'783585'0973   83-3310
ISBN 0-8039-2075-X
ISBN 0-8039-2468-2 (pbk.)

FIRST PAPERBACK PRINTING, 1985

Contents

Preface

This book had its origins in a special seminar on Families and Religions held at the University of Notre Dame during the summer of 1981. All of the chapters contained herein have been prepared especially for this book, and seven of them were presented originally in the summer seminar.

The authors and editors are indebted to Dr. Andrew Weigert, Chairman of the Department of Sociology of the University of Notre Dame, for his encouragement of the idea in the first place, and for his continual friendly criticism and input. We are also indebted to Fr. Robert Austgen, C.S.C., Director of the Notre Dame Summer Programs, for his support of the seminar. And we also are grateful to the University of Connecticut Research Foundation for support in the preparation of the manuscript. The editors also wish to thank the following persons for their help in the preparation of the manuscript: Adele Updike and George Flory, for help in typing and 1000 other tasks that are vital to manuscript preparation; Laura and Raissa D'Antonio, for preparing the subject and author indexes; and Betty Seaver, for editorial help and unflagging good humor at crucial points along the way.

The contributors to this book were selected in part because of their known sensitivity to the subject as well as their expertise. Thus, in fact, some are adherents of the particular religious denominations about which they are writing. They grew up in families with the religious orientation about which they were asked to write. But these essays are in no sense meant to be apologies either for these families or their religious traditions. Rather, the authors' sensitivity to the subject provides the reader an insider's view of families and religious traditions, and of the challenges and tensions posed for these traditions by adaptation and assimilation into American society.

The major thesis is set forth in Part I: The process of modernization in the United States has led to the development of an economic and political system that gives primacy of attention to the individual. The demographic transition that has taken place conjointly with the modernization process has brought about a range of new family and household types, and, consistent with the dominant values of the society, these types focus on the individual and his or her personal concerns. These, in turn, have made obsolete many of the old forms of social control that linked religions so centrally to a group-centered family. In their stead and arising out of the society rather than out of religion have arisen new mechanisms of social support that seem to serve well the variety of new family and household types.

In Part II, we examine the impact of adaptation and assimilation on specific families and religions. We find a range of adjustments and changes among main-line Protestants, Catholics, Jews, blacks, and Hispanics. For all of them, the changing role of women has been a challenge; for some, birth control, divorce, and abortion continue to be troublesome. For others, it's a question of whether religious organizations can provide adequate buffers for families still in the process of adaptation to urban American society. For the religious denominations themselves, an overriding problem is how to translate into an effective normative system their core value of concern for the other.

In Part III, we examine the way that three religious groups are attempting to stand against family change, and against the tide of individualism. The New Christian Right, as Hadden calls them, or the Moral Majority, as they are more commonly called, have been most explicit in rejecting and condemning the family and household types that have emerged during the past 30 years. Their model type is molded out of the pre-World War II traditional religious normative and value system, and they are now trying to use the national political system to turn the tide in their favor.

The Mormons seem at first glance a socioreligious group that has managed to adapt to American society without accepting its modern values and norms as they relate to family life. Yet a closer look shows that they too are struggling against the tide.

We have chosen to include a chapter on the Moonies of the Unification Church as an example of those many smaller social movements in religious circles that have sprung up in recent years, and that clearly struggle against the tide of American individualism and self-centeredness. They offer a way that appears to appeal especially to young and well-educated Americans who find modern family ways unfulfilling.

Americans continue to show a high level of commitment to marriage and family. And they continue to be among the most religious people in the world. In the past, their family life was strongly informed by religion in one form or another. It seems less so today. Generally, the major religions have reacted slowly and reluctantly to the processes of change that have so affected the family. Whether they can now act to develop mechanisms of social support that can enrich and strengthen family life in the decade ahead is one of the key questions emerging from these chapters.

INTRODUCTION
Families and Religions Beset by Friends and Foes

Joan Aldous
William V. D'Antonio

The relationship between families and religions has caught the public's attention in recent years. The diversity of sects and denominations in the United States, the phenomenon that leads us to write of religions in the plural, guarantees lively developments somewhere. The present concern stems from the widely publicized activities of sects such as the Unification Church and its leader, Sun Myung Moon, and more particularly the politics of the "New Christian Right." Both the so-called Moonies and the Moral Majority are dealt with at some length in this volume in chapters by Joseph Fichter and Jeffrey Hadden, respectively.

While Moon and the Moral Majority are attracting much attention, it is important to remember that the great majority of Americans who are church members belong to neither of these groups. Rather, they identify themselves as Jews, Catholics, or members of the long-established Protestant denominations. Thus this book contains chapters devoted to how these religions do and do not continue to influence family lives.

In the following discussion, we put the interest in particular religions and families in broader perspective. We will discuss the common values both institutions share, values that often place them against the tide of values generally characterizing American life. The enduring tension between an emphasis on self-sacrifice for a broader group purpose, one of their concerns, and an emphasis on individual achievement found in other institutions will constitute one of the themes of this introduction. Another theme has to do with the relation between families and religious bodies, specifically with the social control and social support functions of the latter. The discussion of both themes will indicate how the chapters that follow illustrate them, and the differential adjustments being made by various religions and families to the conflicts caused by the clashes between their values and those of other societal structures.

Because of the importance of families and religious bodies, they cannot be forgotten. But the institutions can be sentimentalized, as well as criticized, so that their complexity is overlooked and the very real dilemmas their values and structures present are ignored. We will note how little that sentimentalization, even though it comes from friends of these institutions, helps us to confront and to understand the range and diversity of families and religions that constitute our present society. It is to the sentimentalization of families and religions that we will first address our perspective-setting discussion.

This sentimentalization is most apparent with respect to families. Some 30 years ago, Goode (1956: 3) wrote of the "classical family of Western nostalgia," and this description remains apt. The traditional family with husband-father as breadwinner and wife-mother as housekeeper is one such nostalgic construction. It symbolizes a time when men had much more power. The power was legitimated by the widespread acceptance of patriarchal values, according to which women were expected to center their attention on husbands and children and to maintain the domestic tranquility. Women's economic dependence kept divorce a seldom-used alternative, and planning and parenthood were not associated and unified, and children were better cared for. Moreover, this supposed era of strong families, an era that one wag has located as always being in the decade before each person's birth date, coincided with a United States that had greater control of its economy and its relations with other nations. By concentrating on a "solution" to today's worrisome family problems, people do not have to deal with problems of resource shortages, nuclear weapons proliferation, and the power of multinational corporations. No wonder, then, that the New Right turns its attention to the reinstitutionalization of the traditional family in the broader society, with men as heads of households and women in charge of their day-to-day operations, rather than confronting issues for which solutions are nonexistent or unacceptable.

Such a view of families, however, is quite clearly a product of wishful thinking. Even in earlier periods, there was no one family, traditional or otherwise. Black wives have always had to share the breadwinning role with their husbands, as did wives in immigrant and working-class families (Aldous, 1981; Modell and Hareven, 1973; Smuts, 1959). And, although families in the past may have been more economically interdependent and more stable, people stayed together not always because of love, but because of a lack of acceptable alternatives. In this connection, it is also well to remember that the divorce rate has been rising for the last 100 years (O'Neill, 1973).

The belief that families of the past were centers of concerned child care is another example of rewriting history. It is true that as long as families were production units, children were working along with their parents and under their immediate supervision. But surely no one would wish to return to a family solidarity based on the inexorable demands of the job. There is even some suggestion from the Middletown resurvey project of 1978, notes Elder (1981: 492), that children in Muncie, Indiana, in 1978 had mothers and fathers, whether working or business class, who spent "much more time" with them than did parents of children in 1924 (Caplow and Chadwick, 1979: 331). This was true despite the pronounced increase in the later period of the proportion of business-class wife-mothers engaging in full-time employment outside the home (from 3 to 42 percent) and the continuing high proportion of working-class wife-mothers with such employment (from 44 percent in 1924 to 48 percent in 1978). Too often, family critics judge yesterday's child care as it existed among well-off families rather than among the hard-pressed families intent on obtaining the next meal. Contemporary high standards of child care stem from the shorter working days and greater affluence (two factors Teresa Sullivan mentions in her chapter) that families in all social strata enjoy.

At present, there is a diversity of family types as well as of sects and denominations in the United States. As Table 1 shows, almost one-fifth (17.2 percent) of families are maintained by single parents, about two-fifths (38.3 percent) of families have dual earners, and one-tenth (10.9 percent) of the population lives in nonfamily arrangements. Ultra-rightists, however, are looking to the social control function of religion to force families back into traditional conjugal power arrangements, arrangements that they view as associated with lower divorce rates, less sexual freedom, and better mothers. Women's family roles in such a setup would be prescribed and not a matter of individual choice.

The ultra-rightist sentimentalization of religion does not increase our understanding either. According to this view of religion, its tenets serve to maintain traditional arrangements among convinced communicants and to bring the wavering back into line. Religion, together with old-time families, conservatives see as the repository of the values that made the United States great. Departure from these values, they argue, has led to the present perilous state of the Republic. They remain oblivious to the irony that these values of independence and achievement existed only for white males and that their fulfillment was often at the expense of the collective values central to the existence of both religions and families.

It is true that the code of ethics that religion embodies, along with the norms local religious groups and leaders choose to emphasize from this code, has long served as the basis for social sanctions. It has

TABLE 1   Families by Type and Size: 1978

Type and Size of Family	N (in thousands)	%
Total population	214,159	
in households as family members	190,757	89.1
in nonfamily households	23,402	10.9
Total families	57,215	100.0
Families maintained by a		
Married couple:	47,385	82.8
wife in paid labor force:	21,936	38.3
wife not in paid labor force:	25,449	44.5
Man, no wife present:	1,594	2.8
Woman, no husband present:	8,236	14.4

SOURCE: U.S. Bureau of the Census (1980: 5, 46; 1978: nos. 33, 62, 144, 212, 287, 327) and unpublished 1978 data.

contributed to family solidarity and denominations' continuance, through its emphasis on religious endogamy in marriage, the limiting of sexual intercourse to conjugal relations, and high fertility. Religious sanctions have also operated to support family stability, but sometimes in a context, Joan Aldous argues in her chapter, that assumes traditional marital power relationships. Communicants have conformed to these norms not only because of personal belief, but, as Barbara Hargrove discusses in her chapter on modernization, churches, and families, because of rewarding friendships within the religious body and possible positions of leadership in the group. The fear of gossip and the cutting of emotional ties as a result of nonconformity also keep members in line. These informal sanctions are less ultimate than threats of penalties in the afterlife, but in an increasingly long-lived, present-oriented society, as Sullivan's chapter demonstrates, these informal sanctions may be even more effective.

As a number of scholars, including Hargrove, in her chapter on white Protestant denominations, have noted, religious involvement tends to be associated with conformity to traditional moral codes rather than with diversity in moral perspectives based on individual decisions. Members appear to value conservatism rather than change (Nelson, 1981: 632-633). Hargrove suggests that the charismatic movements within the more liberal main-line Protestant denominations represent conservative lay members' reassertion of conventional values that professional church staff and attenders of denomination conventions may no longer hold. And, as Hargrove points out, these members represent only a minority of all members. The great majority are less liberal.

In other instances the laity and the leadership seem to have drifted apart, with the laity not accepting conservative positions. This is true of Roman Catholics on the issues of birth control, divorce, and the place of women. It is increasingly so for them as regards the issue of abortion, as William D'Antonio and Mark Cavanaugh make clear. Among Jewish leaders, the concern lies in those who have intermarried and are no longer observing religious tenets. Their family behaviors also show differences from those of the religiously committed, as Arnold Dashevsky and Irving Levine note. The fertility rates of these "nonactive" Jews have dropped below 2.0, and they have begun to divorce at the national rate.

The attempt of the New Christian Right to emphasize the social control function of religion in the service of particular family forms runs counter to the main thrust of American life, and to the support features that are common to religions. In a complex, impersonal, bureaucratic society, persons are seeking sources of support for their problems, and families and religions are the most likely sources of affectionate understanding. The religious "ethic of love," as D'Antonio labels this function, is most apparent in the liberal churches, although it is in the smaller, sectlike congregations, with their many associational activities, that close relationships are most easily fostered. It cannot be overlooked, however, that these close relationships provide the mechanism for the exclusionary features inherent in the social control function of religion. Moreover, to rally support, as Hadden discusses in connection with the New Christian Right, it is easier to be against something, such as equal rights for women, or abortions, than for something, such as loving one's neighbor. This is particularly true when the neighbor holds other views, belongs to another religion, and, despite Jesus' example of the good Samaritan, is a neighbor only in a figurative, not a locational, sense. Thus tension exists for religions between the need to maintain a code of ethics, one source of the self-control structure individuals must develop, and the need to supply the unconditional emotional support individuals require in an impersonal society.

Families, like religious bodies, have difficulties providing this support, as high divorce rates and parent-child conflicts indicate. Most persons, whether or not in the "moral majority," hold unrealistic expectations of families. The weaker family members in terms of age and gender, with their lesser access to family resources, have experienced frustration, as have husband-fathers unable to meet the demands of wives and children for power or consumer goods.

Few families enjoy the luxury of controlling their situations. What gets played out on the family stage is affected by what goes on in the workplace and in the school room. Family members with the best will in the world may be unable to get along together in spite of the strictures and beliefs of religious leaders. Psychologist Jerome Kagan (1980: 63) points out that there is little "firm evidence" for the belief that psychological qualities in two-year-olds will be predictive of "similar or theoretically related behaviors" ten years later. Children's development of a self-concept serves to mediate what aspects of those around them they take on, and those around them constitute an ever-expanding set of significant others. These include peers, teachers, and television figures, as well as parents. Parents and especially mothers continue to blame themselves, just as do persons seeking a "quick fix" for problems of delinquency and drug use when children turn out bad. The inability to love one another and to be supportive of other members' emotional needs despite personal longing to do so is a somber aspect of family life that draws families to religion.

While blacks and Hispanics remain our largest and most oppressed minorities, we find in the chapters by Jacquelyne Jackson and Joseph Fitzpatrick that religion has very different meaning and experience for them. In the past, blacks looked to their churches and religious leaders for support to ease the pain of living in a racist society. And when blacks used the boycott and took to the streets and highways to demonstrate their refusal to accept discrimination, religious leaders were in the forefront. But social control also played a part. Martin Luther King, for example, sought to exercise the social control function of churches in the interest of nonviolence among his followers in their push for equal rights.

The Hispanic Catholic tradition is patriarchal and social control oriented. While the tradition remains strong among a minority of Hispanics, Fitzpatrick makes clear that the majority of Hispanics are essentially not active church members, and there is a significant movement toward Protestant Fundamentalism. In addition to promoting strong measures of social control, Fundamentalist churches are noted for their show of love and caring for those who are committed members.

Families and religions are also brought together by a shared set of values that sets them against the tide of the prevailing values in American society. These values can create painful dilemmas for family members that add to the difficulties family members face in attempting to love one another. As D'Antonio discusses in this volume, the primary values in the United States focus on individual achievement, efficiency and equality of opportunity. Hargrove, in her analysis of modernization and religion in the light of the Protestant Reformation, also emphasizes individualism as central to the loosening of control over their members that families and religious bodies have experienced in the last four centuries. Values that judge the worth of individuals in terms of what they accomplish run counter to the collectivist values underlying families and religions. Individuals in these groups are accepted on the basis of ascription, not achievement. Consanguineous and collective ties form the basis for group acceptance, and cooperation and self-sacrifice are emphasized. With such values buttressing their activities, religions and families encourage a diffuse sense of duty, obligation, and caring for their members.

Not all family and denomination members, however, have been equally affected by these values. Men have been caught up in the competitive world of the wage earner, while women have maintained the cooperative world of the homemaker. As the numbers of women employed outside the home increase, they more often face the dilemma, long felt by men, of whether individual or collective values will take precedence. Shall they continue to demonstrate the loving values of the latter or the get-ahead values of the former? As Degler (1980: 472) points out, it is the "humanity and interrelatedness" of family life that is central to the institution. It is also adherence to these family and religious values that prevents women from fulfilling their individual interests in occupational and community spheres. This dilemma, felt by many women and some men, contributes to the inability of both to be loving to other family members. The differential way the dilemma is being confronted by Jews, Catholics, and Protestant denominations is addressed in just about every chapter in this book, with Darwin Thomas's analysis of the Mormons particularly relevant.

Families and religions will continue to abide (Degler, 1980: 473). Unconditional acceptance in some groups is too important for persons to cease being concerned about and involved in the two institutions. This is the case even though there are commitment costs in terms of vulnerability to emotional hurt from group members and failure to achieve in terms of societal standards. Along with the abiding nature of these institutions goes the continuing value tension between them and the broader society. Without these institutions, individuals would lack any alternative to the dehumanizing aspects of a large-scale, impersonal society. The current struggle over primacy and focus of the social control and social support functions of religions indicates the uneasy nature of the relation between families and religions. But without this relation both would be weakened in their attempts to make life more lovable in an often careless society.

REFERENCES

Aldous, J. (1981) "From dual-earner to dual-career families and back again." Journal of Family Issues 2: 115-125.
Caplow, T. and C. A. Chadwick (1979) "Inequality and life-styles in Middletown, 1920-1978." Social Science Quarterly 60: 367-383.
Degler, C. N. (1980) At Odds: Women and the Family in America from the Revolution to the Present. New York: Oxford University Press.
Elder, Jr., G. H. (1981) "History and the family: the discovery of complexity." Journal of Marriage and the Family 43: 489-519.
Goode, W. J. (1956) After Divorce. New York: Macmillan.
Kagan, J. (1980) "Perspectives on continuity," pp. 26-75 in O. G. Brim, Jr., and J. Kagan (eds.) Constancy and Changes in Human Development. Cambridge, MA: Harvard University Press.
Modell, J. and T. K. Hareven (1973) "Urbanization and the malleable household." Journal of Marriage and the Family 35: 466-479.
Nelson, H. M. (1981) "Religious conformity in an age of disbelief: contextual effects of time, denomination and family processes upon church decline and apostasy." American Sociological Review 46: 632-640.
O'Neill, W. L. (1973) Divorce in the Progressive Era. New Haven, CT: Yale University Press.
Smuts, R. W. (1959) Women and Work in America. New York: Columbia University Press.
U.S. Bureau of the Census (1980) Social Indicators III: Selected Data on Social Conditions and Trends in the United States. Washington, DC: Government Printing Office.
————— (1978) Current Population Reports, Series P-20. Washington, DC: Government Printing Office.

Part 1

The Setting

This opening section includes four essays designed to help the reader understand the setting within which the diverse family types and religious denominations are interacting. In the opening chapter, Hargrove examines the modernization process and the impact it has had on the church and the family. Indeed, she shows how its roots are firmly located in the Reformation. In one sense, the values that dominate American society, such as achievement, individualism and success, and rationality and practicality, are direct outgrowths of and one way to define what modernization means. While modernization may have its roots in religion, its consequences have been disruptive of both religion and family life, and Hargrove points to the way this has come about. And while she illustrates how modernization has consistently eroded the authority of religion and family to maintain control over their members, she is not entirely pessimistic. For she does see evidence that as the external constraints have eroded, some of the more liberal churches at least have begun to place more emphasis on support mechanisms and the development of an ethic of love that may yet revitalize the relationship between religion and family.

In Chapter 2, Sullivan approaches the question of the relationship between religion and family indirectly. If the demographic transition can be said to be one of the major consequences of the modernization process, it has seldom been recognized as having the consequences for family life that Sullivan suggests. Her major thesis is that contemporary family behaviors, especially concerning divorce, contraception, abortion, premarital sexuality, and women's greater equality, arise from changed demographics and their impact on corporate bodies such as religion. She speculates that religions' social control mechanisms may have fit well in societies that had high fertility and high mortality rates as their normal way, but these mechanisms are outmoded in modern society.

The demographic transition has made possible long-lasting interpersonal relations, but it has also made possible increasing tension, conflict, and strife among people challenged to develop relationships in a new setting. The transition now allows the family to concentrate on love, nurturance, and support, luxuries until now. The failure to develop intimate, affectional supportive relationships may lead to what Sullivan calls "pseudodeath" and "social death" responses. But on the positive side, she sees the opportunity available to modern peoples to develop long-lasting affectional relations among three and four generations, each of limited numbers. Indeed, she argues that most individuals can only afford a limited amount of affectional bonding; thus, low fertility makes sense emotionally as well as socially, economically, and politically. At the same time, religions need to rethink the issues of family morality in light of the demographic changes and their implications.

In Chapter 3, Aldous probes some of the specific areas of family life and religion in which the relationships have become problematic. She notes that family members have always looked to religion for comfort and support in times of crises, such as death and dying. And today there are added crises of divorce and abortion; clergy from several denominations may find themselves constrained by their official teachings from providing the support needed or desired. The problems are particularly acute in the area of the changing roles of women, confronted as they are by a largely male clergy relying on a patriarchal theology. Aldous concludes with an examination of the possible organizational responses to these challenges, for example, an increase in the number of women in church leadership positions.

In Chapter 4, D'Antonio examines the impact of society's dominant economic and political structures and values on family life and religion. Most families accept and attempt to live by these values and structures, and they have worked them into their lifestyles even though they often cause tension and conflict with the traditional values of family life. Indeed, as D'Antonio suggests, families have generally opted to embrace the societal values over traditional religious or family values. More than that, the overwhelming dominance of individualism has led to social movements involving students and women that have led to more open and permissive attitudes toward sexuality, divorce, and women working. It is in this sense that the efforts of the Moral Majority, the hierarchy of the Roman Catholic Church, the Mormons, and the Unification Church to try to return the society to traditional values are doomed to failure. While the American family life that has evolved is far from perfect, it does fit with the dominant values and structures, and most Americans seem satisfied with the fit. In D'Antonios view, the challenge is not to restore the old ways, but to find ways to strengthen the support structures, to reach out beyond the narrow confines of the small family unit, to encourage religions to preach gospels of love and not of law.

1

THE CHURCH, THE FAMILY, AND THE MODERNIZATION PROCESS

Barbara Hargrove

Processes of modernization have had an ambiguous relationship to organized religion in Western culture. The modern world is socially and psychologically different from the premodern world once defined as Christendom, and one evidence of that change can be seen in alterations of the definition and function of the family and of the church.

CHURCH AND FAMILY IN FEUDAL EUROPE

In pre- Reformation feudal Europe, the family was intertwined in a much wider network of social relations, bounded by inherited definitions of status. Traditional family patterns expressed and reinforced the lifestyle, economic activities, and meaning systems of the particular estate in which each family was embedded. Many of the assumptions about the nature of the family may not have had an explicitly Christian source, but the Christian Church as the established religious institution became the arbiter of feudal values. The Church blessed the marriages, baptized the children, and taught as Christian the values that held in an ordered community the relations of lord and peasant, king and vassal. There was, in fact, only one way other than war to escape the fixed status and traditional activity of one's family, and that was through the Church. Through the parish clergy or the various orders one could become what one's family was not, though even there the strength of family socialization and political power proved great enough that patterns of leadership in the Church tended to reflect the status of a cleric's background.

THE PROTESTANT REFORMATION AND
THE BOURGEOIS FAMILY

The era of the Protestant Reformation accompanied extensive changes in that picture. One need not enter into the ongoing arguments as to whether the Reformation was cause or effect to be able to see that a massive social change had been introduced. It began in the cities, where the fixity of social relations was being challenged by new positions that did not fit the old feudal mode, and it expressed itself in a new openness to inquiry and innovation that resulted in modern science and technology. Technological innovations required new occupational specialties that had no place in the old feudal order, specialities that could not be prepared for in the traditional family, and about which the traditional church had no word or ethic. The new Protestant ideology and ethic provided religious support for the new economic structure, and for changes in family structure and function that fit it.

For example, to become an entrepreneur one must try out new patterns of behavior and engage in work that is not just a duplication of what the family has always done. If it was considered righteous to follow in one's parents' footsteps, this left the person who occupied one of the new roles in a changing society with a religious problem for which there were only two solutions. One could simply agree that this behavior was wrong according to the Church and accept the role of the rebel, or one could find a new way of understanding what kind of behavior was called for by the faith. It is here that Weber's concept of the Protestant Ethic comes into play, for it provided that reinterpretation. If one's primary Christian duty was not obedience to church and tradition, but rather directly to God, and was to be discharged through the pursuit of a vocation formerly defined as secular, then innovations in economic activity and lifestyle could be initiated not out of sinful rebellion but for the greater glory of God. Righteousness was on the side of the innovator rather than of tradition.

Such an attitude was bound to affect the family as well as the church. Just as the family member who became priest, nun, or brother was able to plead religious justification for leaving traditional family activities and relationships, so now economic innovators could claim divine sanction for extricating themselves or their nuclear family units from the extended family patterns that had once demanded loyalty, involvement, and obedience as the religious duties of members.

TWO PATHS TO MODERNIZATION

The process of modernization is frequently equated with economic development, and indeed a certain level of technology and economic organization is required. But in the context of this discussion the more important factors in modernization are those of social organization and world view, what Berger and Luckmann (1966) have defined as "the social construction of reality." It involves a functional appreciation of change, a sense of control that requires the purposeful organization of thought and work, and a goal-oriented instrumentality that may override personal factors or tradition. Moore (1979) defines modernization almost exclusively as a process of the rationalization of life. Perhaps its primary characteristic, underlying all these others, is the element of *planning*, which views segments of human life as problems to be solved, so that planned action can be taken.

The type of modernization most clearly linked with the Protestant Reformation and the bourgeois family is one that emphasizes individual autonomy. The Protestant principle of individual responsibility to God encouraged family patterns of socialization that would turn out individuals capable of taking responsibility for their own lives, acting on a credo resonant with this statement of Berlin (1969: 31):

> I wish my life and decisions to depend on myself, not on external forces of whatever kind. I wish to be the instrument of my own, not other men's acts of will. I wish to be a subject, not an object; to be moved by reasons, by conscious purposes, which are my own, not by causes which affect me, as it were, from outside. I wish to be somebody, not anybody; a doer — deciding, not being decided for, self-directed and not acted upon by external nature or by other men as if I were a thing, or an animal, or a slave incapable of playing a human role, that is, of conceiving goals and policies of my own and realizing them.

Societies that support this individualistic type of modernization have tended to contain three parallel conditions: first, the natural resources necessary for innovation were available; second, political and social structures were at least somewhat supportive; and third, continuing sectarian movements within the religious institution offered new options for religious loyalty and legitimation. This combination is one of two ways in which modernization as a process has been given resources to continue, and nowhere have those circumstances been more evident than in North America, particularly in the United States.

Before continuing to trace that development, it may be useful to take note of its alternative. This begins in the acceptance of the second way of interpreting the escape from traditional feudal social and religious patterns by assuming the status of rebel and nonbeliever. Certainly some of the rationalistic elements of the modern world view can support a secular rather than a religious stance. While Protestantism itself has taken on a considerable amount of secular coloration as it has participated in the modernization of society, full rebellion against religion in the cause of modernization has been most likely to occur in societies where sectarian Protestantism, with its constant development of new religious options, has been least successful. Here, the Marxist alternative that rejects the explicitly religious view has found fertile soil among those who have felt imprisoned in the traditionalism of established religion. Marxism as a political movement has most often linked modernization to the political leadership of the nation-state, supported not by individual entrepreneurship but by governmental programs. Again, the family has been affected, but in a different way. Instead of being fragmented by the breaking off of smaller units pursuing individual goals, the family in these societies has been subsumed under a larger loyalty to the state, which has the right to assign family members to positions or activities that may or may not be consistent with traditional family expectations. Religion, too, has been expected to be subservient to the state, lest its loyalties block the modernization process.

THE AMERICAN CASE

Our focus here is on the United States, where I contend the first type has been and remains the more common form of modernization. Let us take a closer look at the three factors mentioned earlier as important to the growth of modernization here. One need not spend much time arguing the case for the availability — at least until the present — of natural resources to support continuing technological innovation. This has been part of America's taken-for-granted identity. Again, political and social structures have been supportive of innovation and change. Political leadership has been cast much more in the mold of social mobility than that of inherited status. Tax incentives and political power have both been awarded the entrepreneur who is successful, and social status has usually accompanied success as well. Laws have tended in most cases to give precedence to individual rights over family claims, as seen in recent tests of that value in the matter of family members' involvement in some new religious movements.

In fact, much of our economy is built on the kind of individual freedom that can assume that workers are free to move where jobs are available and that activities of the workplace can take priority over family activities. Training for this begins early in life, when the child's school schedule is taken as the structure around which other family activities are planned. Achievement, one of the noted American values, is for the child most often centered in the school rather than in the home, just as in later life it will be understood to be located in the economic or political institution rather than in the family. (This, of course, is a major reason that modern women are likely to find the role of housewife unrewarding; our society does not locate its reward system in the institution in which that role is located.)

Religion in the context of this form of modernization emphasizes, instead of continuing loyalty to a traditional institution of the church, the breaking off into sects, again and again, in continuing schism. Voluntarism, rather than tradition, becomes the central factor in religious belonging. There is a tendency for church-type religion and family as institutions to support one another, and to develop a sense of sacred tradition embodied in families. Voluntarism in religion tends to counter that tendency, positing a religious loyalty that transcends the claims of family and tradition. Personal mobility — social or geographic — is supported in sectarian groups that offer the kind of social interaction and personal formation usually experienced in the family, along with a demand for conversion that burns bridges between former periods of one's life and the new loyalties. While authority and social cohesion are high in the sects, their final impact is to reinforce individualism over group loyalty.

In the United States, the presence of so many religious organizations claiming that kind of voluntarism has occasioned the development of a form of religious liberty that reinforces the understanding of religion as a voluntary activity, and of the churches as voluntary institutions. This is less true in European societies, where ethnic identity is strongly linked to religion. Immigrant patterns in American cities have tended to continue that linkage of religion, ethnicity, and family, at least for a time. The evidence of the different patterns is perhaps best found in Lenski's (1961) study of Detroit in the late 1950s, where he found interaction among Protestants and positive correlations among Catholics and Jews. An important linkage may be assumed in his finding that Protestants had far fewer relatives in the area than did Catholics or Jews (Lenski, 1961: 219-223). It seems evident that they found it easier to move away from families, and that their church membership may have assisted them in the process.

All these issues were particularly relevant to the modernization process in its earlier stages, and much of the traditional system of American values was developed during that part of the process. Underlying such values as those noted by Williams (1955: ch. 2) — achievement, activity, practicality, progress, science, and rationality — is a positive understanding of personal achievement as related to ultimate value, whether or not it is stated directly in the language of the Protestant Ethic. American civil religion contains in its tradition the notion of a covenanted community seeking to create a new social order, but it has long been translated in terms of individual achievement reminiscent of Adam Smith's "invisible hand." Immigrants may have clung to ethnic ways, but they also trusted their children to the American dream, even if it meant leaving some of those ties. Even if religious loyalties had roots in the ethnic community, they could feed voluntarism and social mobility as successful nuclear families moved to suburban parishes oriented more to the formation of new communities than to close ties with tradition. Given the way that religion has been institutionalized as a voluntary society in America, church-type groups such as Roman Catholics and Lutherans have tended to become more sectarian in form, at least to the point of being denominations in a pluralistic religious scene. Economically and socially, the Protestant Ethic has extended to these religious groups as well.[1] American families have come to define themselves less as permanent institutions embedded in the full social system than as launching pads from which new generations may enter that system, and at least in some ways the churches have helped them to reach that definition.

THE NATURE OF MATURE MODERNIZATION

But the modernization process has not stopped with the dividing of extended families and settled neighborhoods into mobile nuclear units pursuing righteous vocations in the secular world. Had it done so, current religious structures probably would not be sensing the kind of dislocation that many are expressing, for their patterns of cooperation with the economic system seem to have been fairly adaptive during earlier phases of modernization, not only in the United States but in the rest of the world.

We must, then, examine how far we have come in the modernization process. For example, it is abundantly evident that patterns of individual entrepreneurship no longer hold dominance in the process. The pursuit of rational science aimed at practical progress has resulted in a type of technology that has required centralization of work into large organizations, just as it has also resulted in the acquisition of a large body of knowledge that requires an organization of persons to master it, having gone far beyond the ability of a single individual or small group to comprehend. As a consequence, both in our understanding of our culture and in our patterns of work we have become specialists, dependent on one another across the chasms of specialized language. We are aware of the vastness of both the available knowledge in our culture and the organization of human effort, but there is no way that we can participate in the totality of either. Rather, we assume that there must be experts, and that these must be arranged in hierarchical order in terms of the amount of access they have to knowledge or to upper levels of the organization. Our value of rationality is expressed in the organization of work and of decision making in such a way that interchangeable parts may be fitted into a product, or interchangeable people into a job description. The entire cognitive style takes up an emphasis on what Berger et al. (1973: 33-53) have termed "componentiality" — that is, a concentration of specific parts — rather than on systems that encompass the whole. In modern systems, these authors say, persons tend to relate to one another on the basis of the particular roles that bring them into interaction, rather than as whole persons; so that over time the individual begins to treat his or her different roles separately, emphasizing those aspects of the personality most appropriate to each role, developing a "componential self."

The anonymity of relations comes to a peak in bureaucracy, where justice itself is seen to be the principle of anonymity, where personnel officers can be "no respecter of persons," but instead must only seek qualifications that fit detailed job descriptions. Human rights thus become the right to be treated anonymously. It is, of course, ironic that movements such as those for civil rights or women's equality, which seek recognition of the individual worth of persons formerly ignored, are transmuted in the modern state into the demand to be treated impersonally.

MODERNIZATION AND
THE TRANSMUTATION OF VALUES

Compartmentalization becomes an accepted form of dealing with the world for those whose self-definition has become "componential," and this, I would argue, has had a significant effect on those values that Williams (1955) identified in the mid-1950s as central to American society. Values such as achievement, activity, efficiency and practicality, progress, science, and rationality fit best into that portion of the self engaged in economic activity, particularly if that activity is directed toward the production of goods.

Berger et al. (1973: chs. 1, 2) make an interesting distinction between the organization of "technological production" and that of "bureaucracy" — the latter probably a poor choice of terms, since technological production is also organized bureaucratically. What is meant by their term "bureaucracy" might better be termed "human services" or some other name that calls to mind activity in which there is no objective, material product, but that nonetheless is necessary to the ongoing life of the society. In this latter portion of the modern society they find orderliness to be a prime value, compared with productivity in their first type. Thus values of hard work may be transmuted to those of proper procedure, style replacing results as the more service-oriented forms of work find it difficult to identify a measurable product by which to evaluate their effectiveness. As the percentage of this type of work has grown, the influence of this style has come to be felt more widely, so that for many workers the primary value of work seems to be faithfully putting in one's time, rather than tied to any scale of productivity. Hard work, then, is removed from the notion of product, and tied more to the idea of time worked or that of working conditions.

The value of material comfort is transmuted at least partially, as an affluent society makes issues of comfort less basic and more likely to become means rather than ends. That is, definitions of the minimal levels of comfort are raised to create demand for products that are necessary to keep in operation the productive organizations, often by making material comfort more of a status symbol than something simply to be enjoyed. Where relations have become too anonymous to provide sure guidelines for judging the status of individuals or families, their level of material comfort is taken as a measure of worth.

Of particular interest is the transmutation of the values of equality, freedom, and humanitarianism. The demand for anonymity in modern organizations has provided a new basis for all three of these values. Equality becomes equal access to positions guaranteed by concentration on objective skills rather than personal characteristics. Freedom in many cases comes to mean the ability to escape personal histories or characteristics such as race, sex, or family background in order to compete for those objectively defined positions. There are other aspects to modern definitions of freedom to be explored later. Suffice it to say now that this value is defined in modern society almost entirely in relation to the right of the individual to escape or transcend any group loyalties in order to create an individually de-signed life plan — a career. Humanitarian mores also become translated into impersonal, anonymous standards. Justice is blind, and charity should make no demand other than that one should meet clearly defined objective qualifications.

This being the case, new values — or at least new interpretations to the names we gave the old values — have come to prominence in American society in the quarter century since Williams published his book on the subject. Perhaps the most persuasive successor to Williams's work is that of Yankelovich in *New Rules* (1981).

The core of the change, says Yankelovich, has occurred in the ideas of self-control and self-sacrifice implicit in the values of achievement, work, and progress. As he puts it, each culture contains a tacit "giving/getting compact — the unwritten rules that govern what we give in marriage, work, community and sacrifice for others, and what we expect in return" (Yankelovich, 1981: 8-10). It is this compact that he sees to have become unbalanced and problematic in American society. One way to put it is to say that what we give up in the anonymous structures of modern society is our very selves, and what we want in return and do not get is the sense of identity that we have lost. It is this that underlies the "culture of narcissism," the self-pursuits of the "me decade."[2] A new value that has risen in importance, then, says Yankelovich, is that of "a duty to myself." Self-fulfillment has become not only a goal, but an obligation.

CHANGES IN SPHERE AND FUNCTION OF THE FAMILY

The way that this is spelled out in the society at large is of particular importance to our topic. It is based on a separation between public institutions that are deemed primary carriers of modernization at this stage — work, government, and to some extent education — and those institutions perceived still to carry some of the more personalistic and wholistic emphases of premodern times — the family and the church. Thus while both family and church were in earlier times institutions that linked individuals with the larger society, they are now sought out as refuges from that society. Lasch's book, *Haven in a Heartless World* (1977), makes this case for the modern experience of the family. It can also be applied to the church: In modern society, both are havens in which people expect to be protected from the ravages of the impersonal public arena, and in which they seek help in the pursuit of a meaningful self-identity. This does not mean that neither institution carries on activities that prepare persons for public involvement; rather, two areas of change have come to light. Those involved in family and church do not necessarily *expect* them to provide such functions; and they no longer have clear channels through which they may advance persons from their midst into the public arena.

As the public arena has become more varied and more anonymous, people have tried to construct in the private realm subworlds of meaning and identity to provide comfort and stability for their lives. Families in earlier times were often penetrated by public affairs and outsiders. Apprentices and servants "lived in." Much of life took place in the street outside homes that provided minimum room for family activities. By contrast, modern families are more likely to carry on private activities in the space behind their homes, protected even from the neighbors by high privacy fences. It is no longer possible to assume that one's subworld is shared by those neighbors, and it becomes important that this one place of security be protected.

This redefinition of family space has had an effect on styles of child rearing. The earlier bourgeois family, as something of a public institution, fit comfortably into patterns of training the young for the kind of self-control necessary to maintain the old giving/getting compact. Rebellion against those constraints, particularly within the emotion-laden content of the family, caused the adolescent to come to a firm sense of self over against that context. It was out of such dynamics that the inner-directed person developed both a clear sense of goals and the motivation to pursue them. In the modern family, however, rigid restraints are seen as inappropriate, especially if they are likely to result in shattering the fragile peace of that refuge from an alien society. Permissive child rearing has become important not only because of the widespread acceptance of psychological theories emphasizing the negative consequences of repression, but also because of the need of adults in the family to perceive the home as a place of comfort and harmony.

CHANGES IN THE UNDERSTANDING
OF RELIGION AND THE CHURCH

Religious institutions have also been faced with incongruities between the functions they have been expected to serve in the past and the means available to them in the present to provide those functions. In modern society, churches have become places where people seek some common world construction, rather than where they celebrate a taken-for-granted community of experience. Often they are caught between the demand for a firm world construction that would require disciplined conformity and the fear that any demand made by the church would shatter the fragile community they are trying to construct.

Generally, comfort is stressed and church discipline is muted if it exists at all. Church members under such conditions do not have a particularly strong sense of religious identity. Rather, they relate to the church more as a "client cult" that offers religious goods and services to a shopping public. This is the pattern defined by Orr and Nichelson in *The Radical Suburb* (1970: chs. 2-5). In that work, the authors trace three types of religious identification. The first, or *savage,* is based on the kind of group loyalty common to tribal religion and still evident in some ethnic religious groups. In fact, traditional parish organization depends largely on this type, where religious affiliation is a part of group identity, a celebration of the individual's roots in the history and present composition of the religious community. It is most easily linked to the traditional sociological concept of the *church* or *ecclesia,* where we find a sanctification of ascribed status, and where one is expected to remain loyal to the religious group as a basis of both public and private identity. The second type, the *conscientious,* is based on a kind of moralism that defines religious identity in terms of behavior, equating action with religious belonging. Like the traditional *sect,* this type creates what Durkheim defined as mechanical solidarity by demanding uniformity of action and belief, even though membership may have been voluntarily chosen rather than inherited. It is a larger concept than that of the sect, since it can indeed include the inheritors of the moralistic ethic who may not experience the religious group as having the high salience the traditional sectarian model requires. In the modern suburb, however, Orr and Nichelson found a third type, the *expansive,* given to tentativeness, openness, and an individual freedom of action, interpretation, and identity that did not preclude church membership or involvement, but did lower the level of commitment to be expected. It is here that religious involvement approaches the nature of the *client cult.*

It seems evident that expansive church people could not be expected to be held accountable for long-range commitments to the church; they also would not find it necessary for religious sanctions to reinforce commitment in other areas of their lives. Tribal religion reinforces all levels of family loyalty as sacred. Conscientious religion reinforces the kinds of personal commitment expected in long-standing marriages and responsible child rearing in the nuclear family. Expansive religion emphasizes emotional gratification in the family, making it possible to approvve dissolution of relationships that no longer provide such personal support, as well as the accretion of other, noncommitted relationships advocated in such concepts as that of the "open marriage." It is in this type of orientation that sexual relations before or outside of marriage are likely to be taken for granted as appropriate outlets. Again, for the expansive, no commitments to the family should be expected to require a woman to continue an unwanted pregnancy or a man to sacrifice all his time and goods for his family.

Such a style can serve the value of the duty to the self, but it may be questionable how much it can assist in the discovery of that self. In modern society, neither the subworld of the family nor that of the church can be depended on to provide a world construction that assures a firm sense of identity in all situations. The demand that they remain isolated in the private realm, where their constructions cannot be challenged, makes it impossible for either church or family to undergird a sense of self in the public arena. At the same time, they make too few demands on the individual to ensure the formation of a sure sense of identity gained through doing battle with those restrictions as one attempts to escape them into the public realm.

SOCIALIZATION AND THE MODERN INDIVIDUAL

The pattern of narrowing the scope of one's world in a search for grounding applies both to institutions and to individuals. Yankelovich (1981: 11) points to the incongruities of the modern search for the self as he discusses the problems of self-centeredness as a basis for self-fulfillment:

> They are caught in a debilitating contradiction: their goal is to expand their lives by reaching beyond the self, but the strategy they employ constricts them, drawing them inward toward an ever-narrowing, closed-off "I." People want to enlarge their choices but, seeking to "keep all options open," they diminish them.

In examining more closely the way such patterns of culture have developed, we begin with the expectation of change within the process of modernization. Particularly in the realm of technological production, new expertise is expected to be generated within the system itself. Thus it becomes impossible to expect knowledge to be passed from generation to generation in the family. Rather, younger members of the family may have more access to new knowledge and skills than older ones may have. The result is a change in patterns of child rearing such as that described in Mead's *Culture and Commitment* (1970: chs. 1, 2). In traditional societies, says Mead, older generations provided a direct model for the young, who could see in their parents and grandparents the contours of their own lives in later years. There the wisdom of the aged was evident, and respect for one's elders a sacred tradition. The older generations were clearly leading the young. In addition, life span in traditional societies has tended to be short enough that it could be assumed that any large project undertaken by one generation would have to be completed by following ones.

The increase in life span in modern societies has not only allowed more generations to be around at the same time, and so to make possible an extended family of perhaps unwieldy size and generational range, but also to allow older generations to complete their own projects, leaving less direct responsibility to younger members of the family to continue particular activities. Mead found, however, that in societies where the rate of social change was increasing, as it does with modernization, the relation between generations may become more of a cooperative activity, as parents and children work together to make sense of their environment. It is at about this stage of modernization that we find the kind of emphasis in the culture defined by Riesman et al. (1950) as "inner-directed," in which the individual is given general direction by older generations, a sort of an "inner gyroscope" setting one's course but leaving one free to make behavioral adaptations necessary to reach valued goals under changing circumstances. Finally, in fully modernized societies the rate of change has become so great that older generations find it difficult if not impossible to set goals for the younger ones. Instead, people develop what Riesman et al. call an "inner radar" that tunes them in to expectations of others around them, so that they become "other-directed." The young, often in contact with more people and newer situations, may have the more sensitive "radar" systems, and hence become the guides of older generations through the minefields of a rapidly changing society (Mead, 1970: ch. 3).

To many people this may seem a hasty overstatement, since not every family shares this experience. However, it must be understood that modernization is felt differently at different levels of the society, so that this may be true of some families without being true for all. The full brunt of change is probably felt most strongly by families most successful in achieving upward mobility through the modernization process — those often referred to as upper middle class or the so-called new class whose economic base is not so much property but modern expertise. For people at this level of modern society, the chief vehicle of inheritance is not the family lands or the family business, but access to educational institutions that will provide the most advanced training in modern skills, attitudes, and values. While it is not always immediately apparent to older generations who value the consequences of a good education for the success of their children, such training is likely to produce a world view at variance with that of the family, and a social base for identity that can replace the family in this important function. The very value commitments of the family may undermine its importance and authority for younger generations.

MARRIAGE AND REALITY CONSTRUCTION

This changing relationship between the young and the extended family creates weaknesses in what Berger and Luckmann (1966) have called "the social construction of reality." If we accept their understanding that human beings organize their world into meaningful systems in conversation with one another, we may then see a kind of double bind in the way the modern person constructs the world. On one hand, the basis of the "componential self" is in the difference among the life worlds of the disparate groups with whom one is in interaction. The world of work may be organized according to very different assumptions from that of the country club or the bowling league, or that of the church or synagogue. Definitions of merit, worth, and meaning change as the landscape of one's day is reinterpreted by each group. The presentation of self will be different in each situation, and with it at least some elements of self-understanding. At the same time, since these other worlds are removed from and often take precedence over the world of one's family of orientation, the modern person is cut off from any meaningful history of interpretations of the world. There is a disjuncture of life worlds over both time and space.

In modernizing societies one of the elements of increased choice has been found in patterns of selection of marital partners. Extricating oneself from traditional society includes escaping from patterns in which marriage has been defined primarily as a family affair, and moving to personal mate selection on the basis of some version of romantic love. Romance still tends to bloom best when partners are found to exhibit some similarity of social class, race, ethnicity, or the like. However, even when such similarities hold, variations in experience and patterns of living have weakened much of the commonality that once could be taken for granted. One can no longer be sure that the life worlds of the two persons have been identical before marriage. Rather, part of the function of romantic love is the construction of a new life world out of materials brought into the marriage by each partner. The intensity of the relationship is needed to make up for the differences the two bring to it. The desire to share as much as possible with the beloved allows the couple to construct a mutual past that was not shared experientially, and so to make more meaningful their present activities and their hopes for the future.

Berger and Kellner (1974: 171), in an article that refers to trends toward earlier marriages in the late 1950s, found the reason for the trend in this need to construct a viable life world separate from that of the family of origin:

> A child raised in the circumscribed world of the nuclear family is stamped by it in terms of his psychological needs and social expectations. Having to live in the larger society from which the nuclear family is segregated, the adolescent soon feels the need for a "little world" of his own, having been socialized in such a way that only by having such a world to withdraw into can he successfully cope with the anonymous "big world" that confronts him as soon as he steps outside his parental home. In other words, to be "at home" in society entails, *per definitionem*, the construction of a maritally based sub-world. The parental home itself facilitates such an early jump into marriage precisely because its controls are very narrow in scope and leave the adolescent to his own nomic devices at an early age.

THE COUNTERCULTURE AS A DEMODERNIZING MOVEMENT

More recently, the age of marriage has risen significantly. Yet the final point made by Berger and Kellner concerning the adolescent being left at an early age to "his own nomic devices" may be seen as an important factor in what came to be known as the counterculture. They mention elsewhere in their paper that the peer group had been growing more important in this situation. One can see the counterculture of the late 1960s and early 1970s as the adolescent peer group magnified into an international focus of identity. Here the young constructed their own world in separation from — and often in opposition to — the world of their parents.

In the counterculture, tradition, whether that of the family or the church, became anathema. In a strange paradox, this celebration of the ultimate in modernity, its "pluralization of life worlds" (Berger et al., 1973: ch. 3), was often accompanied by a rhetoric of demodernization, a rebellion against the forms of technological production and bureaucratic organization that had created the values of choice and variety that they celebrated.

In particular, the counterculture was a protest against the rationality of modernization, as its proponents sought the levels of feeling and response they felt had been repressed in a rationalistic society. Many of the churches had previously participated in the processes of modernization, and had accepted into their own theology basic premises of rationality; now the protest of the counterculture turned against such religion, though often in the name of other, less rational forms of religion. The sense of power and control that had arisen out of the technical prowess of modern production had been an important factor in the development of theological formulations about the "coming of age" of humankind in the modern world that underlay not only the "death of God" theologies but also less extreme celebrations of the "secular city" in the decade of the 1960s. Countercultural religion, while strongly anti-institutional as well as antirational, struck responsive chords among some church people as they sought to reestablish the mysterious, to reclaim festival and fantasy.[3]

Much of the counterculture, however, was problematic for both church and family. There was great variety in the activities of the counterculture, but one common factor underlying all its forms was its anti-institutional bias. All institutions were held suspect, including those of family and religion. Both have served as foci of loyalty and commitment, and so both were viewed as threats to the freedom to experiment that was basic to the values of the counterculture. Tying oneself down to a particular person in marriage was taken to be cutting off one's options. Religious aspects of the counterculture were those of direct experience, mind expansion, celebration — no group loyalties or creedal traditions, but rather private experience. The most negative aspects of the society from the point of view of the counterculture were the institutions of the economy and the government, but family, school, and church were held to be their willing tools.

As the 1970s drew to a close, the counterculture per se tended to fade from the public eye. However, one of the sources of the speculations of Yankelovich that we have been discussing was material from his continuing surveys that showed how counter-cultural values have permeated the society and have become no longer the exclusive province of those he termed "post-affluent" (see Yankelovich, 1974). Many of the styles and values are no longer countercultural, but rather have become part of the culture at large, including the value mentioned above, of "a duty to myself."

NEW DIRECTIONS IN THE 1980s?

Yet in spite of the critique of processes of modernization displayed in our economic system, the focus on freedom, experimentation, and self-awareness was fed by the surplus created by a modern economy. Seldom was any doubt raised about the present and continuing affluence of American society. Then, toward the end of the

1970s, the economic picture changed. Recession, unemployment, and inflation became common typics of conversation. As Yankelovich (1981: 22) has put it, "In a matter of a few years, we have moved from an uptight culture set in a dynamic economy to a dynamic culture set in an uptight economy.."

The result has been that many of those life worlds that people have been enjoying now may seem to have been houses of cards, mere fabrications of overstimulated imaginations. The ground on which we have based our social constructions of reality seems as unreliable as that over some of the sinkholes that have recently been destroying Florida real estate. At the very time that these new values have spread throughout the society, the means for their implementation have become eroded.

So it is that Yankelovich sees the beginning of a movement beyond the focus on a duty to oneself. He applauds the move away from the instrumental values of achievement, practicality, progress, and rationality to a reemphasis on what he terms "sacred/expressive values," or at least to a more even balance between the two types. He finds two facets to the new style. The first involves a hunger for deeper, more lasting personal relationships, the second a willingness to give up some of the benefits of modern technology in order to enhance the sacred/expressive side of life (Yankelovich, 1981: 251-255). His focus seems mostly on that segment of the society most affected by the counterculture, whose affluent base makes it more possible to be willing to give up some of the products of affluence, but, again, these are the people most often looked to as models for their age group.

In this context, the idea of turning again to traditional sources of reality construction begins to appeal, particularly in the light of what they can offer those who are caught up in the responses to modernization that we have been considering. The age group in which the counterculture was focused has been particularly influential in the society, if only because of the numbers of people that age group encompasses. They remain influential, and now that they have reached their thirties, one can see an acting out of the duty to the self as they realize that their postponed commitments in the name of keeping options open are in danger of closing off the option of having children and experiencing a stable family life. At the same time, the next younger age cohort is in many cases seeking stable relationships early in reaction to the chaos they experienced growing up during the unrest of the countercultural years.

Many, then, now seek the family as a source of regulation for their lives. In fact, Yankelovich (1981: 89) points to trends toward an increasing appreciation of traditional patterns of marriage, at least as far as the ideal of the mating couple. Some seek out religion for the same reason, in some cases through new religious movements that offer discipline and commitment, but now more frequently in religious groups at least somewhere near the mainstream. The modern situation, however, raises questions as to whether those institutions can serve the kinds of functions people may expect of them out of traditional definitions of their role in society. To create a stable world, institutions need to be able to regulate both their members and to some extent the context of their activities. It may or may not be possible to look to family and church as regulatory agencies in modern society. They may, in fact, be seen as having become far more regulated by outside forces.

CHURCH, FAMILY, AND SOCIAL CONTROL IN MODERN SOCIETY

In premodern societies, tribal religions showed extensive overlap with families as institutions. It was assumed that both institutions exercised considerable authority over their members, not only during the period of primary socialization that shapes personality and identity, but also in continuing regulation of behavior. The concept of family honor interacted with an understanding of the church as a moral community capable of exercising ultimate sanctions, to provide a framework of personal and public discipline.

With the rise of other institutions that tended to push both family and church out of the public arena, this process has become attenuated. The regulatory function most clearly left to both institutions concerns behavior most private and intimate, particularly sexual relations, and it is in this area that much current conflict has arisen. The secularization of the society has cast into question the moral authority of the church, particularly in relation to its ability to exercise ultimate sanctions. For many modern people the threat of hell or the promise of heaven has little force. Churches that accept a modern role tend to mute such sanctions, offering instead the positive reinforcement that can be given personal relationships within the supportive community of church congregations. There is statistical evidence that marriages lived out within church involvements tend to be more stable (for example, see McCarthy, 1979). It is likely that this is true not only because of the positive support given, but also because of negative sanctions much less ultimate than heaven or hell — gossip, disapproving looks, informal cutting of close ties with miscreants — or rewards given to those who conform to the expected image with greater positive interaction and, perhaps, positions of trust and leadership within the religious community.

Nowhere is this more clear than in current controversies over abortion. To those whose consciousness is thoroughly modern, the practice of abortion is a matter of the right to personal freedom: A woman should be free to exercise control over the uses to which her body is put, and bearing a child is a purely voluntary activity to be accepted or rejected on the basis of personal preference. The positive evaluation given many main-line churches to the whole process of modernization is reflected in their stance on this issue. Many denominations have made statements in favor of freedom of choice, calling into play their value commitments concerning the nature of responsible human action under circumstances in which choice and planning are seen as basic human characteristics.

To people who live in a more premodern world this is a shallow interpretation at best. Those who support the rights of the extended kin group as paramount over those of the individuals see abortion — and often contraception as well — as selfish refusal to exercise one's sacred function of providing future generations of the group. Traditional Roman Catholicism, out of its emphasis on natural law, sees such interference with the processes of nature as violations of a God-given moral code. Mormons, whose theology posits a reservoir of unborn souls waiting their turn to pass through mortal life on their way to higher transformations, reject selfish prevention of the process, particularly since they understand that status in the afterlife is based at least in part on the number of descendents one can claim.

Among conservative Protestants, the issue is often seen simply as one of expressing willingness or unwillingness to obey the will of God, whose power is evident in the fact of conception. Part of the inability of this group to engage in dialogue with more modern people rises out of the casual acceptance by moderns of Freudian definitions of sexual repression as unhealthy, in comparison with a world view that assumes self-control to be an expression of the truly human, and that any sexual intimacy outside marriage violates the will of God, so that contraception or abortion should not even be an issue. Only, perhaps, in the area of responsible family planning might such a subject be raised — if ever.

In general, churches whose orientation is more modern and more lenient in regard to such issues are the ones more likely to have a preponderance of members of the "expansive" type, who would not be likely to accept much church discipline. By contrast, members of more conservative churches are more likely to accept them as agencies of social control. Thus churchly opposition to abortion, contraception, and sexual freedom is more clearly a factor in the lives of members than are the more liberal pronouncements.

One issue raised in this controversy is that of personal preference as opposed to some definition of social responsibility. For advocates of the latter, abortion may be seen as the ultimate in selfishness, the snuffing out of a life in favor of enhancing one's own lifestyle. An exception may be noted among those who use abortion as a method of birth control out of a sense of public responsibility in a world they consider already ecologically unbalanced through excessive population growth. For them, however, there is little defense against the charge that contraception is a far more acceptable form of birth control than abortion, the latter indicating a failure of the former.

Thus the argument, while often originating in church and family, tends to move out into more secular, more public arenas, until the debate centers on legal sanctions concerning abortion or federal support of abortion for the poor. This last has interesting implications, since in most cases the poor are the last to be touched by modern consciousness. Their "savage" orientation, or the sectarian religion most likely to involve the "disinherited," often leads them to view abortion as an evil. Freedom of choice is not a reality in their lives, and so their religion is not likely to stress it. In addition, federal support of both contraception and abortion for the poor has been taken by some minority activists to be a program of genocide practiced by those who exercise authority in the society, who assume that their lifestyle is normative for all.[4] In fact, this is one of the latest of a long string of contacts between poor families and public agencies dominated by social classes in power.

THE FAMILY AS CLIENT
OF CHURCH AND STATE

During earlier stages of the process of modernization in the West, the public regulation of private and family life escaped some of the domination of the state churches of earlier societies and fell to some extent into the hands of sectarian Protestants. Under the assumptions of the so-called Protestant Ethic, small groups of sectarian Protestants exercised strict discipline over their members, reinforcing a moral code of upright living that in the period of early modernization helped families to rise to middle-class status and public participation. Basic to the Protestant Ethic was the Calvinist assumption that those who were God's elect would respond to the moral authority of the sect. So churches of the middle and upper classes continued to develop missions to the poor in their own and foreign lands that stressed not only the religious teachings to which the elect were expected to respond, but also an entire package of education and work opportunities that would assist in the process. Settlement houses as a direct arm of the churches, for example, offered extensive skills training and classes in hygiene, nutrition, and cultural awareness as well as Bible lessons and worship services.

But successful initiation into the process of modernization is usually accompanied by a growing secularization of the consciousness. Church settlement houses and home missions in particular were nearly always associated with an emphasis on public education as a vehicle for the improvement of the life of the lower classes, an education that was at least nominally secular. In cities, political social service activities complemented those of the churches, and settlement houses came to have public as well as church sponsorship. This came about at least in part through negative assessments of the results of interdenominational conflict over styles of service and the loyalty of clients as the society became more religiously pluralistic. Also, the ravages of the Great Depression of the 1930s strained to the breaking point all sorts of private and local charities, allowing federally sponsored programs to come to the fore. The time was probably ripe, in any case, since resentment against being the objects of affluent people's attempts to win favor with their God was often turning into a belief that social welfare is a right of citizenship. Intellectuals whose humanitarianism was more secular than religious legitimated this view, thus withdrawing legitimation from many programs of religious charity.

In the process a number of emphases were changed. One of the primary ones was based on the right of everyone to services provided through public funds. Sectarian services had proceeded on an implicit assumption that the elect or those capable of regeneration would respond and use them as a vehicle to rise to their proper role of full participation in the society. For those not part of God's elect, for the unregenerate, only the goad of poverty could provide motivation for them to make their expected contribution to the work of the world. Public welfare could not make such distinctions. Yet the general attitude had become part of the moral climate, so that it was assumed by many people that those who remained on public assistance were clearly the unregenerate type, not to be expected to regulate their own lives in a moral way.

Children were particularly important in this scenario, since it was thought that they should be insulated from the influence of an unregenerate family life if possible. Again, of course, this was far more explicit among sectarian Christians than among those who worked in welfare agencies. But our child-centered culture developed a child-centered welfare system that has mandated public interference with the functioning of families whose application for social services has defined them as below the social norm. Truancy laws forced families to expose their children to the tempering influence of the public schools, though leaving it open for them to opt for church-sponsored education if they could afford it. Few could. Church-sponsored schools had to deal with the tension between training their own children in their particular moral universe and providing education for the poor that might improve on what their families could provide them. In the long run, the needs of church members' children prevailed. Sunday schools, begun as general education for the poor, turned to religious instruction for members' children; parochial schools began to limit attendance to children of members of the parish or to charge tuition; and some church schools were established, particularly in recent years, explicitly to remove children from the influence of minority students in the public schools.

Again, this process has been attenuated in areas where modernization has been less thorough in its effects. Many ethnic Catholic or Orthodox parishes maintain a relatively closed world for their families, including its educational system. They, like the Mormons, whose devotion to modernization has been limited to the economic sphere, tend to take care of their own poor, ignoring public welfare institutions, and maintaining a world view less responsive to pluralism and secularization.

Meantime, attitudes once religious have been maintained in the secular sphere. Public policy dictates that children should not starve, or be homeless of unclothed, regardless of the shiftlessness of their parents. Thus Aid to Families with Dependent Children became a federal program. But such aid could not be given indiscriminately, so much of the time of the growing welfare bureaucracy has come to be devoted to the establishment of eligibility standards and the enforcement of rules that would prevent either unqualified dipping into the public treasury or the support of a family life assumed to be unhealthy for its children. Thus the regulation of family life has become a public function much more than a religious one.

PUBLIC POLICY AND FAMILY INTERACTION

Changes have occurred under modernization in both the roles played in family interaction and their relative power. When the family was considered truly a public institution, as in premodern times, authority in the family usually led to authority in public activities as a representative of the family. Primary responsibility for the welfare of family members, as well as their behavior, rested with the extended family. This has broken down with modernization as it has separated work from the confines of the home and divided extended families into mobile nuclear subunits. The authority of the head of the nuclear unit is enhanced because that person has direct contact with the public arena now denied those family members who stay at home. Yet the absence of the breadwinner from the home makes that authority less constant, more alien. Thus the common identity and supportive relationships within the nuclear unit tend to be undermined, even while the need for them grows. It is at this point that power relations in the family become an issue, and the subordination of women and children evident.

In general, public agencies with any kind of regulation of family life do not deal with the breadwinner, since if he or she is successful economically there is littel reason for interference. Rather, public agencies deal primarily with issues concerning women and children, or the aged, and have tended to support greater equality in parental roles by developing a relationship with the family in which mothers play the role of advocate. As schools and other public agencies deal with families through the mother, they require that she have a right to speak for the family, and so agencies have been led to emphasize the value of equality in marital roles (see Donzelot, 1979).

In recent years, new public programs have been developed that take the part of women against the power of their husbands, the most evident of which are programs for battered wives. There public agencies seek to correct the imbalance of physical power between marital partners. Similarly, programs are growing that seek to provide protection of children against the abuse of power by parents. In this way public agencies by their actions raise questions about the role of children in the family as obedient subjects of parental will. Modern consciousness, as institutionalized in public service institutions, is clearly giving more value to individual freedom than to group responsibility or conformity.

The call for public agencies to protect family members from violence at one another's hands reflects, also, the erosion of the presence and power of the extended kin group or close neighborhood in affecting the behavior of members, as well as the loss of strength of a religious congregation as a moral force in the lives of its members. In extended families, a fairly large group traditionally has exercised a vested interest in the welfare of each member, as well as a sense of family honor concerning the moral behavior of each. Violence deemed dishonorable or dangerous to the family would be sanctioned powerfully in the extended family, though its definitions of what is dishonorable or dangerous might not always fit modern standards. For example, the violence of family feuds or vendettas is not generally approved by those charged with maintaining peace in the larger society. Similarly, given the emphasis on using modern technology to move toward a risk-free environment, families who allow or encourage members to take serious physical risks are likely to find themselves subject to public pressures.

Again, strict churches that define the rearing of children "in the nurture and admonition of the Lord" in terms of extremely rigid moral or social codes are subject to public pressure in the name of individual freedom. The most clear-cut cases of this sort have involved public pressure to allow medical treatment or advanced education to children that their parents' religion would deny them. There, state intervention is often advocated even by groups that would ordinarily decry it.

While it is often assumed that violence is the lot of the lower classes, more liberal churches often reflect an ethos of support and caring in the family that leaves members stunned if they are faced with domestic violence in their midst. They may be involved in programs aimed at dealing with family problems among the disadvantaged, but often they find it threatening to expand such programs to take care of their own members. Rather, the emphasis is on training priests and pastors in the arts of psychological (pastoral) counseling, expecting full professional commitment to confidentiality, rather than expecting the congregation to provide group support or catharsis. Power relations in the family tend to be ignored in favor of definitions of the primary role of family members as that of psychological support. Individual nurture and support takes precedence over broader group processes, so that the individuation of modern consciousness is supported. Church organizations, often limited to particular age or interest groups, may assist the launching of family members into life patterns at least somewhat separate from those of their families.

MODERNIZATION AND
AN ETHIC OF AUTONOMOUS LOVE

Certainly, for those church members who prefer religious organizations to be powerful public institutions, the process of modernization is likely to be perceived negatively. Modernization has consistently eroded the power of religious institutions to exercise social control. Pluralism has increased the number of voices to which persons are expected to pay heed, and secularization has undermined the sense of special power by which religion has either coerced or persuaded people to conform to its ethic. The fragmentation demanded by modernization has made it impossible for the family to control the careers or activities of members, and modern society's demand for autonomy and equality between the sexes, and to some extent the generations as well, has undermined the authority of the traditional patriarchal family. The rise of the so-called Moral Majority in American politics can be interpreted as a demand for the reassertion of the authority of the church over the family, and of the family over the individual, more in the pattern of earlier stages of modernization. On the other hand, the positive evaluation of modernization that accompanied its economic structure in the form of the Protestant Ethic may have input into later stages of modernization as well, as we look not just to economic organization but to the culture that the process has created.

Yankelovich, for example, has posited as the positive way out of the dilemma of the new values no reversal of the quest for self-fulfillment, but rather some appropriate means to achieve the self-realization that is sought. His term is "an ethic of commitment," and family and religion have been chief foci of commitment in most human societies. The question may well be what forms they will take to enhance a consciousness shaped by modernization at its present stage.

The rebellion against the bigness and anonymity of modern society suggests that external regulation from centralized agencies is no longer acceptable to many Americans. The demand for a reliable world in which one's sense of self is stable suggests that sources of regulation must be found at some intermediate levels. The demand for personalism suggests that regulation will only be acceptable if it comes from sources that treat persons as wholes rather than as fragmented selves. These all point to families and religious institutions as potential subjects of self-enhancing commitment.

D'Antonio (1980: 100-103) has spoken of the increased autonomy of the individual given by modernization as a positive factor, allowing an ethic of love to replace more traditional understandings of marital obligations undergirded by external social controls. There is abundant evidence of popular support for adding "love" to the list of American values presented by Williams (1955). It is probably its reputation as the "love generation" that gave the counterculture the popularity it enjoyed during its heyday. Yet one reason the counterculture floundered was that it had trouble defining what was meant by "love."

For an ethic of love to be concretized, it needs institutional support and definition. Church and family are the institutions usually linked with the notion of love, and are prime candidates to provide social support for an ethic of love, which is very close to Yankelovich's concept of an "ethic of commitment" assumed to be generated by positive feelings rather than external constraints. It would appear, then, that what is called for in the present age is a commitment of religious institutions to an ethic of love as strong as the early Protestant commitment to work, giving theological grounding for loving relationships and institutional examples and support for their maintenance. As the religious work ethic freed individuals from the externally imposed obligations of the traditional kin group or neighborhood so that they could participate in the economic aspects of modernization, so now a religious love ethic might return them to their families as autonomous persons choosing their own commitments.

Some aspects of the current style of the liberal churches noted above could be viewed as positive in this light, though one would need to ask for a more aggressive partisanship for the love ethic than the rather negative approach of "support groups" that simply help one another to cope with modern society. In such a scenario, the local congregation or smaller subparish groups might provide the strongest kind of institutional support. As voluntary associations, these religious groups can be models of the forms of loving commitment undertaken by autonomous individuals that are being sought. As religious groups, these voluntary associations might provide ideological support and ritual celebration of the ultimate bases of love in their own visions of the nature of divine love and human community. Families participating in the activities of such groups could be led to turn their attention beyond their own "havens in a heartless world" to consider the kinds of social involvement for which a love ethic might lead them to volunteer.

This is not a new idea for the churches. Some congregations have long performed in this way, at least in part. Others seem to be struggling to become this kind of action/support group. The sociological model underlying this idea is not new, either. It is the old idea of American pluralism, in which intermediate institutions, many of them voluntary, mediate between the central bureaucracy of the modern state and individuals who separately are powerless to deal with the central structure.

Much of the appeal of the Moral Majority has been to that sense of powerlessness. Late figures indicate a slippage in the popularity of that movement (for example, see Martin, 1981: 7-16), perhaps because its stridency is not meeting the needs of people looking for a positive ethic. If an ethic of love could assist church and family to become relevant to the public sphere, while still retaining a focus on the local and the personal, they might assist the modernization process to overcome some of its negative consequences.

The age groups most affected by the new values accompanying modernization are now forming families, and in many cases are tentatively making contact with churches. It remains to be seen whether they can help mold those institutions into forms that provide both commitment and freedom, both self-enhancement and sufficient regulation to make the world they construct a reliable one, and to make real the new values they are trying to implement.

NOTES

1. Herberg (1955) implies this process in the movement of third-generation immigrants from ethnic churches to those more generically related to the major traditions, which he observed during the height of the movement to suburbia after World War II. More specific evidence is surveyed in Glenn and Hyland (1967).

2. These phrases and others like them have become part of the common language, and have been reinforced by the works of such authors as Lasch (1979), Wolfe (1976), and Marin (1975).

3. The trends of popular religious response to this level of modernization have been ably caught by successive books of Harvey Cox, beginning with *The Secular City* (1965), then moving to *The Feast of Fools* (1969), and more recently *Turning East* (1977).

4. Much of my understanding of this issue has come from private discussions and meetings of such groups as the Welfare Rights Organization. More formal allusions to the issue may be found in Coles (1967), Sherry (1978), and Sabian (1976).

REFERENCES

Berger, P. and H. Kellner (1974) "Marriage and the construction of reality," pp. 157-174 in R. L. Coser (ed.) The Family: Its Structures and Functions. New York: St. Martin's.

Berger, P. and T. Luckmann (1966) The Social Construction of Reality. Garden City, NY: Doubleday.

Berger, P., B. Berger, and H. Kellner (1973) The Homeless Mind. New York: Random House.

Berlin, I. (1969) Four Essays on Liberty. New York: Oxford University Press.

Coles, R. (1967) "Who's to be born: abortion and the laws of the states." New Republic 156.

Cox, H. (1977) Turning East. New York: Simon & Schuster.

————— (1969) The Feast of Fools. Cambridge, MA: Harvard University Press.

————— (1965) The Secular City. New York: Macmillan.

D'Antonio, W. V. (1980) "The family and religion: exploring a changing relationship." Journal for the Scientific Study of Religion 19: 89-104.

Donzelot, J. (1979) The Policing of Families. New York: Pantheon.

Glenn, N. D. and R. Hyland (1967) "Religious preference and worldly success: some evidence from national surveys." American Sociological Review 32: 73-85.

Herberg, W. (1955) Protestant-Catholic-Jew. Garden City, NY: Doubleday.

Lasch, C. (1979) The Culture of Narcissism. New York: Norton.

————— (1977) Haven in a Heartless World: The Family Besieged. New York: Basic Books.

Lenski, G. (1961) The Religious Factor. Garden City, NY: Doubleday.

McCarthy, J. (1979) "Religious commitment, affiliation, and marriage dissolution," in R. Wuthnow (ed.) The Religious Dimension: New Directions in Quantitative Research. New York: Academic.

Marin, P. (1975) "The new narcissism." Harper's (October).

Martin, W. (1981) "The birth of the media myth." Atlantic (June): 7-16.

Mead, M. (1970) Culture and Commitment: A Study of the Generation Gap. Garden City, NY: Doubleday.

Moore, W. (1979) World Modernization. New York: Elsevier.

Orr, J. and F. P. Nichelson (1970) The Radical Suburb. Philadelphia: Westminster.

Riesman, D., R. Denney, and N. Glazer (1950) The Lonely Crowd. New Haven, CT: Yale University Press.

Sabian, M.J., Jr. (1976) "Abortion: the class religion." National Review 28 (January): 28-31.

Sherry, P. (1978) "The class conflict over abortion." Public Interest 52: 69-84.

Williams, R. (1955) American Society. New York: Knopf.

Wolfe, T. (1976) "The 'me' decade and the third great awakening." New York 23 (August): 26-40.

Yankelovich, D. (1981) New Rules: Searching for Self-Fulfillment in a World Turned Upside Down. New York: Random House.

——— (1974) The New Morality. New York: McGraw-Hill.

2

FAMILY MORALITY AND FAMILY MORTALITY
Speculations on the Demographic Transition

Teresa A. Sullivan

If birth and death are the ultimate facts, then one overwhelming characteristic of contemporary society is our relative lack of personal experience of them. Unlike earlier generations, we are not familiar with birth or death. A contemporary woman might experience the birth of two or three children, but many adults never witness a birth. A man or woman can easily reach middle age without ever experiencing the death of a loved one. It is difficult for us to understand what daily life must have been like in a society in which both birth and death are frequent — even commonplace — and where the latter all too often occurs within hours of the former. Life was, as Hobbe noted, nasty, mean, and brutish; but above all, life was short.[1]

For most of human history, high fertility and high mortality have been the ordinary conditions of life. Translated from austere vital rates and statistics into individual experience, this means that most humans have been affected by many births and many deaths (if they themselves lived long enough). Moreover, short lives have been very common. From the society's point of view, "turnover" has been very high. Mechanisms of social control and socialization have had to adapt to relatively large numbers of children, many of whom lived only briefly, as well as to frequent disruptions caused by the deaths of other persons.

Author's Note: This chapter is a revision of a paper presented at the Seminar on Religion and Family in Contemporary Society, University of Notre Dame, June 19, 1981. I am grateful to the seminar participants, especially William V. D'Antonio and Joseph Fitzpatrick, S.J., for their insightful comments. Sherry Young typed the manuscript. The preparation of this chapter was assisted by NICHD Grant HD06160-11A1 to the Population Research Center at the University of Texas — Austin.

The history of social groups and institutions is at least partly the struggle to form collective efforts or "corporate actors" that will outlive their individual members and provide continuity from generation to generation (for a development of this idea, see Coleman, 1974). Much of what is today called "social history" is the story of the transition of corporate actors: great families, dynasties, states. "High turnover" was part of the raison d'etre for the corporate actor and it was also one of the corporate actor's enduring problems. Mechanisms of social control and socialization were vested in corporate actors.

As often happens today in a factory with high turnover, the constant shifting of personnel encouraged harsh discipline. Only after some differentiation of corporate actors could the discipline be relaxed. Nowadays we turn for love and support to family and religion, but this was not always the case for earlier generations. Historians have described the premodern family as an economic institution in which love was neither necessary nor sufficient. By the same token, religious doctrine and authority were called upon for social control as much as for spiritual growth.

The great religious and ethical codes of humankind were formulated against this high-mortality, high-fertiltiy demographic backdrop. Religious and family obligations were linked, and demographic rewards, such as a long life and many children, were promised for the fulfillment of one's duties. In the Decalogue, this link between morality and mortality was explicit: "Honor your father and your mother, that you may have a long life in the land which the Lord, your God, is giving you" (Exodus 20:1).[2]

However, in these days when such demographic rewards are easily within reach, even without religious observance, there is a pervasive sense of "crisis" in the family. Perhaps it is ironic that the sense of crisis seems to be strongest where the demographic circumstances are most favorable. The thesis of this chapter is that many contemporary problems of family morality arise from both the changed demographic context and the subsequent differentiation of corporate actors. To understand this idea, it is necessary first to review the changes in demographic conditions.

THE SHIFT IN DEMOGRAPHIC CONDITIONS

As human history goes, rapid demographic change is quite recent. Notable drops in mortality began to occur in Europe after 1750. Interestingly, although plagues had been viewed as God's judgment upon a society (Aries, 1981; Tuchman, 1978; McNeill, 1976), there were few who saw the deity's hand in the decline of mortality, and even fewer who suggested that the new lower mortality regime was a sign of God's pleasure with human societies. Instead, humankind was given all the credit. The declines in mortality among non-European societies came after several centuries' delay. Much of the current world population "crisis" is the result not so much of increased fertility as of the recent and precipitous decline in mortality rates.

The best indicator of how drastic this reduction in mortality has been is a look at life tables, which are mathematical models of the effects of a given schedule of death rates for every age. At the turn of the century, the expectation of life at birth for the world was 30 years (United Nations, 1971: 32); by 1980, life tables for the world showed that the expectation of life at birth had exactly doubled. If mortality conditions remain constant for the indefinite future, babies born in 1980 could expect to live to be 60 years old, on average.

The shift in mortality conditions from high death rates and low expectations of life at birth to low death rates and high expectations of life at birth has been called the "demographic transition." The study of when and how the demographic transition occurs, its causes and its timing, have been topics of great debate and research among demographers. The study of its consequences has not been pursued so vigorously (Demos, 1970: 180), possibly because the current stage of the demographic transition is apparently without parallel. Institutions evolve slowly, over long periods, and it is perhaps too early to chart the changes that accompany the demographic transition.

The assumption of this chapter is that the demographic context affects the course of family life. One consequence of the demographic transition is likely to be a worldwide change in family life. But the demographic transition has proceeded at different rates in different countries. In Western Europe, the expectation of life at birth is 72 years, and relatively low mortality conditions have prevailed for over 2 centuries. In Western Africa, where the expectation of life at birth is still only 42 years, low mortality is still not the uniform rule. In most African countries low mortality is a development only decades old. Presumably, then, any effects upon family life will be more easily discerned in Western Europe than in Africa. Moreover, existing cultures will affect the type of accommodation made in families. Nevertheless, despite variations in timing and culture, it is possible to discuss at a general level the effect of vital rates of families.

The Demographic Transition:
Changes in Vital Rates

Through the use of life tables, it is possible to model the demographic structure of a society at different stages of the demographic transition. Table 2.1, which was compiled by Hauser (1979: 6), does this. As the table shows, assumptions about the vital rates of a society permit inferences about the age structure, expectation of life at birth, and rate of growth of a population.

We assume that throughout most of human history mortality rates were fairly high and mortality was difficult to control. It is true that human societies always have some limited control over mortality. For example, war, infanticide, and capital punishment are matters over which humans or human societies have control. But for most of human history, the major killers, including congenital and developmental disorders, famine, disease, climatic catastrophes, and nonhuman predators, were beyond the control of humans. Magic, medicine, and religious intercession were among the ways in which humans sought to control mortality, but they met with relatively little success.

The first model in Table 2.1 might well have applied to the earliest human societies. Mortality rates were high, about 50 deaths per 1000 persons per year. Infant mortality was especially high, with perhaps as many as 200 of every 1000 babies not living through the first year of life. As a result, the expectation of life at birth was only 20 years. It increased somewhat for those who survived the first year of life. Fertility rates were also high. (Societies that did not have correspondingly high fertility rates disappeared.) Yet in this "primitive stationary" population, despite high fertility, there was virtually no population growth. Fertility and mortality rates fluctuated from year to year, but over the long run, the numbers of births and deaths remained approximately in balance.

With the limited control over the environment that accompanied the agricultural revolution, human societies could claim for the first time both an economic surplus and a limited rate of population growth — perhaps as much as 1 percent per annum. This situation, the second model in Table 2.1, was maintained with somewhat lower mortality rates, fairly high fertility rates, and slightly longer expectations of life at birth.

The third model describes the beginning of what is usually called the demographic transition. Mortality rates had fallen, but fertility rates remained high. Fertility had evolved strong pronatalist institutions and norms, partly because the technology of control over death preceded the control over births. The control over some previously inescapable means of death occurred at about the time of the Industrial Revolution. The increased economic surplus made possible improvements in public health, sanitation, food availability, and transportation. Mortality dropped fairly slowly in Europe and North America. In the developing world, where the "death control"

TABLE 2.1 Model Demographic Profiles Under Varying Fertility and Mortality Levels

Population Characteristic	Primitive Stationary*	Premodern†	Tran- sitional‡	Modern§	Modern Stationary‖
Birth rate	50.0	43.7	45.7	20.4	12.9
Death rate	50.0	33.7	15.7	10.4	12.9
Annual growth rate (%)	0.0	1.0	3.0	1.0	0.0
Age structure					
Percent under 15	36.2	37.8	45.4	27.2	19.2
Percent 15-64	60.9	58.8	52.0	62.4	62.3
Percent 65 and over	2.9	3.4	2.6	10.3	18.5
Average age	25.5	25.1	21.8	32.8	40.0
Dependency ratio, total	64	70	92	60	61
Youth (under 15)	59	64	87	44	31
Aged (65 and over)	5	6	5	16	30
Percent surviving to age 15	41.0	55.9	78.8	95.6	98.9
Expectation of life at birth (years)	20.0	30.0	50.0	70.0	77.5
Average number of children born to a woman reaching age 50	6.2	5.5	6.1	2.9	2.7
Average number of children surviving to age 20	2.3	2.9	4.7	2.7	2.0

SOURCE: Hauser (1979:6); based on data from stable populations of "west" females. Reprinted by permission.

*Mortality level 1 (for definition of levels, see source).
†Mortality level 5.
‡Mortality level 13.
§Mortality level 21.
‖Mortality level 24.

was not imported until after World War II, the mortality decline occurred very rapidly — almost literally overnight in the case of some countries. The expectation of life at birth soared and, because of the high fertility, the age structure of the population became much different, with relatively more young people. Under these conditions, the population experienced rapid rates of population increase. This is the model that best describes vital rates in many of today's developing countries, especially in Africa.

The fourth model shows a later stage in the demographic transition, when fertility rates have fallen into closer balance with death rates. The fifth model shows the theorized completion of this process, with an expectation of life at birth of 77.5 years. Both because people live longer and because relatively few babies are being born, the age structure changes. The average age of such a society is older. In this model, there is once again no growth in the population, but this time the equilibrium is achieved at a low level of fertility and mortality, rather than at the high rates seen in the first model.

The fourth describes much of the industrialized world. The fifth model does not yet describe any society fully, although some European countries seem to be approaching this model — albeit with annual fluctuations in vital rates. We know little, even in theory, about the transition from the fourth to the fifth model. Although previous transitions accompanied an economic revolution, most demographers write as if current trends, continued for a long enough period of time, will be sufficient to bring today's industrialized societies to the fifth model. The attention of the researchers has been focused instead on ways to hasten the transition from the third model to the fourth in the developing world.

Demographic transition theory describes in broad, sweeping generalizations the basic structure of a society. By itself, it does not describe what happens to the small human groups, where fertility rates are translated into the birth of children or siblings, and where mortality rates are experienced as the deaths of loved ones. Because birth and death are experienced in families, it seems likely that these broad societal changes in vital rates will be reflected in family experience. Our lack of knowledge about how societies move from the fourth model in Table 2.1 to the fifth implies that we have little knowledge about how families will be affected. More generally, family consequences throughout the transition have been little researched and only imperfectly understood. Thus (as the title of this chapter warns) what follows will be speculation upon the micro-level consequences of these macro-level changes.

Family Relationships in
the Late Demographic Transition

As mortality rates have fallen, the most important consequence for family members is the expectation of longer and more certain relationships with family members. Both of these aspects of relationships are important. Even under high-mortality conditions, some relationships do in fact last for a long time because at least some persons are long-lived. But the certainty that any given relationship will last for a long period is much lower. In our society, most parents can confidently expect to see all of their children reach adulthood. As recently as a century ago, 161 of every 1000 babies born in Massachusetts died in the first year of life (U.S. Bureau of the Census, 1975: 57). The rest of the United States was little better. Today's infant mortality rate ranges from 11 to 13 per 1000 babies born in Western Europe or the United States. By the same token, the probabilities of a child's being orphaned or of the early widowhood of married persons have greatly diminished (for details, see Ryder, 1974; Sullivan, 1978).

A first generalization about the effect of the demographic transition is that the conditions for interpersonal bonding were improved. But cultural and other institutional factors affect the actual expression of bonding in a society. Because cultures differ, the effects of lower mortality may be experienced in quite different, even contradictory ways.

An example of contradictory effects is the treatment of children in the early demographic transition. Aries (1962), in particular, is associated with the idea of the "sentimental revolution." The sentimental revolution refers to a profound change in the way in which adults viewed the child. This change was reflected in everything from art to education to clothing. It manifested itself in a subtle change from a distant, instrumental approach to children to a sentimental, affectionate, and ultimately child-centered family.

By contrast, and citing similar demographic data within a different cultural setting, Stone (1975, 1977) has pointed to the rise of patriarchy, with its stern new attitude toward children, in England. Under the influence of puritan religion, parents were admonished to "beat the devil" out of their children — quite literally. Schooling, family norms, and village law combined to reinforce the rights (indeed the responsibilities) of parents to discipline children.

Both of these approaches have been explained by the process of "bonding," which was believed to be facilitated by lower infant mortality and the greater certainty that children would live to adulthood.[3] In Aries's formulation, the bonding led to a sentimental cherishing and indulging of children, and to the setting aside of childhood as a special time of innocence. In Stone's formulation, the bonding, reinforced by religious belief, led to greater zeal in reforming the depraved humanity with which the child was endowed.

As this example indicates, no single set of consequences necessarily flows from demographic change. Although demographic change provides the basic structure within which change may occur, economic, cultural, social, and religious influences may then come into play. What is important about the later stages of the demographic transition is that the basic structure is expanded and enlarged, allowing a greater variety of formulations.

THE FAMILY "CRISIS" AND THE LATE DEMOGRAPHIC TRANSITION

Family Structure

As the discussion above suggests, a narrow demographic determinism is inadequate for discussing a family "crisis." Nevertheless, the low-mortality regime is one factor conducive to greater variation in family forms. This variety will almost surely be seen among cultures, as Aries's discussion for the European continent and Stone's discussion for England suggest. But in addition, a greater variety may spring up within cultures. Greater heterogeneity in family structure is often cited as evidence of "crisis."

There are probably no new family forms within the United States — although some observers might wish to argue about various communal arrangements — but a few household structures that were previously unusual have become much more common. Among them are the unmarried, cohabiting couple (with or without palimony arrangements), various types of single parent-child combinations, joint households of two divorced parents with their children, families with "his-hers-and-ours" sets of children, and single-person households. Demographic structure has not "created" these forms, for they have all existed for centuries. But their incidence is proportionately greater because household structure varies with age and life-cycle stage, and more persons live through the entire life cycle. Moreover, the greater certainty of living through the adult years makes it possible for a young person to postpone establishing a family household.

Changing Functions of the Family

In high-mortality societies, the family tends to be multifunctional: It serves as the labor supply, the source of credit, and the owner of capital, and as the unit of both production and consumption. Families may also play dominant roles in politics, religion, education, and art. For the individual in such a society, one's family name and one's position in that family are likely to determine all rights and privileges. But in addition, the family is always there to provide sustenance, advice, and even collective revenge for any injuries to family members.

One reason for the preeminence of the family in high-mortality societies is that there is relatively little economic surplus to foster the growth of other institutions. Moreover, most lives are too short to permit extensive career building outside the family. While there was rudimentary development of religion, government, and the military, it was not until fairly recently in human history that institutional specialization flourished. The same economic revolutions that facilitated the demographic transition also fostered institutional development. In particular, families were supplanted by other social organizations as units of production and even as agencies of socialization and social control.

As other institutions have specialized, the family has also specialized. In the low-mortality society that makes long, close relationships more possible, the family has specialized in providing warm, affective support and a comfortable haven away from the bustling world of other institutions. The "crisis" of the family is partly one of defining what functions legitimately belong to it and not to other institutions, and partly one of developing techniques for fostering long, loving relationships. In terms of the former task, the family faces competition from the state and from profit-making organizations that perform the same functions — always at a price, either collective or individual. The task of fostering love is not one for which many institutions compete, but it is a difficult task in a world where love has been a luxury. How these elements of the family "crisis" interact can be seen by examining two areas: death and child bearing.

DEATH AND THE FAMILY

Death in the High-Mortality Regime

Through most of history, death has been very common. To be sure, dying was accompanied by its own ritual, but the dying were still integral members of their families. Families, in turn, were accustomed to handling death; although death was probably never routine, it was a commonplace event with which most households were familiar.

Dealing with sickness or death was likely to be a perennial problem, but preventing or postponing death was difficult with the resources available. Today, in countries where death is common, contemporary Westerners are likely to comment that "life is cheap." The more accurate statement might be that extended life is impossible to afford. The striking differences in Eastern and Western world views on life and death may thus reflect their different demographic and economic conditions as much as differences in religious imagery and history.

Death in the Low-Mortality Regime

In the contemporary Western world, where death is relatively rare, it is possible to devote vast resources to personnel and equipment for keeping people alive. Elaborate neonatal intensive care units, kidney dialysis units, and exotic surgical techniques are some ways in which we save lives that only ten years ago would have been thought to be doomed. Although we cannot remove the inevitability of death, we can hope to delay it.

This hope, in turn, justifies the institutionalization of death. New levels of economic surplus finance the institutionalization of death. Doctors and families isolate the sick and dying in hospitals and nursing homes in hopes of helping them. Indeed, women in widely different parts of the world have been honored for "humanizing" death through new institutions — Cecily Saunders of the hospice movement in Britain, and Mother Teresa, who has initiated shelters for the dying in India.[4]

But because of our very unfamiliarity with death, such institutionalization of the dying may serve only to ensure their "social deaths" before the physical death occurs. In much the same way, widows and other bereaved persons must report a sense of isolation and social distance from their friends and relatives. Some ritual isolation of the bereaved is customary in many societies, but one wonders if it becomes less ritualized and thus less manageable where bereavement is relatively uncommon.

The effects of these changes on the family are not easy to trace. The staging of death has, for many families, ceased to be a family function. Moreover, the cathartic or integrating effects of the death of a family member may also be lost to the family. In their place we find different phenomena: "social death" and "pseudodeath."

Social Death. Social death refers to the isolation or ostracism of an individual. The ostracism may be relatively widespread in an entire community, as in the "shunning" practiced by certain religious groups or the "silence" previously employed by cadets at West Point. Or the ostracism may be specific to a particular relationship or set of relationships, as in a divorce. Social death may be inflicted for a deliberate act or pattern of behavior, or it may result from an involuntary condition (as in the isolation of the dying person).

Because human relationships are more likely to be long lasting in the low-mortality society, social death may come to replace physical death as the termination of a relationship. Thus divorce and serial monogamy may replace widowhood and remarriage. However, unlike physical death, social death is not permanent. It can be delayed indefinitely or repealed.

For this reason, a variety of extrafamilial institutions may try to mediate. Counselors of various types, medical specialists, new housing arrangements, and other specialized help may be called upon to relieve family tension. Institutional arrangements may mitigate tensions that arise at predictable points in the family life cycle. For example, day care centers for preschool children and college dormitories for young adults may relieve tensions in the parental home and prevent the "illness" or "death" of a family relationship. However, the fact that such extrafamilial assistance exists may be taken as further proof of the family "crisis."

Pseudodeath. Especially in Western societies, human groupings are often oriented to problem solving. In previous centuries, the family "agenda" of problems might have been full of illness or the impending deaths of various family members. Today, a problem-oriented family agenda is likely to be focused on the relationships within the family. But keeping relationships strong and healthy is not an area in which we have a great deal of accumulated lore and expertise.

It is possible that in some families a new "problem" or "pseudodeath" provides the solution and keeps the family agenda full. The pseudodeath may be the abuse of alcohol, drugs, or food by one family member; it may be violence within the family, or the vicarious thrill of flirting with death through one family member's pursuit of delinquency, dangerous leisure activities, or dangerous substances. Once again, one or more family members are in danger, and the rest of the family may legitimately worry about it. Most recitations of the "crisis" in the family allude to the increase in pseudodeath behavior. But the pseudodeath, like a physical death, can be source of family integration.

To summarize, the low-mortality regime may produce consequences that are interpreted as elements of the family "crisis." These consequences include the loss of death and dying as a focus for family integration, the greater likelihood that relationships will be terminated through social death, and the pursuit of pseudodeath by family members.

CHILDREN IN THE MODERN FAMILY

A central aspect of the alleged family "crisis" is the role of children in the family. Few observers are likely to romanticize "the good old days" of high mortality, with its epidemics and plagues, but there is more nostalgia about the devoted parents with large families that some believe were once common. Thus it is worth considering the social aspects of birth in high-mortality and low-mortality regimes.

Birth in the High-Mortality Regime

The high-mortality populations of which we have knowledge tended to be high-fertility populations as well (the ones that were not did not survive). What this meant for any given family is that the experience of pregnancy and childbirth must have been common, much as death was. Perhaps childbirth was so commonplace that, as Aries (1981) said of death, it was "tame." At any rate, births were common events and difficult to prevent, especially for married women. Births, like deaths, were family events, although the women from the village played supporting roles in the European cultures. "Professional" attendants were common (just as a priest or physician might attend the dying), but birthing was still a home event.

Birth in the Low-Mortality Regime

Many, although not all, low-mortality regimes also have low fertility. The most striking fact about the low-mortality regime is the ability to control the number of births. Demographic studies of historical data reveal that effective fertility control was being practiced well before the advent of the "modern" control measures (the pill, IUD, contraceptive sterilization) and despite the official opposition of corporate actors.

Economic surpluses were growing at the same time that birthrates were declining. In most economically advanced countries, corporate actors were successful in institutionalizing pregnancy and delivery. Medical intervention and government incentives or regulations influenced the transfer of births from homes to hospitals. More recently, a strong countertrend to this institutionalization has occurred, accompanied by demands for a more family-centered birth experience. Because of this movement, births may become an important integrating experience for families — perhaps even more important than formerly, when taboos banished men from childbirth.

Nevertheless, few prospective mothers in the developed countries plan to have more than two children. However profound their experience of birth may be, they do not plan to repeat it more than once. A number of observers see low fertility as one manifestation of a family "crisis." Catholic theologians used to refer to a "contraceptive mentality," but it may be more accurate to refer to an ambivalence about children.

Ambivalence About Children

Both Aries (1980) and Huber (1980) have recently pointed to the very low fertility rates in the Western world. Huber argues that the fertility rate could continue to fall, because women have been provided with so many alternatives to childbearing. Aries notes that although the original drop in fertility allowed parents to cherish and provide for their children with greater diligence — part of the "sentimental revolution" — the later drop in fertility has been motivated by quite different mechanisms. Far from being child centered, Aries argues, we now deprecate children. Childlessness has become more respectable, and motherhood is less esteemed than formerly.

There are many bits of data that could be adduced to support this hypothesis. One need only look at the number of restaurants that forbid children in defiance of the common law responsibility of common carriers. Or one may look at rental housing — over 37 percent of rental units in the United States now forbid children, up 10 percent from only a few years ago. There is increased support for having no children or only one child, and increased disapproval for large families. And birth control has become so noncontroversial that it has been dropped as an item from most national surveys of public opinion.

Certainly this represents a change from the biblical image of children as olive plants set about one's table. Far from being ornaments, children are sometimes viewed as burdens or twenty-year sentences. Periodic studies assess the costs of raising a child to maturity. Other studies allege the occupational disadvantages to workers who are also parents (Montagna, 1977: 390). Nevertheless, zero fertility looks unlikely. Most Americans continue to report that the family is their greatest source of satisfaction, and most Americans still expect to have children, although there is now less heterogeneity in the numbers of children they expect to have. Throughout the United States, there is substantial convergence on the two-child norm (Sullivan, 1981).

The question then becomes whether the two-child norm can itself be taken as a sign of family "crisis," or at least as a sign of decreasing parental interest. Those who would argue that this is a manifestation of crisis point to the intrusion of other institutions into the family's childbearing responsibilities. In Europe, governments provide income, goods, and services to parents of small children, and especially to pregnant women and mothers of infants (Berelson, 1974). Such programs are much smaller in the United States, but the United States has recently seen a substantial expansion in private-sector child care. For example, between 1970 and 1980 the number of 3- and 4-year-olds enrolled in nursery schools nearly doubled, from 1.1 million to 2 million (U.S. Bureau of the Census, 1981). This occurred during the so-called baby bust, when fertility levels were at near-record lows.

Other institutional developments, such as the growth of "parenting seminars" and parents' support networks, may be viewed as quasi-institutional assistance to the family, or as further intrusion into the family's decision making.

These interpretations turn on parental motivation, a variable that is difficult to assess with any accuracy. If parents have few children because child rearing is a low priority and child care is expensive, then the family's functions may be contracting further. But perhaps there is an alternative explanation to low fertility that does not derive from parental selfishness, "the contraceptive mentality," or a family "crisis."

An Alternative Explanation for Low Fertility

It is naive to postulate that the fifth stage of the demographic transition is reached by an equilibrium at which a society "perceives" that its fertility and mortality must remain in balance. But it is possible that a family equilibrium may be desired by individuals as a result of the "bonding" process mentioned above. "Bonding" refers to the relatively long-term and affectionate relationship between members of a family. Most people probably cannot be bonded to too many people at one time; the emotional investment is simply too much. Most of us are extremely close to only a few people at a time. Yet, barring divorce or untimely death, the family members to whom we are bonded are likely to live for a long time. Low fertility may be a way to meet the command to "honor thy father and thy mother" in their old age without straining too much one's emotional (and financial) commitments.

Indeed, low fertility is the only way in which a married couple can limit its commitments. Family members already alive cannot be ignored except at considerable personal cost. And limiting fertility is much more acceptable than taking steps to raise mortality (or even the incidence of "social death"). Some hypothetical data will illustrate this point.

Table 2.2. is based on data taken from Sweden in 1778-1782 and 1965. In the 1778-1772 period, Sweden had a crude birthrate of 34.5 per

TABLE 2.2   Probabilities of Given Numbers of Dependents, Model Family,[a]
Sweden, 1778-1782 and 1965

Mother's Age[b]	1778-82		1965	
	30	35	30	35
Grandparents' generation				
Mother's parents	.40	.28	.80	.70
both alive	(2)	(2)	(2)	(2)
Father's parents	.40	.28	.80	.70
both alive	(2)	(2)	(2)	(2)
Both sets of	.16	.08	.64	.49
parents alive	(4)	(4)	(4)	(4)
Grandparents' generation plus children's generation				
All children	.55	.29	.96	.92
alive	(2)	(3)	(2)	(3)
All children,	.22	.08	.78	.66
one specific set	(4)	(5)	(4)	(5)
of parents alive				
All children,	.09	.02	.49	.45
both sets of	(6)	(7)	(6)	(7)
parents alive				

SOURCE: Calculated from data in Keyfitz and Flieger (1968: 462-463, 508-509).

a. Assumes mothers and fathers were the same age, and were born when their parents were 30 years old. First child is born to mother at age 25, second at age 29, and third at age 30. For children, male and female values of 1_x are averaged.

b. Probabilities assessed at age 30 before birthday of third child. Probabilities assessed at age 35 after birth of three children.

thousand and a crude death rate of 25.9 per thousand, with 31.9 percent of the population under the age of 15. According to Table 2.1, this would have put Sweden somewhere between the first and second models of the demographic transition. In 1965, the crude birthrate was 15.9 and the crude death rate was 10.1 with 20.9 percent of the population younger that 15 — indicators much closer to the fifth model in Table 2.1.

Let us assume that a woman and a man married at the same age, and that both of them were born when their parents were 30 years old. Assume further that the woman became a mother for the first time at age 25 and for the second time at age 29. Assume that a third child was born during the thirtieth year, sometime after the mother's birthday. These assumptions are designed merely to simplify the discussion, but they are not unreasonable assumptions, except for the assumption that spouses are the same age.

The first column of Table 2.2 indicates that when our hypothetical mother is age 30 in 1778-1782, the probability is only .22 that her children and her parents will be alive; by age 35 the probability has

TABLE 2.3   Fertility, Mortality, and Probability of Adult Siblings, Sweden, 1778-1782 to 1965

Year	TFR	Probability All Siblings Survive[a]	Probability at Least Two Siblings Survive[b]	CDR
1778-82	4.5	.08	.20	26
1803-07	4.3	.11	.25	25
1828-32	4.5	.13	.28	26
1853-57	4.3	.14	.31	23
1878-82	4.3	.20	.35	18
1903-07	3.8	.44	.58	15
1928-32	2.4	.74	.74	12
1943-47	2.5	.86	.86	11
1958-62	2.2	.94	.94	10
1965	2.4	.94	.94	10

SOURCE: First and fourth columns from Keyfitz and Flieger (1968: 462-509); second and third columns calculated from data in same source.

a. Assumes number of siblings is equivalent to whole number in first column; female l_x evaluated at age 35.

b. Based on female l_x evaluated at age 35.

dropped to .08. The comparable probabilities in 1965 were .78 and .66. The probabilities that all children and both sets of parents will be alive are .09 for the 30-year old woman in 1778-1782 and .02 for her at age 35. But in 1965, the same probabilities are .49 and .45. Thus the probabilities that a 35-year-old woman would have 7 dependents (in the emotional sense) rose from .02 to .45.

The effect of having the third child is shown by comparing the first and second columns with the third and fourth columns. The probability of having 3 living children at age 35 in 1778-1782 was only .29, but a substantial drop from the .55 for 2 children. By 1965, the probability for 3 living children was very little different from the probability for 2 living children — from .96 to .92. Thus an additional birth in 1965 almost surely guaranteed an additional dependent; moreover, the older generation, the parental generation, was far more likely still to be alive. The probability that at least one set of parents would be alive on the wife's thirty-fifth birthday was only .16 in 1778-1782, but 1.00 in 1965.

Complicating the picture somewhat are the data in Table 2.3 which shows the total fertility rate in Sweden in selected years. Assuming that the average family had the same number of children as the whole number in the total fertility rate, the second column shows the probablility that all of the siblings would survive to age 35 and the third column shows the probability that our hypothetical mother would have a brother or sister survive to age 35. The probability rises from .20 to .94 — an indicator that there might be some help available for the aged parents, but also an indicator that there is yet another family relationship to be considered.

Husbands and wives cannot easily cut off relationships with parents and siblings; the only leeway in their emotional networks may be to reduce the number of children they have. Thus the decline in the fertility rate may represent a kind of personal "equilibrium" in choosing to have closely bonded relationships with a few family members. And what may initially be viewed as a selfish, even immoral attitude toward the next generation may be the result of a complicated but caring network of relationships with older generations.

CONCLUSION

Conventional moral codes were formulated under conditions of high mortality. Low mortality provides more options, and the new options may modify or obscure previous moral positions. Family morality in a time of low mortality is not an easy matter to discuss. The very state of low mortality may make the possible family forms more varied and may distract us into questions about how the family (by which we usually mean a certain model of the family) can survive. If we can look beyond those issues, we may investigate "relationship mortality," an aspect of morality that is of greater importance to contemporary families. And finally, conventional aspects of family morality may themselves contribute to the low fertility that is seen as the end of the demographic transition.

NOTES

1. The famous quotation from Thomas Hobbes is found in *Leviathan*, part I, chapter 13.
2. That the promise should be long life is hardly surprising. Humans have always yearned for long life, although relatively few have achieved it. Long life has been viewed in most religious traditions as a blessing, although its opposite (being more common) was not necessarily considered a curse. In folk tales and traditions, heroic figures have often been long-lived, often much longer-lived than contemporary historical or biological evidence indicates was likely. The exceptionally long lives attributed to the patriarchs in the Hebrew scriptures are one example. But even in more recent times, prominent figures have lived disproportionately long lives. This is not necessarily the result of their excellence, but it does allow several generations of their relatives and countrymen to recognize their excellence (for a series of examples of this principle, see Sullivan, 1979).
3. However, as my colleague Myron Gutmann has noted, this proposition makes strong assumptions about parents' relationships to live children based on relationships to dead children.

4. The irony of this fact in no way detracts from the significance of their contributions. Even institutional shelters for the dying are preferable to no shelter, and hospices are often more compassionate to the dying than are modern hospitals.

REFERENCES

Aries, P. (1981) The Hour of Our Death (H. Weaver, trans.). New York: Knopf.
—— (1980) "Two successive motivations for the declining birth rate in the West" (P. M. Ranum, trans.). Population and Development Review 6 (December): 645-650.
—— (1962) Centuries of Childhood (R. Baldrich, trans.). London: J. Cape.
Berelson, B. [ed.] (1974) Population Policy in the Developed Countries. New York: Mc Graw-Hill.
Coale, A. J. and P. Demeny (1966) Regional Model Life Tables and Stable Populations. Princeton, NJ: Princeton University Press.
Coleman, J. S. (1974) Power and the Structure of Society. New York: Norton.
Demos, J. (1970) A Little Commonwealth: Family Life in Plymouth Colony. New York, Oxford University Press.
Hauser, P. M. (1979) "Introduction and overview," pp. 1-62 in P. M. Hauser (ed.) World Population and Development. Syracuse, NY: Syracuse University Press.
Huber, J. (1980) "Will U.S. fertility decline toward zero?" Sociological Quarterly 21 (August): 481-492.
Keyfitz, N. and W. Flieger (1968) World Population: An Analysis of Vital Data. Chicago University of Chicago Press.
Mc Neill, W. (1976) Plagues and People. Garden City, NY: Doubleday.
Montagna, P. (1977) Occupations and Society. New York: John Wiley.
Ryder, N. B. (1974) "Influence of changes in the family cycle upon family life." Presented at the Symposium on Population and the Family, United Nations Economic and Social Council World Population Conference, Honolulu, August 6-15, 1974.
Stone, L. J. (1977) The Family, Sex, and Marriage in England 1500-1800. New York: Harper & Row.
—— (1975) "The rise of the nuclear family in early modern England: the patriarchal stage," pp. 13-58 in C. E. Rosenberg (ed.) The Family in History. Philadelphia: University of Pennsylvania Press.
Sullivan, T. A. (1981) "Family and fertility," in A. M. Greeley et al., Young Catholics in the United States and Canada. New York: Sadlier.
—— (1979) "Longer lives and life-long relations: a life table exegesis." Concilium 141: 27-38.
—— (1978) "Numbering our days aright: human longevity and the problem of intimacy," pp. 282-294 in D. Tracy et al. (eds.) Towards Vatican III. New York: Seabury.
Tuchman, B. (1978) A Distant Mirror: The Calamitous 14th Century. New York: Knopf.
United Nations, Department of Social Affairs, Population Branch (1971) The World Population in 1970. Population Study 1949. New York: Author.
U.S. Bureau of the Census (1981) Current Population Reports. School Enrollment — Social and Economic Characteristics of Students: October 1980. Advance Report, Series P-20, No. 362 (May). Washington, DC: Government Printing Office.
—— (1975) Historical Statistics of the United States, Colonial Times to 1970. Bicentennial Edition, Part 2. Washington, DC: Government Printing Office.

3

PROBLEMATIC ELEMENTS IN THE RELATIONSHIPS BETWEEN CHURCHES AND FAMILIES

Joan Aldous

Over the years, there has developed a fairly active research tradition relating various aspects of religious and family behavior. Much of this research has been concerned with the social control functions of religion rather than its caring function, a distinction discussed by D'Antonio in Chapter 4 of this volume. For example, religious affiliation, frequency of attendance at religious services, and other measures of religiosity have been shown to be related to such family behaviors as fertility (Spicer and Gustavus, 1974), marital stability (Kunz and Albrecht, 1977), kin contacts (Becker, 1978), and family role definitions (McMurry, 1978). As part of this same research tradition, the effect of family variables on religious behaviors such as parent-child relations or intergenerational similarities in religious beliefs and activities (Weiting, 1975; Montgomery and Montgomery, 1975) have also been examined.

In this chapter however, a different facet of the religion-family relationships will be examined. The mutual interdependence of these two institutions can be seen as an uneasy association in which there are problematic elements for both. In this discussion of the topic, the behavior of the clergy and of families will be examined within the context of church values and doctrine among Christian denominations in the United States. The emphasis will be on families' search for support from religious doctrine and practitioners in times of trouble.

Author's Note: This chapter is a revision of a paper originally presented at the Seminar on Families and Religion, University of Notre Dame Center for the Study of American Catholicism. Joseph Fichter, S.J., William Silverman, and Kathleen Maas Weigert provided perceptive comments on a previous draft.

Issues to be addressed include the women's rights movement, which has disrupted traditional accommodations between religious and family institutions and can have sorrowful consequences for individuals in both groupings. Other events discussed, such as divorce or separation, are for some individuals matters of relief and rejoicing, but are misfortunes for others. Yet the latters' search for help from church functionaries may be frustrated by prevailing church values and doctrine. From the perspective of churches, an enduring issue considered here is the clergy's work with families, which can involve the organized church in the secular world to the extent that traditional religious values are placed in jeopardy.

FAMILIES SEARCH FOR COMFORT

For many families today, the moral attitudes in traditional church doctrines, which clergy taught and enforced through sanctions, seem less clear-cut. The evil of premarital sex, the indissolubility of marriage, and the restriction of women to wife-mother roles are beliefs that no longer go without question, as we shall see later in the chapter. But if families are questioning some of the doctrines churches have traditionally enforced, their very loss of certitude increases families' need for the caring function, for which religion and the clergy have also traditionally been responsible, in times of trouble.

The fleetingness of life, whether one's own or the lives of loved ones, has been the supreme misfortune, and it is within the intimate confines of the family that the most tragic losses for the living occur (see Weigert and Hastings, 1977). Religious functionaries have always served to legitimate as well as to officiate at this final *rite de passage*. The death of a loved one also leads the living to seek comfort from religion and its representatives, one of whose primary responsibilities in the area of pastoral care is to deal with persons in times of grief and to put their loss into meaningful context.[1]

As Sullivan points out in Chapter 2 of this volume, the demographic transition has meant that the biblical standard of three score years and ten is being increasingly met among people in the industrialized countries. Thus the hold on people religion once possessed, because of their fear or hope of what followed death, the control function, has been weakened. Long life leads people to look for happiness in this world and to discount warnings of how their present conduct will affect their fate after death. But the very fact that death is increasingly absent from daily living, due to persons being active longer, can make it more difficult to accept. Among the feeble elderly, death may be a welcome release from present suffering. For their survivors, who have had longer to cherish the deceased, however, death continues to be a source of sadness. Thus the comfort clergy are trained to give, the caring function of the church, continues to be important for moderns unaccustomed and unprepared for death in the midst of life.

Even if persons are born, are married, and die in due time under the aegis of some church official, other events may cloud the atmosphere of family living and increase the importance of churches to the religious. The nature of the human condition is such that life-course events, because of the untoward happenings, occur out of phase or do not occur at all. Family members die too soon or live too long, children are ungrateful when older or overly dependent, love affairs fail to come to fruition, spouses cease to care or care too much, and families unexpectedly fail or unexpectedly succeed. Thus families are faced with emotional strain from unforeseen as well as foreseen events ranging from natural catastrophes to "unnatural" hatreds that cannot be controlled (see Yinger, 1977). Traditionally, churches and their functionaries have been a source of help for families under such unhappy circumstances.

Families are also faced with strains stemming from failure of strongly held expectations to come to pass. Children, despite the best of care, do sicken and die, and spouses ask for divorces. Again families can expect comfort from their churches when cherished expectations are blasted and hopes fail. As Parsons (1952) notes, the strain from the unexpected and the uncontrollable is compounded by the questions of why anyone in God's creation has to experience such tragedies, and, if anyone has to, why those who seemingly flaunt society's standards "flourish as the green bay tree." The discrepancies between expectations and actualities, and between moral standards and the ways of the world, cause families to utilize religion and religious functionaries to make sense of these experiences.

Some immediate problems today's families are facing in getting along with each other, however, are not ones with which all of today's churches are necessarily prepared to deal. No one age may be more religious than another, but Ahlstrom (1978: 14) convincingly argues that some periods make more "excruciating demands for change and adjustment than others even dream of." Such seems to be the present era. Families currently are in such flux that, far from serving with religion as guardians of the social heritage, they are forcing theologians to reexamine long-held positions. Sources of unhappiness frowned upon in traditional church doctrine and formerly seemingly restricted to a few are now becoming more general among families.[2]

Church functionaries in such cases can offer forgiveness to the penitent, but are less able to deal with individuals who accept the new practices but not the "corrective counseling" that the clergy are prepared to offer.

DIFFICULTIES IN THE SEARCH

For spouses, sources of potential misfortune that were less apparent in earlier eras include extramarital sex, separation, and divorce. For adolescents, premarital sexual activity and unwed motherhood are issues. Such phenomena, along with changing gender roles, abortion, and homosexuality, indicate the breadth of issues for which troubled families may be seeking religious solace. A number of these sources, it should be noted, are related to the "new morality," a term apparently used by a theologian at least as far back as 1933 (Newsom, 1933). Unfortunately, as one layperson has written, "men and women now feel free to discuss sex, everywhere except in church" (Mace, 1970: 89).

Sex has been a problem for Christianity for over 1500 years. According to church tradition, sex and shame were associated in the Garden of Eden, so that if it were not for procreation purposes, intercourse should be shunned. Early churchmen saw unmanageable sexual desire as the means whereby original sin manifested itself (Tavard, 1973; Mace, 1970; Kosnik, et al., 1977). Celibacy and virginity, therefore, were the behavioral models early church writers extolled. Even Martin Luther, who did away with the rule of celibacy among the clergy, believed sexual intercourse to result from a lust he likened to leprosy, and so he saw procreation as resulting from a disease (Tavard, 1973).

Some churches have taken categorical stands on issues relevant to sexual behavior, divorce, and gender roles — stands that make it difficult for families experiencing problems in these areas to believe they will receive comfort from the functionaries. Other denominations present no clear messages, but appear to "waffle" on them. The Catholic, Lutheran, and Episcopalian churches have taken the clearest positions on a number of these issues. According to tradition and theological argument, they have held Christian marriage to be indissoluble, and so remarriage unthinkable for the faithful.[3] Thus divorced or remarried members may feel that these churches no longer regard them as members. This is the case even though canon law can be interpreted in such a way that some marriages dissolved through divorce under civil law can be annulled. Remarriages are then possible within the Catholic church (Dedek, 1971). With respect to abortion, the Catholic position is straightforward. It is seen as the destruction of human life and, accordingly, murder. As a consequence, the organized church may not be seen as a source of help for Catholic women who have had abortions and accept the act as legitimate.

The traditional position of the Catholic and Lutheran churches continues to be that premarital intercourse is a sin (Dedek, 1971; Kersten, 1970). Christian laypersons, as well as theologians from other denominations, in the face of increasing sexual activity before marriage, however, have been abandoning categorical positions condemning such behavior (Mace, 1971). A Catholic theologian, Dedek (1971), also has noted that the Bible does appear to label all such behavior as sinful, and that the church has taken no "definite magisterial position" on the matter. Other Catholic theologians have urged that premarital intercourse be judged according to its intent and the relationship within which it occurs (Kosnik et al., 1977). But the Vatican Congregation for the Doctrine of the Faith, in a letter to the United States National Conference of Catholic Bishops, has criticized the book *Human Sexuality: New Directions in American Catholic Thought,* a publication that proposes a more liberal Catholic position on sexual matters. The Congregation warned against church functionaries and laypersons using the book as a source of helpful guidelines. The stand was based on the book's contradiction of traditional church teaching and doctrine (Origins, 1979).

Consistent with the biblical commandment against adultery, extramarital intercourse has traditionally not been countenanced by Christian denominations. Among laypersons in the more liberal Protestant denominations, there appears to be some softening of this injunction under particular circumstances (Mace, 1971). Even liberal Catholic theologians (Kosnik et al., 1977), however, in their pastoral counsel urge the "greatest caution" in addressing this question, because of its presumed threat to marriage.

Pressures from members more conservative than clergy also make it difficult for the latter to depart from traditional ways. A survey of Lutherans in the United States some years ago, for example, showed the clergy to be more liberal than laypersons with respect to the issue of Lutheran ministers performing the marriage of a divorced person. The Lutheran ethic is against divorce (Kersten, 1970). The *National Catholic Register* (November 26, 1978), a conservative United States church newspaper, criticized one of the appointments to the Commission on Marriage and Family Life of the American Catholic Bishops for his criticism of the "church's teaching on marital chastity." The ordination of an avowed lesbian sparked controversy in the Episcopal church while the whole issue of ordaining women within this denomination created a secessionist movement (U.S.

News & World Report, 1977). Churches continue to exercise control over communicants' behavior through sanctions from members as well as clergy. Thus traditional church positions still mobilize enough support to make families unsure of the reception their difficulties that contravene these positions will receive.

The changing roles of women involve not only a more active sexual life, but also a life that includes occupational as well as family roles. This venture outside the home, with its implications for economic independence and filling nontraditional female jobs, has also been censured in some churches. The Mormons and fundamentalist Protestant denominations have seen women's pressure for equal rights and opportunities as going against the devine pronouncement, as expressed in the account of Adam and Eve, that women come under the command of men (Wilson, 1978; Kelsey, 1973). A woman active in the movement for the passage of the Equal Rights Amendment, for example, was excommunicated from the Mormon church (Weathers and Ford, 1979; Shipps, 1980).

The biblical tradition of wives' submission to husbands was further strengthened among such early church fathers as St. Augustine and St. Thomas Acquinas, along with the Protestant reformers, Luther and Calvin, by their belief in women's biological imperative to motherhood (Tavard, 1973). The pronouncement of Pope John Paul II (1979) on women's vocation as that of motherhood continues this tradition.

FAMILIES AFFECTED

Some may urge that this analysis of the difficulties families face in seeking help for their problems from organized religion is overdrawn. First of all, they may say, families that are facing problems arising from sexual behavior, divorce and remarriage, or changing gender roles are families who are not participants in organized religion. The overall statistics in the United States on such rough indicators of family change as divorce and remarriage and the employment of women, however, suggest that the numbers are too large for only those outside organized religion to be involved. Greeley (1978, 1979) reports that a recent U.S. survey showed 18 percent of Catholic adults and 30 percent of Protestant adults were among the ever divorced. Current rates also suggest that 40 to 50 percent of marriages contracted in the 1970s will be dissolved (Farley and Bianchi, 1979). About five-sixths of all divorced men and three-fourths of divorced women eventually remarry (Norton and Glick, 1976). Thus, of the 79 percent of all children under 18 who lived with two parents in 1977, 8 percent lived with a stepparent and an additional 5 percent lived with both natural parents, one or both of whom had remarried. Compared to 1960, the number of children living with a separated parent doubled, the number living with a divorced parent tripled, and the number living with a never-married parent was seven times as great. Although the number of children was roughly the same in 1960 and 1977, the number of children living with both parents in the United States actually declined 10 percent in the 17-year period (Glick, 1979). Such figures suggest that separation, divorce, and remarriage are affecting communicants who are accustomed to turning to religious functionaries in times of difficulty as well as those not participating in organized religion.

The change in the proportion of employed women in the last decade is equally dramatic. In the United States, the number of married women with spouses present who had children under 6 years old, for example, who were working outside the home increased from 23 percent in 1965 to 45 percent in 1980. Comparable figures for women with children 6 to 17 years of age were 43 percent in 1965 and 66 percent in 1980 (U.S. Bureau of the Census, 1980, 1981). Again, these figures are too high to permit the assumption they include only the nonreligious.

But, critics may continue to argue, families in denominations such as Lutheran and Catholic, where heavy emphasis is placed on the community aspects of religion, will not define their problems differently than church functionaries. Families in the more liberal Protestant faiths, they will say, would be the ones likely to seek comfort from churches for problems they define in ways the churches are unprepared to handle. Yet there is evidence that even within the tradition of "Community" churches, members are seeking organizational modifications that go beyond usual patterns of worship. Not only the charismatic movements, but also Bible study groups, along with various position papers and publications (Place, 1978; Ripple, 1978; Kosnik et al., 1977), in these denominations suggest that members as well as clergy are trying to go beyond the traditional organizational patterns of these churches in search of nontraditional answers to current problems.

THE CLERGY AND FAMILY PROBLEMS

The ability of religious functionaries to minister to families in times of misfortune may have been put in particular jeopardy by the kinds of problems today's families are experiencing, but churches' relations to families have long had some elements of ambivalence. Religion has always helped people to cope with the issue of mortality.

In turn, families are critical to the physical immortality of religion (Zimmerman, 1973).[4] Doctrine entrusted to celibates will not generally endure if outside recruitment breaks down and doctrine exists only in written records, as witness the Shakers. Yet this need to serve families to ensure its own continuity can create difficulties for religion. There is an inevitable tension between religious doctrines and the institutions devoted to preserving them. By necessarily being a part of the world in their caring for families, church personnel must accommodate themselves to it at the expense of transcendental concerns (Parsons, 1952; Berger, 1961). In dealing with the anxieties of people, churches become concerned with societal values, values not always those that churches espouse. Where these values are highly secularized, as in the United States, it is difficult for organized religion to remain in a state of tension with the broader society (Berger, 1961). Clergy can work to change these values, but in working with their victims churches may become associated with the values. The relation of churches to families, therefore, is problematic because in dealing with events for which families are seeking meaning, the church and its clergy are implicated in the existing power structure of society, a structure often at odds with religious values (Berger, 1961). Indeed, in "saving" religion for future generations through involvement in the world, the organized church can appear to lose it.

One family affecting churches has to do with women. They are the persons in families most caught up in domestic roles, and are also generally those most involved in organized religion. Women, because they have always had less power and status than men, have been the ones most affected by events over which they lack control. They have been more likely to participate in church activities. Women have constituted a disproportionate part of those in attendance at religious services (Argyle and Beit-Hallahmi, 1975) and have been essential for socializing children into religious belief systems. Mothers generally are the most frequent sources of religious ideas (Argyle and Beit-Hallahmi, 1975; but see Greeley, 1979).

Denominations, in turn, because of their concern for families, have exercised their social control and socialization functions to support the sanctity of the family, thereby strengthening the hands of women traditionally more concerned with the maintenance of marital bonds. Thus church members are less apt to divorce and more apt to say that their marriages are satisfactory (Kunz and Albrecht, 1977). Sanctions against premarital and extramarital sex, which are present in religious codes of personal ethics (Burtchaell, 1977; Kersten, 1970), also have operated to promote conventional family life. They have encouraged continence outside of marriage, or marriage ceremonies when unexpected pregnancies occur. But, although they have shared socialization and social control functions, women and the leaders of organized religion have been separated along gender lines (Smith et al., 1974). This separation has unfortunate implications for organized religion.

The current women's movement, with its focus on gender and sexism, has rendered potentially problematic just those family members that formerly constituted the most unwavering supporters of religion and were most subject to its control. No longer fully committed to family roles as traditionally defined, some women and the changing images of life they are espousing and living have made families less the conservators of traditional gender roles than groups in which altered arrangements are being painfully worked out. Clergymen, particularly in the main-line, more liberal Protestant denominations, can no longer count on families and especially mothers to pass on traditional religious beliefs, with their heavy doctrinal commitment to traditional gender roles, to the next generation.

Clergymen also may be ambivalent about ministering to the divorced, the sexually unhappy, the pregnant single woman, the career-committed wife, and other persons whose situations and perspectives may have been influenced by women's critique of the established social order. The existence of such categories of layper-sons seeking pastoral care demonstrates the flagrant contravention of rules of family life incorporated in the religious doctrine of some denominations. Moreover, the male dominance in the Biblical tradi-tion may make it difficult for some clergymen to accept as legitimate problems arising from women's push for power. When they could minister to women in the congregation on their own terms, terms embodied in the religious tradition, it was easier for those clergymen to be understanding than when women are breaking with this tradi-tion.

The existing discrepancy in family problems and some clergy's ability to cope with them is deepened by those seeking to redress the incongruity of a largely male clergy dealing with a disproportionately female congregation. There are scholars (Reuther, 1974; compare Douglas, 1977) who argue that established religion, with its emphasis on a privatized morality centering on the areas of family and sexual behavior, is part of the world of women and, therefore, of lower status. This, they argue, comes from the split between the family home, the domain of women, and the workplace, where men are in charge — a split that symbolizes the idea of moral humans in immoral society. Women, because of their domestic concerns, are shielded from the compromising hurly-burly of the outside world and can maintain moral standards. The involvement of men in worldly concerns, according to this argument, prevents their active commitment to moral matters. The control function of religion has, consequently, been most apparent with women. Thus these scholars believe that if women were to become religious functionaries, the so-called feminization of religion would be complete with men only peripherally involved, either as members or as the clergy (Douglas, 1977).

Regardless of whether one agrees with this argument or not, it does appear that precedent is against women ministering as equals to male clergy to those caught up in family change. In certain religious groups, notably among Catholics, Orthodox Jews, and Mormons, women are excluded from the priesthood or its equivalent. Even in denominations that have accepted women into the ministry, such as the United Methodist church, they are few in numbers and more apt than men to be part-time workers, paid lower salaries, and employed in smaller churches (Smith et al., 1974; Wallace, 1975). And so the existence of a largely male clergy that ministers to female members caught up in family change adds another problem to the relationship of churches and families.

At the present time, therefore, the relationship of families and organized religion contains problematic elements for both sides. This has been traditionally the case for church functionaries whose ministering to families in times of sorrow involved them in worldly concerns. For families, however, recent changes in sexual behavior coupled with changes in household organization have rendered some clergy less able to deal with the challenges families are encountering. Providing care for families seeking it because of failure to conform to church control presents clergy with difficult dilemmas. They have made apparent the gender difference between a clergy that is overwhelmingly male ministering to the constituency most active in domestic roles, which is overwhelmingly female. Thus problematic elements in the relationship between churches and families are set in sharp relief.

For this reason, however, new accommodations in the family-church relation with respect to current difficulties may develop. More opportunities for women to be active in leadership positions in churches is one example of an organizational response to women's greater participation outside the family (Center for Applied Research in the Apostolate, 1980; Lehman, 1980). "Team" ministries in which men and women work together with families is a strategy being used to bring more women into church functionary roles. There is a greater willingness on the part of the clergy to deal with some of the situations that are contrary to church doctrine. There is now an organization composed of members of the Catholic church who are divorced, as well as a literature devoted to their needs (Ripple, 1978). Annullments of unhappy marriages appear to be more common in the Catholic church also, a means that permits remarriage within the church (Paris *Herald Tribune,* July 28, 1981). Organizational modifications in churches noted earlier, including lay study groups, are examples of attempts by families under the auspices of churches to find religious solutions for contemporary problems. Through such groups, whether families or clergy initiate them, troubled persons can find others experiencing similar unhappy situations and establish support networks. Families minister to themselves and create a sense of community within churches (Kulka et al., 1979). Denominations are also mounting self-surveys, particularly with respect to the thorny issue of women's participation (Garhart, 1976; Participation of Women in Program and Policy Making in the United Methodist Church, 1978; papers at the [Presbyterian] Religious Research Association, 1979) to determine how they can better fulfill their religious mission in the present climate of family concerns.

To what extent the problematic association of families and clergy due to current changes in gender roles and sexual behaviors constitute enduring tension points or occasions for new departures will vary within denominations and across issues.[5] D'Antonio's argument in Chapter 4 of this volume, that the caring rather than the control function should take priority in organized religion, might be relevant here. As Hargrove points out with reference to the argument, such an emphasis encourages primary-type face-to-face affectionate contacts in local congregations. This is a type that would seem particularly congenial to families experiencing problems and seeking comfort in religious fellowship. But a number of fundamentalist denominations that take a traditional approach to womens' role and sexual issues encourage primary group ties among members. These ties, instead of being sources of support to families facing such issues, can be sources of control pushing for traditional solutions. The very closeness of the members makes their negative evaluations more painful. Families who are seeking change in the usual household division of labor or who are having to deal with situations involving unmarried pregnancies, to take two examples, can find themselves no longer welcome in the congregation. Again, the denominations' stands on contemporary issues loom large as to whether clergy and communicants react to families with problems in terms of control or caring. Thus the relations between churches and families are characterized by uncertainty. This uncertainty and the changes it engenders ensure that families and church functionaries will continue to be concerned with the uneasy linkages between the two institutions.

NOTES

1. This chapter is not addressed to the issue of how the functions of religion should be conceptualized. It makes use of the conceptualizations that view religion as providing comfort (Glock and Stark, 1965) and meaning (Parsons, 1952) for laypersons.

2. It is necessary to distinguish between two types of family problems. One type, which has implications for family formation and stability, results primarily from interpersonal relationships within the family or between family members and outsiders. The other type results primarily from structural arrangements in the broader society, particularly in the economy. This type of family problem is one often addressed by churches concerned with issues of social justice. See, among others, publications from the Lutheran Human Relations Association of America (Association of Evangelical Lutheran Churches), the Board of Church and Society (United Methodist Church), the Office for Church and Society (United Church of Christ) and the Encyclical letters of Leo XIII (Catholic Church). This chapter is concerned with the first type of problem.

3. Within the Episcopal church, canon law has been modified to make the issue of remarriage a pastoral rather than a juridical matter. Local pastors now have the major say on decisions concerning remarriage wtihin the church.

4. Religion has also drawn heavily upon family imagery and family rituals for its rationale and sustenance. A 1965 public opinion poll, for example, showed how people use family imagery in their conception of God. When asked how they think of God, 79 percent said they thought of him as a "loving father" (Marty et al., 1968).

5. Structure as well as ideological factors will play a part. The decrease in the number of priests in the Catholic church because of fewer vocations and persons leaving the priesthood suggests an older, more conservative clergy in the future (see the *National Catholic Reporter,* July 17, 1981, for a report of these conclusions from a survey of priests).

REFERENCES

Ahlstrom, S. E. (1978) "National trauma and changing religious values." Daedalus 107: 13-29.

Argyle, M. and B. Beit-Hallahmi (1975) The Social Psychology of Religion. Boston: Routledge & Kegan Paul.

Becker, T. (1978) "Inter-faith and inter-nationality attitudinal variations among youth toward self, family and the collective." Review of Religious Research 20: 68-81.

Berger, P. L. (1961) The Noise of Solemn Assemblies: Christian Commitment and the Religious Establishment in America. Garden City, NY: Doubleday.

Burtchaell, J. T. [ed.] (1977) Marriage Among Christians: A Curious Tradition. Notre Dame, IN: Ave Maria.

Center for Applied Research in the Apostolate (1980) Women and Ministry. Washington, DC: Author.

Dedek, J. F. (1971) Contemporary Sexual Morality. New York: Sheed & Ward.

Douglas, A. (1977) The Feminization of American Culture. New York: Knopf.

Farley, R. and S. Bianchi (1979) "Household structure and welfare: comments about recent trends and data needs," pp. 53-61 in U.S. Bureau of the Census, Issues in Federal Statistical Needs Relating to Women. Current Population Reports, Special Studies, Series P-23, No. 83 (December). Washington, DC: Government Printing Office.

Garhart, M. (1976) Women in the Ordained Ministry. New York: Lutheran Church in America.

Glick, P. C. (1979) "The future of the American family," in U.S. Bureau of the Census, Current Population Reports, Special Studies, Series P-23, No. 78. Washington, DC: Government Printing Office.

Glock, C. Y. and R. Stark (1965) Religion and Society in Tension. Chicago: Rand McNally.

Greeley, A. M. (1979) "The sociology of American Catholics." Annual Review of Sociology 5: 91-111.

—— (1978) Personal communication.

—— W. McCready, T. Sullivan, and J. Fee (1980) "A profile of the American Catholic family." America 143 (September 27): 155-160.

John Paul II (1979) "The dignity of motherhood." Church Documents Quarterly 24: 179-182.

Kelsey, G. (1973) Social Ethics Among Southern Baptists, 1917-1969. Metuchen. NJ: Scarecrow.

Kersten, L. K. (1970) The Lutheran Ethic: The Impact of Religion on Laymen and Clergy. Detroit, MI: Wayne State University Press.

Kosnik, A., W. Carroll, A. Cunningham, R. Modras, and J. Schulte (1977) Human Sexuality: New Directions in American Catholic Thought. New York: Paulist Press.

Kulka, R. A., J. Veroff, and E. Douvan (1979) "Social class and the use of professional help for personal problems: 1957-1967." Journal of Health and Human Behavior 20 (March): 2-17.

Kunz, P. R. and S. L. Albrecht (1977) "Religion, marital happiness and divorce." Journal of Sociology of the Family 7: 227-232.

Lehman, E. C., Jr. (1980) "Placement of men and women in the ministry." Review of Religious Research 22, 1: 18-40.

Mace, D. R. (1971) "The sexual revolution: its impact on pastoral care and counseling." Journal of Pastoral Care 25: 220-232.

—— (1970) The Christian Response to the Sexual Revolution. Nashville, TN: Abington.

McMurry, M. (1978) "Religion and women's sex role traditionalism." Sociological Focus 11: 81-95.

Marty, M. E., S. E. Rosenberg, and A. M. Greeley (1968) What Do We Believe? New York: Meredith.

Montgomery, S. M., and R. L. Montgomery (1975) "Religion practice and orthodoxy among Catholic students as a function of parents' beliefs and religious training." . Psychological Reports 37: 706.

Newsom, G. E. (1933) The New Morality. New York: Scribner.

Norton, A. J. and P. C. Glick (1976) "Marital instability: past, present and future." Journal of Social Issues 32: 5-20.

Origins (1979) "Doctrinal congregation criticizes 'Human Sexuality' book." Vol. 9: 167-169.

Parsons, T. (1952) "Sociology and social psychology," pp. 286-337 in H. N. Fairchild et al. (eds.) Religious Perspectives in College Teaching. New York: Ronald.

Place, M. D. (1978) Divorce and Remarriage: The Church's Response to Marital Failure. Chicago: Association of Chicago Priests.

Reuther, R. (1974) "Male clericalism and the dread of women," pp. 1-14 in R. J. Heyer (ed.) Women and Orders. New York: Paulist Press.

Ripple, P. (1978) The Pain and the Possibility: Divorce and Separation Among Catholics. Notre Dame, IN: Ave Maria.

Shipps, J. (1980) "Mormonism and the media." Christian Century 97 (January): 5-6.

Smith, R., C. Black, B. Hoffman, and S. Burkett Milner (1974) Sociological Studies of an Occupation: The Ministry. Evanston, IL: Murray and Dorothy Leiffer Bureau of Social and Religious Research.

Spicer, J. C. and S. O. Gustavus (1974) "Mormon fertility through half a century: another test of the Americanization hypothesis." Social Biology 21: 70-76.

Tavard, G. H. (1973) Women in Christian Tradition. Notre Dame, IN: University of Notre Dame Press.

U.S. Bureau of the Census (1981) Population Profile of the United States: 1980. Current Population Reports, Series P-20, No. 363. Washington, DC: Government Printing Office.

——— (1980) American Families and Living Arrangements. Washington, DC: Government Printing Office.

U.S. News & World Report (1977) "Churches start facing up to the sexual revolution." September 26: 63-64.

Wallace, R. (1975) "Bringing women in: marginality in the churches." Sociological Analysis 36, 4: 291-303.

Weathers, D. and M. Ford (1979) "Can a Mormon support the ERA?" Newsweek 94 (December 3): 88.

Weigert, A. and R. Hastings (1977) "Identity loss, family and social change." American Journal of Sociology 82: 1171-1185.

Weiting, S. G. (1975) "An examination of intergenerational patterns of religious belief and practice." Sociological Analysis 36: 137-139.

Wilson, J. (1978) Religion in American Society: The Effective Presence. Englewood Cliffs, NJ: Prentice-Hall.

Yinger, J. M. (1977) "A comparative study of the substructures of religion." Journal of the Scientific Study of Religion 16: 67-86.

Zimmerman, C. C. (1973) "Family and religion." Social Science 48 (Autumn): 203-215.

4

FAMILY LIFE, RELIGION, AND SOCIETAL VALUES AND STRUCTURES

William V. D'Antonio

Since the 1960s the United States and the world at large have experienced a veritable revolution in ideas, beliefs, values, and behavior patterns. The war in Vietnam, Watergate, changing sexual mores, rising divorce rates, the women's movement, violence in the family, energy problems, drug abuse, and the Islamic revolution in Iran — all these things and more have shaken our society and its social institutions. The family, one of the institutions, is perceived by many to be particularly threatened. A White House Conference on Families in 1980 brought together an array of persons and organizations concerned about the family. Indeed, the need to restore American family life to its traditional ways became a major theme of the 1980 presidential elections, and legislation now pending in Congress is designed to restore us to those traditional ways.

This chapter examines how the family has been influenced and molded by the dominant social institutions of this society, by the events of recent years, and by the value orientations of the social institutions involved in the events. I hope to make clear our understanding of family life and family values, their relation to religion and to the larger society, and prospects for the future. The major thesis proposed is that the attempt to "restore" the traditional family structure and values by reimposing traditional religious controls runs against the tide. The capitalist economy and the political democracy formed here over two centuries have helped bring about a type of family that now fits too well with them to brook backtracking. In the following pages, I develop this thesis and show why the efforts of today's naysayers are destined to have limited impact.

The chapter begins with a review of what may be called the major value orientations of American society. I consider how they have been affected by events of recent years, note their continued salience, and give particular attention to the impacts these values as well as these events have had on family life and family values.

THE DOMINANT VALUES OF AMERICAN SOCIETY

The early post-World War II period and the 1950s have come to represent, rightly or wrongly, the era of the great flowering of American society, in which attitudes and behavior supposedly reflected the deepest value orientations of the people. In a classic study done at the time, Robin Williams (1955) of Cornell University delineated these core value orientations. Rooted in colonial history, most were closely reflected in the life patterns of the middle class, and working-class people also were trying to instill these values into their children. The public school, business, and government were committed to them — indeed, fostered them. And, to varying degrees, the major religious denominations supported them.[1] A brief review of them here will set the stage for an examination of the changes that have taken place in family life with such dramatic force in the past thirty years. Among Williams' values, nine seem especially relevant to this chapter.

(1) Individual Achievement. Individual achievement has been called one of the key values of this society. Americans came to think of their society as an achieving society. They were urged by their parents, and as parents they urge their children, to achieve good grades in school and victories in athletics, and to become whatever they want to be in the world of work. An important aspect of this value is the primacy accorded to the individual and the individual's efforts. It is central to middle-class family life, and it was strongly preached to and rapidly accepted by the masses of immigrants who came to the United States between 1880 and 1925. Ironically, blacks and other minorities were for many years systematically excluded from participation in the society that would have made this value real for them. We continue to worship achievement and achievers, especially in sports, entertainment, and the world of work in general. We do not often examine individual acheivement's various influences on the family and on family values.

(2) Activity/Work. Closely related to the value of achievement is the so-called work ethic. This value embodies the idea that work is a good thing in itself. Work is especially important as the principal mechanism by which to improve socioeconomic status. One could

expect to get ahead if one were willing to work. It is not an exaggeration to say that in many, if not most, American families, God was believed to be favorably disposed toward those who worked hard. That these individuals got ahead was simply a manifestation of God's rewarding their efforts.

(3) *Efficiency and Practicality.* Linked to the value of work is the value of efficiency and practicality, getting things done, and usefulness. In this sense, the family has been the place people have learned to be efficient and practical, to become motivated to accomplish goals that will "get them ahead." Thus this value has fit nicely with individual achievement and work/activity.

(4) *Progress.* Americans were future oriented; life would be better tomorrow than today. People looked ahead, not back. Progress was seen to result from achievement, hard work, and efficiency and practicality. One consequence of this has been ambivalent feelings about old age. The younger generation invariably has outperformed preceding generations. The elderly are no longer seen as sources of wisdom but as stumbling blocks to progress. Rapid technological change (read: progress) has been a continuing threat to the knowledge and work roles of older people. Also, we demonstrated our belief in this value by continuing efforts to control our environments — physical, social, and personal.

(5) *Science and Rationality.* Americans came to believe that they could master their environment. Science and rationality as means to do so were merely another sign of God's gifts bestowed upon a hardworking, deserving people. This value fits easily with those of achievement, work, and progress. In fact, in one sense, the changes in family life are in no small measure a consequence of the application of science (the pill, better nutrition, health care) and rationality (no-fault divorce). It may be argued that it is at least in part the application of rationality to family life that has fostered the tension and conflict between traditional religion and family values and behavior patterns.

(6) *Material Comfort.* Americans value the "good things" of life. In recent years, critics have noted the degree to which the United States has come to be a consumer-oriented society. Material comfort has been a component of the American Dream, the reward that comes after successful striving for the other values. The business sector promotes it in every possible way; the government gives it its blessing in measuring the gross national product, the standard of living, and the poverty level. Judging by the behavior of all family members, it is a value taught early to the children via television and trips to

supermarkets, discount houses, and shopping malls. It has become a central value of family life. People everywhere desire material comfort, but in the United States, it is supposed to be accessible to all who work for it. It is epitomized in the private ownership of home and auto, and in easy credit. Despite the recession in the auto and home-building industries, Americans in January 1982 reported that they were doing as well as they had been doing in 1981. A total of 24 percent said they were doing *better*, while only 21 percent said they were worse off than they were before Reagan took office.[2]

(7) Equality. From the beginning of their independent history Americans have valued equality, that is, equality of opportunity, but not of result. The objective has been that everyone starts off from the same line, while acknowledging that there are fewer winners than runners in the race for the good things of life.

The idea of equality has had great impact on all aspects of American life, including the family. Its espousal has led to some wrenching tensions, for example, tension over the right of blacks and other minorities to participate on equal terms in the race for unequal results. And, over time, we have had to confront the meaning of equality in politics, regarding the right of women to vote and to hold office, and, most recently, the age of enfranchisement; in the world of work, ensuring that women have equal opportunity to compete for all jobs, with equal pay for equal work; in religion, with the growing demand by women to become priests, ministers, and rabbis; and in the family, as it has involved changing husband-wife roles, and the roles of children vis-à-vis parents. Related to the family in another way has been how the value of equality bears on sexual behavior before, during, and outside marriage. While the sexual revolution of the past generation is not alone a consequence of the ever-growing impact of the value of equality, it certainly owes something to the changing interpretation of this value.

(8) Freedom. Freedom is one of the most cherished of all values. The word itself is almost sacred, and has strong religious connotations for many people. The value owes much to the Protestant belief that individuals must achieve their own salvation, that they must face God alone, without benefit of the confessional or the saints to intercede for them. This value has also been important to Catholics and Jews, although the focus has differed. While the value has clear-cut religious roots, it has permeated all social institutions, and has become secularized in the process. Within the family, it has come to mean training children early to be independent and to be responsible for their behavior. In supporting this value we have come to stress the rights of the individual rather than those of the group. Again, this

value fits with achievement, work, progress, and material comfort, but such an expression of it tends to devalue extended family structure and the obligations, duties, and extensive responsibilities that go with it.[3]

(9) Humanitarian Mores. Williams (1955) notes that Americans developed a pattern of giving aid to the needy, of being charitable to the helpless. It is important to recognize that this value ranks below the other values. The patterns of giving show that American largesse originates in bounty; we are not expected to sacrifice our own material comforts in order to help others.[4] Whatever the roots of this value orientation, it is at least more other oriented than self oriented. Yet it does not imply the idea of caring and sharing that is associated with love.

Together these nine value orientations yield a profile of an aggressive, activist, instrumentally oriented people. The values have a certain degree of consistency: We encouraged our young people to be on their own, to think for themselves, to work hard, to strive to achieve, to believe that they had as much opportunity as anyone else to "make it" if they wanted to, and to be concerned about their own personal happiness. Once well along that road, they should not forget those less fortunate if they were worthy of help.

FAMILY VALUES

While the values just discussed provided the underpinning for the major societal structures within which family members operated, they stood in contradiction to the values that gave meaning to family life. Degler (1980) argues that there has been a long continuity to these family values, and that in important ways they are similar from society to society, at least in the West.

(1) Patriarchal Authority. Since earliest times in the West, father has been the "boss," and mother and children have been subordinate. This arrangement appears to have extended beyond the economic factor of father's working for wages, since it had its origins at least in agricultural society. It has also enjoyed support from the Christian-Judaic religions. Still, there has been a notable decline in both the nature and the extent of father's authority in recent years. If family members are not yet equal, they are certainly not as unequal as they were a century ago. The value of patriarchalism has been challenged, but it still endures, as witness the opposition to the ERA and the many studies that show that wives working full time outside the home do most of the housework.[5]

(2) The Family as Group. Traditionally, the interests of the family as group took precedence over those of its individual members. The value encompasses a sense of broad, diffuse obligation and duty to the group. This value persists in at least a modified form in that the breadwinners share their earnings with the children. Indeed, if father is the only breadwinner, he is required by law to provide support, thus underscoring the importance of this value to the family.

This value has been altered and has taken on new dimensions. Thus children are expected to reflect the good name of the family in school and other activities, but not to support themselves. Parents, for their part, are expected to support children through high school and even perhaps through college. And in times of illness and financial or other crises, families continue to stick together.

(3) Ascription. We gain our membership in the family by the mere fact of birth; we do not have to earn it. And while parents may preach achievement to their children, they are slow to disavow those who do not or cannot achieve.

(4) A Haven of Affection, Warmth, Love. It is especially true in modern times that the family is seen as a haven from the individualism and anonymity of the larger society. It is increasingly perceived as the source of nurturance, love, and affection; many sociologists think that this is the family's crucial remaining function, and if it performs this function well, it thereby justifies itself (Reiss, 1980).

These values are believed to provide the family with a stable, solidary structure, but also to create tension and strain for family members vis-à-vis the larger societal structures and values. The tension may be real, but not necessarily realized. Consider that parents are the first and often the most important agents of socialization for the society. They teach the importance of achievement, independence, freedom, equality, and hard work, and the rewards of material comfort, but it is not at all clear that they perceive such teaching to conflict with basic family values. It is one of the purposes of the following sections to try to show where, how, and to what extent the tension and conflict occur, and with what consequences.

Family values have been and continue to be supported in varying degrees by religious denominations and sects. In fact, as we shall see, it is the conservative religions that have been responsible for a major challenge to the new family patterns that have been evolving in the wake of the events of the past three decades.

RELIGIOUS VALUES

The various chapters in this volume make clear that there is an array of overlapping values that can be thought of as religious values. My concern in this chapter is only with those that focus most broadly on the family and have the widest area of coverage.

(1) Sacredness of Human Life. To be born is good; human life is sacred, and when people bring forth new life they are seen as participating with God in the most sacred of creative activities. During the course of more than 2000 years of Western history, religious leaders have elaborated this value into a very conservative sexual ethic. Because it is a sacred and absolute value to be born, ideally people should:

(a) be married before birth of a child occurs;

(b) be chaste before marriage, and faithful to the partner during marriage;

(c) remain married until death;

(d) avoid actions that prevent impregnation, and that terminate pregnancy by induced abortion; and

(e) avoid homosexual behavior because it is nonprocreative.

The normative patterns that support this value have evolved slowly, and in the past 100 years have come under the most severe attack from the secular society. The changing behavior patterns that have accompanied industrialization and the impact of secular values have led an increasing proportion of Americans to reject some or all of these norms. As the new norms have emerged, they have been defended in the names of freedom, equality, and individualism.

Millions of American families from the entire range of religions still support and adhere to the value of the sacredness of life, and to the norms that reflect it. At the same time, new lifestyles are ignoring or openly rejecting the norms and sometimes the value itself. As Hargrove (Chapter 5, this volume) makes clear, the main-line Protestant church leaders have themselves moved away from a rigid reading of this value. At the least, they are saying that the sacredness of life is not narrowly defined by norms against divorce, birth control, and even abortion. This new direction also seems to open up the area of sexuality itself for discussion.

(2) Patriarchalism. The image of a male God still dominates the language of religion. At the most conservative end of the continuum, religious denominations oppose the ERA, believe the proper place of women to be in the home, affirm the importance of obedience by children to their parents, and assert that women's place in worship is in the pew, and not at the altar. The chapters in this volume reveal both the extent to which this value is still upheld by religions and the extent to which it has been greatly modified or even rejected.

(3) Concern for Others. Some believe that the essence of religion is love; one expression of this idea is that "God is love." the Good Samaritan story teaches that we should love our neighbor and also teaches who our neighbor is. There is no doubt about the continuing pervasiveness of this value in a generalized way, but again the problem arises in interpreting how it is to be manifested. Some insist that the value only has meaning at the individual level; it is a personal responsibility to help one's neighbor. At the most, one tithes in one's own congregation. But one's obligations end there.

Others ascribe a universal meaning to the value: All people are our neighbors, and we must reach out to them in some way. Government can be the instrument, or overseas missions or charities. Concern for others is at the base of the humanitarian mores that have evolved, and that now are in some eclipse in the United States.

While this value has provided varying degrees of social support within and between groups, it has never evolved a theology of sexual love. That may be due in large part to the way that early Christian leaders defined life and love, with the variety of normative restraints mentioned above. It is this failure to develop a positive valuation of sexuality within a basic value orientation that seems to have lessened the role of religion in the modern family. Yet, as we shall see, it is precisely these three values, with their most narrow and traditional interpretation, that the Moral Majority seeks to use to rebuild American family life.

THE VIETNAM ERA:
ITS IMPACT ON FAMILY AND VALUES

The challenge to the American value system became obvious in the late 1960s. Ironically, the decade had opened on a note of hope and optimism, as President John F. Kennedy urged people to dedicate themselves to others. But the decade that began with the Peace Corps as a manifestation of greater interest in others, and that saw the growth of the civil rights movement, the student movement, and the women's movement, ended in the turmoil over Vietnam, violent protests, and the questioning of all major authority structures — religious, political, business. It was a time of confrontation and breakdown at both the macro and micro levels of society. Out of the conflict of this era came the full flowering of the sexual revolution, the drug cultures, hippies, yippies, rising divorce rates, growing acceptance of abortion, and a general tolerance of forms of behavior formerly thought of as deviant, including homosexuality.

It is not possible in this chapter to do more than sketch how the events of the sixties and seventies interacted with each other and with family and societal values. For example, we may say that the beginnings of the modern student movement can be traced to the Berkeley free speech movement of 1964, which began as a request by students to propagandize for political causes on campus. The movement "went national" and quickly escalated into a wide range of concerns about administrative control of student behavior. One important focus came to be the administration's *in loco parentis* role; student demands brought about the collapse of administration authority in this area, and that was followed shortly by the establishment of coed dorms, under the banner of freedom, equality, and individual rights.

Ideas and activities supporting change were happening in the religious sector also. The Roman Catholic church had opened its windows with Vatican II in the early 1960s, and debates over church authority — especially over contraceptive birth control — caught the interest of the young. The pill, a relatively new form of contraception, became a catalyst for hitherto proscribed or feared behaviors because it gave women a more certain control over conception. The debate about it opened up greater freedom and autonomy for the Catholic laity (see D'Antonio and Cavanaugh, Chapter 6, this volume, for a detailed discussion). It represented a rational approach to modern life. By 1968, a majority of Roman Catholic married couples in the childbearing years were using some form of contraception not approved by the church hierarchy. Pope Paul VI overrode the recommendations of the birth control commission appointed to examine the issue. His encyclical *Humanae Vitae* attempted to restore the traditional teaching against contraceptive birth control, but instead severely undercut the authority of the church, and probably further weakened the values of patriarchialism and the sacredness of life.

The civil rights movement was also in full stride, challenging old ways. It embodied such values as equality, democracy, and equal opportunity, and the belief that blacks and Chicanos could now achieve what whites had been achieving, based on ability and not on ascribed qualities. It was an umbrella movement, sheltering sectors of society previously denied the benefits of the American value system. The movement had its inception and major impetus within the black Protestant church, and it received varying degrees of support from main-line Protestant, Catholic, and Jewish groups. This is not to say that societal and religious values were the necessary and sufficient conditions to explain the movement, nor that it owed its success only to religious leaders such as Martin Luther King, Jr. Whatever the initial causes, the values did provide a rationale that caught the imagination of the great majority of the American people.

Let us look briefly now at the way the events of the late 1960s and the 1970s affected the core value orientations of the society.

(1) The value of achievement was challenged for a period of some five or six years. The hippie and yippie movements, the Jesus movement, the turn toward Eastern religions, and experiments with communal living arrangements reflected the extremes of disenchantment with the society, its structures, and its values. But since the mid-1970s and the recession and energy crunch, there seems to have been a return to the ways of the establishment — a return manifested partially in attention to hair styles for men and women, designer jeans, stereos, tape players, and other paraphernalia that attest to the dominance of business in our lives. On the college campus, we see the resurrection of curriculum requirements and the end of pass-fail grading. Business and engineering schools are "in"; their graduates are wooed by corporations with salaries that often exceed those of the professors. Achievement is back in place; and salaries for professional athletes suggest that achievement is good not only for them but also for their owners. At the same time, coed dorms and sexual permissiveness are evidence of the contemporary interpretation of individual freedom and equality.

(2) There has been a questioning and reassessment of work and activity. Increasing numbers of people have come to value leisure and nonwork activities as much as they do work itself.[6] Moreover, work is no longer as seen as a good in itself; rather, people more and more seek and find satisfaction in work to the degree that they are able to control the conditions of work and to participate in the decisions affecting production.

This challenge to the work ethic comes just as the society is beginning to recognize that its industrial infrastructure may not provide the best way to produce for profit. It appears that corporate management, especially in the automobile industry, had been more concerned with short-term profits than with long-term efficient productive arrangements. The recession of 1979-1981 stemmed not from an unwillingness of workers to work but a failure of management to organize and control the quality of work. The Japanese model of work, with which the American is now being compared, suggests a much more group-oriented — even family-oriented — concern for workers, and encourages worker participation in decision making; work is legitimated within an ideology and value system that fosters collectivism and familism. We may be on the verge of changing how we relate work and family life, but the work ethic is hardly nearing its demise.

(3) By the late 1970s we were also questioning the values of science and rationality, progress, and even material comfort: Science and rationality had not brought us to the millennium. And for the first time since the Great Depression, Americans found that change did not necessarily mean progress. Material comfort was suddenly becoming more costly and increasingly elusive for many.

The present situation is one of mixed signals. There are such elements as the energy crisis, pollution, industrial production that is unheedful of its consequences, and inflation. Because science and rationality did not protect or save us from such problems, we question their utility and are cutting sharply the federal monies used to support them. Yet, while science and rationality are challenged by many, for example, the "creationists" versus the "Darwinian evolutionists," their products, such as the pill, sterilization, no-fault divorce, and, yes, the multinational corporation, are worshiped by others. And even the proponents of natural family planning are students of rational methods.

But Americans still value material comfort, even if we no longer believe that every day in every way things are getting bigger and better. The apparent paradox is that recent studies suggest that almost three-fourths of us enjoy a great deal of material comfort, even if it is increasingly a function of two- and even three-person family incomes.[7]

(4) The events of the past decade may have had their most telling impact on the value of humanitarianism. In just twenty years we have gone from the Peace Corps, Vista, the War on Poverty, and Medicare to centering on self and the private sector. The dismantling of the social programs of the 1960s and the incessant, almost obsessive search for "welfare cheats" marks the new directions of the 1980s. Only the "truly needy" deserve humanitarian rescue.

Other evidence of the decline in the humanitarian values is found in studies of the values of college students. In 1969, *Fortune* found that fully 42 percent supported the following statement: "I'm not really concerned with the practical benefits of college. I suppose I take them for granted. College for me means something more intangible, perhaps the opportunity to change things rather than make out well within the system." While such students constituted only a minority of all students, the survey was unusual in that it uncovered for the first time that a high percentage of college students had humanitarian concerns. The editors of *Fortune* predicted that there would be more of these students in the years ahead, but their forecast has not come true. Students are more than ever given over to interest in jobs. The 1970s was a decade of privatism, of individualism without enthusiasm and without illusion.[8]

The roots of American humanitarianism may be in the parable of the Good Samaritan, but its practical results may actually be found in the perceived state of affluence and security of the middle class. Societal programs expanded with the growth and affluence of the middle class, but the events of the 1970s threatened middle-class security, and taxes seemed to make things worse. As the middle class withdrew its support from governmental "good works," those who identified with the Moral Majority gave sums instead to television evangelicals and other right-wing religious groups. They have also been strong proponents of a bigger military. In fact, a significant majority of adults favored increased military spending over tax cuts in 1980 and 1981. Humanitarianism has been displaced by a preoccupation with self and national security.

To sum up, the values that dominated American society during the 1950s have been subject to great stress and strain during recent years. The antiestablishment revolt of the Vietnam years has been put down, and such values as achievement and material comfort retain their attraction. The student, civil rights, and women's movements, supported by such values as freedom, equality, and individualism, met with varying degrees of success. While the values gave these movements legitimacy, economic, political, and religious factors seemed to play a more decisive role in determining the nature and extent of the changes that took place.

THE FAMILY IN A TIME OF CHANGE

To this point, I have written of the family in broad terms, without attempting to define it. For purposes of this chapter, the family may be considered a unit comprising two or more persons who live together for an extended period of time, and who share in one or more of the following: work (for wages and house), sex, care and feeding of children, and intellectual, spiritual, and recreational activities. Persons who live alone because they are single, widowed, separated, or divorced do not constitute families in this sense, but are included because they constitute a significant proportion of all household units (one-fifth). Most families are a variation of the nuclear type; only 30 percent of all families are *fully* nuclear in the sense of having husband, wife, and children under one roof (see Table 4.1).

Throughout most of known history, the common type of family has been the nuclear family. The extended family — that is, three generations of relatives living together — has been an ideal achieved by only a small proportion of any society at any time. The height of extended family life in the United States was probably reached during the early years of the twentieth century, with first- and second-generation ethnic groups, but the figure never exceeded 15 percent of all families. Today only 6 percent are of the extended type.

The figures in Table 4.1 remind us that there are today a variety of social arrangements that may come under the general rubric of family, and to a considerable extent they reflect some of the central values of this society. On one hand, we have couples living together though not married, a reflection of the emphasis on individual freedom and equality. On the other hand, we have elderly people living alone or in couples, no longer expecting to live out their declining years in the bosom of the extended family, but who are supported by pensions, social security, and the like. It is debatable whether their lifestyles reflect any of the traditional family values, or even such societal values as freedom, equality, and humanitarianism. In some cases, at least, their living arrangements suggest a devaluation that goes with aging in a society that measures worth by work, achievement, and rationality.

The contemporary family is small in numbers, and will probably remain so throughout the rest of the century. It seems increasingly to reflect both the societal values of individualism, achievement, and equality and the traditional family values of warmth, affection, and love. And whether despite or because of all the changes, most people seem satisfied with their family lives.

Table 4.2 reports on poll findings that are representative of other polls and related studies: The American people express a high level of satisfaction with family life (Gallup Organization, 1980). There are several explanatory factors. In the first place, we must keep in mind that this profile of American families is of the great mass of middle-class and working-class Americans, whose standard of living is by any measure comfortable. And it encompasses the range of structures noted in Table 4.1.

We must recognize, too, that American family life has come to embody some of the core values of the society in such a way as to produce this high level of satisfaction. Americans have been

TABLE 4.1 Types of Household Living Arrangements	%
Single-parent families	16
Persons who are single, widowed, separated, or divorced	21
Married couples without children	23
Dual-breadwinner nuclear families	16
Single-breadwinner nuclear families	13
No-breadwinner nuclear families	1
Extended families	6
Experimental families or cohabiting families	4
Total	100

SOURCE: U.S. Department of Labor, Bureau of Labor Statistics (1977).

achievers, have worked hard, and have found material comfort to be the reward for their efforts; and they do espouse freedom and equality for themselves in interpersonal behavior. There is a basic consistency in the relation of these values and the family life patterns that have come about in the United States. And, as I will try to show, this family pattern is not inconsistent with the current negative view of such institutions as business and government.

It seems reasonable to suggest that as the institutions of macrosociety (especially government and business) become threatening or lose their legitimacy, the family stands in contrast as a "haven in a heartless world." Thus despite (and in many cases because of) such phenomena as divorce, contraception, and permissive sexuality, the family is seen as *a* source, if not *the* source, of great satisfaction no matter how dispiriting particular experiences. People continue to marry and remarry, and to have children (fewer, however, and in more and more cases, none). The simple functional explanation must be that family is still the best or the only institution, as bad as it may be, that enables people to experience core values of intimacy and security. Accordingly, Americans are striving to resolve the conflict between traditional family values (such as love, solidarity, and group concerns) and those of the larger society (such as freedom, equality, and individualism).

Finally, we should note that the current national debates about sexuality and abortion, ERA, and the like suggest that there is a considerable range in the meaning of satisfaction to American families that more than matches the range in family styles and structures.

TABLE 4.2   Reflections on Various Aspects of Family Life

	Very Satisfied %	Mostly Satisfied %
(1) How satisfied are you with your own family life at this time?	47	44
(2) Which of the following statements best describes how important your family is to you?	the most important element in my life	one of the most important elements
white collar	59	23
blue collar	63	17
(3) How satisfied are you with your present housing?	satisfied	
	84	
(4) How satisfied are you with your children's education?	71	
(5) How satisfied are you with your family income?	62	

SOURCE: Gallup Organization (1980). Used by permission.

CHANGE AND ITS IMPLICATIONS

Let us look now at some specific examples of changes that have taken place in society and their impacts on the family.

The Changing Role of Women. A generation ago, only about 25 percent of married women worked for wages outside the home; today between 55 and 60 percent do so. This move into the labor force has brought about a significant change in women's role relationships within the family and in the larger society. It has intensified the movement toward more egalitarian relations between husband and wife, has influenced fertility patterns, generally to reduce fertility levels, and has greatly influenced childbearing and child-rearing patterns in ways not yet entirely clear. One emerging new pattern is a day-care-type socialization, which can be expected to reduce still further parental influence and increase the influence of the peer group and center groups.

The working wife has also meant additional income to families, either adding to the comfort level, especially in the middle class, or helping to meet basic necessities, as in the working class. But this change is a function of industrialization and an expanding economy as well as a response to the American values of equality, freedom, achievement, and hard work. It has become legitimate for women to strive for these values outside the home. One consequence may be a weakening of some traditional family values, but the change did fit with the institutional demands and the value orientations of an urban, industrial society — at least until now.

From the point of view of an economy, it does not matter who is hired as long as the work is done. The interpretation of our values by the women's movement has allowed women to demonstrate that they can indeed perform tasks in an increasingly automated workplace that negates the male advantage of physical strength and height.

Government and the Family. The government's role in the family life allows another view of change and its implications. Recent Gallup Polls have shown that Americans were more likely to blame government for society's problems than to blame anyone else. And we generally understand that Vietnam, Watergate, school busing programs, and various other actions by Congress, the executive branch, and the Supreme Court have brought about these negative attitudes. Let us look at several actions by government that have had specific consequences for family life.

Social security is firmly a part of American life, including now Medicare and Medicaid. These and other forms of transfer payments provide at least a minimal base of material comfort, freedom, and equality. They may be said to reflect the society's recognition of an obligation to the elderly. The task is removed from the home and made impersonal, but, again, fits with the values of freedom and equality. Parents do not expect their children to take care of them directly, and young people find it easier to accommodate the elderly in this way than by taking them in as boarders. Both sides gain some freedom. The cost in the meaning and satisfaction of social relationships may be higher than we think at the present, but that is a different matter. This is the first time in history that such large numbers of elderly have been alive, so we really are facing a new situation (Sullivan, Chapter 2, this volume, presents some provocative ideas about this new demographic phenomenon).

In some ways, the most important things the government has done to support family life have been to provide mortgage loan monies and to allow deductions for mortgage interest and property taxes on federal income taxes. It is no wonder that Americans express satisfaction with their housing! And it is another index for them of the reality of the core values, but they fail to appreciate the role of government in making homeowning possible.

The government has also fostered affirmative action laws, voting rights laws, and other legislation that has given new meaning to the core values of freedom and equality for minorities and women. And then there are the government actions relating to abortion and divorce. People who believe that abortion and divorce are major reasons for the decline in family life in the United States blame the legislation and judicial opinions of recent years.

Divorce. Until 1970, divorce laws in the United States were very stringent. Indeed, they had not changed much since 1890, when there were few divorces. But despite the laws, divorce rates climbed almost continuously during this century. The post-World War II period 1946-1948 saw a record number of divorces. Restrictive divorce law as a social control mechanism was no longer effective because it did not fit with the urban, industrial society, with its dominant business orientation, the values that had evolved with that orientation and with increasing longevity. Divorce law was changed to *reflect* different behavior, not to cause it. And, as a result, the law was brought into greater conformity with values like freedom and equality. Precisely how family life has been threatened thereby is not at all clear. That is, family life as it has evolved in this kind of society seems to have elicited the new divorce law. In the process, the legitimacy of the absolutism of religious values has crumbled.

The values of freedom, individual autonomy, equality, achievement, practicality and work, and progress and material comfort all give or make sensible the possibility of divorce in contemporary society. How can we unravel this complex issue and see it in its essence?

Married women have been a part of the paid labor force since before the turn of the century. But the traditional norm and the reality were that the great majority of married women worked in the home and in the kitchen. Indeed, women's place in the home was seen as a core family value supported by religion. Nevertheless, the society has never hesitated to set aside that value when it needed the paid labor energy of women. When World War I drained manpower from industry, womanpower was drained from the home to industry. World War II saw an even greater number of women (married and not) move into the paid labor force.

People in families did not sit around and plot to have women move into the labor force. Indeed, they continued to preach traditional norms and values, even as the movement continued inexorably. It proceeded because of the changing nature of the world of work, the kinds of jobs being created, shifting attitudes toward family size and the availability of more reliable methods of birth control, revised notions about material comfort and the amount of money needed to achieve it, and the rising number and percentage of women attending college and being led to think of careers other than that of wife and mother.

Thus not a single factor but a variety of factors were at work and influencing each other to bring about new attitudes regarding divorce and the actual decisions to divorce. Structural events, such as the wars, the expanding economy, and the growth of public universities and colleges, mixed with such events as the invention of the pill to set up conditions for change in the microworld of the family. The post-World War II baby boom was an exception to a long-term pattern of decreasing fertility and family size, and it was inspired by the sense of release and affluence following World War II.

In traditional society, divorce was seen as a violation of sacred rules, and especially as a threat to community solidarity. A group bond was being broken. Now the values focus on the individual and the right to personal happiness. Divorce is recognition of the failure of a couple to establish or maintain a worthwhile, reciprocal relationship. An unhappy married person demands freedom to dissolve the marriage. Thus, if we are to be concerned about the causes of divorce, we must look to the way societal structures and values impinge on family members. It simply will not do to see divorce arising in shortcomings of individuals, greed, or lack of concern for the group. It is, rather, the result of a core value, freedom, winning out over a less central traditional value, familism and group solidarity — and an even more abstract religious value, the sacredness of marriage.

Abortion. The issue of abortion is much more complex than that of divorce. Questions of biology mix with philosophical and theological questions about the meaning and sacredness of life. The government's support of the right of a woman to have an abortion is a recognition of the pluralist nature of the society. It also affirms that government does not recognize the absolute value of life once conceived. Again, the government's position seems consistent with some of the major value orientations of the society. What other family values may be threatened thereby, and how, is not readily apparent.

Abortion is as old as history, and known in almost all societies. And, in all societies, the rich have access to medically safe abortions; the poor do not, and must put lives at risk to obtain them. Further, societies that have the most stringent antiabortion laws are often the societies least likely to have broad-scale support for the living needy. Perhaps more than any other issue, abortion pits a traditional, core religious value (sacredness of life from the moment of conception) against secular societal structures and values.

From a comparative viewpoint, how has abortion, legal or illegal, throughout most of history affected family life and family values? Does its practice mean that people place a lower value on life and on children? Data from South America indicate not. A study in Chile showed that women who had abortions were more likely to be those who believed they already had all the children they could care for (Romero, 1966); it was a form of birth control used to protect the family. Research in the United States on the personal and social consequences of abortion has not provided evidence of harmful effects on family life (Lamanna, 1980). All we can do here is point out that government action in regard to abortion is consistent with the core secular values of this society, and it has been supported, in varying degrees, by some of the major Protestant denominations. Still, its challenge to the traditional core religious values ensures that abortion will remain controversial.

RELIGION, FAMILY, SOCIETY

We come now to the role of religion. We recognize that in the West the values that came to identify the family were derived in some measure from Greek, Roman, and Hebrew cultures. Whether they were a function of the primarily agricultural economies or not, they presented models of family life that were patriarchal and that defined proper male and female roles, sexual conduct, and parent-child relationships. Thus, at the micro level of the family, they have acted as mechanisms of social control and social support. There is much evidence that there were periods when these mechanisms were more breached than practiced, but they did persist (Gordon, 1978). And it is to American Protestantism that many of the macro-level core values cited in this chapter can be traced. The Puritan work ethic and self-responsibility as an embodiment of the value of freedom came to permeate all segments of the society. One can say that American Catholics, especially those under age 45, have manifested their allegiance to these core American values by their approval of contraceptive birth control and divorce despite the church's official opposition. The traditional religious values prohibiting birth control and divorce are not sustained in today's society. Indeed, there is considerable disagreement among the major religious groups about *which* traditional values should continue to be supported.

There are several ways to assess the importance and influence of religion in a society; in general, the measures separately or together suggest that the United States is among the more religious societies (Carroll et al. 1979). And, despite tensions created by the economic and political systems and by the turmoil of the 1960s and 1970s, data suggest that Americans continue to be a religious people (PRRC, 1980). Two-thirds of all Americans not only express quite a bit or a great deal of confidence in organized religion, but have more confidence in religion than in any other social institution outside the family. There is a notable falling off in expressed religious preference among young adults, and they are less likely than older adults to say that religious beliefs are important to them — and much less likely to attend church weekly (see Table 4.3).

Overall, church membership in the United States has risen steadily during the past three centuries; 73 percent of those who identify themselves as Protestants say they are members of particular church congregations, as do 83 percent of all Catholics. Only 34 percent of Jews identify themselves as members of synagogues. While there has been some falling off in church attendance (mostly among Catholics) and in church membership (mostly among Protestants), the overall picture reveals religion to be still important to most Americans. How that translates into behavior is less clear.

A majority (75 percent) of Americans say that the place for the spiritual and religious development of the child is the home, not the church (PRRC, 1980). Yet, Gallup Polls show that only 45 percent of parents claim that religion in the home had strengthened relationships with their children a great deal. And only one-third said that religion in the home had helped their children a great deal in handling daily problems. As expected, among parents who themselves had experienced a strong religious atmosphere in their home lives as children and who considered themselves to be very religious, 63 percent said that religion had helped strengthen family relationships and 62 percent said it had been very helpful to their children.

A survey of teenagers suggests that parents do indeed have continuing influence over children in matters religious. Consider the following data (PRRC, 1980: 63-72):

95 percent believe in God or a universal spirit

85 percent say their religious beliefs are very (42 percent) or fairly (43 percent) important

68 percent say they have had the feeling of being in God's presence

71 percent are church members

TABLE 4.3   Measures of Religious Commitment in the United States, 1978

	National Sample	
	Adults %	Young Adults (18-24) %
(1) Confidence in organized religion (great deal or quite a bit)	65	66
(2) Religious preference		
Protestant	60	48
Catholic	29	30
Jew	02	02
all others	01	10
none or no affiliation	08	10
(3) Importance of religious beliefs to respondent (very or fairly important)	84	72
(4) Attended church	41	28

SOURCE: PRRC (1980: 20-72). Used by permission.

47 percent attended church within the week prior to the interview

87 percent said they had ever prayed, 39 percent said they prayed frequently

At the same time, 77 percent said that a person could be a good Christian or Jew without going to church or synagogue, and 48 percent thought the influence of religion on American life was decreasing.

In summary, it seems clear that family and religion continue to have a close relationship in some respects. As the chapters in this volume make clear, religions offer a range of social support and social control mechanisms. The family continues to absorb and pass them along. But, as these chapters also indicate, religion's role as social control agent for society seems to be called into question at least in regard to the absolute value some religions place on sacredness of life. And, as we shall see shortly, that absolute value so far has meant a negative, restraining, or at best reluctant approach to sexuality.

Organized religion does not speak with one voice in American society, at either the micro or macro level. Nor do the various groups and denominations always manage a close consonance between their values and their social structures. For example, local autonomy within Protestant congregational denominations and sects has greatly hindered or slowed the ability of ministers to translate the norm "love thy neighbor" into programs for racial integration. The laity simply

78/80

withdraws financial support, votes out the ministers, or disbands the parish (Woodrum, 1978).

The "New Christian Right" seems to have the massive support of its followers on the issues of abortion, divorce, and premarital sex. Its position fits well with that of the Catholic hierarchy (and to some extent the laity) in the shared attack on what they call "secular humanism," but they part company on other manifestations of humanitarian values. The Catholic leadership supports most of the social legislation of the past forty years, including strong labor unions, while the New Christian Right has opposed such legislation. Still, both sides use political means to try to restore traditional family values and behaviors.

Most religious groups and their leaders give at least tacit support to United States-style capitalism, and have been very slow to see it as in any way responsible for "the evils" they decry. Catholic schools and colleges are at least successful as the public and other private schools and colleges in producing graduates who fit smoothly into the corporate structure at all levels.

Religion, or more precisely religiosity, does predict differences in attitudes and behavior regarding such phenomena as interreligious marriage, fertility, abortion, premarital sex, and divorce, but the relationship is not one to one; social class, education, and occupation are often more important variables (Heiss, 1977). The amount of the variance religion explains has been steadily decreasing. And, as with the abortion issue, there is a growing consensus among the laity across religious lines, in at least some instances.

But what about religion as a support mechanism for marriage and family? That is, to what extent does religion itself foster such values as meaning, intimacy, love, and concern for others?[9]

LOVE, FAMILY, AND RELIGION

Love is a central tenet of the Judeo-Christian tradition, but it is nowhere listed as one of the core values of American society.[10] Yet, Americans hold love to be the central reason for marrying and having children, and college students see it as very important in their lives. Love, then, is among the core family values. In the context of the contemporary American family, love has developed an individualistic meaning. It is a phenomenon of interpersonal relations between two people and, by extension, to their children. One loves one's spouse, one's parents, and one's children, and, to a lesser extent, one's other relatives (D'Antonio, 1980). In the traditional family, love involved a relationship with an extended number of relatives, and carried with it a strong sense of duty and obligation, honor, and commitment to the welfare of the group. Today love has a more intensive affective meaning, and is less encompassing; its meaning is consistent with the core values of the society. As Reiss (1980) points out, in the traditional family system love was only one of the functions of the family; in the contemporary family system, with its many forms, love may be the only function. And within the marital or cohabiting unit, it has taken on a strong sexual component in the search for self-actualization. Religions have been struggling for the past century to come to terms with this new family pattern. They have gradually conceded that sex is an act good in itself for the pleasure it gives to the participants and not simply because it is open to procreation. But even as religions and their leaders have come to accept sexuality as a good within marriage, they are having to confront the fact that a significant proportion of the laity have extended the notion of acceptable sexuality to nonmarital contexts.

Most religions of the West have extolled the value of a single standard of sexual morality: abstinence before marriage and fidelity within marriage. At the same time, they have acquiesced at the practical level in a double standard that permits the male varying degrees of sexual freedom before and during marriage. Reiss (1980) has delineated two new patterns of sexuality: "permissiveness with and without affection." It is these patterns that have most severely challenged the traditional religious value because they have achieved a certain normative legitimacy in the society. They have also helped raise the issue of homosexuality as an alternative lifestyle. As Aldous (Chapter 3, this volume) notes, the more progressive theologians among Catholics and Protestants have been struggling to develop an ethic of developmental sexuality and personality growth that changes the focus away from the negative control mechanisms (sex as sinful, immoral behavior) and toward greater concern for the integrity of the individuals. It is this movement toward accommodation that the New Christian Right and other traditional leaders most strongly oppose. But, on the face of things, they will not prevail. These new sexual patterns, with and without love, are a product of this society and its structures and values; they have not emerged from a communist conspiracy. And, so far at least, there is no evidence that these patterns are the causes of child abuse, wife beating, alcoholism, or drug addiction. What can be said about them is that they do not follow traditional family models and absolutist religious norms.

The current permissive atmosphere regarding sexuality results from structures and values of the secular society, not from religious bodies suddenly giving more emphasis to Solomon's "Song of Songs" than to the Ten Commandments. Neither the threat of "hellfire and damnation" nor the idea that there is something superior about virginity — such as implied in the phrase "Mary pure and undefiled" — has much impact on the majority of people today. More hopeful would be a social ethic that, while celebrating sexuality, emphasizes the dignity, integrity, and interdependence of men and women. This means, among other things, as much concern for the other's well-being, pleasure, and happiness as for one's own.

In a recent study of university students, 70 percent said that love was the most important ingredient in religion; an additional 17 percent said that it was the second most important ingredient (Wright and D'Antonio, 1980). What did they mean? Is this the love that they see as so central to modern marriage? Is it a more generalized feeling that relates to Christ's injunction, "love thy neighbor"? Or is it only a vague feeling that love and religion should have a close relationship?

Let us hypothesize that these students are fairly representative of college students today in the United States, and that they learned something about the relationships between religion and love from their parents as well as from religious leaders and through readings. We may then ask whether there may be in fact a potentially greater concern and caring for people constituting the community beyond the family than is suggested by the core values of American society. If so, the question becomes, How can such a love be manifested within families and, through family members, to the larger social structures? There is little evidence now that love in the broad sense of commitment to and caring for others has a place in the economic and political institutions that dominate our society. Indeed, it seems out of place with the value orientations discussed above, which are the foundation for the structures, if not also, in part, the outcomes of the structures. The structures of modern society, and the values that undergird them, greatly restrict what the family is and can be. And thus they have come to restrict the meaning of "community." These values also seem to make love, nurturance, and caring the central functions of a highly individualized family life today. Not everyone is pleased with this turn of the wheel. For example, it seems to encourage, as a further consequence, interreligious marriage, which may be seen as dysfunctional to the maintenance of traditional religious and family life patterns. This tension is discussed in several of the chapters that follow.

The professional and upper segments of the middle class enjoy varying amounts of freedom and autonomy in their occupational and other social roles. In their families this freedom is blended with a desire for love to be a vital interpersonal relationship. A strong sense of freedom and equality, together with a level of achievement that allows for material comfort, has created a family lifestyle satisfying to those groups but dismaying to the Moral Majority. The poor, some 25 to 30 million people, do not share this lifestyle. Their family life is not sustained by the system or its values. They are constantly threatened by recession, inflation, and welfare programs that do little more than act as palliatives. And they are at present not part of any community to which a majority of Americans feel any deep commitment. So love as an interpersonal relationship remains without any structural support or plausibility in the larger society. In the present political climate, we are reminded of our humanitarianism and are urged to help the truly needy. But we are told that governmental structures do not work. And economic conditions encourage us to look out for ourselves.

We may predict a number of things about the family in this decade: There will be more childless couples, more people remaining single for longer periods of their lives, and more single-parent families. We will surely find a predominance of one- and two-child nuclear families, and perhaps some increase in families of the extended type caused by "doubling up," as the economy dictates shelter arrangements. And there is evidence that some 5 percent or 6 percent of the population will experiment with various forms of extramarital cohabitation. These patterns reflect the impacts of American society's structures and values on people, and their responses.

The majority of Americans find their own family lives satisfying, but perceive that those of their neighbors are falling apart. They say something like this: " My divorce and remarriage have given me a new lease on life, but all that premarital sex, women pushing for ERA, and millions of divorces are sure signs of the moral decay of the family." They may not recognize consciously that the positive consequences for them of the values of equality, freedom, and individualism become negative consequences for others when those others are viewed collectively, that is, as the society. Nor do they recognize the degree to which the legitimacy of these values is tied to dominant economic and political structures.

In today's setting, the social control mechanisms that religious groups used for so long to keep their adherents — and by extension the society — in line have begun to fall into disarray. In the chapters that follow, we find evidence of the various ways in which these mechanisms have collapsed in recent years. The struggle of the Moral Majority to restore the mechanisms seems doomed because, in fact, less than one-third of the adult population supports them. The irony is that the Moral Majority supports the social structures and the ideology of the larger society that make improbable coexistence of traditional family structures and values.

It is time for religious denominations to give more emphasis to social support and nurturance mechanisms. To do so does not mean abandoning values and patterns of life that are crucial for the survival of the family. On the contrary, I argue that the changes of the past century have made it more possible than ever before for more people, women and men, to realize their human potential. We now have an opportunity to draw out the love and caring features of religious teachings. The chapters that follow examine some of the ways that this is or is not being done.

NOTES

1. It is an assumption of this chapter that these values were derived at least in part from historical events occurring in business, government, and religion; in turn, these values are seen as influencing events themselves. When people believe things to be real, things can and do have real consequences for them.

2. See the nationwide survey authorized by the Conference Board of New York to learn how consumers see their economic situations. The fact is that the greater majority of Americans, especially as families, continue to do well, and to improve their standard of living, albeit at a slower pace than formerly (see Lightman, 1982: 1).

3. See Hillery (1968) for a more detailed discussion of this and related points.

4. On October 1, 1980, Robert McNamara, outgoing president of the World Bank, chided Americans citizens for their very limited support of the poor of the world: In 1980, only .18 of 1 percent of GNP, barely half of the amount donated by the other industrialized nations (see Hartford Courant, 1980: 1). The point is that Americans simply want to believe they are charitable; in reality, their charity is very limited. The same criticism has been made of America's "giving" patterns to private charities such as the United Way, Catholic Charities, and the like (see National Catholic Reporter, 1980: 21).

5. See Gagnon and Greenblat (1978: 260ff.) for a summary discussion of the literature.

6. For example, a poll taken in Connecticut by the University of Connecticut Institute for Social Inquiry, published August 22, 1980, reveals that almost half the respondents said they preferred activities that gave them personal satisfaction and pleasure to working hard (see University of Connecticut, 1980).

7. Caplovitz (1979) studied the impact of inflation on the American people and found that at least through the mid-1970s, most were coping successfully. One reason might have been the high rate of home ownership, reaching almost to 75 percent of families. Property values were keeping up with inflation, but most people were paying interest rates well below the high rates of the late 1970s. It is the poor, the near poor, and young marrieds (who rent) who have suffered most from the events of the past five years.

8. Bellah (1978) sees the decade as one of utilitarian individualism devoid of any other-oriented religious spirit. See also Yankelovich (1981), who argues that even as

the economy has taken a downturn, the new norms urge us to do what we want to do, to seek autonomy, self-fulfillment, and love now. See Hargrove (Chapter 5, this volume) for further discussion on this point.

9. A recent study found that most research published in the major journals on the scientific study of religion focused on the social control aspects of religion related to family. Thus it was not surprising to find that most references to religion in sociology of family texts have been to its social control functions and not to social support functions. There is rarely a reference to religion in chapters on love (see D'Antonio et al., 1982).

10. In his classic study, *The Religious Factor*, Lenski (1963: 222ff.) reports on a survey that asked which of the following is the most important value to instill in a child to prepare her or him for life: (1) obedience; (2) to be well liked or popular; (3) to think for oneself; (4) to work hard; and (5) to help others when they need help. Personal autonomy (3) was most frequently chosen, obedience was next, and helping others was third.

REFERENCES

Bellah, R. (1978) "Religion and legitimation in the American Republic." Society 15: 16-23.

Caplovitz, D. (1979) Making Ends Meet: How Families Cope with Inflation and Recession. Beverly Hills, CA: Sage.

Carroll, J., D. W. Johnson, and Martin E. Marty (1979) Religion in America: 1950 to the Present. San Francisco: Harper & Row.

D'Antonio, W. V. (1980) "The family and religion: exploring a changing relationship." Journal for the Scientific Study of Religion 19, 2: 89-104.

———— W. Newman, and S. Wright (1982) "Religion and family life: how social scientists view the relationship." Journal for the Scientific Study of Religion 21 (September): 218-225.

Degler, C. (1980) At Odds: Women and the Family in America from the Revolution to the Present. New York: Oxford University Press.

Fortune (1969) "What they believe." January: 70-71.

Gagnon, J. and C. S. Greenblat (1978) Life Designs. Glenview, IL: Scott, Foresman.

Gallup Organization (1980) American Families — 1980: A Summary of Findings. Princeton, NJ: Author.

Gordon, M. (1978) The American Family in Social-Historical Perspective. New York: St. Martin's.

Hartford Courant (1980) "United States criticized by McNamara on aid to poor." October 1: 1.

Heiss, J. (1977) "Social traits and family attitudes in the United States." International Journal of Sociology of the Family 7 (July/December): 209-225.

Hillery, C. (1968) Communal Organizations. Chicago: University of Chicago Press.

Lamanna, M. A. (1980) "Science and its uses: the abortion debate and social science research," pp. 99-158 in J. T. Burtchaell (ed.) The Abortion Parley. Kansas City: Andrews & McMeel.

Lenski, G. (1963) The Religious Factor. Garden City, NY: Doubleday.

Lightman, D. (1982) "Public feels it's done well, despite economic statistics." Hartford Courant (March 12): 1.

National Catholic Reporter (1980) "Charities funding." October 3: 21.

Princeton Religion Research Center [PRRC] (1980) Religion in America: 1979-1980. Princeton, NJ: Author.

Reiss, I. (1980) Family Systems in America. New York: Holt, Rinehart & Winston.
Romero, H. (1966) "Chile," pp. 235-247 in B. Berelson et al. (eds.) Family Planning
    and Population Programs. Chicago: University of Chicago Press.
University of Connecticut, Institute for Social Inquiry (1980) General Attitudes to
    Life and Work. Connecticut Poll 8, Release 3. Storrs: Author.
U.S. Department of Labor, Bureau of Labor Statistics (1977) News release. US DL
    77-191. March 8.
Williams, R. (1955) American Society. New York: Knopf.
Woodrum, E. (1978) "Towards a theory of tension in American Protestantism."
    Sociological Analysis 39 (Fall): 219-227.
Wright, S. and W. V. D'Antonio (1980) "The substructure of religion." Journal for
    the Scientific Study of Religion 19: 292-298.
Yankelovich, D. (1981) New Rules: Search for Self-Fulfillment in a World Turned
    Upside Down. New York: Random House.

Part II

Struggling in the Tide

The five essays in this section focus on specific religious denominations and families. In the opening essay, Hargrove compares the structures and values of such main-line Protestant families as the Congregational, Episcopalian, Presbyterian, Methodist, and Lutheran. We find out that over time these churches and their followers have moved away from ethical positions against divorce, abortion, and nonmarital sexuality to positions of support and comfort in such situations. These adaptations have occurred over a period of some sixty years. Indeed, in some cases it would appear that the church leaders and teachings are more progressive and supportive than are many of the laity.

Perhaps the close congruence between the American political and economic systems and their Protestant heritage is nowhere better exemplified than in the model Protestant family that has emerged as the American family prototype, with its emphasis on freedom, equality, achievement, and rationality.

In Chapter 6, D'Antonio and Cavanaugh reveal in sharp detail the growing gap between official Catholic teachings about marriage and family, and the actual behavior of American Catholics. American economic and political systems set the stage for the assimilation of immigrant Catholics, and Vatican II, the election of John F. Kennedy as president, and the great debate over the pill all helped bring about the downfall of traditional church teachings for a majority of American Catholics. Church leaders have made only modest efforts so far to recognize the importance of social support mechanisms as regards family life, and one important consequence has been a significant falling off in church membership, especially among the young. Even on the key issue of abortion, substantial numbers of Catholics dissent from the official teaching. It seems fair to say that the majority of Catholics today are very much like their Protestant counterparts in choosing for themselves what they still believe and what values they will support.

Chapter 7, by Dashefsky and Levine, presents yet another picture of the dynamics of adaptation to American society's values and structures. Jews embraced the values of American society like no other immigrant group; and they have succeeded like no other. But as Dashefsky and Levine point out, Jews are now beginning to worry about the cost to the Jewish family of all their success, for this acceptance has brought with it increasing rates of interreligious marriage, increasing rates of divorce, and fertility rates below the rates of replacement. Thus the survival of the Jewish family is threatened not by extermination from without but by acceptance and assimilation.

For most Jews, the key issue has not been abortion, nonmarital sexuality, the roles of women, or even birth control, but survival. Dashefsky and Levine seem to be saying that Jewish leaders are proposing a blend of support and control mechanisms to foster intimacy, meaning, and autonomy while teaching the positive values of Jewish life. Indeed, some of the recommendations in this chapter are generalizable to American family needs in general, for example, creation of quality day care centers for employed parents and the teaching of family skills in high school and college.

In Chapter 8, Jackson reminds us of how little we actually know about the role of the black churches in black family life. Of course, the churches and their leaders played a key role during the 1950s and 1960s in making clear to both blacks and whites that the core values of American society were values to which blacks as well as whites could aspire. The churches were thus a crucial support mechanism for blacks, whether they were church members or not.

It appears that black churches, while formally espousing the same traditional Christian teachings on matters of sex, abortion, and divorce, have been much less concerned with social control in these areas. Rather, these churches have been sources of support for an oppressed people. At the same time, their greater tolerance for and sensitivity to matters of nonmarital sexuality and divorce seem to be precursors of patterns slowly emerging among main-line Protestants and Catholics.

In the final chapter of this section, Fitzpatrick examines the problems faced by our newest large immigrant group, Hispanics. Nominally of Roman Catholic tradition, Hispanics comprise a range of subcultural variations, including especially Mexican, Puerto Rican, and Cuban. The traditional ways of these cultures stand in sharp contrast to those of the United States, and already signs of conflict and tension proclaim the problems that lie ahead as the second generation attempts to live between two worlds.

Hispanics, like earlier immigrants, come to this country with a strong sense of family and with deeply held values about male dominance, the importance of respect, and personalism. These are heading for an inevitable clash with American values, and it seems only a matter of time before they give way. But Hispanics are not able to look to the Roman Catholic church for much help. Their Catholicism is weak, and less than 40 percent can be said to be adherents in any meaningful sense. In many ways, the Catholic parishes of U.S. cities are as alien to them as is the society in general. Thus the picture Fitzpatrick paints of this potentially large U.S. Catholic population is mixed at best. Hispanics seem headed for major kinds of family disruption in their quest for a place in the mainstream of American society.

5

FAMILY IN THE WHITE AMERICAN PROTESTANT EXPERIENCE

Barbara Hargrove

PROTESTANTISM AND
THE NORMATIVE AMERICAN FAMILY

The heritage and actions of the Protestant churches vis-á-vis the family have had an ambivalent cast, in spite of consistent profamily rhetoric. The early reformers were clear in their denunciation of the high place given celibacy in the medieval Roman Catholic church. In place of the "counsels of perfection" being applied only to a few who were called to a higher life that included virginity, Luther rejected the idea of second-class status for any of the baptized. He found marriage to be the good and normal way of life, and the family a school of faith. In the family, he said, one daily practices the grace-full life of loving service as in no other living arrangement. He himself rejected the vow of celibacy he had taken to become a monk, married a former nun, and raised a large and boisterous family. In fact, his actions and teachings, along with those of other reformers, changed much of the Christian understanding of sex roles that had been prevalent in late medieval times.

Doctrines that celebrated the special virtue of celibacy had not only elevated the position of priests and monks in relation to married men, but had also given a particular place in the church to celibate women, where they could exercise a number of roles other than housewifely ones. Yet the fear of women was great among men who so prized celibacy, and by the late middle ages these virginal women were almost wholly cloistered. The reformers, in affirming the goodness of marriage and family life, allowed the emergence of the

Author's Note: For material in this chapter I am deeply indebted to my colleague, Dr. Larry Graham, Assistant Professor of Pastoral Care and Counseling at the Iliff School of Theology, and members of our winter 1981 class in church and family. Larry has read and commented on this chapter and my other chapter in this book, and "good woman" from the cloister. However, the positive evaluation of the family made it most common to assume that the place of greatest service for the pious woman was in the home. Said Luther:

> If a mother of a family wishes to please and serve God, let her not do what the papists are accustomed to doing: running to churches, fasting, counting prayers, etc. But let her care for the family, let her educate and teach her children, let her do her task in the kitchen. . . . If she does these things in faith in the Son of God, and hopes that she pleases God on account of Christ, she is holy and blessed [translated in Douglas, 1974: 295].

Luther's doctrine of the two spheres of life left marriage in the sphere of human fallenness, thus to be controlled by the state. In this way a secular legalism replaced the rigidities of canon law. Marriage was held to be an irrevocable legal contract, so that divorce could not be permitted — nor could the annulments that Roman Catholicism had allowed to be substituted. Calvinists were not enamored of the idea of a separate and coequal sphere for the secular government. They held to a positive evaluation of marriage, including the function of mutual support and love. They were more likely, however, to accentuate scriptural teachings concerning the "headship" of the man and the duty of the wife to submit to him. Children were also expected to be submissive to their parents.

Reformation churches that later became state churches supported family norms not only because they had developed a theology supportive of the family, but also because their position as legitimate social institutions made them feel responsible for the public order. The rearing of children who were self-controlled and oriented to the good of the society was both an act of piety and a service to the society. The sects of the radical reformation were less supportive of established social institutions, so that while most of them also supported the family as preferable to celibacy, they also permitted a wider range of roles to family members.

Anabaptists, for example, accepted the idea of the "counsels of perfection" for all members, assuming that all who were baptized in their faith would be expected to obey all the commands of the New

---

served as an active sounding board for the ideas expressed in both. Specific members of the class who gathered some of the denominational information presented here include: Mary Lou Morgan, Unitarian-Universalists; Diane Lewis, the Episcopal church; Bette Hutchinson, the United Presbyterian Church; Grace Bonar and David Larimer, the United Methodist Church; Linda Martin, the United Church of Christ; Joan Ham, the Lutheran Church in America; and LuAnn Bigler, the Nazarene church. Other members of the class whose specific denominational work was not used were also helpful in discussion of the issues.

Testament, no matter how rigorous. They did not read it, though, to demand celibacy (Bainton, 1952: 100). Thus their definition of marriage was that of a covenantal relationship between two persons already equal in God's sight, each of whose first commitment was to God rather than to one another. Marriages in the "old church" were not considered any more valid than the infant baptism they had received there, so many were remarried after their new baptism. Divorce became easier because it could be put to the test of continuing faithfulness to the original religious covenant as well as to the mutual covenant of the couple. This definition of the nature of marriage had long-lasting results. "The Anabaptist emphasis on the covenantal principle and the freedom of conscience for all adult believers," says Williams (1962: 506), "constituted a major breach in patriarchalism and a momentous step in the Western emancipation of women."

As is the case in many movements that rebel against established institutions, there were in the radical reformation many experiments with new forms of marriage and family life, but these tended to fall away as the heirs of the movement became more integrated into the mainstream of the society. That pattern has been carried over into American society among such inheritors of the radical reformation as the Amish, whose families appear to us to be particularly traditional.

Yet the heritage of the reformation has introduced into Protestantism the concepts of freedom of conscience and adult commitment in ways that create strains in family loyalty, particularly in reference to the extended family. American culture has been a fertile ground for nurturing this heritage, particularly through the experience of the settlement of the continent and the invention of the evangelical style. Picking up on the ideas of the radical reformation, in particular, evangelicalism, has put the primary understanding of the nature of Christianity upon the voluntary commitment of the individual to Christ and to a Christian way of life. Should his or her family's style of life or value commitments be judged non-Christian or sub-Christian, the individual is urged to break family ties, at least as soon as it becomes evident that the family will not follow the convert into the church. This is most evident in demands made on converts from non-Christian cultures by Protestant foreign missionaries. Domestically, the primary application of the demand to rise above one's family heritage has been found in evangelistic work with members of social classes that are lower than that of the evangelist — or those few who would listen who hailed from families of the corrupt rich. But however seldom exercised against families whose style of life is familiar to that of the religious group, the evangelical call is to individuals, and their primary commitment is expected to be to God rather than to any human community.

Deep in its understructure, the Protestant principle sets limits on its support of the family. Even inheritors of the Calvinist concern that their religion be expressed in a righteous soceity begin with the assumption that it is the righteous individual who serves God through social responsibility. Thus inherited communities, including the family, are always subject to prophetic rebellion in the name of a righteous God.

The ways in which this ideal has developed in American society are particularly instructive. The American myth maintains that the nation was started by people escaping traditional societies in pursuit of religious freedom. Founders may have emigrated from Europe as families, but usually as nuclear families — husband, wife, and minor children — leaving behind more extended kin, neighborhood, and other communal groups. European settlement of the American continent was affected by those who were willing to pull up roots, and they often gave religious reasons for doing so.

THE FRONTIER EXPERIENCE
AND FAMILY VALUES

Coming to the continent, however, was just the beginning. Succeeding generations recreated the pattern in the great migrations westward, and it is here that the American Protestant attitude toward the family was most clearly forged. The first people to move west were not often the "family type." Most were men noted for individualism, adventurers and relatively rootless. In general, the first women on the frontier were not the family type, either, but were entertainers, saloon girls, prostitutes, who provided diversion without commitment for men seeking just such companionship. Religion, at least in its institutional forms, was seldom evident. When the land was deemed safe for families and women and children came to live in it, they brought with them ministers and teachers, and set about civilizing the wilderness, including its earlier residents. Family and church, then, were linked closely in the culture of the West. Yet again, since there was a high proportion in the population of unchurched individuals, the evangelical demand for personal conversion came to its most highly developed stage here, penetrating through the teachings and practices of the churches. Even as families struggled to provide a religious tradition for their children, they did so in churches strengthened by the several Great Awakenings, by camp meetings, revivals, and traveling evangelists.[1]

On the frontier, the nuclear family was the essential unit of survival. Taming what was perceived to be a wild and savage land, breaking sod, clearing forests, planting, harvesting, building, all the activities of human settlement took the full energies of men, women, and children. They depended on one another for their very lives. The settlement patterns encouraged by homestead laws required that each family live on the acreage it was claiming, so independent family units were separated geographically from one another.

Frontier churches were a source of values that reinforced and celebrated family autonomy and interdependence. They tended to be small and to exercise the level of social control usually attributed to sects, concentrating on moral issues particularly relevant to family life. These included role behavior that reinforced the division of labor by age and sex that had provided for the physical and emotional needs of all; obedient and hardworking children knew themselves as indispensable parts of a going concern, and their churches helped them to know that it was good. When it was not, the churches tended not to support the individual who rebelled. Rather, the independent and irresponsible life of many of the earlier settlers, as symbolized by the frontier saloon, was seen as a primary evil. So churches fought against strong drink, gambling, dancing, and prostitution in the name of a Christian, family-centered society. To be a Christian was to raise a healthy, strong family, capable of overcoming the challenges of nature to create an ordered and viable civilization.

Many of those attitudes outlasted the frontier. The call to be a civilizing agent turned many churches toward later immigrants with the same messages they had applied to the uncivilized western settlers: Strong drink and gambling were sins that destroyed family life; only (Protestant) church membership could ensure the virtue of a young woman; personal conversion was the basis of a lifestyle on which the American family could rest. They could not see that some immigrants, also clustered together in a hostile (social) environment, might seek family unity through familiar practices that might include drinking or dancing with members of neighbor families; nor could they see that other churches that did not demand a personal conversion experience might provide the basis of personal virtue. Nor did they in most cases take note of broader social ills that might force men to strong drink or women to prostitution. The primary responsibility of the churches was judged to lie in the inculcation of private virtue of a type that would strengthen the family by reinforcing personal commitment and strengthening the individual to resist outside forces that might erode responsible behavior.

The definition given the family, however, was a circumscribed one, generally limited to the nuclear unit. The family was not seen as an end in itself, but rather as the instrument through which righteous individuals would be produced, who could then take their appropriate places in the work of the world, all to the glory of God. This heritage may still be felt, for no matter what pronouncements particular Protestant churches may feel called upon to make in support of the family, they are always tempered with considerations of the rights and responsibilities of the individual. At the same time, whatever may be said about broader social issues will always meet with some responses that these can be dealt with only by producing better individuals, individuals responsive to moral codes created to build and strengthen the normative American family.

DENOMINATIONAL DIFFERENCES

Other experiences have also contributed to the stance of American Protestant churches toward the family. Among other things, different denominations were differently involved in the westward expansion of the nation. The Episcopalian and Presbyterian churches demanded that their clergy be highly educated, and so kept their denominational strength in more urban centers, where both clergy and laity could enjoy the fruits of what they considered a higher culture. They tended to expect theological pronouncements, whether they concerned the family or any other issue, to conform to the tenets of rationality and the world view of an educated elite capable of leading the masses into a more refined and intelligent Christianity. When they did go out to the frontier, they tended to carry with them a high commitment to education and to cultural upgrading of the areas in which they worked.

Colleges founded by these and other denominations were created after the frontier had been pacified, in an effort to bring enlightenment to new generations growing up far from the centers of urban culture and refinement. Sponsored by churches, these colleges nonetheless were conceived as tools to allow the young to rise above their church-member families, both economically and culturally. This, however, was not inconsistent with family values. The value of progress led parents to hope that their children would surpass them in learning and in style of life. Only then would they be able to claim success as parents.

These values were fairly widespread among denominations that would come to be the mainstream of American Protestantism. Methodists, for example, having become a denomination just in time to participate in the westward migration, quickly adjusted their form of organization to fit the situation, and advanced with the people through the invention of the post of circuit rider. While many Methodist churches were frontier sects in the classic sense, their form of organization tended to keep denominational decision-making power in central locations that came to reflect an urban provenance, so that Methodist leadership has also come to represent urban, educated ways, and the attempt to pass them on through colleges and other institutions.

Congregationalists, dominated as they were by their New England heritage, were largely identified with the educated classes, even though the "Old Light, New Light" controversies that shook them and the Presbyterians were evidence of a split between urbanity and homegrown evangelicalism.[2] Other denominations with a congregational polity but a different heritage, such as the Baptist churches, have tended to reflect more directly the values and lifestyles of the localities in which they are found.

Lutherans, for the most part, came to America enough later than the other groups to have missed the full force of the frontier experience. Immigrant Lutheranism, like immigrant Roman Catholicism, reflected a strong ethnic identity, and so tended to support traditional family structures, particularly in rural areas where its adherents could become the dominant group. At the same time, these immigrants — and here especially the urban ones — brought with them many facets of the European culture that educated Americans were trying to emulate.

The relationship of the family prototypes celebrated in American Protestantism and the churches that grew among American blacks was particularly agonizing. Having been kept by the institution of slavery from regularizing their family life, emancipated blacks were cast among the unrighteous for lack of family virtue, so that racism was given religious sanction. Black churches, then, were caught between enforcing a particularly stern moral code to prove the Christian respectability of their members and ministry to those who through custom and economic need were kept from living up to that code. This vital and sensitive issue needs more thorough research and explication than can properly be done here. For that reason, specific material on the black churches will not be presented here (see, however, Jackson, Chapter 8, this volume).

The subject does, however, bring up the place of caste and class in religious life, and one factor of class that continues to affect the position of denominations on family and other ethical issues. On the whole, blacks and native Americans have been the two groups excluded from the class fluidity that accompanied the settlement of the North American continent. Among whites, exploration and development made rich people out of poor ones, and they as well as the less favored sought to establish their superiority (or equality) through education. Parents sought and often still seek to establish the family's status through the quality of their children's education. Yet education provides a very individual, as opposed to group or family, kind of access to the culture. Whether education has been oriented toward the technology that would provide material progress or the liberal arts out of which a more cultured style of life might be developed, it has become a tool of individual social mobility. Education became the pathway to freedom, freedom defined as the opportunity of the individual to make choices concerning his or her occupation, style of life, and companions.

Thus, while the evangelical aspects of the frontier encouraged individualism, the educational emphasis of urban centers also encouraged their own kind of individualism. The importance of the frontier family as a civilizing influence set limits on the amount of free will that could be tolerated in those matters most relevant to the strengthening of the nuclear family; this constraint was less applicable to those who left families to obtain higher education or to move to urban centers in pursuit of new careers. Local congregations as a whole have continued to emphasize values of personal and family morality, and to reinforce traditional roles known to have produced a stable family life. Educated urban people, freed from some of those patterns, also found themselves involved in larger issues of the society, and have come to emphasize ethical questions around those issues more than those concerned with the private sphere. As denominations have become larger, and their programs more complex, more and more denominational leaders have been drawn from the more urban group, who have had the specialized training that is needed to deal with organizational complexity in the modern world. Hence, in many Protestant churches there are two sources of information concerning values and attitudes toward the family — official denominational statements reflecting the viewpoint of denominational leadership, and what is actually preached and practiced at the local level. At each level, there are denominational differences, but patterns of relationship between congregation and denomination remain important.

CURRENT DENOMINATIONAL
STANDS ON FAMILY ISSUES

Traditionally, the churches have supported the nuclear family in a number of ways. They have defined monogamous heterosexual marriage as an honorable estate and have defined other types of sexual union as less than honorable. They have defined the rearing of children to be a prime function of the family and hence, at least, have cast suspicion on married couples who seek to avoid that responsibility, particularly through abortion, but often through contraception as well. They have tended to provide religious sanction for cultural definitions of age and sex roles that strengthen accepted family structures, including the dominance of parents over children and of the husband over the wife. Yet in each of these areas, the accent on individualism and its necessary correlate, freedom of choice, has affected Protestant stands. The interaction between church teachings and cultural trends has been affected both by the theology of particular denominations and by their organizational structure. We may best see this by considering specific ways in which denominations have treated issues related to the family. What follows, then, is a survey of some recent statements from some denominations. No attempt has been made to find parallel statements on each issue by every Protestant denomination. Again, what is presented here concerns a reasonable number of churches of the so-called mainstream, generously defined, whose cultural situation, theological position, and form of organization may be taken as representative, rather than a complete survey of all denominations. On the whole, the issues usually addressed by the churches concerning areas related to the family include definitions of the Christian family; male and female roles in church, family, and society; definitions and practices concerning marriage, divorce, contraception, and abortion; homosexuality; and the rights of children.

The Unitarian Universalist Association. This liberal group is on the fringes of the mainstream, often rejected as a member of Christian councils because its polity does not require members to profess a belief in the divinity or lordship of Jesus Christ. In this denomination, individual freedom of choice is given theological standing: The final arbiter of all truth is the individual conscience. It should come as little surprise, then, that the Unitarian-Universalists offer perhaps the widest definition of the family and the roles through which it is supported of all the churches surveyed. In the association's newspaper of January 1981 we find this statement: "A family is a unit of two or more people who interact physically and emotionally in a mutually beneficial manner." Even more explicit in its openness is the following paragraph from a mimeographed handout presented at a Unitarian-Universalist (U-U) workshop, "The Changing Family: The Responding Church," led by Pauline Boss of the University of Wisconsin in the winter of 1980:

> The family is no longer defined by what it looks like or who serves in what role, but by how it works, how it adapts to change, how whoever happens to be in the family at a given time acts upon others and is acted upon. . . . We must stop defining families which are

different as problems. They are resources, just as any other unit, individual or collective, in our church is a resource, just as individuals in or out of family units are resources.

National resolutions of the Unitarian Universalist Association have been promulgated supporting the right of choice concerning birth control and abortion and for rights for homosexuals, and against sex discrimination toward working women, and against child abuse and neglect. At the local level, programs in at least some U-U churches reflect a similar openness. Some have provided camps for couples and "singles who will act as couples." An "extended family" program in some congregations provides a structure of relationships among their members explicitly designed to replace family units for those whose patterns of living do not include such traditional forms. Some churches provide divorce rituals, seeing the need for a rite of passage in this case as well as in marriage. Some, though a smaller number, also provide rituals for couples planning to live together without the permanent bonds of matrimony, who nonetheless want to celebrate their relationship in the community. In all these ways, the Unitarian-Universalist churches support freedom of choice for their members, affirming them in whatever family or nonfamily patterns they may choose.

Freedom of choice extends to their form of government, which tends to be congregational, with the central organization exercising little power over local congregations. Unitarian-Universalist churches are dominantly urban, much less likely than most denominations to reflect the more family-centered culture of small town or rural America. The influence of the frontier experience is felt only in the openness to the new, not in a reaction to that openness. The predominant background of members is one of high education and occupational positions not unlike those of denominational leaders in general. Under these circumstances, denominational statements probably reflect the attitudes of members more accurately than those of most denominations.

The Episcopal Church. Except in such areas as parts of Virginia, where it served as a state church long enough to attain a more broadly based constituency, the Episcopal church also has a membership heavily skewed toward the well educated and the well-to-do, toward those for whom freedom of choice is a live option in many areas of life. However, the theological and structural supports for individualism and voluntarism are considerably weaker than among the Unitarian-Universalists.

The Episcopal church, as has been noted, was not a dominant force on the American frontier during the period of westward expansion. Its understanding of threats to the family was not developed out of the antisaloon modality, but rather from a tradition as a state church whose support of the institution of marriage and the family came out of mutual reinforcement expected of two established social institutions. Thus the weight of church tradition has been conservative, even though the lifestyle of many members would appear to push them to more liberal opinions. It does not come as a surprise, then, that dissension in the church on a number of family-related issues has been open and strong.

Anglican tradition, of which the American Episcopal church is a part, inherited from its Roman Catholic roots an antipathy to divorce. Episcopal affiliation with Protestantism has made it easier to relax some of the prohibitions, so that there has gradually been a softening in this area. In 1973, new canons were adopted that allowed easier access of divorced persons to marriage within the Episcopal church.

However, issues regarding the family have remained problematic. In 1978, a National Conference of Episcopalians on Families was held, in which a number of recommendations to the denomination indicated a growing openness to a more flexible definition of the family. The opening statement of the report of this conference, for example, says, "The family, under God, is alive and well *in its many forms*" (emphasis added). A later statement reads, "Our basic assumptions about the family need re-examination." One outgrowth of the conference was a recommendation by the Executive Council of the denomination that each diocese establish a Family Life Commission, and that "every program and policy of this Church be formed with a conscious concern for its effect on family life."

In the matter of sex roles, the Episcopal church also exhibits considerable tension. There are in its membership many women of high professional competence, whose areas of interest have included not only the entire range of secular institutions, but also the church. For example, Cynthia Wedel, an Episcopal lay woman, has served as moderator of both the National Council of Churches and the World Council of Churches. Yet the struggle for legitimation of women in the primary professional roles of the church has not been fully resolved. In 1973, after the General Convention once again failed to accede to their request for ordination, eleven Episcopal women were "irregularly" ordained by three dissident bishops. Whether through pressures developed from this and subsequent similar acts or in spite of them, the next General Convention allowed the ordination of women — in dioceses and by bishops who were willing to accept them. Since that time, the number of women priests has risen speedily, more speedily perhaps than changes in the societal structures in which they work. Many are finding that their professional duties make difficult the kind of family life supported among their male colleagues. In a culture that still expects the man of the family to have a higher-status occupation than his wife — if, indeed, she is employed outside the home — and that assumes that decisions to move will be made to foster his career, the pressures of the role of parish priest and of the search for a position within the system are made particularly difficult for married women, more difficult even than for partners in other types of dual-career marriages. On the other hand, single women who are priests suffer from the same kinds of strains — lack of personal support, criticism for being "different" — that are experienced by singles in most professions, with the added burden of congregational expectations about ministers' families providing role models and helpful participation in church life. This problem, of course, is not limited to women in the Episcopal priesthood, but is exacerbated by their tenuous legitimacy in the denomination.

Another point of Episcopal tension concerns the attitude of the church toward homosexuals. At the 1976 General Convention, it was stated that "homosexual persons are children of God who have a full and equal claim with all other persons upon the love, acceptance, and pastoral care and concern of the Church," and that their civil rights should be defended. Beyond that, the issue of the place of the homosexual in the church was remanded to a study commission, charged with "serious study and dialogue in the area of human sexuality (including homosexuality), as it pertains to various aspects of life, particularly living styles, employment, housing and education" (Executive Council of the Episcopal Church, n.d.: 357). The issue of accepting homosexuals as priests was left for consideration after hearing the report of the commission, with the hope expressed by the Executive Council (n.d.: 359) that "no bishop will ordain or license any professing and practicing homosexual until the issue be resolved by the General Convention." A resolution of sorts was reached by the 1979 General Convention, allowing the ordination of "qualified persons of either heterosexual or homosexual orientation whose behavior the Church considers wholesome" (Executive Council of the Episcopal Church, n.d.: A51-A52). Wholesome sexual behavior, however, was defined by the Convention in the traditional mode of chastity except within the bonds of heterosexual marriage, so that while marriage is honored for heterosexual priests, celibacy to the point of complete chastity is demanded of the homosexual seeking ordination.

However, the issue is far from settled. A minority of bishops have lodged a formal protest, claiming that they cannot accept these recommendations, since one of the vows they took as bishops was to "encourage and support *all* baptized people in their gifts and ministries" (emphasis in original). Their statement includes the following:

> We have no intention of ordaining irresponsible persons, or persons whose manner of life is such as to cause grave scandal or hurt to other Christians; but we do not believe that either homosexual orientation as such, nor the responsible and self-giving use of such a mode of sexuality, constitutes such a scandal in and of itself [Executive Council of the Episcopal Church, n.d.: A57].

In all these ways, then, traditional definitions of the family and sexuality are being challenged, with strong feelings on both sides of the issue. Also involved here are the workings of the Episcopal form of government. Matters of serious policy must be passed by both the House of Bishops and the House of Delegates, the latter formed by representatives of the priesthood and the laity. On the whole, the House of Bishops has tended to pass the more liberal policies on family matters, though not all bishops agree with the majority. It has been the House of Delegates that has held the line against such issues as the ordination of women, reflecting perhaps some priestly job insecurity, but also the greater conservatism of parishes that are mostly composed of members of nuclear families who are concerned about the erosion of the legitimacy of that form of living as normative. The range of Episcopal variation, however, has limited debate on some issues such as abortion, where it is assumed that consideration of a denominational policy would be more divisive than helpful.

The United Presbyterian Church in the USA. The United Presbyterian denomination is an amalgam of several smaller ones whose involvement in evangelical Christianity has varied. Its form of government is representative, and lay people have an equal number of delegates to that of clergy in deliberative bodies at all levels above the local congregation. In practice, this hardly means that they have equal power, since particularly in the basic unit, the presbytery, lay people usually rotate attendance, while clergy are continuing members, more aware of issues and the channels by which they are dealt with. Nonetheless, the high level of lay participation in governance of the church has reinforced the Presbyterian emphasis on lay education. Family issues must be presented in ways that will convince a constituency probably more conservative in this area than the professional denominational leadership. Presbyterian pronouncements, hammered out in the political forums of the system, tend to deal either with particular situations the denomination cannot avoid, or with broad generalities that may be interpreted differently by different constituencies. While Presbyterian literature does not deal specifically with trying to define the structure of the family, the nuclear heterosexual model seems taken for granted while the church turns its attention to social justice for those whose lifestyles come under suspicion because they do not fit that model. In the Westminster Confession, a basic document of United Presbyterian beliefs, marriage is sanctified for the "happiness and welfare of mankind." Nurture is treated as a primary family function, with an emphasis on the individual as a relational being. For example, in 1978, in response to a study on homosexuality, the denomination affirmed the importance of ministry to single persons and supporting patterns of friendship between people who are of the same or the opposite sex, then went on to what can be construed as a model of marriage and the family as "committed choice of life-mates, joyous and loving fidelity within marriage, the establishment of homes where love and care can nurture strong children able to give loving service for others" (General Assembly of the United Presbyterian Church, 1978: 265).

On matters of public justice, the United Presbyterian Church has taken stands in favor of the Equal Rights Amendment and other issues concerning the economic equality of women. It has endorsed freedom of choice in the matter of obtaining an abortion, although in 1980 several overtures came to the General Assembly asking for wording that would make it very clear that their 1972 action was "prochoice," and not "proabortion." Conservative trends within the church are never absent, though justice remains important. The denomination has gone on record supporting laws and methods of intervention that might prevent sexual and domestic violence. Laws supporting the rights of children also have been urged, and their individual status affirmed. For example, in 1977, the General Assembly (1977: 595) adopted a paper that stated, "Children are full persons in God's sight. They are therefore entitled to a fully human life."

Women have been ordained to the ministry in the United Presbyterian Church since its inception, and in its largest predecessor since 1956. However, their full equality in parish ministry has been slow to come. The Presbyterian system allows each congregation to choose its own pastoral leaders from among qualified candidates, and a person cannot be ordained unless he or she receives a "call" from a parish or to some other church position. Presbyteries hold both an advisory role and veto power over congregational selections, since a pastor when called becomes a member of the presbytery, not the congregation. Congregations, unused to female professional leadership, have been slow to call women pastors. Small and struggling churches who come to recognize that they "cannot afford anything better" are most likely to call women. Few women have attained positions as senior pastors of affluent and influential congregations.

Homosexuality is still a problem for Presbyterians, who have refused to ordain anyone known to be a practicing homosexual. At the same time, they join other main-line churches in affirming the civil rights of homosexuals and their right to a supportive ministry of the church. Study groups continue to deal with this issue and others related to the family. Their reports will be used to inform the church in its decision-making processes, rather than be set forth as church policy.

The United Church of Christ. The United Church of Christ (UCC) is a denomination formed in 1957 by a union of the Congregational Christian churches with the Evangelical and Reformed church. Its form of government is considerably looser than the Presbyterian, giving less power to central judicatories, a legacy of the congregational polity in which a majority of its constituency were steeped. Thus, again, the need to educate members is great if the church is to follow its professional leadership. In 1977, the United Church of Christ published *Human Sexuality: A Preliminary Report,* which has been hailed in many church circles as a particularly balanced and definitive look at issues relating to the family and sexuality. In addition, a number of stands have been taken by the General Synod of the denomination.

While the UCC study recognizes the nuclear family as the type most supported by law and culture, it goes on to say: "We feel the need for the church to explore more critically the policies that limit or preclude the existence of nontraditional, yet relatively stable, living arrangements" (United Church of Christ, 1977: 189). The document also supports the idea of no-fault divorce, if sufficient protection can be provided any children involved in the situation.

In 1976, the subject of women in church and society was given top priority for the General Synod. The United Church of Christ has been supportive of women's rights and of programs increasing their ability to participate in society as equals with men. Women have been ordained in the UCC since the denomination was formed, and for many years before that in constituent groups. However, like the Presbyterians, they are subject to the whim of local congregations in order to serve as local pastors; and, like the Presbyterians, women are consequently overrepresented in staff positions and special ministries, and underrepresented in the parish ministry.

The study on human sexuality arose primarily out of the concern of the church about the issue of homosexuality. The 1975 General

Synod adopted a broad policy statement in favor of civil rights for gay and bisexual persons, saying as it did so:

> The purpose of this pronouncement is to make a statement on civil liberties. It is not within the province of this pronouncement to make an ethical judgment about same-gender relationships [General Synod of the United States Church of Christ, 1975: 69].

The human sexuality study does not make specific pronouncements, since it is intended to be a preliminary study for the use of the church in making up its mind on these issues. It is a report to the church as a whole, intended to be the objective material out of which decisions might be reached. It does seem to lean, however, in the direction of greater acceptance and legitimation of nontraditional styles of life. In discussing, however indirectly, the question of the ordination of homosexuals to the ministry, the report says this:

> Those whom we ordain are not finally "ours" to ordain. God calls to ministry. We share in that calling, honor it in another and in ourselves, and celebrate it in acts of ordination [United Church of Christ, 1977: 231].

Since the form of government of the United Church of Christ leaves the actual approval of individuals seeking ordination to regional associations, there are some avowed homosexuals who hold clergy status in the denomination. Clearly, the entire church has not yet approved such appointments, and some members hotly contest them. But the denomination seems to be moving consistently in that direction, as it has in the direction of more openness to changing family and sexual patterns in general.

The United Methodist Church. Like the United Presbyterians and the United Church of Christ, the United Methodist Church (UMC) is made up of several mergers of smaller bodies. The latest merger (1968) was with the Evangelical United Brethren Church, which had its roots primarily among German immigrants to the Midwest who arrived after the period of frontier settlement. These people, then, have had less direct identification with American history, or at least the frontier segment of it, than have the more indigenous Methodists. The latter, however, have been divided by varied experiences in different regions of the country, solidified for a time in separate denominational structures that were only merged at midcentury. In spite of their differences, Methodists have often been taken to be the most solidly middle class of the denominations, and as such are thought to be guardians of middle-class morality, a morality steeped in traditional family values. Yet, like most middle-class people, the Methodists have placed a high value on education, and have put into positions of denominational leadership members of the educated classes, classes whose devotion to those family values is far more tenuous. The organizational structure of the UMC allows leaders to speak for the denomination with less general participation than is required by the Presbyterian system and with more authority than is given denomination's statements of social principles have substituted for more abstract theological approaches. With this much variation in background and power, as one would suspect, the United Methodist Church is the locus of considerable controversy over some family issues, but it has spoken as a church in a generally liberal tone.

The 1980 Book of Discipline gives the following definition of the family:

> We believe the family to be the basic human community through which persons are nurtured and sustained in mutual love, responsibility, respect, and fidelity. We understand the family as encompassing a wider range of options than that of the two-generational unit of parents and children (the nuclear family), single parents, couples without children. We affirm shared responsibility for parenting by men and women and encourage social, economic, and religious efforts to maintain and strengthen relationships within families in order that every member may be assisted toward complete personhood [United Methodist Church, 1980: 89].

While marriage is affirmed by the church as a lifelong commitment, divorce is recognized, though "regrettable," and the right of divorced persons to marry is affirmed. Some experimental work has been done on rituals for the divorced. The Book of Discipline goes on to say, "We affirm the integrity of single persons, and we reject all social practices that discriminate or social attitudes that are prejudicial against persons because they are unmarried" (United Methodist Church, 1980: 90).

Abortion is a subject of considerable anguish. It is stated that belief in the sanctity of unborn human life brings reluctance to approve the practice; yet, "we recognize tragic conflicts of life with life that may justify abortion." Supporting the legal option of abortion, they add that any decision concerning an abortion should be made "only after thoughtful and prayerful consideration by the parties involved, with medical, pastoral, and other appropriate counsel" (United Methodist Church, 1980: 91).

The stand of the United Methodist Church (1980: 90) on homosexuality is relatively clear:

> Homosexual persons no less than heterosexual persons are individuals of sacred worth, who need the ministry and guidance of

the Church in their struggles for human fulfillment, as well as the spiritual and emotional care of a fellowship which enables reconciling relationships with God, with others, and with self. Further, we insist that all persons are entitled to have their human and civil rights ensured, though we do not condone the practice of homosexuality and consider this practice incompatible with Christian teaching.

As for the role of women, the Book of Discipline notes, "We reject social norms that assume different standards for women than for men in marriage" (p. 90). In its own life, the UMC has accepted women into full ordination since its inception, and in the uniting branches since 1956 for the Methodists and longer for the Evangelical United Brethren. The first woman bishop was elected in the UMC in 1979. The power of bishops and district superintendents to appoint pastors to the pulpits of local congregations has been used in dioceses led by advocates of sexual equality to place a higher percentage of women in the parish pastorate than has generally been true in denominations that give local congregations power to call their own ministers. Even in this denomination, however, few women have become senior pastors of large and influential congregations.

In its official statements, the United Methodist Church has adopted a consistently liberal line (except, perhaps, in its dealing with homosexuals) and has upheld the rights of women, children, youth and young adults, the aging, the handicapped, racial and ethnic minorities, and religious minorities. Its greatest problem may be with its own conservative religious minority, for whom some of these liberal statements are problematic. Their disaffection has swelled the ranks of the evangelical Good News Movement within the denomination, as will be noted later.

The Lutheran Church in America. Lutherans, like Episcopalians, carry in their tradition a history of having been a state church. They differ from American Episcopalians in two salient respects: The majority of their constituency comes from immigrant groups whose arrival in America was significantly later than that of the English; and the primary areas of Lutheran dominance are more midwestern and rural than in the urban East where the Episcopal Church has had a long history. While this is less true of the Lutheran Church in America (LCA) than its far more conservative sister denomination of the Lutheran Church/Missouri Synod, there are still more likely to be more forces for traditionalism in this body than among the inheritors of the Anglican tradition.

Perhaps an indication of this is the fact that the latest available social statements of the Lutheran Church in America on the family are dated 1970. Most churches are driven to making statements about things that have become problematic for them; apparently this Lutheran group has not felt extreme pressure on the family for the past decade. In those statements, it is recognized that the family appears in many forms, but, regardless of form, it is held that the family is "intended by God to be that basic community in which personhood is fostered" (Lutheran Church in America, 1970: 3). Significantly, the passage goes on to say, "The family should not become centered on itself, but should be seen as a base from which its members move out into society." Thus while supporting the family's traditional role of nurture, the LCA has affirmed a less traditional support for social mobility.

Marriage is defined by the LCA (1970: 1) as a "covenant of fidelity — a dynamic, life-long commitment of one man and one woman in a personal and sexual union." Divorce is recognized as a formal recognition of the brokenness of that covenant:

> To identify the legal action of divorce as sinful by itself obscures the fact that the marital relationship has already been mutually undermined by thoughts, words, and actions. Although divorce often brings anguish to those concerned, there may be situations in which securing a divorce is more responsible than staying together [Lutheran Church in America, 1970: 4].

The church is urged, when faced with individuals desiring remarriage, to "concentrate upon the potential of the new rather than the collapse of the former marriage."

As regards contraception, the LCA (1970: 5) states, "People have a right not to have children without being accused of selfishness or a betrayal of the divine plan; and every child has a right to be a wanted child." Abortion is considered a serious matter, but it is stated, "On the basis of the evangelical ethic, a woman or couple may decide responsibly to seek an abortion" (p. 5) if economic, psychological, medical, family, legal, and social conditions indicate this to be the right course of action.

On the subject of homosexuality, the statements are guardedly ambiguous. This being the case, it may be best simply to reproduce the entire paragraph on the subject:

> Scientific research has not been able to provide conclusive evidence regarding the causes of homosexuality. Nevertheless, homosexuality is viewed biblically as a departure from the heterosexual structure of God's creation. Persons who engage in homosexual behavior are sinners only as are all other persons — alienated from God and neighbor. However, they are often the special and undeserving victims of prejudice and discrimination in law, law enforcement, cultural mores, and congregational life. In relation to

this area of concern, the sexual behavior of freely consenting adults in private is not an appropriate subject for legislation or police action. It is essential to see such persons as entitled to understanding and justice in church and community [Lutheran Church in America, 1970: 4].

As to the role of women, the LCA statement on marriage finds it biblically defined as "a communion of total persons, each of them living for the other." It does not go beyond that to discuss specific gender-related roles. In its own life, the LCA has been relatively slow to grant women professional equality, having ordained its first women in 1970.

In sum, in its official statements, the Lutheran Church in America does not give evidence of the level of conservatism regarding the family that might be predicted from its history and tradition. In its own structures it may come closer to that expectation, but it would still be classified within the liberal camp on the issue.

The American Baptist Convention. Of all the major main-line denominations, the Baptists are most in the free church tradition of local church autonomy. Yet even here, and particularly among the American Baptist branch, the influence of professionals in the denominational organization has grown steadily (Harrison, 1959). Because of the free church form, groups who have resisted that liberalizing influence have tended to break off into separate denominations or independent congregations, leaving the American Baptist Convention (ABC) as the most liberal of the Baptist bodies.

Their commitment to local autonomy has tempered any tendency to make denominational pronouncements on all issues related to the lives of their members, and many that are made are carefully worded political statements devised to be "all things to all people." In spite of this, they have in such statements been quite supportive of the rights of women in the society and in the church. The Convention has supported the Equal Rights Amendment and a time extension to secure its passage. In regard to its own life, the denomination passed a resolution urging affiliated organizations and churches to reverse the declining number of positions in churches held by professionally trained women, establish policies and practices in elections and appointments in order to give more adequate opportunity to women to participate fully in the governance of the church, and to give equal status to women in positions of major responsibility within the church.

The American Baptists discussed a policy statement on family life in 1981 that claims family relationships to have been ordained by God as the primary human community in which God's love can be expressed, which should:

> (a) enhance the most intimate personal relationships and the dignity of each person in the family; (b) provide for, nurture, and guide children without inhibiting the realization of their God-given potentials; (c) establish God's creative, forgiving and redemptive purposes for all persons and the social order.

The statement goes on to say:

> There is a variety of patterns of behavior and structure for family life for persons, groups, and various cultures of the world. We commend those churches that serve as a "larger family" in their ministries to the needs of both traditional and non-traditional forms of family life [Lee, n.d.].

Such mention of "non-traditional forms of family life" may have been the reason the statement was not passed by the Convention, since it could be interpreted as opening a door to homosexuality. Most churches have been forced to wrestle with this issue explicitly when persons who are avowed homosexuals have sought ordination within the denomination. Since ordination in the Baptist tradition is a local matter, the Convention has not had to make rulings about the issue. At the same time, no open homosexuals are known to be in the ABC pastorate.

Earlier in the period of discussion of the issue, the ABC passed a carefully worded statement in favor of freedom of choice regarding abortion. Currently there are pressures to make sure that the church is not in favor of abortion, only of freedom of choice, as noted above in the case of the Presbyterians.

There are a number of denominations in the so-called mainstream that are not discussed here, but a quick survey indicates that their stands and statements fall somewhere into the same general area as those we have noted. The main line as a whole represents the largest number of American Protestants. However, it is time to consider those not represented there and, in doing so, those formally represented by the mainstream who are in disagreement with their denominations on many of the issues related to the family.

THE EVANGELICAL COUNTERPOINT

The word "evangelical" is one that most Protestant churches would claim, but in today's world it has come to be used primarily to designate one branch of Protestantism, one distinguished from the so-called mainstream. This branch of Protestantism takes two forms.

On one hand, there are a number of denominations that claim the title, and have in recent times organized themselves into a national cooperative body, the National Association of Evangelicals, to compete with the main-line National Council of Churches. However, their foundation is in the concept of personal freedom of conscience that is the primary heritage of the radical reformation. This has encouraged the creation of congregations independent of any denominational structure. It also has encouraged individual dissent from stands taken by church organizations in which one holds membership. This makes it much less possible to discuss specific evangelical stands by considering denominational statements.

While issues concerning the family are likely to show a particularly high degree of consensus in evangelical circles, even here evanglical Protestants are not more a monolithic force than are the mainstream denominations. Quebedeaux (1974) has divided the evangelical branch of Protestantism into five types: closed fundamentalists, open fundamentalists, mainstream evangelicals, charismatics, and the radical evanglicals of the left. In their attitudes toward the family, they range from liberal to rigidly conservative. Such evangelicals as Donald and Lucille Dayton, Letha Scanzoni, and Nancy Hardesty have traced evangelical history, supporting wider roles for women, as well as examining biblical references that support more open family and sexual styles. Scanzoni and Hardesty's *All We're Meant to Be: A Biblical Approach to Women's Liberation* (1974) is a far different approach from that of, for example, the Moral Majority. In *Is the Homosexual My Neighbor? Another Christian View* (1978), Scanzoni and Virginia Mollenkott make a strong case for an affirmative response, in the process giving evidence that not all evangelicals write off such issues as inappropriate for Christian thought and action. They, of course, would be classified on the far liberal pole of evangelical thought, representative of a minority.

Most people who classify themselves as evangelicals are reasonably well represented by some of the evangelical denominations. On the whole, the social sources of such denominations are two: some are relatively new organizations formed in established denominations and some have remained relatively isolated from those denominational drifts by geographical or ethnic boundaries.

The Nazarene Church. Founded as a denomination in the late nineteenth century, the Nazarene church is an outgrowth of the holiness movement, which took styles of living very seriously as one of the reasons for their leaving such main-line denominations as the Methodists. The denomination seems to be moving along the usual path of conservative social stance toward the main-line accommodation, but their position at the present time seems clearly within the evangelical camp on family issues.

Marriage is defined by the Nazarenes as heterosexual and lifelong, and divorce is allowed only for adulterers. Only the innocent party in such divorces is free to marry within the church. The primary function of the family is seen as home building, and parenthood is expected to be an element of that task. Abortion for the sake of personal convenience or population control is condemned. Only in the case of a life or death situation, medically defined, is it allowed. Homosexuality is flatly declared incompatible with Christian morality. Roles in the family are traditional ones, with a strong preference for women to remain in the home, at the center of the home-building enterprise.

The Southern Baptist Convention. This large denomination represents the denominational source of evangelical churches in relative isolation from the urban, academic forces that have molded the nature of the more liberal Protestant denominations. Developed in a South that for several generations held itself aloof from the sinful ways of the industrial North, the Southern Baptist Convention's churches have escaped those regional bounds to gain membership among those who would prefer that simpler, more structured existence even if they do live in urban industrial surroundings. As the native South of the denomination has industrialized, the centers of the denomination may be more liberal than its periphery, but it remains conservative in comparison with the so-called mainstream.

Statements of the Southern Baptists are clear on family matters, and perhaps are most representative of the evangelical stance. Definitions of the family are not spelled out. The nuclear family is taken for granted not only as normative in American culture but God given. In a resolution passed at the 1981 convention protesting the upcoming White House Conference on the Family because previous conferences had undermined the "biblical concept of the family," Southern Baptists declared flatly, "The family has been clearly defined in God's Word and accepted by the Jewish and Christian society of America for over two hundred years" (Southern Baptist Convention, 1981: 47). Concerning roles within the society and the family, that same convention passed another resolution recognizing the increased role of women in the society outside the home, and their right of fairness in employment, but closed with the resolution that the convention, "affirming the biblical role which stresses the equal worth but not always sameness of function of women, does not endorse the Equal Rights Amendment" (Southern Baptist Convention, 1981: 33).

Similarly, the 1980 convention protested against legislation in favor of children's rights, claiming the right of every child to adult guidance and saying, "To give children all adult rights would burden their immature and inexperienced minds with responsibility of forming judgments and far-reaching decisions which are difficult for even the most mature adult" (Southern Baptist Convention, 1980: 55-56).

Southern Baptists are opposed to abortion except to save the life of the mother, and in 1981 passed a resolution condemning the "permissiveness of the new morality," particularly as seen in sex education and the distribution of birth control information and "devices" to minors (Southern Baptist Convention, 1981: 55).

Their stand on homosexuality is clear: "All such practices are sin and are condemned by the Word of God." Their only kind word to homosexuals is the assurance that "the Bible also offers forgiveness for those who will seek it and receive it" (Southern Baptist Convention, 1980: 55).

On the whole, such statements represent the general orientation of the majority of those who consider themselves evangelicals. Many recognize the changing nature of the family, even among their own members, and the need to deal with such issues in counseling and supportive acts. However, the more militant evangelicals are very sure of their stand against anything that would change what they see as traditional and God-given family patterns. If it seems impossible to live up to the ideal, they tend to blame the society and the liberal churches for the tensions thus created. For them, there is no compromise with emerging forms of the family, changing sex roles, or abortion. All these changes are viewed as a Satanic attack on the very foundations of Christian morality, to be resisted at all costs. Not only is the nuclear family in its heterosexual form taken as the norm, but it is also defined as having a very specific structure of roles and relationships. The work of Larry Christenson, widely influential among evangelicals, is exemplary concerning this pattern. According to Christenson, "headship" is the responsibility of the father, decreed by God in the whole structure of the universe:

> God's fatherhood operates according to a principle which, like his fatherhood, is eternal. It is the principle of *headship*. He has built the headship principle into the structure of creation, and with particular reference in family life: "The head of every man is Christ, the head of a woman is her husband, and the head of Christ is God" (I Cor. 11:3). To be a father, according to the model of God, is to be a "head" [Christenson, 1977: 21].

The authority of the father is rooted in his submission to Christ, and is to be exercised with love and gentleness, but also with firmness, even to the use of spanking. The role of children is obedience. Says Christenson, "The obedience of the children is not a 'sometime' thing. It is a settled issue, because Christ expects it."

The position of the woman in the family is one of submission. Says Christenson (1977: 22):

> In purely human relationships, subjection often carries with it the stigma of inferiority. Not so in a Christian marriage. It is formed on a better model. Husband and wife are one, as the Father and Son are one. The wife is fully equal to the husband, as Christ is equal to God; yet she remains submissive to her husband in all things, as the Son is submissive to the Father.

On the subject of women's liberation, Christenson (1977: 23) says:

> American women today are not subjugated and oppressed, in need of "liberation." How anyone could grow up in our culture during the past 40 years and arrive at such a notion is incomprehensible. It is precisely the *absence* of male authority which plagues American culture.

This movement from the strictly theological and the private realm to broader cultural and political issues is widespread. Family values have been made a strong platform of the Moral Majority, led by the Reverend Jerry Falwell of television fame, but also of evangelicals less politically inclined and less militant. The only consolation that some take is in their premillennial theology, which would see in current changes of family patterns one more bit of evidence of the social corruption that will usher in the Second Coming of Christ and the rapture of the faithful.

As can be inferred from some of the material above, evangelical opposition to abortion may be as total as that in some Catholic quarters, but their concern is less with the natural rights of the fetus than with the casual sex they assume has created the unwanted pregnancy. Promiscuous sex is a primary target, and is considered to be thoroughly depraved in its homosexual forms. The world of the hard-line evangelical is one in which civilization is defined as control, particularly self-control. If the changing culture is treated by mainstream Protestantism as its products and responsibility, in the pattern defined by Niebuhr (1951) as the church of the "Christ of culture," these evangelicals assume the traditional stance of the sect, that of the "Christ against culture."

THE INTERPENETRATION OF THE TWO TYPES

The irony of the distinction between mainstream and evangelical Protestants lies in the persons making up the evangelical subculture, for many of them are members of main-line Protestant denominations. In some cases they are organized as identifiable caucuses within their denominations — Concerned Episcopalians, the Presbyterian Lay Committee, the Methodist Good News Movement, and the like. They may also be simply individual and relatively invisible dissidents within the ranks. They join with members of independent congregations and some evangelical denominations to decry the loss of traditional family values. They may send their children to independent Christian schools in order to avoid the corruption of the public schools, a corruption they see particularly in pressure toward sexual promiscuity from peers and in the sex education classrooms.

Who then are these evangelicals? In a 1980 Gallup poll, 19 percent of the American adult population responded affirmatively to all three of the questions commonly used to distinguish the evangelical perspective: claiming to be "born again," activities aimed at sharing their faith with other people, and a literal belief in the Bible. Between 38 percent and 44 percent gave assent to at least one of those questions. The stereotype of the evangelical as an older person was not fully supported: Gallup found 45 percent of those classified as evangelicals to be over the age of 50, but 21 percent were between the ages of 18 and 21. As expected, the South accounted for the most — 50 percent, in fact — with 23 percent in the Midwest. However, stereotypes concerning educational background must be handled with care, for Gallup found about one-fifth to have some college background, and while that survey does not make the distinction, many have earned graduate degrees (see Emerging Trends, 1980). They might, then, be expected to be members of the "educated classes," as the discussion here has named them. The distinction may parallel Yankelovich's (1972) findings in his polls of collegiate youth a decade ago, when he distinguished between the "career minded" and "post-affluent" students. Most of the "career minded" sought higher education because of the demands for specialized knowledge in an increasingly technological society. The "post-affluent," by contrast, were more likely to major in the humanistic disciplines that are less directly linked to specific occupations. We may need, then, to distinguish the "humanistically educated classes" from those whose higher education has been more instrumental, preparing them for a life within the world of industrial or business work rather than that of the academy, the arts, and the humanities.

It is the more humanistically educated who seem to be particularly supportive of changes in family values, and those whose occupational positions deal with human services and ideas. Persons who go into theological education, particularly at its higher levels, tend to be oriented more toward the humanistic disciplines; for many of their fellow humanistic graduate students, the church has become irrelevant. Instead, the church has become the habitat of those whose social attitudes are more conservative, who also take religious participation more seriously (see Kelley, 1972). Their church involvement reflects in part a desire for clear-cut and traditional societal forms, including a family life that is reliable and unchanging, a "haven in a heartless world."

Professional church staff may often not reflect the opinions of their constituency, and those lay members who are free to attend denominational conventions may be overrepresentative of the liberal or leisure classes as well. Many of the conservative caucuses seek to reverse this tendency. Thus family values have served as a focus for intrachurch as well as interchurch conflict. The direction in which main-line Protestantism has been moving has been clearly toward a liberalization of policies in regard to the family. There are some indications, however, that political movements within the denominations, aided by paradenominational organizations and churches not of the mainstream, may reverse that trend.

NOTES

1. These "awakenings" were periods of religious fervor that swept across the nation first in the mid-1700s, and again in the early 1800s, with numerous other local outbursts. They were characterized by fervent preaching to mass audiences, with resultant great numbers of conversions. The awakenings, though not limited to any particular denomination, had the result of strengthening newer sects-turning-denomination, such as the Methodists and the Baptists (see McLaughlin, 1978: 45-140).

2. These controversies were generally confined to the clergy and the seminaries, and reflected the strains put on such denominations as the Congregationalists and the Presbyterians by the Great Awakening. They contrasted the staid orthodoxy of more settled areas with the evangelical fervor of the new forms that were more popular in more recently settled areas. The primary source of contention was the appropriate-ness of "experiential religion" (religious experience). It was these controversies among the leadership that led to the competitive disadvantage of the denominations noted in note 1 (Ahlstrom, 1972: 287-293).

3. The free church tradition was based theologically on assumptions concerning the freedom of God to act in human life unconstrained by social forms. This found one expression in a suspicion of any organization beyond the local fellowship. As Harrison (1959: 19) says, "Baptists believed that the greatest threat to God's freedom . . . was an ecclesiastical order supported by magisterial power." Thus local autonomy, as well as church-state separation, remains a basic value, and denominational staff and structures are deemed only advisory.

REFERENCES

Ahlstrom, S. E. (1972) A Religious History of the American People. New Haven, CT: Yale University Press.

Bainton, R. L. (1952) The Reformation of the Sixteenth Century. Boston: Beacon.
Christenson, L. (1977) "Families need a head," pp. 21-24 in Viewpoints: Christian
    Perspectives on Social Concerns: The Family in Crisis. Minneapolis:
    Augsburg.
Douglas, J. D. (1974) "Women in the contenental reformation," in R. Ruether (ed.)
    Religion and Sexism. New York: Simon & Schuster.
Emerging Trends (1980) Gallup poll. Vol. 2 (October). Princeton, NJ: Princeton
    Religion Research Center.
Executive Council of the Episcopal Church (n.d.) Social Policy of the Episcopal
    Church. Regularly updated publication of Church and Society. New York:
    Author.
General Assembly of the United Presbyterian Church (1978) Minutes of the General
    Assembly of the United Presyterian Church in the United States of America.
    Seventh series, vol. 12. Part I: Journal. New York: Office of the General
    Assembly.
————— (1977) Minutes of the General Assembly of the United Presbyterian Church
    in the United States of America. Seventh series, vol. 11. Part I: Journal. New
    York: Office of the General Assembly.
General Synod of the United Church of Christ (1975) Minutes, Including Addresses,
    of the Tenth General Synod of the United Church of Christ, June 27-July 1.
    Minneapolis: Author.
Harrison, P. M. (1959) Authority and Power in the Free Church Tradition.
    Princeton, NJ: Princeton University Press.
Kelley, D. (1972) Why Conservative Churches Are Growing. New York: Harper &
    Row.
Lee, Rev. A. (n.d.) Mimeographed sheet, personal communication. Calvary Baptist
    Church, Denver.
Lutheran Church in America (1970) "Sex, marriage, and family." Social Statements,
    the Lutheran Church in America. (Adopted by the Fifth Biennial Convention,
    Minneapolis, June 24-July 2.) New York: Division for Mission in North
    America, Lutheran Church in America. (pamphlet)
McLaughlin, W. G. (1978) Revivals, Awakenings, and Reform. Chicago: University
    of Chicago Press.
National Conference of Episcopalians on Familes (1978) A Policy/Strategy
    Statement. (Conference held November 13-16.) Denver: Author.
Niebuhr, H. R. (1951) Christ and Culture. New York: Harper & Row.
Quebedeaux, R. (1974) The Young Evangelicals. New York: Harper & Row.
Scanzoni, L. and N. Hardesty (1974) All We're Meant to Be: A Biblical Approach to
    Women's Liberation. Waco, TX: Word.
Scanzoni, L. and V. Mollenkott (1978) Is the Homosexual My Neighbor? Another
    Cristian View. New York: Harper & Row.
Southern Baptist Convention (1981) Annual of the Southern Baptist Convention,
    Los Angeles, CA, June 9-11. Nashville: Executive Committee, Southern
    Baptist Convention.
————— (1980) Annual of the Southern Baptist Convention, St. Louis, MO, June
    10-12. Nashville: Executive Committee, Southern Baptist Convention.
United Church of Christ (1977) Human Sexuality: A Preliminary Report. New York:
    United Church Press.
United Methodist Church (1980) Book of Discipline. Nashville: United Methodist
    Publishing House.
Williams, R. (1962) American Society: A Sociological Interpretation. New York:
    Knopf.
Yankelovich, D. (1972) Changing Values on Campus. New York: Washington
    Square.

6

ROMAN CATHOLICISM AND THE FAMILY

William V. D'Antonio
Mark J. Cavanaugh

This chapter examines the relationships among the family, the Roman Catholic church, and the societies within which they have coexisted over the past 2000 years. We will note that at times the relationship has been so close that we can speak of the Catholic family as the prototype of the family within Western society. At other times, the family that was Catholic often stood out against the society. More recently, we find distinctive subcultural differences among Irish, Latin, and Slavic Catholic families, despite the common value, belief, and normative systems uniting them. And now in the present, ethnic differences are giving way to differences between traditional and modern catholic family types.

We begin with a brief historical overview, sufficient to place the emerging Catholic family in its Judeo-Roman-Greek setting. We note how the teachings of Jesus and the early followers developed an ethic of marriage, sexuality, and family life that came to dominate Christendom for more than 1000 years. The Reformation, followed by the Counter-Reformation and the Council of Trent, then gave new direction to the relationship between the Catholic church and the family. We conclude our examination with a close look at the tumultuous events of this century that have so greatly shaken the traditional relationships, and we ponder the meaning of the growing gap between church teachings and laity behavior in matters relating to marriage and family.

In effect, the Catholic family as a type slowly evolved from other societal types during the early centuries of the Christian era. It became institutionalized as a type as the Roman Catholic church gained hegemony over the Holy Roman Empire and developed its bureaucratic structure. The Reformation and the Council of Trent further institutionalized, even rigidified the type. At the same time, with modernization and the migration of peoples to the Western Hemisphere came an increasing differentiation of subtypes built on ethnic differences. Yet these differences became submerged into what was perceived by the 1940s as a model American Catholic family.

It is now clear that the 1960s, especially with the aid of Vatican II, have led us to the emergence on the one hand of a new type, and, on the other, of an effort to reaffirm the traditional pre-World War II type. This struggle defines the current state of affairs. U.S. Catholics, like their non-Catholic neighbors, have been greatly influenced by the structures and values of the secular society, and this influence has led millions away from the traditional Catholic family type. Indeed, as we will see, it may be difficult now to see just how the family that is Catholic differs from the family that is not. This fact poses serious problems for the Roman Catholic church as an organization to the degree that organizational strength and health depend on families for support.

Despite the gap between church leaders and followers on matters relating to marriage and family, there is no evidence that people are less religious today than 40 years ago. Thus we must wonder whether we are moving into an era in which issues of sexuality, marriage, and family become the means by which the church becomes transformed, including especially its authority structure, but also its values and beliefs, and the norms deemed appropriate to give them meaning. The relationships among family, religion, and society continue to be close, but the lines of influence are more complicated. And these influences seem to be leading us toward a church and family relationship that is more concerned with social support and a respect for personal autonomy tempered by a sense of social responsibility and interdependence.

THE EMERGENCE OF THE CATHOLIC FAMILY

The norms, values, and beliefs that came to characterize the early Christian family were strongly embedded in their native Hebrew, Greek, and Roman cultures. One of the most important features of those cultures was the emphasis on patriarchal authority. Thus, despite the fact that Christ had preached that women were co-heirs of the Kingdom, and despite the fact that women apparently served at least as deacons in the early Church, the societies within which Christianity grew provided the major patriarchal ethos that so strongly shaped the nature of the family down to modern times.

The Influence of St. Paul

Along with the societal influence came the influence of St. Paul as the first great interpreter of Christ's message. It is evident that St. Paul believed that Christ's return to earth was imminent and that his glorious return would mark the final judgment day. St. Paul prized celibacy above marriage in the belief that people free from marriage could concentrate on the life of the spirit and prepare themselves properly for the second coming of Christ. Marriage could only be a distraction.

At the same time, Paul seemed to recognize that this counsel was one that many, if not most, people could not abide. So, while he urged them to be, as he, bachelors, he accepted marriage as an acceptable alternative, for as he said, it is better to marry than to burn with unfulfilled passions. He even acknowledged that widows could marry if they wished to do so. And in a key passage, Paul likened the relationship between husband and wife to that of Christ and the Church. He said: "Let wives be subject to their husbands as to the Lord; because a husband is head of the wife, just as Christ is head of the Church . . . just as the Church is subject to Christ, so also let wives be to their husbands in all things" (Eph. 5:23-33).

Now it may be argued in contemporary thought that the relationship between Christ and the Church, if it is one of love, cannot imply dominance of one over the other. But given the patriarchal nature of the times, it is not surprising that this passage came to be translated into norms that assured that women, while idealized in one sense, would be the subordinate, weaker sex for the next nineteen centuries in the teachings of Church leaders and in the minds of their followers. Even the Reformation did not radically alter that fact for three centuries.

St. Paul also preached the importance of love and fidelity, and reiterated Jesus' prohibition against divorce, although he did seem to allow divorce when one of the spouses was non-Christian and the couple could not live in peace and harmony.

Perhaps the most important consequence of St. Paul's teaching was the negative evaluation given to human sexuality. Although the biblical story of creation seems to affirm sexuality, and erotic sexuality is found in Solomon's Song of Songs, the fact is that since St. Paul, the Christian message has focused on a spiritual life in which sexuality has been at best problematic.

St. Augustine

Between the second and the fifth centuries, the Church leaders gradually evolved a theology of marriage and sexuality that recognized marriage as a sacrament blessed by Christ, but that saw sexuality as redeemable only as it led to procreation, the true end of marriage. The early classic statement on marriage was written by Augustine, and it became the foundation stone for the Church's teachings into the twentieth century. Augustine had a mistress for years before his conversion and subsequent life as a celibate priest, and we can only ponder how his later teachings were influenced by his youthful sexual activities. According to St. Augustine:

> The purpose of marriage is none other than the begetting of chil-
> dren. Indeed, our sexual desires are nothing more than the
> unfortunate effects of original sin. Every child is literally born of his
> or her parents' "sin" because procreation is possible only with the
> seductive aid of physical lust [McBrien, 1980: 791].

The reader should bear in mind that, despite such strong attitudes, the Church never went so far as to condemn marriage. For a great while, many priests were married; it is significant, in fact, that celibacy was not imposed upon the clergy for quite some time. (No universal law can be traced earlier than the first Council of the Lateran in 1123.)

Such ambivalence toward marriage persisted even into medieval times, by which time the family had become the primary social unit and the locus of religious festivals, feasts, and celebrations. Certainly it was upon the network of the life cycle that the sacramental system was hung; Catholic sacraments pinpoint birth through baptism, by which the infant is entrusted to the care of the community; the "attainment of reason," which allowed a young person to enter the community, symbolized by being allowed to partake in the Eucharist; the passage into adulthood through confirmation; the committing of oneself to a vocation such as matrimony or holy orders; and prepara-tion for death. Admittedly, this system of sacraments did undergo a long evolution and was not well developed until the Council of Trent.   A sublimated form of family life became idealized in monasticism. To this day, many religious congregations and orders speak of maintaining a family spirit or ideal within the community, despite the fact that such communities are usually of one sex. Bene-dict's rule confers upon the head of the community the title of abbot (from *abbas,* father), and the nomenclature with which Catholics address clergy and members of religious orders is strongly familial.

Marriage was proclaimed a sacrament of the church in 1439 at the Council of Florence, and this position was reaffirmed by the Council of Trent in 1563. Trent was largely a response to the Protestant Reformation, which had denied that marriage was to be considered a "true sacrament." The Protestants nevertheless upheld its sanctity, but they specifically rejected the church's right to any authority over marriage (a position not uncommon among American Catholics of today) and they approved divorce. Trent strongly rejected these teachings: "The Tridentine perspective remained normative for Catholic theology, canon law, and pastoral practice until the Second Vatican Council. Meanwhile, Trent's teaching was vigorously reaffirmed by Pius XI's *Casti Connubii* in 1930 which set forth as marriage's primary purpose the propagation of life" (McBrien, 1980: 791).

Impact of Roman Law on the Family

It is worth mentioning here that in the Middle Ages, as now, civil law had a profound effect upon the norms of family life. Remy (1979: 5), for example, has discovered the drastic effect upon the status of women and children that the reintroduction of Roman Law had at the end of the thirteenth century:

> In the Middle Ages there was a definite demarcation line separating different types of family life. South of the Loire, and including the Mediterranean countries, social life was regulated by what is customarily called written law and felt more the effects of Roman Law. To the North, and influenced rather by the Celtic and Germanic traditions, were the countries based on customary law. . . . To the extent that these traditions held sway, and above all, therefore, to the north of the Loire, women and children enjoyed autonomy and public recognition. Official acts bear the signature of the father, the mother, and the oldest son; if the father died, the mother acted as guardian; fiefs, even the most important, had to be passed on to women; children could attain their majority at a very early age. In the customary family, the authority of the father was that of a guardian and manager. He never had complete authority over either persons or over goods.

The progressive adaptation of Roman Law excluded women from public life to the point where they became "juridically powerless." The actions of a particular woman had to have the approval of her husband. "The family," writes Remy (1979), "adopted the personality of one of its members: the father, who became by degree the *pater familias* of Roman law, a proprietor with control over persons and goods."

The growth of Roman Law was linked both to the rise of market towns and the decline of feudalism. Further, Parsons (1964: 180), in an interesting footnote, links the celibate priesthood with the decline of feudalism and the hereditary principle in medieval social organization: "There was never more than a precarious balance between the Church and secular power structure, and this was fraught with high tensions. The victory of either would destroy the other. It is probably of fateful significance in Western civilization that it was a victory for the church, because if the balance had tipped the other way, the hereditary principle in social organization would probably have been consolidated, not attenuated."

In response to the decline of feudalism, the church began to exercise an increasing influence on family life, in an effort to regain the control it exercised during early Christendom and that had been threatened by the Reformation and modernization. The powerful movement toward the rights of individuals was modernistic and antithetical to the church. For example, the religious campaign against premarital sex dates from the sixteenth century; prior to this, as Remy (1979: 9) has demonstrated, the engagement or betrothal carried great weight:

> If the Church frowned on the unblessed marriage, she did not forbid it. Very often, above all in the country, the church marriage took place when the woman was pregnant, sometimes toward the end of her pregnancy . . . intercourse took place as a kind of test of fertility. One only married the girl when she was pregnant.

It was in light of this that Trent declared the sacramentality of marriage and decreed that all marriages should be celebrated by a priest in a church of the parish where one of the partners lived. This was not an easy adjustment. Since the theology of marriage for Catholics has always been that the partners confer the sacrament upon each other, the sacrament has been associated throughout its history not only with the official liturgy but with local customs and traditions to a degree not experienced by any of the other sacraments. In the early centuries after Christ the presence of a priest or a bishop was not mandatory, although there is some evidence that by the fourth and fifth centuries priestly solemnization was not uncommon. "The papal decree of the fourth century laid down that the lower orders of the clergy were bound to have their marriages solemnized by a priest. For the laity, the priests' presence and blessing was looked upon in the nature of the Church's approval" (Hardon, 1975: 533). Local customs and practices varied widely until the Middle Ages, when "the exchange of vows had to take place, under pain of nullity, in the presence of the pastor or his delegate, who questioned the bridal couple as to their mutual consent, and in the presence of two other witnesses. Nevertheless, before Trent there was no universal law of the Church on what is called the form of marriage (i.e., under what ecclesiatical conditions the contract would be valid). The decrees of Trent on marriage assured that, for Catholics, the Church was the sole arbiter of valid marriages, although she had no power at all regarding betrothal and she became increasingly opposed to premarital relations. Trent remained the norm until Vatican II" (Hardon, 1975: 533).

Though the picture is quite complex, it was largely in this form that Catholicism began to be transplanted to the United States. This Catholicism was strongly centered in the parish and "emphasized the sacraments of baptism and confirmation, attending Sunday Mass, receiving communion once a year, and annual confession of one's sins. Numerous devotional practices were encouraged, religious confraternities were multipled, and the catechism became the handbook of faith" (Dolan, 1977: 27). The point is that the church still held considerable influence over the family, and though, in Europe, it may have been losing its control, it quickly filled the need for security experienced by the immigrants: It was a social, spiritual, and educational haven in an often alien America.

ETHNIC DIVERSITY AND THE EMERGENCE OF THE AMERICAN CATHOLIC FAMILY

The Catholic church in the United States is dominated by descendants of German, Irish, Italian, and Polish immigrants. There are also significant numbers of descendants of other Latin and Slovakian groups. The Germans are the oldest, with their roots going back to the early 1800s, but they are also the most assimilated now.

The Irish, who began to migrate to the United States in large numbers during the 1840s, soon became the dominant group. They, as the Germans, brought a strong parish and churchgoing tradition with them, and by the late 1870s, they were in the process of creating the Catholic parochial school system, and then the Catholic college system. The Irish honed their political skills in the political parties of the major cities, and by the early 1900s they had also gained control of the Catholic church structure in the United States, a control that they maintain to this day.

The Italians, whose numbers rose into the millions and whose descendants now almost equal the number of Irish Catholics in the United States, brought a Latin tradition much at variance with the rigid, almost puritanical Catholicism of the Irish. Indeed, the Italian peasants who migrated to the United States had the highest illiteracy rates of any of the European groups, and the weakest formal ties to the Catholic church. But they brought a very strong and cohesive family system, which they used as a buffer between themselves and their alien surroundings. And they, like the Poles and the other immigrant groups, sought comfort and protection within their own neighborhoods. They created their own self-help organizations and celebrated the feast days of their native villages.

The factor that came to distinguish the Catholic church in America was the parochial school system. Parish life came to focus in the school in such a way that the school itself became a major force for social cohesion of the family. As the system developed, along came the Catholic colleges and universities and hospitals, so that Catholics educated and trained their own doctors, lawyers, and nurses, providing a mechanism for social mobility in an often hostile urban environment.

The Italians did not find the Irish-dominated church and school system congenial, and in the early years there was much antagonism between these two largest Catholic ethnic groups. However, in the years after World War II, Italians began to use the parochial school and college system as much as the other Catholic ethnic groups, and today it is probable that one major consequence of this particular kind of assimilation into American society is that Italian, Irish, Polish, and other ethnic groups (except the Hispanics) share a general Catholic and family culture that is clearly evident despite their continuing ethnic differences in other ways.

Herberg (1955: 150) summarizes this Catholic assimilation process in the following words:

> Unlike American Protestantism, Catholicism in America was never a religious movement. Its story is that of a foreign church, or rather a conglomerate of foreign churches, recruited from the successive waves of overseas immigration, finally emerging into one of the great "American religions." This remarkable transformation of a group socially and culturally alien into a thoroughly American religious community provides a significant clue to the inner history of Catholicism in the United States.

The disruption of family life that immigration created was fierce, and it is not surprising that the church, which had begun to formalize beliefs on family life, as a refuge for millions of Catholic immigrants, began to mold and shape the American Catholic family. Parents were encouraged to train their children for the responsibilities of family life, but were also encouraged to pray that at least one of their children would enter the priesthood or religious life. Among the Irish, it was common for one of the sons to become a priest. The net result was a predominantly Irish American clergy, and an American church with an ear for Rome that is not even found in European Catholic countries.[1]

Among the immigrants, the church preserved traditional values and beliefs, built churches, schools, and encouraged voluntary associations, all with the central purpose of "strengthening the family and of (maintaining) a social discipline grounded in family life" (O'Brien, 1981).

Much has been written about the experiences of the immigrants in their newfound home. First of all, there is no doubt that the church provided for the family a complex network of religious and social organizations that educated them, provided strength and support, provided them with political power, and assisted them in an ongoing effort to become assimilated into American society. The church was omnipresent for the immigrants: On one block in New York City (where one of the writers taught the latest Catholic immigrants for several years) those structures and institutions that for nearly 100 years supported immigrant groups are still going strong, and one can find there the church, a Catholic school, a Catholic hospital, a funeral parlor and liquor store (both run by the same pillar of the parish), a convent, and a monastery for the brothers who taught in the school. A family, in the parish's heyday, could (and many did) live their whole lives on the street and not be wanting.

The apparent strength of the family prompted little direct attention on the part of the church; many of the problems encountered by immigrant families were (rightly) attributed to the effects of immigration. When it became clear, however, that such problems were going to persist, and that some of them might even have stemmed from the church's own efforts at assimilation, the institutional church began to focus with greater clarity on family life. Certainly, the immigrants should become assimilated, but they were to be mindful that they should never go as far as to allow the "Godless secularism" in American society to influence them. The church, as the traditional upholder of sacred values, would provide the anchor in the storm of American Godlessness. The tone of ecclesiastical messages on the family became somewhat more strident, and

> whereas they [the bishops] had once attributed the problems Catholic families faced to conditions, mainly poverty, they now implied that such problems arose from character. If there was divorce, disruption, or difficulties in the Catholic family, it was a result of personal failures to live by the Catholic moral code. . . . Devotion to the duties of family life — fidelity, sexual restraints, child bearing and provision of proper religious education — was thus a religious obligation and a civic duty. . . . So, in the greatest of ironies, self-proclaimed pro-family bishops and evangelists, by shifting from external condition to personal character, from self-help organization to a moralistic ideology, ended up endorsing the separation of morality from social and economic life which was a major source of the problems they deplored [O'Brien, 1981].

This brings us to the present, and to some of those issues that continue to have impact on the family in the present day. These will be explored in the next section.

CHURCH TEACHINGS
IN THE TWENTIETH CENTURY

During this century, there have been several important official Catholic church teachings on marriage and the family, as well as a number of other less official statements and studies. The most important of these teachings is the Encyclical of Pius XI titled *Casti Connubii (On Christian Marriage)*. All other more recent teachings and statements such as *Humanae Vitae* (1968) and Pope John Paul II's response to the bishops (issued December 15, 1981) have been reaffirmations and elaborations of *Casti Connubii*.

Casti Connubii: **Affirming Tradition**

Casti Connubii formalized a number of principles: (1) The prime purpose of marriage is the procreation and rearing of children; (2) conjugal love is also an important purpose of marriage; (3) parents may for licit reasons limit the size of their families; and (4) the only licit form of family limitation is abstinence, absolute for nonmarried people, and periodic for married couples. Thus the rhythm method of birth control was declared to be the only natural way to limit fertility. In the words of the encyclical itself, "Any use whatsoever of matrimony exercised in such a way that the act is deliberately frustrated in its natural power to generate life is an offence against the law of God and nature, and those who indulge in such are branded with the guilt of a great sin."

Casti Connubii further emphasized that the proper place of woman was in the home, that marriage was a sacrament indissoluble except by church annulment, and that any expression of sexuality outside of marriage was also a grave sin. *Casti Connubii* was developed in major part as a response to the Lambeth Conferences of the Protestant Churches, held in England during the 1920s. These conferences led the main-line Protestant churches to adopt the position that contraceptive birth control was a legitimate option for married couples, and that the couples themselves were in the best position to determine what methods to use. Further, from these conferences came the gradual acceptance of divorce and of the right of women to work outside the home.

Clearly, from the point of view of Catholic laity, the dominant thrust of *Casti Connubii* was one of control over behavior, rather than of support of conjugal love. When people talked about *Casti Connubii* they talked about its teaching on birth control, not about its doctrine of marital love or of the importance of responsible parenthood.

During the next two decades, panel teachings on marriage and family were elaborations on *Casti Connubii,* which was popularly thought by many church leaders as well as followers to be an infallible teaching, that is, an absolute truth not subject to error, and thus not subject to change.

Vatican II: The Struggle Between Tradition and Change

The seeds of change were sown, however, in the wider world with which the church struggled to maintain contact. Pope John XXIII called for a council of church leaders to open the windows of the church to the modern world, and Vatican II came into being. During the days of the council (1962-1965), "the pill" became available to the public, and because of its mechanism of action, many theologians, some bishops, and lay leaders seized upon it as a possible licit form of birth control.

Pope John XXIII established a special birth control commission to examine the issue apart from the regular meetings of the Vatican Council. Pope Paul VI allowed the birth control commission to continue its deliberations. The council itself developed a special paper on the "Church in the Modern World," in which it acknowledged a population problem and, while also acknowledging the official teachings of *Casti Connubii,* affirmed the prime importance of conjugal love in marriage, of the right of women to sexual satisfaction in marriage, and of the importance of responsible parenthood. The debate over sexuality in marriage and birth control became increasingly public during these years.[2]

In July 1968, Pope Paul VI finally acted, after it had already become known that a majority of the members of the birth control commission, which included cardinals and bishops, as well as some laity and theologians, had recommended a change in the church's teachings, to allow couples to decide the means of birth control most suitable to their needs and behavior. In July, the Pope issued his *Encyclical Humanae Vitae,* which reaffirmed the traditional teaching on birth control that had been established in *Casti Connubii.* The encyclical also affirmed the primary importance of conjugal love and of sexuality in marraige, and of the importance of responsible parenthood in these times. But the focus of attention of the public was on the question of birth control. As we shall see shortly, the document had a tremendously negative impact on the teaching authority of the papacy. Despite many pleas from all sides, Paul VI stuck to his position.

There was hope and expectation that John Paul II would move the church gradually away from the traditional position of *Casti Connubii* and *Humanae Vitae,* but such appears not to be the case. Almost from the beginning of his pontificate, John Paul II has spoken out strongly in support of the traditional teachings. He has been most outspoken in his opposition to divorce, which he has called a cause of the breakdown of the family; he has been outspoken in his opposition to abortion, and to nonmarital sexuality. In December 1981, he responded formally to the request of the special synod of the bishops held in the fall of 1980 and focused on problems of the family. In this case, a majority of the bishops had already reaffirmed the church's traditional teachings on all matters related to marriage and family. Only a minority asked for "clarification" on matters of birth control and divorce. The Pope supported the majority in very strong terms.

At the same time, while the Pope has stressed again the prime responsibility of women to the home, he has attempted to assert in personalistic terms the rights of women to be loved as persons and not lusted after as sex objects. And he has also attempted to give positive emphasis to marital sexuality. Whatever his intentions, however, it is clear that his teachings are seen as restraining and controlling and not as providing support and compassionate understanding for those who would remarry after divorce, or those who would use forms of contraception other than rhythm.

In summary, it may be said that during the past fifty years, official Catholic teachings on marriage and family have been modified only slightly in the matter of the primary purpose of marriage, but not at all on other key issues.

The Catholic Laity and Church Teachings

In 1961, on the eve of Vatican II, Lenski published his now classic *The Religious Factor.*[3] He found that: (1) Catholics were more involved with kin, Protestants with neighbors. Catholics were less spatially mobile than Protestants and Jews. Protestants had higher divorce rates than Catholics, and also higher remarriage rates after divorce. Family life was more durable among Catholics. Lenski suggests that this might be explained in part by the fact that Catholics had fewer nonfamily ties than Protestants. Thus they came to see family ties as more crucial to their well-being than did Protestants. A divorce for a Catholic might mean loss of all significant group ties. This was much less likely to be the case for Protestants. Thus Protestants could "afford" divorce; Protestantism encouraged autonomy and participation in voluntary associations that provided social support outside the family.

(2) Protestants and Jews were more likely than Catholics to see personal autonomy as the primary value in preparing children for life. This was true across all religious and class lines. Lenski relates this finding directly to vertical mobility; those who were autonomous were more vertically mobile. Commitment to this value apparently made for more achievement orientation. The differential response to the value of personal autonomy was a key finding for Lenski, for he also sees personal autonomy as a vital element in defense of American democracy. It fosters respect for freedom and support for voluntary associations. A reliance on obedience, on the other hand, would correlate with restraints on individual freedom, as well as on one's capacity to be competitive in school and in the world of work.

(3) Lenski reports the well-known finding that Catholics had more children and wanted more children than did either Protestants or Jews. Here Lenski notes the negative impact of large families on social mobility. It was more difficult for large families to be mobile because it was more expensive for such people to sponsor their children through college. Thus, since college was more and more the vehicle for vertical mobility through the world of work, those opting for large families, for whatever reason, were inadvertently making it more difficult for their children to succeed in this society. According to Lenski, it was not that Catholics did not accept the materialistic values of American society or value good jobs with high incomes as much, but that certain features of their beliefs and practices as Catholics (larger families, close-knit ties to family, obedience to church more than to personal autonomy) put them at a disadvantage in the competition with Protestants. His data, gathered during the 1950s, showed that Catholics were living by their teachings fairly closely.

Research of the past 20 years designed to test further Lenski's hypothesis and empirical findings is extensive in nature. The key points as they bear on the family-religion relationship show significant convergences in the behavior of Catholics and Protestants (Greeley, 1976a; Roof, 1979; Arney and Trescher, 1976; Westoff and Jones, 1977; McCarthy, 1979; Riccio, 1979):

(1) Regarding birth control, Protestant and Catholic differences in attitudes toward the use of various contraceptives have all but disappeared. Recent studies show that as many as 85 percent of Catholics reject the right of the church to teach on birth control.

(2) Regarding family size (number of children wanted and actual family size achieved), again, differences between Protestants and Catholics have all but disappeared. Westoff (1979: 231), in a survey of birthrates over the last 50 years, has shown that on questions of fertility and contraceptive behavior, there has been a "dramatic move

toward convergence" between Protestants and Catholics. This was evident for several decades before World War II. It reflected the broad process of assimilation that the Catholic church, of course, encouraged, although it continued to stress the importance of large families and the procreative purpose of intercourse. The trend was reversed somewhat during the baby boom, but this was a general pattern; in any case, this rise in fertility was followed by an equally dramatic decline that was "undoubtedly accelerated by the growing popularity of the pill during the moral ambiguity of the mid-sixties preceding Humanae Vitae." We should expect that the two-child family will remain the norm for the foreseeable future.

(3) Catholic and Protestant separation and divorce rates are converging. In 1978, Catholics were reported only three percentage points behind Protestants in the divorce rate; at the same time, McCarthy (1979) found that active Catholics were less likely to divorce but more likely to seek annulments. The number of annulments (a church declaration of an invalid marriage) has dramatically increased in the last ten years: 442 annulments were recorded in 1968; in 1977 the same source reported 18,603. In the same period, the number of "dissolutions of marriage" requested by Americans and granted by the Holy See jumped from 3,062 to 32,100 (Pfnausch, 1978: 352).

(4) Differences between Catholics and Protestants on the several measures of vertical mobility (income, education, and occupation) have either disappeared or are disappearing. Actually, some Catholic ethnic groups, such as the Irish and German, have higher educational, occupational, and income means than do other Catholic groups, such as Italians, Poles, and Hispanics. They also have higher mobility scores than some Protestant denominations, such as Baptists, Lutherans, and Methodists, and are close to the Congregationalists and Presbyterians.[4] The general direction for Protestants and Catholics in the broadest categories is toward convergence.

Other findings on American Catholics are also instructive. Membership is currently estimated at about 50 million. Within this population, a marked downward trend in religious practice can be observed. Greeley (1979) found an average mass attendance of 42 percent per week (as opposed to 72 percent in 1963). Approximately one-third of all Catholic males in the country went to church once a week, while only 25 percent of the men and women under 30 years old attended at that rate. More than one-fourth of the Catholics in the country said at that time that they never went to church, including two-fifths of those under 30, and almost half of the men under 30 said that they attended church only once a year or less. Within the larger population, Greeley has identified a group he calls "communal Catholics," who strongly identify with the church but who disagree with it on sexual ethics, racial integration, and allied issues. Communal Catholics may be either devout or nondevout; "the critical difference is that even the non-devout have no inclination to identify as anything else but Catholic and the devout have little inclination to yield much credibility to the Church as an official teacher" (Greeley, 1979: 104).

These findings tell us something about the dramatic changes that have taken place in Catholicism during the past 25 years, changes for which Lenski's (1961) theoretical perspective was simply not adequate. For example, a key feature of Lenski's analysis was the place personal autonomy had in differentiating Catholic and Protestant attitudes and behavior. Current Catholic attitudes and behavior regarding birth control, abortion, and divorce are the clearest indicator that whatever the differences between the two major religious groups were in the 1950s, American Catholics have responded to societal structures and values by developing their own variant on autonomy.

John XXIII became Pope in 1958, and in some important ways turned out to be less than traditional and much more than ordinary. He set Vatican II in motion, and with that came a series of documents (schemas) on the church in the modern world that encouraged the laity to apply critical thinking and personal autonomy to matters such as sexuality and birth control. The church allowed itself a protracted five-year examination of the birth control/pill issue. It turned out to be an exercise in personal autonomy that could not be overcome by the reiteration of traditional teachings presented in *Humanae Vitae*. An ever-growing data base supports the hypothesis that the 1968 papal encyclical on artificial contraception, Paul VI's *Humanae Vitae*, marked the beginning of the end for absolute church authority. As Greeley (1976a: 134) put it:

> The change in birth control thinking (i.e., greater acceptance of artificial contraception for Catholics . . . is clearly the most important factor at work in the decline of Catholic devotion and practice during the last decade, with related declines in divorce and respect for the papacy combining with birth control to account for *all* the deterioration in mass attendance, support for a priestly vocation in one's family, and Catholic activism.

Greeley's work strongly supports the proposition that in the decade between 1963 and 1974 two forces, one the "positive dynamic" of Vatican II and the other the strongly negative effect of *Humanae Vitae*, were operative.

Left to itself, the Council (Vatican II) led to an increase of about one-sixth in Catholic religious practice. Left to itself, the encyclical would have led to a decline of almost one-half. The net result is a decline of almost one-third as far as the active Catholic scale is concerned. . . . Far from causing the problems of the contemporary American Catholic Church, the Council prevented them from becoming worse [Greeley, 1976a: 139].

Modern Catholic writers and thinkers have professed their belief that the traditional church simply could not survive the twin pressures of Vatican II and higher education. Their thesis is that Catholics had become better educated with even larger numbers in secular colleges, and, since Vatican II had encouraged "self-directive" thinking, the church had in effect recommended that people move from the most ' primitive type of moral thinking, based on fear of punishment, to the most mature, interiorized principles. But the net result was something the church may never have bargained for: independent educated people, who strongly identify with the church but who often disagree with its official stance, especially on issues of personal morality. This rebelliousness, and the apparent inability or unwillingness of the bishops to confront it has led conservative scholars such as Monsignor George Kelly to declare the present situation a scandal caused by accommodation to the pressures of a secular society.

It is clear now that the authority of the Catholic church is no longer automatically linked with the authority of God. And, if sexual issues have been primary in bringing about this change, other actions taken by the bishops themselves have also added to the collapse of authority. For example, there is the event that has been referred to as the "meat on Friday" syndrome, a reference to the devotional practice of abstaining from meat on Friday as a penance.

The elimination of meat on Friday [*sic*] revealed the benign corruption of authority and the false perspective on sin that had previously governed the enforcement of ecclesiastical regulations. Even the unlettered recognized that something was wrong and shook their heads as they realized that they had taken their Friday avoidance of meat so seriously. How could they have believed, until a group of bishops took a vote, that such a trivial violation would weigh in the same scales of eternal justice with the worst violations of God's law and the human spirit [Kennedy, 1980: 21]?

Abortion

It has frequently been said that abortion is for Catholics of the 1980s what birth control and divorce were for the 1960s. There is some evidence that this may be the case. There has been a steadily increasing acceptance of abortion during the 1970s, but with the degree of acceptance depending both on degree of religious commitment and on the nature of the particular abortion-possible situation. Baptists and Catholics are most alike in their attitudes. They give overwhelming support to abortion in cases of health, birth defects, and rape (Family Planning Perspectives, 1980). But as late as 1978, less than a majority of Catholics, Baptists, and other fundamentalist Protestants were willing to support abortion for reasons of low income, not wanting to marry, or not wanting another child.

It appears that only a small proportion of Catholics autor atically support the official church teaching of absolute opposition to abortion. Rather, it would appear more likely that, like most Americans, they are trying to reason out each issue, and to judge it on its social merits rather than on the basis of an absolute religious teaching.

There is an interesting anomaly in the struggle between the forces of tradition and those of change that have characterized so much of what has happened in the Catholic church in the past twenty years: While the leaders insist on reaffirming the traditional teachings, they still acknowledge the principles of the inviolability of the individual conscience and of the possibility that people might err in their judgments. If nothing else, this principle has allowed American Catholics, brought up and socialized into the American value system, to think the issues through for themselves and to come to judgments different from those of the hierarchy.

The question of the future of the Catholic family looms large. Certainly, the trend toward Americanism cannot be reversed, as the Catholic population, once small but separate, grows larger and more indistinguishable from other U.S. populations. Those social forces that are currently intruding on the American family — the corporate world, the economy, government intervention — will continue to affect the Catholic family.

What can be expected? Though the ostensible relationship between the family and the institutional church is supposedly one of mutuality, there is clear evidence of strain, as shown in the previous discussion; as we shall see, there are also some hopeful signs.

To begin with, it is probably quite naive to expect that church teachings are apt to change within the next decade, or, for that matter, at all. Given the church leadership's historical stance of caution, and the church's rootedness in its own traditions, in natural law, in the Christian respect for life and for the principles found in Scripture, we do not see the leadership bending very far. Nonetheless, there are a few examples of tendencies toward change that merit mention.

EMERGING SYSTEMS OF SOCIAL SUPPORT

Though not a product of the hierarchy per se, the Catholic Theological Society's *Human Sexuality* (Kosnik et al., 1977) represented a modern attempt to reconcile the cleavage between sex and religion. The report, as it is called, was hailed by social scientists and many theologians and clergy at the same time it drew fire in traditional circles. It states in part that

> sexuality further serves the development of genuine personhood by calling people to a clearer understanding of their relational nature, of their absolute need to reach out and embrace others to achieve personal fulfillment [Kosnik et al., 1977: 85].

The authors are attempting to achieve an approach to sexuality that is "creative and integrative" rather than the more traditional "unitive and procreative." No longer should an evaluation of human sexual behavior be based on abstract and absolutist predetermination of sexual expression as being intrinsically evil and always immoral. On such grounds, the authors of the report refuse to find contraception a moral evil.

Human Sexuality should be understood as an important step in the direction of new teachings emphasizing love, nurturance, and personal responsibility. Also of interest is a document issued jointly by the Bishop's Committee for Ecumenical and Interreligious Affairs of the National Conference of Catholic Bishops and the Caribbean and North American Council of the World Alliance of Reformed Churches (Presbyterian and Congregational). Dialogue between these two groups has continued without interruption since 1965 (a rather positive effect of the Vatican Council) and the statement produced here, from the third joint session, is from a document called *Ethics and the Search for Christian Unity*. In actuality, the document is two position papers, one on abortion and the other on human rights. The abortion statement is significant for several reasons: (1) It bears the stamp of the U.S. Catholic Conference of Bishops, the highest authority in the American church, and is a clear indication of that body's willingness to openly confront a pervasive and difficult problem; (2) it takes into account current understandings of human sexuality and has a keen ear toward empirical research; (3) it clearly and emphatically states both Catholic and Presbyterian positions, and further explains when and why they differ and agree; and (4) the statement mentions, and takes some responsibility for, "ecclesial traditions which devalue women."

The statement on abortion, in part, reads:

> Women are too narrowly regarded in terms of their reproductive functions. Women encounter problems of poverty, inequality of opportunity, and sexual exploitation. If our churches are to be credible in addressing abortion, they must take the lead in accepting women as full and contributing members of the human and ecclesial communities. They must work to develop supportive networks to which pregnant women have a rightful claim. We recommend extensive, open discussions in the churches on the reproductive functions, on responsible sexuality, on the social aspects of pregnancy and child rearing and on the new problems raised by prenatal diagnostic information as well as the pervasive sexual bias influencing many of our ecclesial and social institutions [U.S. Catholic Conference of Bishops, 1980].

The explanatory and accompanying statements acknowledge respective traditions without being overburdened by them. The document, though brief, is impressive, and may well serve as a model not only for continued dialogue between the churches on those topics related to marriage and the family, but also for future church thinking with regard to the family.

At the parish and diocesan level, there are a number of steps being taken, with and without official approval, that focus on development of social support networks. For example, one of the most popular and successful in recent years has been the "Marriage Encounter" movement. Married couples go together on weekend retreats designed to help them improve their interpersonal relationships. Various Protestant and Jewish groups have adopted the model to fit their own needs.

Premarital counseling has been greatly increased, and sex education programs have been developed with a broad focus on interpersonal relationships and the importance of developing socially responsible attitudes toward members of the opposite sex.

Many parishes and dioceses now offer counseling and organized social programs for divorced Catholics, and some even for divorced and remarried Catholics. And while the Pope continues to insist that the divorced and remarried can only receive the sacraments if they live as brother and sister, it is well known that many clergy on the local level do not make such distinctions. They are more concerned with offering help to restore such couples to feeling good about themselves as active members in the life of the church.

On a less controversial level, the church has been increasingly active in developing programs on behalf of the elderly and the poor.

Indeed, some parishes located in areas populated primarily by the elderly are enjoying boom conditions. A variety of social support programs are emerging to deal with the needs of the elderly and the poor.

Unfortunately, the church has been much slower to develop day care centers for children of working couples. This is an area in which it can do a great deal, because many of its buildings are in central-city areas that are in the greatest need of day care centers; we may expect much more movement along these lines in the coming years.

Our response to the question, "How is the contemporary Catholic family doing?" must depend on the questioner's paradigm: If one is asking how the ideal family, the family found in the papal encyclicals and bishops' statement is doing, if one is inquiring about the typical Catholic family circa 1960, then the answer must be "not very well." But if one is asking how the Catholic family is doing given the complexity of modern capitalistic society, given the "invasion" of the family by government, corporate life, and the media, we would answer that it is doing well, whether in spite of or because of the fact that it is no longer dominated by the institutional clerical hierarchy.

Catholics may not always have obeyed the church's official teachings on premarital sex and contraception, but in the 1930s, 1940s, and 1950s, they could be found in the confessional on Saturday, thus acknowledging the legitimacy of the church's teachings. In the 1970s and 1980s they no longer consider these teachings valid or binding on their consciences. Thus what most distinguishes Catholics from Protestants and Jews now is not so much behavior as it is the consonance between behavior and the teachings of their respective religions. Main-line Protestant and Jewish denominations have changed their teachings to bring them into line with changes in behavior; the Catholic laity is changing with little or no sign that the church leaders will significantly modify their teachings. Indeed, one can say that the most recent statements of John Paul II point to a return to earlier positions, not unlike those of the Moral Majority.

Thus, it seems quite fair to say with Fichter (1977) that "the church is being modernized in spite of itself. It appears that the changes are occurring at the bottom of the structure. . . . American Catholicism is experiencing adaptation at the grass roots. The most significant aspect of this change is the switch of emphasis in the basis of moral and religious guidance. Dependence on legislation from above has largely switched to dependence on the conscience of the people." Like other Americans, Catholics continue to exhibit strong religious interests. But they look to religion now not for a system of laws that seem totally irrelevant if not harmful to marriage and family life, but for principles of love and nurturance that will help them to lead a satisfying life in a complex and difficult time.

NOTES

1. The Irish took very seriously the teachings from Rome, and saw them as laws to be obeyed (attendance at Sunday mass and avoidance of meat on Fridays, for example) under penalty of serious sin. Italians and other Latin Catholics continued to see such teachings as ideals that they, as mere weak human beings, could not hope to obey, and thus need not worry about.
2. Probably the most accurate and complete statement of the issue is to be found in Hoyt (1968).
3. The discussion of Lenski is derived in part from D'Antonio (1980); in this essay, Lenski's classic work is examined in detail.
4. Roof (1979) carried out a partial reexamination of Greeley's (1976b) study on ethnicity, denomination, and inequality, and found only partial support for Greeley's claim that Catholics have achieved parity with Protestants in matters of class and status.

REFERENCES

Arney, W. R. and W. H. Trescher (1976) "Trends in attitudes toward abortion, 1972-1975." Family Planning Perspectives 8 (May/June): 107-124.
Burtchaell, J. [ed.] (1980) The Abortion Parley. Kansas City: Andrews & McMeel.
Carroll, J., D. Johnson, and M. Marty (1979) Religion in America. New York: Harper & Row.
Cogley, J. (1973) Catholic America. Garden City, NY: Image.
D'Antonio, W. V. (1980) "The family and religion: exploring a changing relationship." Journal for the Scientific Study of Religion 19, 2: 89-104.
Dolan, J. (1978) Catholic Revivalism. Notre Dame, IN: University of Notre Dame Press.
——— (1977) The Immigrant Church. Baltimore: Johns Hopkins University Press.
Family Planning Perspectives (1980) "Abortion attitudes, 1965-1980: trends and determinants." Vol. 12 (September/October): 250-261.
Fichter, J. H. (1977) "Restructuring Catholicism." Sociological Analysis 38, 2: 154-164.
Goode, W. (1964) The Family. Englewood Cliffs, NJ: Prentice-Hall.
Greeley, A. M. (1979) Crisis in the Church. Chicago: Thomas More.
——— (1976a) Catholic Schools in a Declining Church. Kansas City, MO: Sheed & Ward.
——— (1976b) Ethnicity, Denomination, and Inequality. Beverly Hills, CA: Sage.
——— (1976c) "200 years and counting." Critic 34 (Summer).
Handy, R. T. (1972) Religion in the American Experience. New York: Harper & Row.
Hardon, J. (1975) The Catholic Catechism. Garden City, NY: Doubleday.
Herberg, W. (1955) Protestant, Catholic, Jew. Garden City, NY: Doubleday.
Hoyt, R. C. [ed.] (1968) The Birth Control Debate. Kansas City, MO: National Catholic Reporter.
Kennedy, E. (1980) "Stand out of our light." Notre Dame Magazine 9 (October): 21.
Kosnik, W., W. Carroll, A. Cunningham, R. Modras, and J. Schulte (1977) Human Sexuality: New Directions in American Catholic Thought. New York: Paulist Press.
Lenski, G. (1961) The Religious Factor. Garden City, NY: Doubleday.
Lasch, C. (1979) The Culture of Narcissism. New York: Norton.
McBrien, R. P. (1980) Catholicism. Minneapolis: Winston.
McCarthy, J. (1979) "Religious commitment, affiliation and marriage dissolution," in R. Wuthnow (ed.) The Religious Dimension. New York: Academic.

Neill, T. and R. H. Schmandt (1957) History of the Catholic Church. Milwaukee:
    Bruce.
Nevins, A.J. (1972) The American Catholic Heritage. Huntington, IN: Our Sunday
    Visitor Press.
Noonan, J. (1965) Contraception. New York: New American Library.
O'Brien, D. (1981) "How different is a Catholic family?" National Catholic Reporter
    (May 15).
Parsons, T. (1964) The Social System. New York: Macmillan.
Pfnausch, E. G. (1978) "The question of tribunals." America 139 (November 18):
    352.
Remy, J. (1979) "The family: contemporary models and historical perspectives," in
    A. M. Greeley (ed.) Concilium. New York: Seabury.
Riccio, J. A. (1979) "Religious affiliation and socioeconomic achievement," in R.
    Wuthnow (ed.) The Religious Dimension. New York: Academic.
Roof, W. C. (1979) "Socioeconomic differentials among white socioreligious groups
    in the United States." Social Forces 58, 1: 280-289.
U.S. Catholic Conference of Bishops (1980) Ethics and the Search for Christian
    Unity. Washington, DC: U.S. Catholic Conference, Publications Office.
Westoff, C. (1979) "The blending of Catholic reproductive behavior," in R. Wuthnow
    (ed.) The Religious Dimension. New York: Academic.
—— and E. F. Jones (1977) "The secularization of U.S. Catholic birth control
    practices." Family Planning Perspectives 9: 203.

7

THE JEWISH FAMILY
Continuity and Change

Arnold Dashefsky
Irving M. Levine

You may recall that in the musical about Eastern European Jewish life, *Fiddler on the Roof,* the protagonist, Tevye, compares life in his village of Anatevka to a fiddler on the roof trying to keep his balance. What prevents the fiddler from falling off the slanted roof and what keeps the Jewish people by analogy from losing their balance in a changing world? "Tradition!" Tevye says. "Without our traditions our life would be as shaky as a fiddler on a roof." Of course, the paramount integrative institution of traditional Jewish society was the family.

A discussion of the evolutionary changes of the Jewish family requires an understanding of the dramatic transformations of Jewish societal and communal life across nearly four millennia of history. In the first section of this chapter, an overview of that history is provided to demonstrate effects on the continuity of the Jewish community and the persistence of Jewish identity to which the family has been linked as the central institution.

THE EVOLUTION OF THE JEWISH FAMILY:
BIBLICAL AND POST-BIBLICAL ROOTS

The evolution of the Jewish family is congruent with the evolution of Jewish society throughout the history of the Jewish people. That

Authors' Note: Thanks are due to Bernard Lazerwitz and Howard M. Shapiro for valuable insights provided on this topic over a long period of time. In addition, the authors wish to thank Dana Kline and David Zeligson for their research assistance and Linda Snyder and Celeste Machado for their help in typing the manuscript.

history can be divided into two halves, the Biblical period, more familiar to many, and the even more important post-Biblical period, from the point of Jewish history.

While it is not possible to present an accurate sociological description of Jewish societal and familial life in Biblical times because of the absence of hard data, an examination of literary passages of the Bible can provide a rough idea of family life.[1] Whatever one's own religious and theological views, it is important to understand that the Hebrew Bible, or *Tanach*,[2] is at one level a literary document that sees Jewish history as a trinitarian relationship among the People of Israel *(am yisrael)*, the Land of Israel *(eretz yisrael)*, and the Religion or Law of Israel *(dat yisrael)* as embodied in the keeping of the precepts of the Torah. A large portion of the time these three elements are not synchronized, that is, the Jewish people are not living in the land and observing the Torah.

Jewish family life was rooted in the culture of the ancient Near East and as such was patriarchal, patrilocal, patrilineal, polygynous, and endogamous (Patai, 1977). The stories of the Bible, beginning with the patriarch Abraham, reveal a view of Jewish life rooted in a pastoral nomadic or seminomadic existence but not anchored to an independent political state. These wanderings across western Asia took place, it is thought, between 2000 and 1500 BCE (Before the Common Era). The stories emerged as a part of the Hebrew oral tradition and were recorded centuries later and included in the Bible. These migrations included the sojourn in Egypt, the Exodus, and the subsequent conquest of Canaan. With the conquest is evident a transformation of Jewish societal life from nomadic sheepherders to sedentary farmers. Eventually these farmers formed an independent nation with an urban population in cities, such as Jerusalem, as revealed in the stories of David and Solomon, who established the first Jewish commonwealth about 1000 BCE. This Jewish commonwealth survived civil war, insurrections, and partial conquest of the northern kingdom by the Assyrians until the Babylonian occupation and destruction of the Temple (the center of Jewish religious life), culminating in the exile of many Jews, such as the prophet Jeremiah.

In the Biblical metaphor God is viewed as the parent who punishes the child, the *People* of Israel for not obeying the *Law* of Israel, and exiles them from the *Land* of Israel. Mirroring this view of God as the father, the Jewish family in Biblical times was patriarchal in structure. In this period, the epics are pastoral in nature, reflecting the nomadic or seminomadic existence of the patriarchs who tended their flocks.

Marriage as seen in the Bible was for the purpose of companionship and procreation and was fundamentally monogamous, as in the story of Adam and Eve, even though polygamy appears under extenuating circumstances or among the upper class. While the wife was viewed as the property of her husband, as was the custom of nomadic Middle Eastern peoples, Jewish tradition established a contractual basis between husband and wife and accorded the wife certain protections as specified by the husband's ten obligations toward his wife and the four rights owed to him.[3] The frequent expressions of the prophets against the oppression of the widow and the orphan suggest an idealized concern for the weak that may have been more honored at times in its breach than in its observance.

The entire Biblical period spanned nearly two millennia, from the early patriarchal tales in the Torah to the last sections of the Prophets and the Hagiographa, or Writings. In the subsequent period Jewish life was dominated by the decline of the priestly class and the emergence of the rabbis as arbiters of Jewish religious life and law, embodied in the *halachah* (the religious code of conduct that defined the Jewish normative system, literally, the way or path of religious practice); hence the first post-Biblical phase of Jewish history is called the *rabbinic period.*

Modern scholars believe that the Hebrew Bible was standardized in its present form during the Roman period at the beginning of the Common Era. During this period the *Mishnah,* the oral law or rabbinic commentary on the Torah, was written down. In addition, the Talmud, consisting of the *Mishnah* and its commentary, the *Gemara,* was compiled. From these sources we learn of the importance of priestly families adhering to strict genealogical standards as well as the purity and mutual responsibility of individuals in family life. Rabbinic writing is replete with pithy aphorisms that express this integral relationship, such as, "whosoever, brings disrepute upon himself brings disrepute upon his whole family" (Num. R. 21:3). Consider another example, "A family is like a heap of stones. Remove one, and the whole structure can collapse" (Gen. R. 100:7).[4]

In Judaism, unlike in Christianity, which valued celibacy, marriage and the family were praised. According to Rabbi Hillel, the minimum number of children was two, one boy and one girl. Indeed, marriage and family life were seen as full of joy and blessing. The Talmud includes such statements as "He who has no wife lives without joy, without blessing, and without goodness"; and "Of that man who loves his wife as himself, honors her more than himself, who guides his sons and daughters in the right way, and arranges for their early marriage, Scripture says, 'and thou shalt know that thy tent is peace'" (Job. 5:24).[5]

The post-Talmudic period in Jewish history overlaps the Middle Ages[6] in European history. During this *medieval period,* rabbinic literature consisted of *sh'elot v'tshuvot,* answers to questions about

Jewish religious law submitted by questioners to rabbinic authorities. They are commonly called the *Respona,* and contain valuable economic and social information. During this period, for example, monogamy was rabbinically sanctioned as the religiously prescribed form of marriage, even though it had been the common practice among Jews for centuries. The axis of Jewish life shifted from Palestine and Babylonia to the Muslim-controlled areas of Spain and the Mediterranean basin under the Moors. Here Jewish intellectual life flourished in a healthy and protected interchange with Islamic thought and culture as exemplified by the Jewish physician and philosopher, Maimonides, Moses Ben Maimon.

During the emergence of the early modern period of exploration and scientific discovery, anti-Semitism led to the expulsion of the Jewish people from Western European countries (such as Spain in 1492), and they migrated to Eastern Europe. These Jews turned inward and developed a rather rigid Orthodoxy that only began to buckle as the French Revolution of 1789 heralded a new *modern period.* The effects of the Revolution gave Jews their first opportunity to participate as full and equal citizens in the life of their country. Under certain conditions it meant that Jews could leave the urban ghetto and small village, or Eastern European *shtetl,* and participate politically, economically, socially, and culturally in the life of the larger society. It was a period of unprecedented opportunity for Jewish people and a time of unparalleled threat to the perpetuation of Jewish tradition. This modern period of emancipation and enlightenment produced the great German Jewish philosopher, Moses Mendelssohn, who was a strictly observant Jew; ironically, his grandchildren, including the composer, Felix Mendelssohn, were raised as Christians.

The best summary of the significance of the family in traditional Jewish life is expressed by the author of the article on the family in the *Encyclopedia Judaica* (1971: 1172):

> The constant insistence upon the value of the family as a social unit for the propagation of domestic and religious virtues and the significant fact that the accepted Hebrew word for marriage is *kiddushin* ("sanctification"), had the result of making the Jewish home the most vital factor in the survival of Judaism and the preservation of the Jewish way of life, much more than the synagogue or school.

Through the various sayings and stories, legends and folklore, the rabbis traditionally instructed Jews in the basic values of Jewish family life, which was closely intertwined with Jewish religious life. As Heinrich Heine, the German poet, has suggested, the Jewish people have a "portable religion," which can be easily transported in their wanderings; it is the Jewish home. In the modern period further equality brought with it the possibility of further assimilation. Nowhere could this tension and its effect on the family be more interesting to observe than in the United States.

THE AMERICAN JEWISH FAMILY: 1654-1984

While Jewish life in America can be traced more than three centuries back to 1654, when a small group of Portuguese Jews fled Brazil to the Dutch province of New Amsterdam, in reality most of the population and its characteristics have roots barely a century old.[7] During much of the European colonial domination of America, Jews were a rather small population of Spanish and Portuguese origin, called *Sephardim,* numbering about 3000 at the time of the American War of Independence. Economically, they were primarily part of the merchant class. Socially, they assimilated to Anglo-Saxon culture and experienced little anti-Semitism as legal bars to political participation were eventually removed. Religiously, they maintained the dignified Orthodoxy they brought with them. Politically, the Jews initially experienced restrictions, but as time progressed these declined. With respect to marriage and family life among the very small Sephardic community, many intermarried, as did the first American Jew, Jacob Barsimon. This situation of a small Sephardic Jewish population continued for nearly 175 years (more than half the period of Jewish settlement in North America), from 1654-1825.

It is estimated that in 1825 about 10,000 Jews resided in the United States. During the next 50 years, from 1825 to 1880, the population increased 25-fold, swelled by large numbers of German Jews escaping the instability and upheaval in Central Europe. While the Sephardic Jews were relatively comfortable, the German Jews adjusted economically by relying on peddling as a primary means of making a living. Socially, they assimilated but maintained a separate religious community, carrying on the tradition of German Jews or *Ashkenazim,* which initially was Orthodox. As the years went by and the numbers increased, Reform Judaism was introduced from Germany. This denomination gained a greater number of adherents particularly as the migration of Eastern European Jews began in the last quarter of the nineteenth century. Reform Judaism became an attractive option because it permitted a sharp distinction between the relatively uneducated, more traditional Eastern European immigrants and the more established German Jews, while retaining a unique Jewish religious expression. During this period, anti-Semitism was not widespread. What characterized this period was the great amount of freedom German Jews enjoyed, and this extended to marriage and family life as well, with intermarriage not uncommon but not as great as among the smaller Sephardic community (Sachar, 1958).

In the 40-year period between 1880 and 1920 (about 12 percent of the total period of Jewish sojourn in America), the population grew about 1200 percent, from approximately 250,000 to 3,000,000. This tidal wave of humanity was part of the great Atlantic migration from Southern and Eastern Europe to the United States. In the case of the Jews they fled the increasing anti-Semitism of the czarist regime beginning in 1881 and subsequent pogroms, uprisings, and the Bolshevik revolution. Economically, these Eastern European Jews adjusted by becoming factory workers and artisans. Socially, they assimilated to American political and economic norms but maintained separate territorially defined communities in part imposed by external hostility and in part by internal choice. Like the Germans, the Eastern European Jews were also Ashkenazim (in contrast to the Sephardim), but they maintained their own generally more rigid interpretation of Jewish law. This migration produced a distinctly American denominational innovation — Conservative Judaism. (Both Orthodoxy and Reform were imported.) Politically, the mass migration of Jews and others was associated with growing anti-immigration sentiments, racism, and anti-Semitism, which already existed in Europe. During this period, for example, a Jew was lynched in Georgia for alleged rape and only vindicated when an eyewitness exonerated him nearly seventy years later, in 1982. In terms of the family this period marked the beginning of the weakening of the authority and control exercised by the family and particularly the father over the children as they became more American than their parents.

The period following World War I, 1920-1945, marked the end of open immigration to the United States and the slowing of the growth of the Jewish community. The Jewish population of the United States grew from about 3 million to 5 million. Economically, Jews became more mobile, moving from manual occupations to clerical and sales positions and to the free professions. Socioculturally, assimilation increased, even though Jews continued to reside in identifiable neighborhoods. Politically, anti-Semitism peaked as America participated in the war to overcome the racist Nazi regime in Germany. Religiously, this period marked the rise of Conservative Judaism, which had emerged in the second decade of the twentieth century as a middle road between the existing alternatives of a rigid Eastern European Orthodoxy and an assimilated German Reform. Politically, Jews experienced more anti-Semitism; and increased exclusivistic practices barred Jews from certain neighborhoods, resorts, clubs, businesses, and professions. As far as the family was concerned, this period marked an erosion of the significance of the extended family in kinship relations and the growing independence of the nuclear family.

The contemporary, postwar period began with two traumatic and dramatic events that once again transformed Jewish life: the destruction of much of the European Jewry (one-third of the total world Jewish population) in the Holocaust and the rebirth of an independent Jewish commonwealth in the State of Israel in 1948 for the first time in nearly 2000 years. Between 1945 and the present the Jewish population of the United States grew from 5 million to 5.9 million (1980) but the proportion of Jews in the U.S. population began to decline, from 3.7 percent in 1937 to 3.5 percent in 1947 (Sklare, 1971) to 2.6 percent in 1980 (Chen Kin and Miran, 1980). Economically, Jews continued their upward mobility, extending themselves in the business and professional strata; nevertheless, this mobility involved a shift from less to more bureaucratized modes of employment and its associated loss of autonomy in the workplace. Socioculturally, with the rising affluence of American Jews, assimilation increased along with a greater residential dispersion in various regions of the country as well as within metropolitan areas. Politically, overt anti-Semitism declined in terms of employment and social practices, and more Jews gained office as both elected and appointed officials. In the religious sphere of Jewish life, the Conservative movement consolidated itself as the largest denomination (24 percent), but Reform Judaism began to emerge as the fastest-growing denomination (17 percent). Orthodoxy was the least popular denomination (7 percent) among American Jews belonging to synagogues (Lazerwitz, 1979).

Is the American Jewish family that distinctively different from the American family in general? Is it just the *American* middle-class family *par excellence*, or is it a variation of the traditional *Jewish* family? To some extent it is both. The American Jewish family is an amalgam of traditional Jewish roots transplanted to the fertile but rocky soil of the United States. For example, in the contemporary period the family embodies the American middle-class version of the nuclear family, yet it retains the Jewish characteristics of the interdependence rather than the separation of generations. As Sklare (1971: 87-89) has suggested, there is a movement away from this *extension* of family ties. Nevertheless, the growth of the *Havurah* (religious fellowship) movement may be distinctively Jewish response to this American challenge in that the Havurah represents a surrogate family that provides a sense of togetherness in the observance of Jewish festivals and rites of passage.

A question that frequently arises in reviewing the Jewish experience in America is how Jews managed to become so successful so quickly in comparison to other groups that arrived at the same time (between 1880 and 1920) from Eastern or Southern Europe. Table 7.1 shows, for example, that one-third of American Jews in 1971 were professional owners and managers. Sometimes the question may imply that the success of the Jews can be explained by their stereotypical characteristics of being "too sly, too cunning in business, and too smart!" (Stereotypes generally include a positive redeeming virtue.) If we compare the situation of Jews to other religioethnic groups that arrived at more or less the same time, we find that Jews when they arrived were more urbanized, literate, and occupationally suited for the rapidly industrializing post-Civil War U.S. society. While migrants from other countries came from rural agricultural backgrounds where literacy was not common, Jews came from small towns and big cities; and while they generally could not read or write English, they could read or write Hebrew or Yiddish, Polish, Russian, or some other language. Moreover, the Jews found an ongoing Jewish community that had roots more than 200 years old. Furthermore, while many other migrants also came with a minority religious background — Catholicism — they initially encountered more anti-Catholic sentiment than anti-Semitism. In addition, Jews had less strong opposition to birth control than Catholics and more quickly limited their family size, which aided upward mobility. Finally, Jews came to the United States with thousands of years of accumulated sociocultural heritage in adapting as a minority group in a new society going back to the Babylonian and Roman Exiles. By contrast, for the disadvantaged Catholic migrants who arrived at about the same time this was the first experience with minority group status, that is, with living in a land where the language, religion, and culture that predominated were not their own. Of course, for Jews, as for some other groups, the principal institution that simultaneously provided socioemotional support as well as instrumental adaptiveness in a precarious new situation was the family.

The fact that each succeeding generation of American Jews became more assimilated was true for the Sephardim in the seventeenth and eighteenth centuries, the German Jews in the nineteenth century, and the Eastern European Jews in the twentieth century. The major factor in halting the "straight line" of assimilation to the dominant Protestant culture was each successive wave of migration. While Jews go back over 300 years in American history, much of the organizational and denominational basis of Jewish life today is less than 100 years old.

What this brief overview of the family in the context of world and American Jewish history points out is the evolutionary nature of the social, cultural, and religious life of the Jewish people. The great

TABLE 7.1 Demographic and Social Characteristics by Denominational Identification and Affiliation of Jewish Adults, NJPS, 1971

Characteristics	Total Adult Sample	Orthodox Member	Conservative Member	Conservative Not Member	Reform Member	Reform Not Member	No Identification
Sex — % Women	56%	57%	51%	54%	68%	56%	50%
Age							
20-39 Years	30%	27%	27%	20%	24%	48%	37%
60 and Over	27%	36%	24%	38%	24%	19%	29%
Family Status							
Married with Children under 16 Years in Household	43%	30%	57%	29%	57%	38%	38%
Generations in U.S.							
Foreign-Born	21%	52%	24%	27%	7%	11%	17%
Both Parents U.S. Born	20%	5%	16%	13%	25%	24%	37%
Socioeconomic Status							
College Grads.	35%	23%	34%	18%	52%	40%	41%
Professional	33%	31%	30%	23%	39%	38%	38%
Owners and Managers	29%	29%	44%	43%	20%	16%	17%
Family Income							
$20,000 or more	24%	16%	24%	12%	33%	28%	28%
n	4,305	399	1,160	616	841	548	475

SOURCE: Lazerwitz and Harrison (1979: 659). Reprinted by permission.

migrations and transformations have of necessity forced change on the Jewish family structure. The major problem for Jews throughout their history has been how to maintain — and for scholars, how to explain — the cohesiveness of community and the persistence of identity. Traditionally it has been the family that has linked individual Jews to the chain of generations of Jewish religious and communal life. Will it continue to be that cohesive link in 1984 and beyond? In the subsequent sections the current state of the American Jewish family will be assessed from a variety of perspectives, and the basis for an answer will be framed.

DEMOGRAPHIC DIMENSIONS: FERTILITY AND MORTALITY

The Hebrew Bible or *Tanach* provides in the first chapter the traditional Jewish view of family size: "Be fruitful, and multiply, and replenish the earth" (Gen. 1:28). With this commandment the rabbis explained the obligations to provide for the care of children, including daily needs, education, and training for a trade or profession. Originally all these applied to sons only, but in later times they applied to daughters as well. In recent generations, as American Jews have become more middle and upper-middle class, they have adopted the custom of smaller family size, being concerned more with the quality of care and education of the children than with the quantity of births or high fertility.

Of course, it is a long way from the Biblical view of fertility in the Book of Genesis to *Look* magazine's article on "The Vanishing American Jew." (Morgan, 1964), which noted the decline of Jewish fertility among other variables as contributing to the disappearance of American Jews. Fortunately for American Jews, *Look* disappeared before they did. Nevertheless, the issue of Jewish fertility remains very central to the size and proportion of the Jewish population in the United States.

Goldstein (1974, 1980) has reviewed the available literature comparing Jewish fertility to that of other Americans. He reports that as early as the late nineteenth century the Jewish birthrate was lower than that of other religious groups. Reliable data on the American Jewish population as a whole are difficult to obtain. While the decennial U.S. Census is forbidden by law to ask questions about religion, a sample population survey was conducted in 1957. It confirmed the previous findings of other more small-scale studies. While the cumulative fertility rate (of women 45 years of age and over) was 3.1 for Catholics and 2.8 for Protestants, it was only 2.2 for Jews. This figure is very close to the 2.1 figure usually associated with the notion of zero population growth (ZPG), which needs to be sustained for 70 years. Indeed, Goldstein (1974: 107) concludes: "For the immediate future, all available evidence continues to point to inadequate birth levels among Jews, insuring little more than token growth. This being so, the total Jewish population is not likely to increase rapidly beyond its present six million level."[8]

The natural increase of a population is not just dependent upon fertility but also on *mortality*. Goldstein (1974: 102) reports that "differences exist between the age-specific death rates, life expectancy, and survival patterns of Jews and of the total white population, generally more so for males than for females." For example, Jewish mortality is lower in the younger age categories and higher in older age categories. Nevertheless, Goldstein (1980, 1974) concludes that the existing differences are not sufficient to account for the slow rate of natural increase of the Jewish population. Lower-than-average fertility for Jews compared to the rest of the American population remains an important aspect of family life and continues to be an issue of concern in the organized Jewish community.[9]

Indeed, while most Jews have adhered to the ZPG movement, consciously or not, others have argued that Jews have a special right to exempt themselves from this moral and social concern, since one-third of the world's Jewish population was destroyed by the Nazis during the Holocaust. They have emphasized that on the eve of World War II there were 18 million Jews in the world, and by the end of the war only 12 million remained. In the ensuing postwar period, over nearly 4 decades, the world Jewish population is estimated to have risen only to about 14 million. At that rate with no increase in fertility it will take another 75-80 years for the world Jewish population to reach the level it had already attained in 1939!

SOCIOLOGICAL SCENE: MIGRATION AND MOBILITY

As the introductory sections have suggested, migration is central to an understanding of the dynamics of Jewish history, society, and family life. The first extant written attempt to explain the emergence of the Jewish people begins with the twelfth chapter of Genesis (12:1): "Get thee out of thy country, and from thy kindred, and from thy father's house, unto the land that I will show thee." The emergence of an independent Jewish state with its own legal system was associated with a second migration, the Exodus from slavery in Egypt. Successive waves of suffering, oppression, destruction, exile, and return migration punctuated the course of Jewish history so frequently that migration has become a regular pattern of Jewish life.

While much of the migratory experience of Jews has been of necessity, today much migration is by choice (see Elazar, 1982).

In the American experience immigration has served to invigorate the institutions and culture of American Jewry, as in the case first of the German and later of the great Eastern European migration. Nevertheless, such migration has slowed down in the contemporary period. Indeed, while in earlier periods the migrants were more traditionally oriented than the natives, recent migrations of Soviet and Israeli Jews have brought less traditionally oriented persons. Much of the significant migration in the Jewish community has been internal, either of interurban or intraurban types.

The behavioral dimensions of migration and geographic mobility can take many forms. One indicator is place of birth. As Goldstein (1974) has pointed out, a number of studies in Detroit, Providence, and Springfield found that from two-fifths to two-thirds of persons living in these communities were born elsewhere.

A second dimension of mobility involves the regional redistribution of population. Farber et al. (1981) report that since World War I the northeastern and north central states have lost Jewish population to the southern and western regions, especially Florida and California. For example, between 1930 and 1980 the northeastern states' Jewish population has declined from 68 percent to 57 percent of the national total, and the north central states from 20 percent to 12 percent. In the same period the population in the South grew from 8 percent to 16 percent, and the West had a whopping increase from 4 percent to 15 percent (1930 figures from Farber et al., 1981; 1980 figures from Chenkin and Miran, 1980).

A third indicator of mobility is length of residence. Here Goldstein (1974) reports a high degree of residential mobility based on studies in Boston and Milwaukee, where approximately 50 percent to 60 percent of the population had lived at their current address for less than ten years.

Within urban areas a fourth aspect of geographic mobility has been the suburbanization movement, which began to flourish in the post-World War II period. Goldstein and Goldscheider (1968) found that Jewish suburbanites have higher rates of intermarriage, nonaffiliation, and no Jewish education, and lower scores of ritual observance than city residents. Nevertheless, most research suggests that synagogue (or church) attendance tends to increase as people move to the suburbs.

A fifth dimension to understanding mobility and migration is that of the density of the Jewish population. In a study of the Jewish community of Columbus, Ohio, Mayer (1970) found only about one-fourth of the population lived in a neighborhood that was 50 percent

Jewish. Nevertheless, respondents preferred living in sections with a higher proportion of Jews, such as a 50-50 split. Jews living in the more concentrated areas tended to have higher levels of traditional beliefs and practices. Yet in a study of St. Paul, Minnesota, Dashefsky and Shapiro (1971) found that living in a Jewish neighborhood was significantly correlated with a higher level of Jewish identification only for an older generation studied, not for the younger generation. This was so even though 77 percent of the older generation lived in the Jewish neighborhood, and only 45 percent of the younger generation did. Perhaps the interpersonal dimension (the number of close friends who are Jewish) may be more crucial than the ecological dimension (residence), especially in small to medium-sized Jewish communities.

What has precipitated these rapid changes in migration and mobility? Largely they have resulted from economic changes in the larger society and in the Jewish community. The growth of industrial, commercial, and technological enterprises in the South and West has produced a demand for highly educated personnel. At the same time, second-, third-, and fourth-generation Jews were increasingly pursuing higher education, which is the gateway to other jobs. The result has been a growing dependence of Jews in the professional and managerial sectors on employment in bureaucratic organizations, such as corporations, government agencies, and universities, where transfers and career growth frequently require repeated moves.

What then are the effects of mobility on the individual and family life? Some research suggests that it takes as long as five years for a migrant to achieve the same levels of participation in a community as a native (Zimmer, 1955). Consequently, mobility may attenuate ties to Judaism and the Jewish community, and further reduce socioemotional support to the family on the move.

On the other hand, the movement of migrants into smaller Jewish communities may serve to heighten the family members' own sense of Jewish identity and in turn strengthen the Jewish community.[10] As Goldstein (1974: 139) has stated: "All this suggests the need for greater concern with the role of migration than of intermarriage in the future of American Judaism. The latter may largely be only a by-product."

SOCIAL PSYCHOLOGICAL PERSPECTIVE: FAMILY AND IDENTITY TRANSMISSION[11]

It is a sociological axiom that the family is the basic agent of socialization. However, some sociologists note a lessening influence of the family on its members. While recognizing that the family "has been the prime mechanism for transmitting Jewish identity," Sklare (1971: 99) argues further: "This system of identity-formation is currently on the decline. The emerging crisis of the Jewish family in identity-formation is in part due to the newer limitations on the family as a socialization agent — limitations that affect all other Americans as well." Even if one grants this, it appears that the family is still the most important factor in Jewish identification. Furthermore, the family is not only the chief "mechanism" by which this attitude is transmitted, but the most important *source* of Jewish identification as well. In other words, the content of family life, the attitudes and practices of family members, contain many of the transmitted elements of Jewish identification. This appears to be what Sebald (1968: 290) means when he writes, "Jewish family life is interwoven with ethnic practices, thus giving children the immense psychological benefit of a number of meaningful rituals and ceremonies that mark religious observances, holidays, family events, and rites of passage."

Starting with Mead (1934), the notion of the attitudes and expectations of others as a central element in the formation of an individual's attitudes has been central to sociological social psychology. The literature on roles emphasizes the effect of expectations on the individual's behavior (see Biddle and Thomas, 1966) and those of significant others are the most important. Based on this perspective, Dashefsky and Shapiro (1974) assessed the degree to which family members perceived by their respondents as significant others expected them to participate in Jewish activities during adolescence. The measure used, an Index of Jewish Expectations (IJE), was correlated to the Jewish Identification (JI) scale and was statistically significant.[12]

The Index of Jewish Expectations indicates something of the extent to which the family's, and particularly the parents', attitudes were important for Jewish identification. It does not reveal, however, the extent to which individuals actually engaged in Jewish-related activities with their parents. A number of leading attitude theorists have argued and provided evidence for viewing behavior as a determinant of attitudes in contrast to the more popular opposite view (Festinger, 1957; Bem, 1970). They see attitudes as forming to coincide and be consistent with the actual behavior of the individual. Dashefsky and Shapiro (1974) measured Jewish activities undertaken with one's parents during adolescence. They found that their Index of Jewish Activities was significantly correlated with the Jewish Identification Scale.[13]

Family members constitute the primary significant others and reference groups for most Jewish adolescents. The family provides both the mechanism and the content for Jewish identification. This is true in spite of much popular reference to the "generation gap." Dashefsky and Shapiro found the family's expectations that their son participate in Jewish activities (measured by an Index of Jewish Expectations) and the actual activities that the adolescent engaged in with his parents (measured by an Index of Jewish Activities) to be determinants of Jewish identification. Both family expectations and activities with parents were significantly related to the Jewish Identification scale. Focusing on individual family members as significant others, they found that those respondents having older brothers had significantly higher JI scale scores than those who did not. The most important individual in the family was, however, as one would expect for sons, the father. In particular, the father's religiosity and the father's own JI scale score were related to the respondent's JI scale score.

In sum, Dashefsky and Shapiro found family, peers, and Jewish education in that order to be key determinants of Jewish identification. Indeed, in their final regression analysis of family influence over Jewish identification, they were able to explain 28 percent of the variance in their measure of Jewish identification. Of this total amount, family variables explained about two-thirds or 18 percent, with friends' expectations explaining 6 percent and Jewish education 4 percent. This means that the family was 3 times as important as friends, and 4.5 times as important as Jewish schooling. These prior socialization variables, however, become less significant in the explanation as they provide a framework for subsequent adult patterns of Jewish identification through religious organizational involvement, primarily in synagogue life.

While the family remains the most important agent of socialization to Jewish identification, its ability to function in this way depends in part on the internal dynamics of the life-cycle change and the external pressures of societal change. Sklare and Greenblum (1967) report that when the children reach school age, more active involvement in the Jewish community is noted. Cohen (1981), in analyzing data from a 1975 Boston community study, found a decline in Jewish involvement associated with the growth of alternative households — singles, childless, and divorced. Nevertheless, while the family plays the primary role in identity formation more or less effectively (depending on the stage of the life cycle or degree of conventionality), other communal institutions provide a framework for reinforcing Jewish identification (Waxman, 1982). Such institutions would include the synagogue, Jewish schools, and youth programs after school and at summer camps. All of these socialization factors may leave a lasting imprint on Jews that distinguish them from their neighbors.

CLINICAL CONTEXT:
PSYCHOLOGICAL ASPECTS OF
CHILD REARING AND FAMILY LIVING

From a clinical point of view, religioethnic attachment involves conscious and unconscious processes that fulfull a deep psychological need for identity and a sense of historical continuity. It is transmitted by an emotional language within the family and reinforced by the surrounding community (Giordano and Giordano, 1977). It is a profound and abiding aspect of human experience.

As McGoldrick (1982) has suggested, there are a number of factors that influence the way ethnic or religioethnic patterns surface in families:

(1) the reasons for immigration, that is, what the family was seeking and what it was leaving behind (religious or political persecution, poverty, wish for adventure, and so on)'

(2) the length of time since immigration and the impact of generational acculturation conflicts on the family;

(3) the family's place of residence — whether or not the family lives or has lived in a homogeneous neighborhood;

(4) the order of migration — whether one family member migrated alone or whether a large portion of the family, community, or nation came together;

(5) the socioeconomic status, education, and upward mobility of family members;

(6) the political and religious ties to the group;

(7) the language spoken by family members;

(8) the extent of exogamous marriage; and

(9) the family members' attitudes toward the values of the group.

Religioethnic differences not only persist as family life phenomena but are probably more crucial in the area of child rearing than previously believed. Research to date indicates that different groups do differ not only in their behavioral approaches to child rearing, but in their expectations and aspirations for their children as well (see Bartz and LeVine, 1978; Caudill and Frost, 1972; Freedman, 1979; Greenglass, 1971). For example, Freedman's (1979) research indicates that these differences do not disappear after a generation or two, but can be observed in fourth- and fifth-generation Americans. Thus, based on the differing structures of families in our culture, it is understandable that different cultural trends would affect these forms differently.

Some of these trends may be described psychodynamically, especially in the case of the Jews. Because of their socioeconomic status, Jews are more likely to rely on some forms of psychotherapy. For example, Herz and Rosen (1982) state that Jews are also more willing than members of other ethnic groups to accept a family definition of their problems. Moreover, Jewish parents tend to have democratic relationships with their children and less rigid generational boundaries than most other groups. Psychotherapists describe Jews as placing high value on verbal explanations and reasoning in child rearing. Therefore, therapists are asked to be alert to the meaning of parents' desire to reason out issues and to be sensitive to the pride that Jewish parents take in their children's verbal skills, intelligence, and ability to think things out logically (Herz and Rosen, 1982).

Clinicians list some typical characteristics of Jews who are in therapy that reveal aspects of family life:

(1) Jews will value talk, insight, and recognition of complex levels of meaning.

(2) They value the gaining of wisdom and have a long tradition of consulting with a wise person, or several wise people, always remaining themselves the final judges of the opinions they hear.

(3) Raising successful children is the major responsibility of the parents, particularly the mother; and underachievement or more serious problems are often felt to reflect not only on the family but on the ethnic group as a whole.

(4) Parents are expected to make great sacrifices for their children, and when children grow up they are expected to repay their parents in *naches*, a special pleasure one gets only from the success and happiness of one's children (Herz and Rosen, 1982).

Jewish-Americans, in particular, seem more affected by the "crisis of expert testimony" than other groups. Many Jewish parents seem preoccupied with doing what is "psychologically right" for their children. Jewish parents (and particularly Jewish women) also seem to have particular difficulties with separation issues. Based on the strong dependence that Jewish women have traditionally sustained with their children (Blau, 1974), some now appear highly conflicted about the desirability of leaving their children to pursue personal careers or goals and often seem guilty over whichever path they choose.

Indeed, one of the most popular themes in depicting Jewish family life has been that of the self-sacrificing Jewish mother, who raised successful sons as doctors, lawyers, professionals, and businessmen. These same women today, however, who have internalized the values of success and education, now have the opportunity to succeed on their own (Herz and Rosen, 1982). Perhaps the extent to which their husbands support them in their choices and the children in child rearing will determine the specific outcome.

By contrast, Irish-American women, for example, appear very concerned with issues related to discipline. Right and wrong are very important to the value system in which these women grew up, and changing from a traditionally "strict" family style is often confusing and difficult for them. Nevertheless, respect for the authority of the father remains very important in black, Italian, and Hispanic families. How to integrate this respect into new family patterns perhaps more permissive and egalitarian than their own families seems especially stressful.

Observers have noted significant differences between those who are actively involved in a religioethnic community and those who are not. Parents living within a tight-knit community seem on the surface less conflicted than those who do not live in such communities. Thus, for example, one does not find readily apparent the same soul-searching about child-rearing practices among many Orthodox Jewish parents. There is an acceptance of a basic value system rooted in an entire system of belief. Thus there is some place to turn for support as the community sets a standard and strives to support members in their attempts to sustain themselves within the value system.

This sense of security has also been observed among Irish Catholics who have maintained strong ties to the church and among blacks who are actively involved in church life. Moreover, clinicians and parents alike report that religioethnic background and family history become quite influential in times of stress. People report that they act in ways totally out of character with their *intended* child-rearing style when they are under stress. They "hear themselves saying things that their parents said" and that they "swore they would never say" to their own children. Lack of awareness of the strong influence of one's past often leads to guilt and ambivalence about a person's ability in child rearing.

What concerns many leaders and members of the organized Jewish community is how to reconcile changing sex roles and still retain the relatively successful model of family cohesion and high achievement of children. The retention of these prized elements of traditional family life seem threatened by the growing incidence of separation, divorce, and intermarriage. Additional research may yield clues to a better understanding of the dynamics of Jewish family cohesion and disruption.

THE EROSION OF JEWISH FAMILIAL
AND COMMUNAL LIFE:
ROLE OF DIVORCE AND INTERMARRIAGE

In their study of Eastern European Jews, Zborowski and Herzog (1952: 290) comment on the sacredness of marriage in Jewish society:

Marriage is both the climax and the threshold. From birth on every step is directed with an eye to the [k]hupa [marriage canopy], and if that goal were missed, life itself would seem to be bypassed. Once attained, however, marriage is merely the background for the great goal, the great achievement, the great gratification — children.

Indeed marriage is seen in Jewish tradition as a sacred act, and the Hebrew word for it, *kiddushin,* comes from the Hebrew root, *holy.* While divorce is permitted in Jewish religious law, it traditionally has not been regarded positively. In his qualitative study, *Divorce and the Jewish Child,* Cottle (1981) even found one child who thought divorce was against Jewish law and not permitted.

Many popular commentators and scholars have suggested that in the past decade or two a crisis has gripped the Jewish family. Forces that have disrupted the cohesiveness of the American family in general have penetrated to the Jewish family. Indeed, as one sociologist has suggested, the Jewish family is on the "SCIDs," that is, *s*ingle, *c*hildless, *i*ntermarried, and *d*ivorced; still, Jews have increased in numbers, as the New York Jewish population survey reveals (Cohen, 1982).

No current national data exist, however, to compare Jewish and non-Jewish divorce rates. Nevertheless, Goldstein (1974), in examining the 1957 U.S. sample census that included a question on religion, found that the proportion of divorced persons in the total population was nearly twice as great as the proportion for Jews. For males the proportion divorced for the total population was 1.8 percent, compared to 1 percent for Jews; for females it was 2.3 percent for the total population and 1.4 percent for Jews. In their study of the Providence Jewish Community, Goldstein and Goldscheider (1968: 108) found a "*lack of* clear-cut generation changes and the general stability of Jewish families in such generation."

Relying on more recent data (NORC surveys of 1977-1978), Cohen (1981) reports that the proportion of ever divorced in the 35-44 age group was 20 percent for Protestants, 15 percent for Catholics, and 10 percent for Jews (the highest proportion for any age category, with 5 percent for the 55-64 age category being the lowest percentage). While these percentages are substantially higher for Jews than reported overall in the 1957 U.S. sample census, they are also higher for non-Jews. Certainly they are not as high as some might expect, given the reports in the mass media. This may be so because the popular figure frequently cited is the ratio of current divorces to marriages, rather than the ratio of divorces to ever-married individuals. As Cohen (1981: 144) concludes, "While Jews (like Christians) are divorcing more frequently than they have in the past, they are still divorcing less often than their non-Jewish counterparts. Moreover, the proportional gap between Jewish and non-Jewish divorce rates has been remaining steady, since non-Jewish rates have climbed faster than Jewish ones."

The effects of divorce on the religioethnic identity of the children appear varied. As one teenage boy told Cottle (1981: 5): "When my father told me they were separating and would probably get divorced, one of the first crazy thoughts I had . . . was well, you don't have to be Jewish anymore." On the other hand, a teenage girl told Cottle (1981: 21): "I'm staying [at the temple religious school] because everything having to do with being Jewish is the only thing not being moved around."

The equally vexing question of intermarriage, and its effects on Jewish family life, has been the subject of much controversy in the organized Jewish community as well as among the researchers who study it. The traditional Jewish response of the parent whose child intermarries has been to observe many of the practices associated with mourning for the deceased. In addition, conversion of non-Jews has generally not been encouraged.

Most studies have found a relatively low *overall* rate of intermarriage. According to Lazerwitz's (1981) analysis of the 1971 National Jewish Population Survey (NJPS), 7 percent of ever-married Jews had or were intermarried.[14] Generally, intermarriage in the Jewish community is viewed as the marriage of one spouse not born of Jewish background and one spouse who is of Jewish background. This is a sociocultural definition and not a Jewish legal or religious definition.

Local community studies usually reveal an increase of proportions of intermarried persons for more recent generations. The most dramatic evidence of a possibly radical change in Jewish adherence to endogamy was the NJPS finding, as reported by Lazerwitz (1981), that the proportion of Jewish persons who intermarried in the most recent period was 14 percent of married Jews under age 35 (twice the overall rate). Some recent community studies have found even higher rates.[15] Such intermarriage is more likely to occur for individuals who have achieved only low levels of Jewish education, have lived in areas of lesser Jewish population, and have come from backgrounds with low levels of religious observance and other forms of Jewish identification.

The increased intermarriage raises the question of whether it is a threat to Jewish family cohesion and Jewish community survival. As a study prepared for the American Jewish Committee by Mayer and Sheingold (1979: 30) found: " Differences of religious background do not seem to contribute to estrangement from parents or to conflicts in family decision-making, including decisions about child-rearing. Relationships between both born-Jewish and born-Gentile respondents and their parents were consistently reported to be close and harmonious. "

With respect to the effect of intermarriage on Jewish community survival, however, there is a falling off of the intention to give a Jewish education, comparing in-married (85 percent) to intermarried persons (71 percent) as reported by Massarik and Chenkin (1973). Furthermore, in-married adults are more religiously observant than those in mixed marriages and more organizationally involved.

Nevertheless, it is important to note that a major variable explaining the subsequent relationship of the intermarried family with respect to the Jewish community depends on whether the Gentile spouse converts to Judaism. As Mayer and Sheingold (1979: 29) found:

On every index of Jewish attitudes and practice, couples whose born-Gentile spouses have converted to Judaism scored higher than other intermarried couples. Indeed, based on what is known about the religious and ethnic life in endogamous marriages, the family life of conversionary marriages is more consciously Jewish, both in religious practice and in formal and informal Jewish acculturation of children.

The factor most responsible for the Jewishness of intermarried families — including the conversion of the born-Gentile spouse — would seem to be the extent of Jewish background, knowledge and commitment of the born-Jewish spouse.

Finally, Mayer and Sheingold (1979: 30) conclude:

The findings summarized above tend to reinforce the fear that intermarriage represents a threat to Jewish continuity. Most non-Jewish spouses do not convert to Judaism; the level of Jewish content and practice in mixed marriages is low; only about one-third of the Jewish partners in such marriages view their children as Jewish; and most such children are exposed to little by way of Jewish culture or religion.

All of this suggests that despite much research on the subject of intermarriage, there is still more research that needs to be done, especially to examine its effects on the children.[16] But as Gold-scheider (1982: 39-40) has reminded us:

> It is not the level of Jewish intermarriage per se that challenges the sociodemographic survival of Jews in America. . . . Rather it is the specific demographic context within which intermarriage rates operate in America that is of paramount significance. The combination of low fertility, geographic dispersion, minimum potential sources of population renewal . . . declines in family cohesion, *and* relatively high intermarriage rates have resulted in issues associated with the demographic vitality of Jewish Americans.

All of this evidence suggests that intermarriage, divorce, and the other factors cited are symptoms and not causes of the erosion of Jewish familial and communal life in a rapidly changing society wherein urbanization, secularization, bureaucratization, industrialization, and assimilation have predominated during the recent past. Certainly more research is needed to uncover the complex interrelationships of the variables studied. Indeed, the facts suggest that the family alone is not able to function as a socialization agent as effectively as in the past without external supports.

FAMILY CONSERVATION:
THE JEWISH EXPERIENCE AND ITS IMPLICATIONS
FOR OTHER RELIGIOETHNIC GROUPS

The significance of the family for Jewish life has been that it has served as the crucial link in building a relationship between the Jewish identity of the individual and the larger Jewish community. Now, perhaps more than ever, the family in general needs to have the social support of other communal institutions within the particular religioethnic community as well as society at large.

The case of the Jewish family is particularly illuminating because despite its centuries of sociocultural experience in cushioning minority group status, it is afflicted by all of the woes of modernity, with some special strains brought about by the even greater rapidity in Jewish life of occupational, geographic, and sex-role changes. Jewish adaptability has in the past been a virtue, but current adaptations may have disastrous consequences for Jewish family life.

In addition, the Jewish family's nurturing function has been weakened by the diminution of close relationships with grandparents and other relatives and the emotional intensification of relationships between parents and children. Sklare (1971: 100) acknowledges that while the Jewish family may have been weakened in its capacity to rear and sustain emotionally stable individuals, "it is the shrinking contribution of the family to Jewish identity-transmission that constitutes its essential weakness." This weakness arose due to the combination of high acculturation of Jewish parents and the limited access to more Jewishly committed and competent relatives. Sklare notes that even the extended family has been diminished in its capacity to assure Jewish distinctiveness, partly as a result of the process of acculturation and also because of the effects of the growing rate of intermarriage. Very few Jewish family networks do not have non-Jewish members, whose presence tends to result in some dilution of the centrality of Jewish customs and practices.

Beginning in the 1970s, there was a reaction against the disintegrative drift in the Jewish community and a movement to preserve Jewish family life. A new consensus emerged even among "liberal" Jewish analysts, rooted in Tevye's call in *Fiddler on the Roof:* "Tradition." How to integrate tradition with change became a concern not just of the more traditional Jewish groups but also of the less traditional.

In *Consultation on the Jewish Family,* the American Jewish Committee (1977: 3) discusses the relationship of the family to Jewish identity and community:

> It is fruitless to compare "traditional" and modern families in an arbitrary fashion. It is important, however, to consider and define the acceptable range of Jewish family structures at various periods and recognize the changing norms. It would then be possible to recognize a variety of family structures which are "resonant with Jewish perspective" and allow for continuity.

> If the Jewish family is to serve as a vehicle of Jewish identity transmission, then it must be expected to resist external pressures of current trends and apply some of the constraints of tradition.

The organized Jewish community has had some experience in adapting to the changing needs of families. While some of these experiences may apply more to the specific needs of the Jewish family, the following series of suggestions may have application to other religioethnic communities. These suggestions are based in part on a report by the American Jewish Committee's Jewish Communal Affairs Department on the consultation mentioned above (American Jewish Committee, 1977: 18-20).

The first set of suggestions focuses on creating structural conditions for helping families cope with changing roles, by:

(1) upgrading parenting and recognizing the societal benefits of child care by providing *social security coverage* and/or other *pension and disability benefits* for the primary homecare person as well as supporting in particular the responsibility of the father as a nurturant parent;

(2) providing *quality day care facilities;*

(3) promoting *flexi-time job opportunities;*

(4) developing *family support systems* by bringing into the home retired men and women as surrogate grandparents;

(5) encouraging the development of *extrafamilial support systems,* such as the Marriage Encounter movement (and the Jewish community's *Havurah* or fellowship movement), which are ongoing group structures that provide an opportunity for the intimate expression of family and/or marital solidarity;

(6) creating *"welcome wagon"* programs (such as the Jewish community's "shalom wagon") within the particular religioethnic community to integrate newcomers; and

(7) recognizing the special needs of *single and divorced persons* and providing special programs for them oriented toward coping with family living as well as integrating them into community events frequented usually by intact families.

The second set of suggestions focuses on offering cultural opportunities through educational programs, by:

(1) providing *family education programs* that emphasize sharing aspects of the particular religiocultural tradition in a relaxed and informal family setting at a weekend retreat (a "Shabbaton" in the Jewish community) or an afternoon family holiday preparation program (as in a "Hanukkah workshop," where the families work together to make holiday ceremonial objects and prepare for the observance of the holiday in the home);

(2) elevating the stature of *formal religioethnic education* for youth with an emphasis on the positive experiential aspects of the particular tradition and the role of the family (as in the "Hebrew school");

(3) supplementing the formal with *informal religioethnic education* through teen and youth programs after school, on weekends, and in summer camps (as in Hebrew-speaking and other Jewish religious and cultural camps);

(4) utilizing the *mass media* to illustrate ways in which the religioethnic tradition can enrich family living; and

(5) offering *courses in family-living* skills in high schools and colleges — both public and private.

Many of these kinds of activities need to be pursued not just in the specific religioethnic community but in the general community as well. Governmental agencies can have a role to play in protecting young children and ensuring them the opportunity for healthy development. Private religious and welfare agencies certainly should have a role in the establishment of national as well as local family centers to focus attention on the family. Such family centers could coordinate needed research, assess social policies, provide public relations, and develop educational and training programs for effective family living (American Jewish Committee, 1977: 20). Indeed, the American Jewish Committee, for example, took its consultation report seriously and established a National Jewish Family Center shortly thereafter.

Finally, we come back to the issues raised in the beginning sections of this chapter. Will the family disintegrate? Will the fiddler fall off the roof? Will the cohesiveness of community and the persistence of identity endure among Jews? It appears likely that the family will endure although the proportion of conventional families in the population will decline. It is likely that the Jewish family, though altered — as it was many times before — will continue as the primary socialization agent, although it will need more assistance from other societal agents and communal support systems to function effectively.

You may ask whether this is a pessimistic or optimistic account of family life. Do you remember the difference between the pessimist and the optimist? As one pundit put it, "The pessimist sees the difficulty in every opportunity; the optimist sees the opportunity in every difficulty." Perhaps, through wise planning and investment of resources, the community can create the support systems to sustain the family to "stay on course" in a time of change. Thus, in that way, the fiddler will not fall from the roof.

NOTES

1. The *Encyclopedia Judaica* (1971) article on the family provides a detailed account of the traditional Jewish family as seen in the Bible and post-Biblical literature and provides a basis for this section of the chapter.

2. TaNaCH is a Hebrew acronym used to refer to the Bible. T stands for *Torah*, or the Five Books of Moses ("Pentateuch"); N for *Neviim*, or the eight books of "Prophets"; and CH (K) for *Ketuvim*, the Hagiographa or eleven additional "Writings."

3. The common Biblical and modern Hebrew word for wife is *ishah*, or "woman," and the Hebrew word for husband is *baal*, or "master." Nevertheless, one rabbi observed that when the Hebrew letter *yod* is removed from the word for man *ish*, the remaining letters spell the Hebrew word for "fire," *esh*. Similarly, remove the Hebrew letter, *hai*, from the word "woman," *ishah*, and the remainder also spells the Hebrew word for fire, *esh*. But the two removed Hebrew letters *yod* and *hai* spell a Hebrew word for God, *Yah*. This implies, sermonized the rabbi, that when God departs from the marriage, only the fire of contention remains.

4. Quoted in the *Encyclopedia Judaica* (1971: 1170).

5. Quoted in the *Encyclopedia Judaica* (1971: 1171).

6. An excellent account of Jewish life in the middle ages is provided by Abrahams (1958).

7. A good social history of American Judaism is provided by Glazer (1957), whose work provides the basis for this section of the chapter.

8. Other reports such as that of Della Pergola (1980) estimate that Jewish fertility in the early 1970s was below replacement level. Cohen (1981) also reports lower Jewish fertility compared to Protestants and Catholics based on an examination in part of NORC General Social Surveys 1972-1978. There is, however, about one-quarter of the Jewish community who tend to have higher fertility than the rest; these are persons who attend synagogue frequently and who have an Orthodox or Conservative preference (Lazerwitz, 1980). Indeed, Waxman (1982) suggests that some segments of the American Jewish population, such as members of the various Hasidic sects and other Orthodox Jews, are underrepresented in sample surveys; and they tend to have much larger families than is typical of the rest of Jews.

9. For a more in-depth analysis of Jewish mortality and fertility with comparisons to Protestants and Catholics see Goldscheider (1982).

10. Additional details are available in Goldstein (1980) and Goldscheider (1982).

11. This section is adapted from Dashefsky and Shapiro (1974: 53-55, 58), with permission of the coauthor.

12. $r = .30$.

13. $r = .24$.

14. Massarik and Chenkin (1973) report 9 percent also using NJPS data.

15. For example, Farber et al. (1979) report that for persons aged 20-24 in metropolitan Kansas City in 1976, 70 percent of males and 45 percent of females had intermarried (as reported by their parents). Of those aged 25-29, 39 percent of males and 23 percent of females had intermarried, and of those aged 45-64, 30 percent of males and 6 percent of females had intermarried. Of course, Kansas City is not necessarily a prototypical community.

16. At the time of this writing, the American Jewish Committee was in the process of evaluating recent data on the effects of intermarriage on the children.

REFERENCES

Abrahams, I. (1958) Jewish Life in the Middle Ages. New York: Meridian. (Originally published in 1896.)

American Jewish Committee (1977) Consultation on the Jewish Family: Its Role in Jewish Identity and Continuity. New York: Institute of Human Relations.

Bartz, K. W. and E. S. Le Vine (1978) "Childrearing by black parents: a description and comparison to Anglo and Chicano parents." Journal of Marriage and the Family 40 (November): 709-719.

Bem, D. J. (1970) Beliefs, Attitudes and Human Affairs. Belmont, CA: Brooks/ Cole.

Biddle, B. J. and E. J. Thomas (1966) Role Theory: Concepts and Research. New York: John Wiley.

Blau, Z. S. (1974) "The strategy of the Jewish mother," pp. 167-187 in M. Sklare (ed.) The Jew in American Society. New York: Behrman House.

Caudill, W. and N. Frost (1972) "A comparison of maternal care in infant behavior in Japanese American and Japanese families," pp. 329-342 in U. Bronfenbrenner (ed.) Influences on Human Development. Hinsdale, IL: Dryden.

Chenkin, A. and M. Miran (1980) "Jewish population in the United States," pp. 170-171 in M. Himmelfarb and D. Singer (eds.) American Jewish Year Book, Vol. 81. New York: American Jewish Committee.

Cohen, S. M. (1982) "The demographic dimension." Presented at the International Center for University Teaching of Jewish Civilization, Jerusalem, June.

────── (1981) "The American Jewish family today," pp. 136-154 in M. Himmelfarb and D. Singer (eds.) American Jewish Year Book, Vol. 82. New York: American Jewish Committee.

Cottle, T.J. (1981) Divorce and the Jewish Child. New York: American Jewish Committee.

Dashefsky, A. and H.M. Shapiro (1974) Ethnic Identification Among American Jews. Lexington, MA: D.C. Heath.

────── (1971) The Jewish Community of St. Paul. St. Paul, MN: United Jewish Fund and Council.

Della Pergola, S. (1980) "Patterns of American Jewish fertility." Demography 17, 3: 261-274.

Elazar, D. (1982) "Jews on the move: the new wave of Jewish migration and its implications for organized Jewry." Journal of Jewish Communal Service 58 (Summer): 279-283.

Encyclopedia Judaica (1971) "Family." Vol. 6: 1164-1172.

Farber, B., L. Gordon, and A.J. Mayer (1979) "Intermarriage and Jewish identity: the implications for pluralism and assimilation in American society." Ethnic and Racial Studies 2 (April): 222-230.

Farber, B., C.H. Mindel, and B. Lazerwitz (1981) "The Jewish American family," pp. 350-383 in C.H. Mindel and R.W. Habenstein (eds.) Ethnic Families in America. New York: Elsevier.

Festinger, L. (1957) A Theory of Cognitive Dissonance. New York: Harper & Row.

Freedman, D. (1979) "Ethnic differences in babies." Human Nature 2 (January): 36-43.

Giordano, J. and G. Giordano (1977) Ethnocultural Factors in Mental Health. New York: American Jewish Committee.

Glazer, N. (1957) American Judaism. Chicago: University of Chicago Press.

Goldscheider, C. (1982) "Demography of Jewish Americans: research findings, issues, and challenges," pp. 1-55 in M. Sklare (ed.) Understanding American Jewry. New Brunswick, NJ: Transaction.

Goldstein, S. (1980) "Jews in the United States: perspectives from demography," pp. 3-59 in M. Himmelfarb and D. Singer (eds.) American Jewish Year Book, Vol. 81. New York: American Jewish Committee.

────── (1974) "American Jewry, 1970: a demographic profile," pp. 97-162 in M. Sklare (ed.) The Jew in American Society. New York: Behrman House.

────── and C. Goldscheider (1968) Jewish Americans. Englewood Cliffs, NJ: Prentice-Hall.

Greenglass, E.R. (1971) "A cross-cultural comparison of maternal communication." Child Development 42, 3: 685-692.

Herz, F.M. and E.J. Rosen (1982) "Jewish families," pp. 364-392 in M. McGoldrick et al. (eds.) Ethnicity and Family Therapy. New York: Guilford.

Lazerwitz, B. (1981) "Jewish-Christian marriages and conversions." Jewish Social Studies 43, 1: 31-46.

────── (1980) "Religiosity and fertility: how strong a connection?" Contemporary Jewry 5, 1: 56-63.

────── (1979) "Past and future trends in the size of American Jewish denominations." Journal of Reform Judaism 26 (Summer): 77-82.

────── and M. Harrison (1979) "American Jewish denominations: a social and religious profile." American Sociological Review 44 (August): 656-666.

McGoldrick, M. (1982) "Ethnicity and family therapy: an overview," pp. 13-30 in M. McGoldrick et al. (eds.) Ethnicity and Family Therapy. New York: Guilford.

Massarik, F. and A. Chenkin (1973) "United States National Jewish Population Study: a first report," pp. 264-306 in M. Fine and M. Himmelfarb (eds.) American Jewish Year Book, Vol. 74. New York: American Jewish Committee.

Mayer, A.J. (1970) Columbus Jewish Population Study: 1969. Columbus, OH: Jewish Welfare Federation.

Mayer, E. and C. Sheingold (1979) Intermarriage and the Jewish Future. New York: American Jewish Committee.

Mead, G. H. (1934) Mind, Self and Society. Chicago: University of Chicago Press.

Morgan, T. B. (1964) "The vanishing American Jew." Look (May 5): 4288.

Patai, R. (1977) The Jewish Mind. New York: Scribner.

Sachar, H. M. (1958) The Course of Modern Jewish History. New York: Dell.

Sebald, H. (1968) Adolescence: A Sociological Analysis. New York: Appleton-Century-Crofts.

Sklare, M. (1971) American Jews. New York: Random House.

————— and J. Greenblum (1967) Jewish Identity on the Suburban Frontier. New York: Basic Books.

Waxman, C. I. (1982) "The family and the American Jewish community on the threshold of the 1980's: an inventory for planning," pp. 163-185 in M. Sklare (ed.) Understanding American Jewry. New Brunswick, NJ: Transaction.

Zborowski, M. and E. Herzog (1952) Life Is With People. New York: Schocken.

Zimmer, B. (1955) "Participation of migrants in urban structures." American Sociological Review 20, 2: 218-224.

8

CONTEMPORARY RELATIONSHIPS BETWEEN BLACK FAMILIES AND BLACK CHURCHES IN THE UNITED STATES
A Speculative Inquiry

Jacquelyne Johnson Jackson

Myths abound about the religiosity of blacks and about the interactive and additive effects between black families and black churches. Blacks are often described as being extremely religious. Some people even believe that religion is far more important to blacks than anything else, including their families. Black churches are typically depicted as pillars of their communities and as effective agents of social control over the lives of black families.

A reasonable and customary response to the above kinds of generalizations is that they seem plausible, ergo they are true. They make sense because they fit the popular image of blacks as religious beings readily controlled by religious leaders who are decidedly more literate than the masses, a notion more apt for a feudal society in medieval Europe than for today's democratic society of the United States of America. Those generalizations also fit a racist attitude growing out of slavery, to wit, that the Christian religion is an effective mechanism for controlling blacks, provided that the blacks understand full well and accept the inapplicability of the Christian principles of equality and individual freedom to them.

But a critical question now concerns the validity and reliability of those types of generalizations about current relationships between black families and black churches. Given the voluminous literature available about black families, the dearth of empirical research about the black families-black church relationship is surprising. But relatively few contemporary investigators of black families have been concerned about the interactive or additive effects between familial

Some of the quoted material in this chapter is reprinted by permission of Schocken Books Inc. from *The Negro Church in America* by E. Franklin Frazier. Copyright © 1963 by The University of Liverpool. Copyright © 1974 by Schocken Books Inc.

and religious institutions involving blacks. Correlatively, the precious few investigators of sociocultural and psychological characteristics of black churches have rarely amassed empirical data about relationships between black families and black churches.

Most of these few studies have focused on cults founded by blacks, such as those headed by Father Divine or Sweet Daddy Grace (see Fauset, 1974), or where most of the participants were black, such as in the People's Temple, headed by James Jones, or the studies have emphasized a theoretical or historical orientation (see Frazier, 1974; Jackson, 1980; Johnston, 1954; Sernett, 1972; and, for a useful condensed history of the early years of black churches and a critique of current works then available about black church, see Nelsen and Nelsen, 1975). A few works have concentrated on the Black Muslims, founded by the late Elijah Mohammed, now headed by one of his sons and known as the World Community of Al-Islam (see Lincoln, 1961).

Few black sociologists have been involved in the sociology of religion. Even fewer black theologians have obtained the sociological or anthropological training that is necessarily antecedent to producing relevant studies about relationships between black familial and religious institutions.

The provision of definitive statements about current relationships between black families and black churches now is largely impossible. Concrete data that are *sine qua non* for that purpose are practically nonexistent. Therefore, this chapter presents only some tentative judgments about those relationships. But these judgments are grounded in considerable knowledge about black families and reasonable familiarity with the literature about black families and black churches. An important caveat is that this chapter is primarily concerned with extant relationships between black families and black churches, as opposed to a review or critique of literature about black families or black churches, or any racial comparisons. An underlying premise is that the development of blacks throughout their life spans is fostered when their families and their churches are effectively involved in their socializing processes.

For present purposes, the concept of "black families" refers to an aggregation of two or more persons related by blood, marriage, or adoption, who reside within the same household, provided that the householder is black. For instance, a white mother residing as a householder with her black son does not constitute a black family. Also eliminated from the definition of black families are members of coresidential units where the cohabiting adults are not legally married. The proportion of such units among blacks is not, however, significantly large.

The concept of "black churches" raises some definitional questions. Should it be restricted operationally to those churches that are not formally affiliated or connected with white religious denominations, such as the African Methodist Episcopal church? Or should it be extended to predominantly white denominations with some black churches, such as the United Presbyterian Church, U.S.A.? The concept of "black churches" is operationally defined herein to refer only to those churches established by or for blacks, where the controlling power is vested entirely within black hands. This definition conforms well to the idea that "the Negro church was created as a result of the refusal to submit to the indignities of a false kind of 'integration' in which all power was in the hands of white people" (National Committee of Negro Churchmen, 1968: 267).

The first of the four major sections of this chapter provides a brief demographic profile of the current black population. The nonfamilial data presented are contrasted with data for whites. The second section contains a very limited demographic and historical profile of black churches. In the third section, certain key issues pertaining to contemporary families are discussed as they may relate generally or specifically to black families. These issues include premarital and extramarital sex, abortion, illegitimacy, sex roles, divorce, economic support for dependent family members, and the aged. The selecion of these issues followed largely the directives set forth by the editors of this book. The last section focuses specifically on the roles or functions of black churches in abetting or hindering the development of black families. Necessarily included is some discussion of the involvement of black churches in the civil rights movement of the 1950s and 1960s and in contemporary political elections.

DEMOGRAPHIC PROFILE OF THE BLACK POPULATION

Table 8.1 contrasts data for blacks and whites by size, age, residential location, education, employment, occupation, and income. The bulk of these data are for the noninstitutional population, with the employment data confined to the civilian segment.

In 1980, the 26.5 million blacks and 188.3 million whites constituted about 12 percent and 83 percent, respectively, of the total resident population of the United States. Both the black and white populations are aging, but blacks remain younger, by about 6 years in 1980. A majority of blacks and whites are metropolitan dwellers. Residing in central cities was far more common among blacks (56.0 percent) than among whites (23.7 percent). While the educational

STRUGGLING IN THE TIDE

TABLE 8.1 Selected Characteristics of Blacks and Whites in the United States, 1980

Characteristic	Black	White
Resident population*	26,488	188,341
% of total resident population	11.7	83.2
Median age (years)	24.9	31.3
Noninstitutional population[a]	25,473	188,207
Residential type		
% in metropolitan areas	77.3	66.3
% in central cities	56.0	23.7
Education for those 25 or older		
% high school graduates	51.2	70.5
% with some college education	20.4	32.9
% with 4 or more years of college	7.9	17.8
Labor force status, 16 or older		
Females: Total number[a]	9,616	75,162
total number in civilian labor force[a]	5,107	38,544
% in civilian labor force	53.1	51.3
% unemployed	14.0	6.5
Males: Total number[a]	7,807	68,495
total number in civilian labor force[a]	5,490	53,627
% in civilian labor force	70.3	78.3
% unemployed	14.3	6.1
Occupation, 16 or older and employed		
Total number[a]	9,098	86,380
% white-collar workers	36.6	53.9
% blue-collar workers	37.3	31.1
% service workers	24.4	12.1
% farm workers	1.7	2.9
Income and poverty in 1979		
Median income of persons with income, 15 or older:		
female	$4,023	$4,394
male	7,745	12,357
% of persons 15 or older below the poverty level:		
female	31.4	9.5
male	20.8	6.2

SOURCE: U.S. Bureau of the Census (1981a).

a. In thousands.

level of both races has risen greatly over time, the relative position of blacks remains below that of whites. Among persons over 25 years of age in 1980, a slight majority of blacks, compared to about 70 percent of whites, were at least high school graduates.

The rates of labor force participation among those over 16 years of age were only slightly higher among black (53.1 percent) than among white (51.3 percent) females, but somewhat lower among black (70.3 percent) than among white (78.3 percent) males. More than one-third of employed blacks, compared to more than one-half of employed whites, were white-collar workers in 1980. Not surprisingly, then, a larger proportion of black than white church members are not white-collar workers.

The proportion of farm workers among blacks is smaller than that among whites. Extremely few blacks today are farm workers. Also, decreasing proportions of blacks are rural dwellers, as noted above. The paucity of black residents in rural areas has a number of significant implications for the development and maintenance of black churches within those areas.

Among persons over 15 years of age with any income in 1979, the median incomes, as usual, were lowest among black females, followed in ascending order by white females, black males, and white males. When measured by the poverty index, black females remained at the bottom, followed next not by white females, but by black males. The magnitude of black poverty in 1979 was threefold that of whites.

Data about the marital statuses of blacks over 14 years of age, by age and sex, in the United States show a considerable decrease between 1970 and 1981 in the percentages of black females of any age who were married and living with their husbands. For instance in 1970, a majority of women 25-54 years of age lived with their husbands. In 1981, only a minority of women in any age category lived with their husbands. The decrease in the proportion of men living with wives was not as dramatic.

Because most marriages in the United States are racially endogamous, the marital statuses of black women are generally affected by the black sex ratio, or the number of black men per every 100 black women. Based on data adjusted by the U.S. Bureau of the Census for the net census undercount, the 1970 black sex ratio of 96.2 declined slightly to 95.1 in 1979. But, using more recent population data (U.S. Bureau of the Census, 1982) for the total population of the United States, including persons abroad, the 1970 black sex ratio of 91.8 declined only slightly to 90.6 in 1981. As may be evident, precise data about the sizes of the black population by sex prohibit the determination of the exact sex ratio. Male excessiveness occurs among blacks under 20 years of age, while female excessiveness dominates in the remaining years. For example, in 1981, the black sex ratio for those between 20 and 29 years of age was only 93.4. Further, a growing number of blacks are not marrying when or soon after they reach adulthood. In 1981, for those between 20 and 24 years of age, 68.8 percent of black females and 80.2 percent of black males had never married, as was true for 35.7 percent of black females and 49.1 percent of black males between 25 and 29 years of age, and 20.7 percent of black females and 24.2 percent of black males between 30 and 34 years of age.

Table 8.2 contains selected familial characteristics of blacks in the United States in 1979 or 1980. In 1980, there were about 6.3 million black families, almost all of which were nonfarm families. Most of the farm families lived in the South. A slight majority of black families were husband-wife families. About two out of every five were female headed, with no husband present. Black female-headed families, only slightly smaller than husband-wife families in size, had substantially less income. On average, then, black female-headed families were poorer than black male-headed or spousal-headed families.

About 42 percent of black children under 18 years of age in the civilian, noninstitutionalized population lived with both of their parents in 1980, compared to almost 44 percent of their counterparts residing only with their mothers. Almost 11 percent of those children lived with other relatives only, and over 1 percent lived only with nonrelatives. Far fewer than one-third of the mothers with children present under 21 years of age, and with absent fathers, had been awarded child-support payments. Of those entitled to such payments, almost two-thirds had difficulty in receiving their payemnts. The 1979 mean payment, moreover, was only $1294 for the 12 months, a small sum in light of the estimated costs of child rearing.

Among women ever married, 15 to 44 years of age, in the 1979 civilian noninstitutional population, childlessness was about 12 percent. It is often forgotten that some black women are childless, a factor well worth noting for a number of reasons, but especially for those developing social policies for older blacks, a number of whom are childless.

The kinds of data presented above have varying implications for relationships between black families and black churches. Illustratively, structural implications for rural churches can be seen in the links between their generally small membership sizes and the sparse black rural population. Many black rural churches are served by circuit ministers holding several pastorates. Weekly services at any given church are rare. Circuit ministers increasingly reside in urban areas, as opposed to living among their rural congregants. Often, they also hold other jobs, sometimes full time, during the week.

TABLE 8.2   Selected Familial Characteristics of Blacks in the United States, 1979 or 1980

Characteristic		*Median Income (dollars)*
Total number of families, 1980		
(in thousands)	6,317	
% nonfarm	99.2	
% in central cities	56.1	
% in South	52.1	
Type of family, 1980		12,674
% married couples	53.7%	18,593
%female householder, no husband present	41.7%	7,425
% male householder, no wife present	4.6%	12,557
% of all families (excluding military		
families) with no earnings	19.0	
Average family size, 1979		
Husband-wife family	3.87	
Female householder, no husband present	3.63	
Male householder, no wife present	3.08	
Housing tenure, 1979, % owners		
All families	52.2%	
Husband-wife family	65.2%	
Female householder, no husband present	34.4%	
Male householder, no wife present	53.3%	
Living arrangements of children under 18		
years of age, 1980, civilian noninstitu-		
tional population:		
% living with both parents	42.2	
% living with mother only	43.8	
% living with father only	2.0	
% living with other relatives only	10.7	
% living with nonrelatives only	1.3	
Child-support payments for women with own		
children under 21 present from absent father		
Number of women, 1979 (in thousands)	1,895	
% awarded support payments	28.8	
% awarded payments who received payments	63.0	
Children ever born per 1,000 women, 18-44		
years, civilian noninstitutional population, 1979	1,927	
% childlessness for women ever married,		
15-44 years, civilian noninstitutional		
population, 1979	12.4	
Divorced persons per 1,000 married		
persons with spouse present, 1980		
Females	257	
Males	151	

SOURCE: U.S. Bureau of the Census (1981a, 1981b, 1980).

The location of most blacks in central cities has increased greatly the potential for relatively large memberships in some of the most popular churches, typically Baptist or Methodist. For ministers of those churches with political inclinations (and particularly for holding elective offices), these churches can provide a base of operations.

Substantively, the rising educational levels of church attendants, as well as the continuing problems of unemployment and poverty, have some effect on sermonic content and on church programs. The growing presence of female-headed households and of the aged also suggests a need for more diversification in church programs. Many black churches have already responded in varying ways to these challenges. Some have developed child care centers, nursing homes for the elderly, and the like. But, for the most part, relatively little church aid has been given in these directions, points more fully discussed in the culminating section.

DEMOGRAPHIC AND HISTORICAL PROFILE OF BLACK CHURCHES

Not only is relatively little known about the relationships between black families and black churches; relatively little is known about black religion itself, including the changing statuses of the tremendous variety of black churches over time. Mitchell (1975: 13) notes aptly that "the fact is that there have been no scholars of Black religion, per se, until recently, because the beliefs did not originate in academic settings and were not thought to have scholarly significance."

Using the present definition of black churches, the first black churches arose out of the Free African Society, whose founders included Richard Allen and Absalom Jones. Most of the few works available on black churches contain some historical notations. Those notations typically rely upon Woodson's (1921) account, as did Frazier[1] (1974: 32-33), who writes:

> The most famous of the Negro preachers in the North was, in a sense, Richard Allen because of the role which he played in the organization of an independent Negro church organization. Allen was born a slave in Philadelphia but was sold to a planter who took him to Delaware. He early came under the influence of Methodist preachers and was converted in 1777. He was allowed to conduct prayers and preach in the house of his master who became converted. In the same year, he and his brother were permitted to purchase their freedom from their master, who had become

convinced that slavery was wrong, for $2,000 in depreciated Continental currency.

After becoming free, Allen engaged in odd jobs but remained intensely religious and became a preacher in 1780. In recognition of his talents as a preacher he was allowed to travel with white ministers and given assignments by Bishop Asbury. When he went to Philadelphia in 1786 he was invited to preach in the St. George Methodist Episcopal Church. When Allen observed in Philadelphia the need of the Negroes for religious leadership and an organization, he proposed that a separate church be established for Negroes. His proposal was opposed both by whites and Negroes. However, when the number of Negroes attending St. George Methodist Episcopal church increased, Negroes were removed from the seats around the wall and ordered to sit in the gallery. Mistaking the section of the gallery which they were to occupy, Allen, Absalom Jones, and another member were almost dragged from their knees as they prayed. They left the church and together with other Negro members founded the Free African Society.

After Richard Allen and Absalom Jones organized the Free African Society, they differed as to whether Negroes should model their church organization after the Methodist or after the Protestant Episcopal Church. Allen was of the opinion that the Methodist form of worship was more suited to the religious needs and form of worship to which the Negroes had become accustomed. As a consequence of this difference between Jones and Allen, Jones organized the African Protestant Episcopal Church of St. Thomas but the majority of the Negroes who had seceded from the white church followed Allen. Allen organized the Bethel Church for which an old building was purchased and dedicated in 1794. Bishop Asbury ordained Allen a deacon and later he became an elder. The movement begun by Allen under the name of African societies spread to other cities where so-called African Methodist Episcopal Churches were set up. There was some cooperation among the leaders of the separate church organizations in the various cities. As a result, the representatives of these churches met in Philadelphia in 1816 and established the African Methodist Episcopal Church [as a connectional church]. At this meeting Allen was elected bishop and a book of discipline was adopted which embodied the same articles of religion and rules as the Wesleyans.

The above passages indicate clearly that the founding of independent black churches by free blacks grew out of racial disharmony. Moreover, these passages suggest strongly the development of parallel organizations — organizations segregated or separated racially, but not by religious tenets or rules.

But neither the African Protestant Episcopal Church of St. Thomas nor Bethel church was the first black church in the United

States. According to Mays and Nicholson (1933), the first Negro church was founded in Silver Bluff, South Carolina, sometime between 1773 and 1775, and, about 1779, a Negro Baptist church was established in Savannah, Georgia. But whether the origin of black churches is dated from the establishment of independent black churches by free blacks, or the development of black churches by blacks (with the permission of a slave owner) for blacks, black churches have existed in some form in the United States for more than 200 years. During that time, their proliferation has been absolutely nothing less than phenomenal, although relatively few of them today have substantially large memberships. Most black churches are still relatively small, with congregations typically under 300 active members.

Unfortunately, no accurate or comprehensive portrait of contemporary black denominations or their memberships can be drawn. The most recent data from the U.S. Bureau of the Census about the religious affiliations of Americans are old. Collected in March 1957, the data are not specific to blacks, but to nonwhites. Well over 90 percent of nonwhites were then black, but it is scientifically inaccurate to characterize the nonwhite data as black data. The specific question asked on a voluntary basis in that 1957 survey about religious affiliation was "What is your religion?" (U.S. Bureau of the Census, 1958). Table 8.3 contains the responses of the civilian, nonwhite population over 14 years of age, by sex, in that survey. It shows that over 89 percent of the females and 85 percent of the males were Protestants, most of whom were Baptists. In fact, about 3 of every 5 nonwhites in that sample indicated that they were Baptists. The next largest proportion were Methodists, about 17 percent for each sex. These data suggest that about 80 percent of blacks over 14 years of age in the United States in 1957 were Baptists or Methodists. Of the extremely few nonwhite members of the sample reporting "no religion," the proportion was somewhat higher among males than among females. Although the proportion of blacks today with a religious affiliation of Baptist or Methodist may be somewhat lower than 80 percent, the overwhelming percentage remain in one or the other of those broad denominational categories.

In the eighteenth century and the early part of the nineteenth century, Baptists and Methodists were usually more successful in Christianizing blacks than were their fellow evangelical Protestants. Their greater success may have been due in part to the fact that the Baptists and Methodists initially opposed slavery, a position that they typically and swiftly reversed as they encountered southern whites. Ironically, that very reversal gradually helped the Baptists and

TABLE 8.3   Religion Reported for Nonwhites Over 14 Years of Age, by Sex, in the Civilian Population of the United States, March 1957

Reported Religion	Female	Male
Protestant	89.4	85.4
Baptist	62.0	59.1
Methodist	17.5	17.0
Presbyterian	0.8	1.0
Lutheran	0.2	0.3
other Protestant	8.9	8.0
Roman Catholic	6.6	6.4
Jewish	0.1	—
Other	1.5	1.5
None	1.7	5.4
Religion not reported	0.7	1.3
Total	100.0	100.0

SOURCE: U.S. Bureau of the Census (1958).

Methodists to obtain greater access to plantation blacks. This generalization, expounded by Frazier (1974), is typically repeated in the few available works dealing with the historical origins of the prevalence of Baptists and Methodists among contemporary blacks. Futher, as Frazier suggests during and following slavery, and up to this very day, blacks tend to be more attracted to the Baptist than to other denominations, perhaps because the local autonomy of each Baptist church increases their hegemonic opportunities, at least within their communities. The custom of being Baptist is now fairly well entrenched in a number of black communities, but a growing number of blacks of upper-middle-class status especially are found in the Episcopal church or other predominantly white denominations with high prestige. Most often, however, the specific churches attended by these blacks are entirely or predominantly black and usually served by a black priest or minister.

Mead (1980: 42) provides some limited data about black religious identification:

Today, out of approximately 20,000,000 blacks in the United States, better than 10,000,000 are in the South, and 44 percent of the total black population are church members. They are grouped into a large number of churches and denominations. There are more than 30 recognized and entirely different black denominations, some with less than 20 members, but seven-eighths of our total black population [presumably with religious affiliations] is either Methodist or Baptist. Nearly 8,000,000 black Baptists are found in the two major conventions: 5,500,000 in the National Baptist Convention of U.S.A. Incorporated; and 2,668,799 in the National Baptist Convention of America, usually called the "unincorporated" body.

This passage suggests somewhat the considerable diversity of black religions, a diversity as varied as the sociocultural characteristics of blacks.[2]

Also, a comparison of Mead's statistics with the 1957 survey by the U.S. Bureau of the Census suggests that there may have been a proportionate drop in black church membership between 1957 and 1980. Despite the acceleration of gospel singing and clapping among a notable proportion of contemporary black college students and other blacks as well, the decrease in church membership seems probable. But it should be emphasized strongly that data indicating the size of black church membership and the religious preferences and affiliations of blacks are not available.

As previously noted, some blacks are affiliated with white or predominantly white denominations. Generally, blacks began worshiping in these denominations on an integrated basis, as judged by seating, gradually moving first from a segregated seating pattern within the church and then to racially segregated churches. In some few instances, however, worship remained on an interracial basis, as in the case of Baha'i. Types of denominations or religious bodies falling into both the racially segregated and integrated bodies of predominantly white religious institutions also include the Church of Jesus Christ of Latter-day Saints (Mormons), the Protestant Episcopal church (more generally known as the Episcopal church, an alternate name adopted by its 1967 General Convention), Friends (or Quakers), Jehovah's Witnesses, Seventh-day Adventists, Roman Catholic church, Mennonites, Moravian church, Muslims (separate entirely from the World Community of Al-Islam), United Presbyterian Church in the U.S.A., Unitarian Universalist Association, and the United Church of Christ.

A major issue that may be raised about black participation in predominantly white religious institutions concerns the characteristics that distinguish them from blacks who only maintain religious membership in all-black institutions. Contributory factors obviously include socioeconomic status, geographical location, and migratory status to that geographical location. It may be hypothesized that blacks of high socioeconomic status, whose incomes are derived largely or entirely from salaried (as opposed to self-employed) positions, are more likely than other blacks to flock to the predominantly white churches, even if specific churches within those denominations have a history of racial segregation. This may be particularly true of blacks whose religious affiliation in their adult years differs from that of their childhood years.

Over time, some blacks have belonged to a variety of sects or cults, such as the Father Divine movement. Father Divine, himself married to a white woman when he died, forbade marital relations between his followers within his "kingdom." His movement flourished especially during the worst years of the Depression in the 1930s. The United House of Prayer represents an outgrowth of the Sweet Daddy Grace movement, whose group during much of his lifetime was known as the House of Prayer for All People. Additionally, metropolitan areas with relatively large black populations frequently contain a number of storefront churches that have been typically organized by a single individual and that attract a limited number of participants.

An obvious point made above is the considerable heterogeneity of religious participation by blacks, a heterogeneity often masked by the traditional characterization of blacks as primarily Protestants by social scientists and religious scholars. The great diversity of religious beliefs and practices of blacks prevents categorizing them easily into a single "black box." Attempts to do so have limited greatly our current knowledge and understanding of relationships between black families and black churches.

KEY ISSUES AFFECTING CONTEMPORARY FAMILIES

In the absence of any known consensus on the order and priority of issues facing black families, one presumption is that the key issues related to black families and black churches deal with such topics as premarital and extramarital sex, abortion, illegitimacy, sex roles, divorce, and the economic well-being of family members. These issues are ultimately inseparable from the effects of racism on the quality of life available to blacks. Dealing with racism, in turn, involves some consideration of the political roles of black churches on the local, state, and national levels. In the discussion that follows, specific attention is focused on these issues, primarily on a speculative level.

Premarital and Extramarital Sex

An assessment of the Christian and non-Christian beliefs of the various religious bodies to which blacks typically belong suggests strong taboos against premarital and extramarital sex. But there are many variations on this theme. The folklore among many blacks is that some black ministers (albeit a minority) encourage both premarital and extramarital sex among their members by their own behaviors. That is, they engage in premarital or extramarital sex, sometimes with members of their congregations. This pattern is still sufficiently widespread to raise questions about discrepancies between "what I say and what I do" when ministers are perceived as role models.

With the probable exception of the cult leaders' own behaviors, the cults seem to have been more successful than are traditional black denominations in curbing premarital and extramarital sex. Fauset's (1974) study of five black religious cults in Philadelphia in the early 1940s does not speak directly to this question, but he notes that fornication and adultery were taboo, as were such behaviors as lying, stealing, backbiting, indulgence in athletic games, movies, wearing short dresses, chewing gum, and gambling. Perhaps because participation in a cult is more intensified, time consuming, and exhaustive than is participation in a religious denomination, control of sexual behavior is more critical in gaining control of the individual. Cults tend to seek fuller control of the individual's entire life. Denominations are far less involved in the totality of the life of an individual member. Many denominational pastors typically see their members only when they attend formal worship services. Cult leaders have much more frequent interaction with their members. Thus sexual control may be used as a weapon for mind control within the cults, as opposed to its being used to promote piety.

Preachings against premarital sex within many black churches were sometimes accompanied by sly remarks akin to "A shoe should not be bought unless it fits," or, more coarsely, "Try on the shoe before you buy it." It is difficult to determine to what extent black churches actually condemn premarital sex, particularly in light of shifting attitudes affected by technological developments in contraceptives. But most black churches probably condemn promiscuity. They probably tolerate extramarital sex conducted discretely, but condemn it if a scandal erupts. The gaps between religious beliefs opposing premarital and extramarital sex and the personal beliefs of religiously affiliated blacks is probably greater among men than among women, largely because women have been subjected to differential standards of sexual conduct during their formative years. Clearly, empirical investigation is needed about these gaps and the factors affecting them.

Whatever the prevailing religious philosophies of blacks about premarital and extramarital sex, both have increased in recent years. This increase, of course, is not unique to blacks, but is a part of the larger social fabric. When undesired consequences occur, such as illegitimate children or marital disruption, a question arises about the social control of black churches over blacks. This, too, is an empirical question.

Abortion and Illegitimacy

Most black churches seem to oppose abortion for many reasons, ranging from concerns about black genocide to religious beliefs about murder. But the rates of abortion and illegitimacy have typically risen among blacks, as well as nonblacks, in recent years. One problem in dealing with abortion and illegitimacy is that the moral pronouncements are usually made by males, while females are those most intimately involved. Almost nothing is known about the interaction of female-male attitudes related to abortion and illegitimacy.

What is known, however, is that most males who are absolutely opposed to abortion do not seem to exhibit significant behaviors related to providing money and other support to affected females. For example, far too many black males do not connect the critical question of *not* aborting with support for the resulting infant. Moreover, most blacks still typically blame women, and not men, for pregnancies, even when the women did not intend to become pregnant. Many religious pronouncements in this area also blame women more readily than men.

While many black churches remain opposed to both abortion and illegitimacy, their ministers are rarely involved in "prolife" movements. Neither, for that matter, are their congregants. Involvement by black ministers to make certain that abortions remain illegal, or are declared illegal, is rare. When the subject is abortion, most black ministers and their congregations are publicly silent.

One norm violated with increasing frequency pertains to illegitimate births. Illegitimacy is definitely frowned upon by most black churches. Why, then, has there been such a significant growth of illegitimate births among blacks since at least the late 1930s? Frazier's (1939) analysis of black families is helpful here. Elsewhere, Jackson (1973: 198) describes a portion of Frazier's analysis:

> The [black] matriarchate's prestige was not to rise "in the City of Rebirth," although this family type inherited from slavery continued to exist on a relatively large scale. Urbanization induced family desertion and "outlawed motherhood" as well, for Blacks themselves were developing negative attitudes toward illegitimate children. Blacks of the dominant family types in the city frowned upon illegitimacy. These included the upper class, the Brown middle class, and the patriarchal Black proletariat, all distinguishable from

the matriarchal Black proletariat. The small group of families comprising the upper classes were readily distinguishable from the masses by their higher moral standards and their superior culture. The Brown middle class, a new class developing during the rapid urbanization around World War I, could be differentiated from the upper class through their newness, their salaried positions by and large [often with both spouses employed], and their tendency toward egalitarian, rather than patriarchal, family authority.

Illegitimate births seem to be most pronounced among members of the matriarchal proletariat. This black underclass has few, if any, effective role models of fathers functioning according to the prevailing American norms.

Black churches probably exercise little social control over the matriarchal proletariat, due partially to the relatively low level of their participation in on-site religious activities. Also, it is quite likely that many black churches, and particularly the major established denominations, are lukewarm or generally unreceptive to the matriarchal proletariat who are poor and residing in metropolitan areas. In the absence of sufficient data to support the aforementioned generalizations, an attitude of a minister in a city where 65 percent of black births were illegitimate in 1980, as reported by Williams (1981), is illuminating and thought provoking:

"I think 50 percent of the children I christen are illegitimate," says the Rev. Knighton Stanley of the People's Congregational Church on 13th Street NW [Washington, D.C.]. "It's no fault of the children, of course. The children aren't so much illegitimate as the parents are illegitimate. I would not deny any illegitimate child the right to be christened but I wish the parents would not force me to christen the child at the 11 o'clock service before my son and daughter."

In light of the significantly large number of black churches in the nation's capitol, an important inference is that those churches do not or cannot act as effective agents of social control in curbing illegitimacy. What remains to be determined is the cause of that failure, or if, indeed, such attempted control is the responsibility of black churches. I think not.

Determining the cause of the increased proportion of illegitimate births in localities such as the District of Columbia also requires some consideration of the changing demographic composition of their black residents. For example, the movement of middle- and upper-class blacks outside of the District and, to a lesser extent, a similar movement of the patriarchal black proletariat into the surrounding suburbs of Virginia and Maryland, would necessarily lead to rising illegitimacy rates within the city. More simply put, as fewer and fewer black women who are married give birth in the city, the proportion of unmarried black women giving birth increases. Many more of the married women whose counterparts previously lived in the city now use hospitals outside the District. Thus their infants are not recorded as having been born in the District. The black matriarchal proletariat are those least likely to have migrated to the surrounding environs, or, more properly within the present context, are those least likely to have given birth outside of the District. That group represents a growing proportion of blacks in central cities. It should be expected that the changing socioeconomic status or marital status of a black population within a given area will have some impact on the frequency and percentage distributions of illegitimate births within that population.

Sex Roles

According to Genesis (2:18), after the Lord God made Adam, He said, "It is not good that the man should be alone; I will make him an help meet for him." So the Lord God (Genesis, 2:21-24)

> caused a deep sleep to fall upon Adam, and he slept; and he took one of his ribs, and closed up the flesh instead thereof;
>
> And the rib, which the Lord God had taken from man, made He a woman, and brought her unto the man.
>
> And Adam said, This is now bone of my bones, and flesh of my flesh: she shall be called Woman, because she was taken out of Man.
>
> Therefore shall a man leave his father and his mother, and shall cleave unto his wife: and they shall be one flesh.

These verses essentially explain the dominant view of black denominations about sex roles. Women, made from men, are subservient to men. Given the patriarchal character of both American Christianity and the plantation system, it is not surprising that black churches would reflect the traditionally subservient view of women.

Nor is it surprising that many black women of the past and the present have accepted subservience as morally right. Zilpha Elaw, born in Pennsylvania and reared largely by Quakers after the death of her parents, was a black woman who united herself with the Methodist Episcopal church in 1808. Later becoming a minister or at least a ministerial traveler, several of her observations are decidedly on point. Marrying in 1810, Elaw (1846: 13) later noted that her husband was

> a very respectable young man, in the general acceptance of the term, but he was not a Christian, — that is, a sincere and devoted disciple

of Christ, though nominally bearing His name. Oh! let me
affectionately warn my dear unmarried sisters in Christ, against
being thus unequally yoked with unbelievers.

Or again, after having indicated that a father's guardianship and
government of his daughter continued until her father surrendered
her to the care and government of her husband, Elaw (1846: 14-15)
stressed:

> That woman is dependent on and subject to man, is the dictate of
> nature; that the man is not created for the woman, but the woman for
> the man, is that of Scripture; these principles lie at the foundation of
> the family and social systems; and their violation is a very immoral
> and guilty act.

Frazier's (1974: 39) analysis of the Negro church indicated that,
following slavery, "the new economic position of the man was
consolidated by the moral support of the Negro church." This new
economic position involved patriarchal control over the family, as
well as economic responsibility for the family. But the husband and
father also needed and controlled the labor of his family, as in farming
operations. In Frazier's (1974: 39-40) words,

> There was, of course, moral support for a patriarchal family to be
> found in the Bible and this fact contributed undoubtedly a holy
> sanction to the new authority of the Negro man in the family.
> However, there were more important ways in which the Negro
> church gave support to Negro family life with the father in the
> position of authority. . . . The leaders in creating a new community
> life were men who with their families worked land or began to buy
> land or worked as skilled artisans. It is important to observe that
> these pioneers built a church as well as homes. Many of these
> pioneer leaders were preachers who gathered their communicants
> about them and became the leaders of the Negro communities. This
> fact tends to reveal the close relationships between the newly
> structured life of the Negro and his church organization.

Already established prior to the cessation of slavery, the black
church was, aside from the black family, probably the only black
institution already structured at slavery's end. But it was structured,
as Frazier indicates, to provide male authority. While Wilberforce
University had been established as a black institution before the end
of slavery, soon thereafter a number of black educational institutions
arose, including Howard, Johnson C. Smith, and Shaw universities,
and St. Augustine's College. The last three of these were church

sponsored. The emergence of .these institutions and the growing educational levels of blacks, as previously noted, are factors that have lessened considerably any overall hegemony black preachers may have enjoyed in black communities.

The significant heterogeneity of black churches, including their doctrinal variations, makes it difficult — in fact, impossible — to generalize about their positions on sex roles beyond the typical pattern of a belief in the subordination of females to males. Certainly within the church, the preferred sex for the position of minister or spiritual leader is male. The 1970 census showed that 96.1 percent of the 12,850 black clergy then in the United States were male. The top-level administrative positions in most black churches are still held by males. Historically, women were rarely, if ever, permitted to function as trustees or in similar capacities. Female participation in administrative or official roles of the church, such as on a Steward Board in an African Methodist Episcopal church (AME) is only slightly more prevalent today. The vast majority of laypersons holding official positions within black churches are still male, despite the generally greater preponderance of women among church members. Women have typically been more involved in housekeeping chores, Sunday schools, and missionary work within the churches. Black churches generally follow traditional role segregation by sex, perhaps a reflection of the adherence of both sexes to patriarchal authority, buttressed often by religious beliefs and customs.

Black churches do not have a single position on the Equal Rights Amendment movement. Some support it, others oppose it, and still others remain neutral. As for other social issues, the positions of black churches require localization. An AME church on one street in New York, for example, may support an issue, while an adjacent AME church may not. These positional variances must be considered in light of doctrinal tenets and autonomy of given churches, applicable characteristics of ministers and congregations, and the prevailing Zeitgeist.

Perhaps the World Community of Al-Islam is the largest black religious body in the United States today to prescribe and proscribe familial behavior. In addition to segregated seating by sex during worship, the prescribed sex roles within the family are typically segregated by specific tasks. But both spouses are urged to work together cooperatively to benefit themselves, their children, and their religious community.

Several informants with wide experience in particular types of black churches, most notably Baptist churches in metropolitan areas, indicate that most black churches have not taken specific positions on the issue of sex roles from the pulpit, have remained essentially conservative in their views, or both. But in the instances of the relatively few black ministers who also hold or seek public offices, it is quite likely that they favor the ERA for women when they think that position will enhance them politically. Since those opinions were obtained from the informants, an incident occurred that sheds some light on certain relationships between religious positions and the acquisition of public appointments. Specifically, in 1982, a middle-aged black conservative minister from Pennsylvania was nominated by the president of the United States for appointment to the U.S. Civil Rights Commission. A number of factors ultimately led to his withdrawing his nomination, one of which was probably negative reaction to his publicly stated opposition to the ERA.

Divorce

Historically, most black churches seemed to have been opposed to divorce, adhering to a traditionally American belief that divorce was sinful. But the relationships between black families and black churches in considering divorce should be shifted more nearly to whether black couples contemplating divorce seek pastoral counseling. Today, not only do most blacks not view divorce as sinful, but most of them probably reject pastoral counseling about divorce.

Economic Support for Dependent Family Members

Historically, too, a number of black churches helped to form and maintain beneficial societies to assist needy blacks. Frazier (1974: 41), among others, describes broadly their functions, including their germination of "secular insurance companies." Many black churches today continue to provide some economic support for dependent members and other needy individuals. But direct aid is not nearly as great as it was some decades ago. Indirect aid, instead, has grown. For example, black churches now are more likely to support legislation considered to be beneficial to black economic conditions and to urge their members to vote for political candidates most in tune with those needs. They are also more likely to refer needy individuals to community agencies. The age-old tradition of proffering small amounts of food to poor families for Thanksgiving or Christmas continues in many churches, but on a smaller scale than in previous years.

Also, needy black families are much less likely today to seek financial aid from their churches. Many of them are not even church members or are not frequent attendants. Black families requiring financial aid are much more likely to seek help directly from public agencies or from private agencies in the secular sphere.

The Aged

Somewhat over 2 million blacks in the United States were over 65 years of age in 1982. Their religious affiliation tends to be higher than that of young blacks. To the extent that their health permits, their religious attendance is also generally better. This may be especially true of rural blacks. The increasing emphasis on problems of the aged has not gone unnoticed by most black churches, but far fewer are directly involved in providing specific services to the elderly or in planning specific ongoing church programs for them. Most black churches are also not involved in nonprofit ownership and operation of long-term care facilities for the aged, partially because many of these churches are located in areas too small to generate a sufficient number of patients to justify the operation of a nursing home. A few black churches, chiefly in metropolitan areas, have, however, sponsored long-term care facilities for many years. It is likely that more black churches will become involved in various types of programs for the elderly in the near future. A contingency factor may be the availability of federal funds for seed monies.

Several years ago, a unit of the Progressive Baptist Conference sponsored an enlightened conference on aged blacks, attended mostly by interested ministers. Some consideration was given to the role of the aged in black churches and to how those churches might help upgrade the quality of life for the aged. One conference participant, a Baptist minister and a rest home owner in a southern town, had participated in two summer workshops I had directed on aged blacks. Since then, he has promoted a workshop session on aged blacks at his annual conventions. He reports that the interest was initially minimal, but that it has increased dramatically as more and more black ministers and laypersons become aware of the aging of the black population and its implications for their churches.

A reasonable presumption is not only that more black churches will focus on the needs and problems of the aged in future years, even though, to date, no national body of black churches has developed a specific task force to concentrate on the aged. It is also likely that black churches of black denominations will focus more heavily on retirement pensions not only for their ministers, but also for their layworkers in the future, including their choir directors and janitors.

FAMILIAL AND POLITICAL ROLES OF BLACK CHURCHES

Two commonplace myths today are that black churches represent the gravitational centers of black communities and the avant-garde for black equality. These myths contain a grain of truth, but empirical research is needed to determine the precise community and advocatory roles that black churches *qua* black churches play, including those that remain neutral to or oppose civil rights and other efforts designed to bring about black equality.

Frazier (1974: 51) long ago noted the general conservatism of the Negro church when he stated that:

> The Negro church with its own forms of religious worship was a world which the white man did not invade but only regarded with an attitude of condescending amusement. The Negro church could enjoy this freedom so long as it offered no threat to the white man's dominance in both economic and social relations. And, on the whole, the Negro's church was not a threat to white domination and aided the Negro to become accommodated to an inferior status. The religion of the Negro continued to be other-worldly in its outlook, dismissing the privations and sufferings and injustices of this world as temporary and transient. The Negro church remained a refuge despite the fact that the Negro often accepted the disparagement of Negroes by whites and the domination of whites.[3]

Lincoln (1974), who distinguishes between the Negro church and the black church, opined that the Negro church conceptualized by Frazier was dead. That Negro church died, according to Lincoln (1974: 106-107), "because the norms and presuppositions which structured and conditioned it are not the relevant norms and presuppositions to which contemporary Blacks who represent the future of religion in the Black community can give their asseveration and support." Recognizing at least the ambivalence of many Negro churches on the issue of civil rights, Lincoln (1974: 108) contends that the black church "has produced some of freedom's most celebrated leadership . . . but the Negro Church *qua* Church traditionally courted such a conservative image as to have seldom been considered a threat to prevailing social values." In general, both Frazier and Lincoln agree that Negro churches are typically conservative. But Lincoln's definition of the black church infers a certain stance toward freedom, reinforced by action, that is not even true today of most churches. Consequently, his assertion that the Negro church is dead is rhetorical and not empirically valid.

Left unanswered, too, in Lincoln's assertion is whether the black churches were responsible for producing some of those most cele-brated leaders, or whether those leaders needed the element of a membership base for followers. Another element is whether the independence of black churches can produce opportunities for blacks who can become leaders on controversial issues, largely because their economic well-being is not dependent on wages or salaries from white or white-controlled employers.

Impressionistic judgments and informal interviews with a dozen or so black scholars on at least "nodding terms" with black churches (as distinguished from the earlier informants, whose knowledge of an experience with black churches were much greater) suggested strongly that Frazier's version of the Negro church is very much alive today. Relatively few black churches have been actively involved in black protest movements over time. Much of the prominence, they contend, that has been given to Martin Luther King, Jr., is often vicariously and erroneously attributed to black churches per se, as opposed to specifically supporting congregations.

Individuals knowledgeable about the emergence of the Montgomery bus protest of the mid-1950s and its subsequent history know that it did not originate within a black church. Instead, one black church and eventually a number of black churches were used as meeting sites. At that time, racial segregation prevented black access to city-owned public places of adequate size for the meetings, and it is doubtful if the white board of education would have permitted the Montgomery Improvement Association to have used public school buildings. But not all black churches in Montgomery were even supportive of the bus protest, nor would all black churches have permitted the use of their premises for mass meetings. In the 1950s, these phenomena were characteristic of other places in Alabama as well, such as Tuskegee, Birmingham, and Selma. They were not unheard of in other places outside Alabama.

One important consequence of the Montgomery bus protest[4] was that it brought together a variety of individuals with and without religious affiliations, representing various races and socioeconomic statuses. It helped to focus national and international attention on the fact that basic provisions of the Constitution of the United States of America were being violated. Further, it culminated legally in *Gayle v. Browder,* 352 U.S. 903 (1956), which technically overturned the separate-but-equal doctrine of *Plessy v. Ferguson,* 163 U.S. 537 (1896). *Gayle* represented a significant victory for a local movement led by a black minister. The movement also caused many Americans and others of all races to question critically the real meaning of Christianity, including the equitable brotherhood of humankind.

Aside from the long-established efforts of the National Association for the Advancement of Colored People to increase the number of black registered voters and actual voters, several religious bodies also encouraged registration and voting. The most notable black religious organization engaged in this task was the National Baptist Convention, U.S.A., Inc., under the leadership of Dr. Joseph H. Jackson, its president from 1953 until 1982. Jackson also underscored the federal role by noting that "the Federal Government should take a great responsibility in determining and protecting citizenship rights" (National Baptist Voice, 1975: 1, 3).

Another issue concerns the fact that black religious leadership in civil rights or related movements is heavily dependent on the extent to which black religious leaders are financially independent of whites. While not ignoring the significant financial contributions of many individual whites and white organizations to black civil rights movements or movements for economic equality, most *true* black leaders have been heavily dependent on blacks, and not on whites, for their financial well-being. In this regard, for example, one could question whether Jesse Jackson, president of PUSH, based in Chicago, Illinois, represents a true black leader, or one who more nearly owes a considerable amount of his imagery as a leader to the predominantly white media.

By and large, there are only two major groups within the black community whose economic well-being is solely or more nearly in black than in white hands. The first group usually contains self-employed professionals, such as physicians and dentists. It also contains most salaried black ministers, some of whom may also be dependent on whites for their additional earnings in other jobs. The larger black churches or those with predominantly middle-class congregations are less likely than their opposites to have a minister employed outside the church.

Perhaps some distinction should be made between outside employment by black ministers that is merely for additional income and that which is devoted to an issue considered to be relevant for blacks. For example, the Rev. Leon Ralph, a former member of the California State Legislature and an active pastor of a church in California, has also been employed by the Federation for American Immigration Reform, based in Washington, D.C. He commutes between his two jobs primarily because he is vitally interested in helping to bring about effective federal action on immigration control. One of his serious concerns is the negative impact on the employment of blacks in the secondary labor market by the continued stream of illegal aliens.

While many black churches were not actively involved in the black civil rights movements of the 1950s and 1960s, some others were. Morris (1981: 748) has argued that the black southern student sit-in movement of the late 1950s and early 1960s was clearly connected to the black church:

> The black church served as the major institutional force behind the sit-ins. . . . Nearly all of the direct-action organizations that initiated these early sit-ins were closely associated with the church. The church supplied these organizations not only with an established communication network, but also leaders and organized masses, finances, and a safe environment in which to hold political meetings. Direct-action organizations clung to the church because their survival depended on it.

Certainly those black churches that were active in the black civil rights movement also aided, even if only indirectly, black families. The sit-in movement, for example, enabled many black parents to use racially desegregated public facilities when they were on a shopping spree downtown or when they traveled away from home.

One can also inquire about the extent to which black churches help black families achieve the dominant American values, described by D'Antonio in Chapter 4 of this volume. The only study on this subject I was able to locate that provided some empirical insight was by Scanzoni (1971). His data generally suggest that his 1968 block-quota sample of 400 black husbands or wives who had been married for at least 5 years and who lived in Indianapolis, Indiana, tended to feel that their churches had been helpful to them in their marital selections and successes, as well as in helping them to acquire dominant American values. Scanzoni (1971: 126) concludes that most of his respondents benefited through the provision of church services that supplemented their familial resources, thereby aiding "them in performance of adult roles and thus in their later marital stability."

Unfortunately, Scanzoni's (1971) results cannot be generalized to the larger population of blacks married for more than five years in 1968, nor to all black families in 1968, let alone to black families today. Thus we have come full circle, back to our starting point, acknowledging the limited amount of research about contemporary relationships between black families and black churches, a subject definitely in need of rational and empirical investigation.

CONCLUSIONS

This chapter began on a speculative note because a reasonable review of available literature showed that relatively little was known about contemporary relationships between black families and black churches. Many of the generalizations about black religious attitudes and behaviors simply have not been validated. Many of the generalizations about the interaction between families and religion among blacks also remain unvalidated.

It is quite clear that the physical structures of black churches were used frequently years ago as the equivalent of community centers, political halls, and the like. Greater access to other physical structures has undoubtedly lessened the demand by black groups to use black church facilities for nonreligious purposes. But we do not know empirically about the shifts in the use of various physical structures for nonreligious, and even for religious, purposes. As a final illustration, the significant growth of well-educated blacks in many different disciplines has lessened greatly the dependence that blacks may have had on their ministers in years past, a number of whom were themselves poorly educated. It seems probable that the status and prestige of ministers in black communities has declined considerably over the years. This decline in status and prestige is associated with a number of factors, but what are those factors?

Because I have raised far more questions than I have answered, perhaps the most feasible way to end this chapter is to suggest some needed research on the topic of institutional relationships between black families and black churches, a topic that could be feasibly approached with a normative orientation.

(1) Major research priority should be given to the development of a cross-sectional study of the descriptive characteristics of black families and black churches. Such a study would employ a nationwide, representative sample. Given the frequent tendency of many social scientists to make racial comparisons, it may be feasible to include white families and churches as subjects in this survey.

In light of the current reductions in public funding for social research, I do not suggest a longitudinal study or a study encompassing also a longitudinal design. It may also be feasible to consider less costly types of studies that could lead toward greater knowledge and understanding of black family-black church relationships, perhaps through dissertational research.

(2) Within a selected geographical area, a study could be undertaken to determine the specific uses made of church facilities over a period of time. One concern would be the extent to which black churches double as community centers today.

(3) Also within a selected geographical area, a feasible study could be undertaken to determine the sermonic content related to public policies and public issues. A content analysis of the sermons of black ministers could yield useful information about the influence of demographic characteristics of the ministers and their congregations on sermonic selection and acceptance.

(4) A study in social stratification might be undertaken to determine the hierarchy of social status and prestige blacks within a given community assign to the ministerial and other occupational positions. Then, using only the ministers within the given community, further description and analysis could help determine the rankings assigned to specific ministers and the factors influencing those rankings.

(5) A description and analysis of blacks who are and who are not members of churches could help greatly in shedding light on distinguishing characteristics. Further, the data could also be examined to determine distinguishing characteristics among blacks of various denominations, and among blacks professing the same denomination but who attend predominantly black or predominantly white churches of that denomination within a given city. Also, it may be useful to distinguish between active and "paper" members of black churches, with the latter being defined as those who join a church but rarely attend or contribute to church activities.

(6) The above study could also extend to a determination of the expectations that blacks hold about what black ministers and black churches ought to do to aid their families. The specific question concerns the functions of black churches vis-à-vis black families.

If and when the kinds of studies suggested above are completed, I suspect that the tremendous heterogeneity of both black families and black churches will make it difficult to generalize about them across the board, principally because, in reality, there really is no "black church" or "black family." Instead, there are black churches and black families.

NOTES

1. Woodson's (1921) work is probably the chief reference on which subsequent social scientists of black churches have relied for historical information. Frazier, a noted sociologist who was also black, died before the publication of his work on the Negro church. I do not know if he had completed the manuscript in its entirety at that time. In a memoir in the original and subsequent publications of that work, Everett C. Hughes, a white sociologist, characterizes Frazier's career as having been "devoted . . . mainly to the study of two American institutions, the Negro family and the Negro church" (Frazier, 1974: 5). Although Frazier notes the support of Negro churches for the establishment of patriarchal authority in some black families

following the Civil War, he never describes or analyzes in any detail relationships between the families and the churches. His works related to this subject generally do not provide historical or empirical data to document clearly his conclusions. But this criticism is not an effort to downgrade Frazier's work as a sociologist. With the possible exception of W.E.B. Du Bois, Frazier remains the most prescient and perceptive of all black sociologists, living or dead.

2. In *The Black Church in the U.S.*, Banks (1972: 49), cites the following membership statistics for blacks by religious affiliation:

Statistics in 1916 for the four major all-black groups were: Baptists, 3,196,623; AME, 545,814; AMEZ, 456,813; CME, 202,713.

The 1971 World Almanac gives this breakdown for 1970: National Baptist Convention, USA, Inc., 6,487,003; National Baptist Convention of America, 2,668,799; Progressive Baptist Convention, 521,692; AME, 1,166,301; AMEX, 850,389; and CME, 66,718.

These statistics do not tell the complete story, of course. Pentecostal and apostolic churches are omitted; figures for some groups are difficult to obtain.

Today nearly one million Negroes are in the major white churches. Latest figures are found in the Negro Handbook of 1966. They are: Methodist Episcopal, 373,327; American Baptist, 200,000. There may be some overlap here because some National Baptist churches are dually aligned, belonging both to the Negro conventions and to the white convention. They are listed as follows: Congregational, 38,000; Christian Churches (Disciples of Christ), 800,000; Protestant Episcopal, 73,867; Seventh Day Adventist, 167,892; United Church of Christ, 21,859; United Presbyterian, USA, 6,000. Add to these the nearly 800,000 black Roman Catholics and the many other smaller Protestant groups and we estimate there are two million Negroes belonging to predominantly white denominations, compared with the estimated twelve million belonging to black denominations.

Also, Mead (1980) does not provide a comprehensive listing of all black denominations or cults. Those that are listed include the African Orthodox church; Black Baptists (whose different conventions include the National Baptist Convention of the U.S.A., Incorporated, the National Baptist Convention of America, the Progressive Baptist Convention [organized in 1961, following a dispute between Martin Luther King, Jr., and the National Baptist Convention of the U.S.A., Inc.], the National Baptist Evangelical Life and Soul Saving Assembly of the U.S.A., and the National Primitive Baptist Convention of the U.S.A. [formerly the Colored Primitive Baptists]); Bible Way church; World Wide (a Pentecostal body); Black Muslims (now the World Community of Al-Islam); Fire Baptized Holiness church; Free Christian Zion Church of Christ; Black Jews; Kodesh Church of Immanuel (the vast majority of whom are black); African Methodist Episcopal church (the denomination founded by Richard Allen); African Methodist Episcopal Zion church; African Union First Colored Methodist Protestant church, Inc.; Christian Methodist Episcopal church (established in 1870, it was known as the Colored Methodist Episcopal church until 1954); Independent African Methodist Episcopal church; Reformed Methodist Union Episcopal church; Reformed Zion Union Apostolic church; and the Union American Methodist Episcopal church.

It may also be noted that for the past few years, ecumenical discussions have been occurring between several predominantly white and all-black denominations, including especially the African Methodist Episcopal Church.

3. This position may seem to be congradictory to that taken by Escott (1979). Escott, however, was merely concerned with the religion of the Negro slaves, as recalled by blacks during interviews held in 1927, 1929-1930, or 1936-1938. Perhaps the most difficult problem here, as Escott (1979) mentions, is memory. Inasmuch as

the Civil War ended in 1865, with the Emancipation Proclamation having preceded it by 2 years, the youngest subject to have been born a slave would have been at least 62 years old at the time of interview and born in the year in which the Civil War ended. It is very doubtful that the recollections Escott includes about religion (but not about churches, an important difference because Frazier's work was focused on churches, and not on religion per se) can be regarded as accurate representations of slave religion. Further, Escott (1979) fails to recognize that much of the "long-term memory" of the aged is selectively rehearsed memory, and memory that may well have been distorted to be made more pleasurable over time. Thus, Escott's work should not be regarded as valid on the subject of slave religion. Rather, it represents a codification of the recollections of some former slaves as they reported those recollections to interviewers. Escott's (1979: 116) characterization of the role of ministers during slavery is that they "were a force that strengthened the slave community and worked for its liberation." He does not provide any evidence whatsoever to support his view. It is extremely doubtful that most black ministers who were slaves performed in that fashion, although one cannot discount at all the significant role of Nat Turner, whose rebellion ended with his death.

4. For an empirical study of the Montgomery protest and the Montgomery Improvement Association that contains a description and analysis of data collected from a sample of the MIA members during the time of the protest, see Clarke (1962).

REFERENCES

Banks, W. L. (1972) The Black Church in the U.S. Chicago: Moody.

Clarke, J. J. (1962) These Rights They Seek. Washington, DC: Public Affairs.

Elaw, Z. (1846) Memoirs of the Life, Religious Experience, Ministerial Travels and Labours of Mrs. Zilpha Elaw. London: Zilpha Elaw. (Sold by T. Dudley, 19 Charter-House Lane, and Mr. B. Taylor, 19 Montague St., Spitalfields.)

Escott, P. D. (1979) Slavery Remembered. Chapel Hill: University of North Carolina Press.

Fauset, A. H. (1974) Black Gods of the Metropolis. New York: Octagon.

Frazier, E. F. (1974) The Negro Church in America. New York: Schocken.

——— (1939) The Negro Family in the United States. Chicago: University of Chicago Press.

Jackson, J. H. (1980) A Story of Christian Activism: The History of the National Baptist Convention, U.S.A., Inc. Nashville: Townsend.

Jackson, J. J. (1973) "Black women in a racist society," pp. 185-268 in C. V. Willie et al. (eds.) Racism and Mental Health: Essays. Pittsburgh: University of Pittsburgh Press.

Johnston, R. F. (1954) The Development of Negro Religion. New York: Philosophical Library.

Lincoln, C. E. (1974) The Black Church Since Frazier. New York: Schocken.

——— (1961) The Black Muslims in America. Boston: Beacon.

Mays, B. E. and J. W. Nicholson (1933) The Negro's Church. New York: Russell & Russell.

Mead, F. (1980) Handbook of Denominations in the United States. Nashville: Abingdon.

Mitchell, H. H. (1975) Black Belief. New York: Harper & Row.

Morris, A. (1981) "Black southern student sit-in movement: an analysis of internal organization." American Sociological Review 46: 744-767.

National Baptist Voice (1975) October issue.

National Committee of Negro Churchmen (1968) "Black power: a statement by the National Committee of Negro Churchmen, on July 31, 1966," pp. 264-271 in F. Barbour (ed.) The Black Power Revolt. Boston: Extending Horizons.

Nelsen, H. M. and A. K. Nelsen (1975) Black Church in the Sixties. Lexington: University Press of Kentucky.

Scanzoni, J. H. (1971) The Black Family in Modern Society. Boston: Allyn & Bacon.

Sernett, M. C. (1972) "Black religion and American evangelicalism: white Protestants, plantation missions, and the independent Negro church, 1787-1865." Ph. D. dissertation, University of Delaware.

U.S. Bureau of the Census (1982) Preliminary Estimates of the Population of the United States, by Age, Sex, and Race: 1970 to 1981. Current Population Reports, Series P-25, No. 917. Washington, DC: Government Printing Office.

—— (1981a) Population Profile of the United States: 1980. Current Population Reports, Series P-20, No. 363. Washington, DC: Government Printing Office.

—— (1981b) Money Income and Poverty Status of Families and Persons in the United States: 1980. Advance data from the March 1981 Current Population Survey. Washington, DC: Government Printing Office.

—— (1980) Household and Family Characteristics: March 1979. Current Population Reports, Series P-20, No. 352. Washington, DC: Government Printing Office.

—— (1958) Religion Reported by the Civilian Population of the United States: March 1957. Current Population Reports, Series P-20, No. 79. Washington, DC: Government Printing Office.

Williams, J. (1981) "Illegitimacy." Washington Post (October 6): A-21, column B-E.

Woodson, C. G. (1921) The History of the Negro Church. Washington, DC: Associated.

9

FAITH AND STABILITY AMONG HISPANIC FAMILIES
The Role of Religion in Cultural Transition

Joseph P. Fitzpatrick, S.J.

By the middle of the twenty-first century, a majority of Catholic families in the United States may be of Hispanic background. Therefore, it is important to gain some perspective about the relationship of religion to the Hispanic family in its adjustment to life in the changing society of the United States. Among earlier Catholic immigrant groups the Catholic parish was a basic element in the strong, stable immigrant communities — the little Dublins, the little Italies, the little Polands — that gave solidarity and permanence to the immigrants in their adjustment to American life. It gave strength and stability as well to the families in transition. There are reasons to believe that religion will not be able to play the same role for Hispanic families that it played for the families of earlier Catholic immigrant groups. What will the consequence be for the Hispanic families and for the church? Will there be a process to replace it?

THE DEMOGRAPHIC SITUATION[1]

The Hispanic population is the fastest-growing population in the United States. It increased from 9,072,602 in 1970 to 14,600,000 in 1980, an increase of 61 percent. The increase in the total population was 11 percent. Whatever the ambiguities in identifying the Hispanic population, the increase is significant, and it will continue. Newly arriving immigrants with visas for permanent residence are predomi-

Portions of this chapter are taken from Joseph P. Fitzpatrick, PUERTO RICAN AMERICANS: The Meaning of Migration to the Mainland, © 1971, pp. 82, 90-92, 94-96, 99, 115-117. Reprinted by permission of Prentice-Hall, Inc., Englewood Cliffs, N.J.

nantly from Mexico, the Caribbean, and Central and South America. This increase of "legal" immigrants will continue. Central and South America have among the highest rates of population increase in the world; economic distress and political turmoil will exert pressure on people to move; the large group of relatives and friends already here will provide a strong magnet to draw others. If the "undocumented" were added to this "reported count," the number of Hispanics would be much higher. It is a reasonable estimate that Hispanics already constitute one-third of the Catholic population of the United States. If the trend continues, they will be the dominant Catholic population by the middle of next century.

The Hispanic population is a very young population in contrast to the general population of the nation. The median age of the general population in 1980 was reported by the U.S. Bureau of the Census (1981b) at 30 yars of age. (The median divides the population in half; half above, half below that age.) The median age of the Hispanic population was 23.2, almost 7 years younger. The median age of the Puerto Rican population was 19.9. Whereas 32 percent of the total U.S. population was under 19 years, the percentage of Hispanics below 19 years was 44 percent; of Puerto Ricans it was 51.4 percent (U.S. Bureau of the Census, 1980c). When these populations reach marriageable age, even if they have small families, it will compound the numbers in the population. Meantime, the numbers of older Catholics of European background are declining.

Hispanic families tend to be large families. Casual observation reveals that. The U.S. Bureau of the Census (1981b) reported that 30 percent of Hispanic families had 5 or more persons, compared to 17.1 percent of all families in the United States.

Hispanic families are poor families. The Bureau of the Census (1980a) reports that the median family income for Hispanic families in the United States in 1978 was $14,716, in contrast to that of all families, $21,623. Median family income of Puerto Ricans was $8,282. Only 7 percent of all white families in the United States were below the poverty level; of Hispanic families, 21 percent were below the poverty level; of Mexican families, 19 percent were below the poverty level; and 40 percent of Puerto Ricans were below poverty (U.S. Bureau of the Census, 1980a). If the Catholic church in the United States wishes to make a "preferential option for the poor," as the church has done in Latin America, the option will be largely for the Hispanics. If present trends continue, therefore, the church of the next century will be predominantly a church of the young, rapidly increasing, poor Hispanic families.

DIVERSITY AMONG HISPANIC FAMILIES[2]

There is a tendency in the United States to speak of Hispanics as if they are similar because they all speak Spanish. They are not.

Color

Mexicans and some Central and South Americans come from Indian or Mestizo background. (Mestizo is the offspring of Indian and European parents.) Cubans of the 1960 migration and many South Americans are largely caucasoid; Puerto Ricans and Dominicans range in color from completely white to completely black. The racial issue creates serious problems for Hispanic families who are colored. Although racial discrimination is present in all areas of the Caribbean and Central and South America, it expresses itself in different ways from its expression in the United States. In the former areas it is closely associated with consciousness of class differences, whereas the sharp focus on color in the United States, and the discrimination associated with it, are difficult for Hispanics to take. Hispanics differentiate American blacks from blacks of their own nationality group. A black Puerto Rican is called Puerto Rican among his people, in contrast to an American black, generally called *moreno*. Hostility and fear often mark the relations of Puerto Ricans and American blacks. No such hostility exists between white and colored Puerto Ricans or Dominicans.

Education

Cubans of the 1960 migration are at an educational level closest to that of the total United States. Among Cubans over 25 years of age, about 50 percent have finished high school; among Puerto Ricans, 36 percent; among Mexicans, 34.3 percent (U.S. Bureau of the Census, 1980a). This improves among all groups in the second generation (those born here of parents who were born abroad). But the second-generation population is so young that relatively few have reached the age of 25.

Location

As is commonly known, Hispanics of different backgrounds are concentrated in different parts of the nation: persons of Mexican background in the Southwest; persons of Cuban background in Florida; persons of Puerto Rican or Dominican background in the Northeast.

Although some characteristics are found in all Hispanic groups, the above factors affect their experience in the United States and will involve a different process of adjustment for the families of diverse background. Persons from middle-class or upper-middle-class backgrounds in Cuba or Central or South America will have many of the characteristics associated with middle-class families everywhere. Families that come from a background of slavery will have been affected by the influence of slavery. The pre-Columbian Indian cultures have influenced families from Mexico and families of Indian background in Central or South America, whereas little of this remained in Puerto Rico, Santo Domingo, or Cuba. Nevertheless, the Spanish colonial influence has had a profound impact on all families of Hispanic background.

Preeminence of the Family

Among the features of this influence that may still be found in varying degrees among Hispanic families, none is more important than the commitment to the family as group.[3] The family is the central social group for them. Thus, for example, they have struggled to maintain the chaperonage system during courtship, despite the inroads of modern urban life. Young people are still expected to seek parental approval for purposes of courtship.

Included in this type of family is a strong sense of the superior authority of the male. This pattern of male dominance is manifested especially in the double standard of morality. The "good" woman is supposed to be protected by the males in the family so that she may be a virgin at marriage, while the male is permitted to seek out "loose women" before marriage and even perhaps have a mistress while married.[4]

Despite this legacy, there is a considerable amount of research evidence that there is much nonmarital sexuality among Hispanics and that this often results in consensual or free unions.[5] Thus the Hispanic legacy as regards sexual mores has been modified in the course of time.

SLAVERY[6]

A word must be said about slavery. This particularly affected Puerto Rico, the Dominican Republic, Cuba, and the coastal areas of the Caribbean. Slavery was a milder institution in the Spanish colonies than in the United States. But slavery in the Western world has had a devastating effect on family life. Little effort was made to provide for the stability and permanence of the slave family; men and women, relatives, children, were bought, sold, exchanged, and shifted with little or no regard for permanent family union. Slave women were defenseless before the advances of free men.

The usual consequences of slavery in the broken family life of blacks have been as evident in Hispanic areas as elsewhere. A number of features of Spanish colonial culture modified the effects to some extent. Consorting with a woman who was not one's wife was a practice of upper-class men in this society and was not confined to black women. Therefore, the extramarital relationships of white men and black women tended to follow a pattern similar to that of white men with white women. Cultural patterns formed around these relationships that provided some advantages to the women and children involved in them. However the mother-based family — the family with children of a number of fathers and no permanent male consort — has been a common phenomenon in areas where slavery prevailed.

One feature of slavery in the Spanish colonial areas was the intermingling and intermarriage of persons of different color. This was the result of the primary emphasis on class. Color was simply one indicator that a person was lower class. Thus, among lower-class whites and blacks, intermarriage was much more common than it was in the United States. As a result among these peoples a range of color is found from completely black to completely white.

DOMINANT CULTURAL VALUES[7]

In an extraordinary way the Spanish were able to inculcate into their colonial people a range of values characteristic of the Spanish tradition. They are surprisingly widespread, and surprisingly persistent. They constitute a culture decidedly different from that of the United States. They are the values around which tension and conflict will emerge under the impact of the way of life of the United States. They are not specifically "family values," but since all values are communicated primarily through the socialization that occurs in the family, it is important to list them here.

Personalism

The basic value of Hispanic cultures is a form of individualism that focuses on the inner importance of the person. In contrast to the individualism of the United States, which values the individual in terms of his or her ability to compete for higher social and economic status, the Hispanic culture centers attention on those inner qualities that constitute the uniqueness of the person, and the person's goodness or worth in itself. In a two-class society where little mobility is possible, people are born into a social and economic position. Therefore, they define their value in terms of the qualities and behavior that make a person good or respected in the social position in which they find themselves. A poor farm laborer is a good man when he does those things that make a man good on his social and economic level. He feels an inner dignity *(dignidad)*, about which the Hispanic is very sensitive; he expects others to have respect *(respeto)* for that dignidad. All persons have some sense of personal dignity and are sensitive about proper respect being shown them, but this marks the Hispanic culture in a particular way. Hispanics are much more sensitive than Americans to anything that appears to be personal insult or disdain; they do not take to practical jokes that are likely to embarrass, or to party games in which people "make fools of themselves."

Personalism and Efficiency

It is this personalism that makes it difficult for Hispaniscs to adjust easily to what Anglos call "efficiency." For them, life is a network of personal relationships. They trust persons; they rely on persons; they know that, at every moment, they can fall back on a brother, a cousin, a *compadre*. They do not have the same trust for a system or an organization. Anglos, on the other hand, expect the system to work; they have confidence in the organization. When something goes wrong, the Anglo reaction is: "Somebody ought to do something about this"; "Get this system going." Thus Anglos become impatient and uneasy when systems do not work. They respond to efficiency. Hispanics become uneasy and impatient if the system works too well, if they feel themselves in a situation where they must rely on impersonal functions rather than personal relationships. Personalism is one Hispanic value that thus comes into sharp conflict with traditional American values of independence, freedom, and self-fulfillment. This represents conflict between individualism as it is institutionalized in the Hispanic culture in contrast to American culture. The conflict will be explored later in this chapter.

The Padrino

Related to personalism is the role of the *padrino*. The padrino is a person, strategically placed in a higher position of the social structure, who has a personal relationship with the poorer person in which he provides employment assistance at time of need and acts as an advocate if the poor person becomes involved in trouble. The padrino is really the intermediary between the poor person, who has neither sophistication nor influence, and the larger society of law, government, employment, and service. He is a strategic helper in times of need, but the possibilities of exploitation in this relationship are very great. The poor person can become completely bound to the padrino by debt or by obligations to personal service to such an extent that his life is little better than slavery. The role of the padrino has decreased in Hispanic areas, but the tendency to seek a personal relationship in one's business affairs is still strong.

Machismo

Another aspect of personalism is a combination of qualities associated with masculinity. This is generally referred to as *machismo,* literally, "maleness." Machismo is a style of personal daring (the great quality of the bullfighter) by which one faces challenge, danger, and threat with calm and self-possession; this sometimes takes the form of bravado. It is also a quality of personal magnetism that impresses and influences others and prompts them to follow one as a leader — the quality of the conquistador. It is associated with sexual prowess, influence, and power over women reflected in a vigorous romanticism and a jealous guarding of sweetheart or wife, or in premarital and extramarital relationships. (For references to machismo, see Stycos, 1955.)

Sense of Family Obligation

Personalism is deeply rooted in the individualism that has just been described; it is also rooted in the family. As explained above, Hispanics have a deep sense of that network of primary personal relationships that is their family. To express it another way, they sense the family as an extension of the person, and the network of obligations follows as described above.

Sense of the Primacy of the Spiritual

Hispanics generally refer to American culture as very materialistic, much to the amazement of Americans, who are conscious of human qualities, concerns, and generosity in American culture that are missing in the Hispanic. What the Hispanics mean is that their fundamental concerns are not with this world or its tangible features. They have a sense of spirit and soul as much more important than the body, and as being intimately related to their value as persons; they tend to think in terms of transcendant qualities, such as justice, loyalty, or love, rather than in terms of practical arrangements that spell out justice or loyalty in the concrete. On an intellectual level, they strive to clarify relationships conceptually with a confidence that if these can be made intellectually clear and precise, the reality that they express will have those relationships. They think of life very much in terms of ultimate values and ultimate spiritual goals, and express a willingness to sacrifice material satisfactions for these.

In contrast, the American preoccupation with mastering the world and subjecting it, through technological programs, to domination by human beings, give to Hispanics the sense of reversing the system of values, of emphasizing the importance of mastering the physical universe rather than seeking the values of the spirit. It is striking to note how much more attention and prestige are given in Hispanic areas to gifted writers and artists. It is precisely the sense of obligation to dominate the world that leads inevitably to a decline in the elemental sense of the sacred that is so much a part of the spiritual attitude of Hispanics. The Anglo-Saxon sense of vocation is rooted in a particular awareness of the meaning of the scriptures taught, "Increase and multiply and 'fill the earth — name all the plants and animals and dominate them." The Anglo-Saxon feels a deep obligation to change the world, not simply to adjust to it.

Fatalism

Connected to these spiritual values in Hispanics is a deep sense of fatalism. They have a sense of destiny, partly related to elemental fears of the sacred, partly related to a sense of divine providence governing the world. The popular song, *Que Será, Será* ("whatever will be, will be") is a simple expression of it, as is the common expression that intersperses so much of Hispanic speech: *si Dios quiere* ("if God wills it"). The term "destiny" recurs frequently in popular songs. This quality leads to the acceptance of many events as inevitable; it also softens the sense of personal guilt for failure. If, after a vigorous effort, an enterprise does not succeed, the Hispanic may shrug his or her shoulders and remark: "It was not meant to be."

Sense of Hierarchy

The Hispanics have had a concept of a hierarchical world during the whole of their history. This was partly the result of the two-class system, in which members never conceived of a world in which they could move out of the position into which they were born. Thus they thought of a relationship of higher and lower classes that was fixed somewhat as the various parts of the body were fixed. This concept of hierarchy contributed to their concept of personal worth as distinct from a person's position in the social structure.

TRANSITION TO THE MAINLAND

The institution that faces the most direct shock in the migration to the United States is the family, and the progress of Hispanics can be measured to a large extent by a study of the family. However, no general description is sufficient to explain the experience of Hispanic families; their experience has been extremely diverse.

Many Hispanics are descendants of people who were residents of the Southwest when it was Mexican territory; their history and traditions go far back beyond the time the Americans appropriated the territory and began to move to the Southwest. Puerto Ricans are citizens of the United States, but they come, without restrictions, from a language and cultural area very different from that of the mainland. Most Cubans have come in the past twenty years as refugees from the Castro revolution. Dominicans have come more recently, many of them without documents (the so-called illegals), leading a hidden life in fear of deportation. Mexicans move in and out by the millions, some with documents, others without. Many Central and South Americans are here temporarily, supporting families at home, and hoping one day to return themselves. Many of them also have no documents.

These varied experiences exert enormous strain on family life. For example, the gainful employment of women outside the home is a common feature of Hispanic families. This is not a response to the pressure for upward mobility, as is the case with American families; it is more often the pressure for survival. According to the 1980 data, more than 50 percent of Cuban women (over age 20) and of Central and South American women were in the labor force. At that time, this was much higher than the 40 percent of non-Spanish white women. Of Mexican women, 50 percent were then in the labor force, as were 37 percent of the Puerto Rican women (U.S. Bureau of Labor Statistics, 1981: 198). A recent study of Cubans in New Jersey found a rate of 70 percent of married women in the labor force, much higher than the rate for all married women in the United States (Rogg and Cooney, 1980: 15).

THE PROCESS OF ADJUSTMENT

The most extensive analysis of data about Hispanic families is found in Jaffee et al. (1980). These authors analyzed all available data from the 1970 census. Focusing especially on language, fertility, and intermarriage, they found an increasing convergence with the dominant patterns of American society. With each passing generation, the use of Spanish language declines: one-third of U.S.-born Hispanics switch from their mother tongue to English as the "language usually spoken at home" (Jaffe et al., 1980: 75). Fertility declines with successive generations and higher levels of education, and approaches the average fertility rate of the United States. Studying the prevalence of U.S.-born wives of Hispanic background, Jaffe et al. (1980: 66) found the following percentage of wives who had married non-Hispanic whites: wives of Mexican descent, 16 percent; of Puerto Rican descent, 33 percent; and of Cuban descent, 46 percent. The authors conclude: "With each passing decade they [Hispanics] are being brought closer to the mainstream of social change and economic development of the larger society until eventually there will be a merging. . . . In another generation or two, they will be almost indistinguishable from the general U.S. population" (Jaffe et al., 1980: 22).

Fitzpatrick and Gurak (1979) recently published a study of Hispanic intermarriage in New York City in 1975, using official marriage records from the Office of the City Clerk (Table 9.1). Rates of intermarriage with non-Hispanics are high for Cubans, Central Americans, and South Americans. Rates are very high for all except Puerto Ricans in the second generation, but the numbers are too small to provide a reliable indicator of a trend. The decline in intermarriage among second-generation Puerto Ricans is the surprising finding of this study, a decline from a high rate of 1949 and 1959 — above 30 percent — to the relatively low rate of 18.2 percent for brides and 8.1 percent for grooms in 1975.

No satisfactory explanation of this decline has been given. It is possible that the large numbers of second generation Puerto Ricans — 5690 persons marrying in 1975 — and their concentration in certain sections of New York City may be important factors. For second-generation Dominicans, whose numbers are much smaller — 76 persons marrying in 1975 — the rates of intermarriage with non-Hispanics are very high: 32.4 percent of the brides; 35.9 percent of the grooms. If intermarriage is a major indicator of structural and cultural assimilation, as is generally accepted, the intermarriage rates, with the exception of second-generation Puerto Ricans, indicate a rapid assimilation to American society.

Type of Wedding Ceremony

One other indication of change can be found in some of the evidence we have about type of marriage ceremony. In their definitive study of Mexican Americans, Grebler et al. (1970: 477) found that

TABLE 9.1   Intermarriage with Non-Hispanics Among All Hispanic Marriages in New York City, 1975, by Nationality, Sex, and Generation

	All Hispanic Marriages		*Second-Generation Hispanic Marriages*	
	Brides %	*Grooms* %	*Brides* %	*Grooms* %
Puerto Ricans	15.0	11.9	18.2	8.1
South Americans	22.3	16.1	53.2	52.7
Dominicans	7.8	6.0	32.4	35.9
Central Americans	22.9	23.7	63.9	48.5
Cubans	32.4	22.8	59.7	48.5

SOURCE: Fitzpatrick and Gurak (1979: Tables 9, 10).

among Mexicans in Los Angeles County marrying in 1963 for the first time, less than half married in Catholic ceremonies. In their study of all Hispanic marriages in New York City in 1975, Fitzpatrick and Gurak (1979) found low rates of Catholic marriage.

There was a high rate of second marriages among these that may partially explain the low rate, namely, divorced persons remarrying. But that still leaves a low rate of Catholic marriages. This requires explanation that is not yet available. Rates of Catholic marriage must also be compared with rates in the countries of origin. For example, in Puerto Rico in 1975, only 31 percent of all marriages were Catholic marriages. Therefore, the low rate in New York does not necessarily indicate a change resulting from the shock of adjustments to U.S. culture.

Changes in Values

Much more important than the above statistical descriptions of Hispanic families in the United States is the study of changes in values that they face. Probably the most serious is the shift in roles of husband and wife. There is abundant evidence that this is a common experience of immigrants. But, as indicated above, the rate of gainful occupation outside the home is high for immigrant families. It is provoked by a number of things. First, it is frequently easier for women than men to get jobs in the cities to which Hispanics are coming. This gives the wife an economic independence that she may never have had before, and if the husband is unemployed while the wife is working, the reversal of roles is severe. Second, the impact of American culture begins to make itself felt more directly around the work experience. Hispanic women from the poorer classes are much

TABLE 9.2   Catholic Ceremonies in Hispanic Marriages, New York City,
1975, by Nationality, Sex, and Generation

| | Both Generations | | Second Generation Only | |
	Bride %	Groom %	Bride %	Groom %
Puerto Ricans	26.4	26.1	33.1	33.6
South Americans	18.3	17.7	39.1	20.5
Dominicans	22.2	20.3	37.8	28.2
Central Americans	15.3	14.0	23.5	26.2
Cubans	35.1	32.0	33.7	40.2

SOURCE: Fitzpatrick and Gurak (1979: Tables 18, 19).

more involved in social, community, and political activities than they
were in their nations of origin. This influences the wife gradually to
adopt the patterns of the mainland.

Even more direct and difficult to cope with is the shift in role of the
child. Hispanic families have frequently lamented the patterns of
behavior of even good boys in the United States. Hispanic parents
consider them to be disrespectful. American children are taught to be
self-reliant, aggressive, and competitive, to ask "why," and to stand
on their own two feet. A Hispanic child is generally much more
submissive. When the children begin to behave according to the
American pattern, the parents cannot understand it. A priest who had
worked for many years with migrating Puerto Ricans remarked:
"When these Puerto Rican families come to New York, I give the
boys about 48 hours on the streets of New York, and the difference
between their behavior and what the family expects, will have begun
to shake the family."

The distance that gradually separates child from family is indicated in much of the literature about Puerto Ricans in New York. In
the autobiography of Piri Thomas, (1967), *Down These Mean Streets,*
it is clear that his family — and it was a good strong family — had no
way of controlling him once he began to associate with his peers on
the streets. The sharp contrast of two life histories presented by
Meyerson (1965) also demonstrates the difficulties of a Puerto Rican
family in trying to continue to control the life of a boy growing up in
New York. His peers become his significant reference group. A
considerable number of scholars and social workers attribute much of
the delinquency of Puerto Ricans to the excessive confinement that
the Puerto Rican families impose in an effort to protect their children.
Once the children can break loose in the early teens, they do so
completely.[8]

Probably the most severe problem of control is the effort of
families to give their unmarried girls the same kind of protection they

would have given them back home. When the girls reach their early teens, they wish to do what American girls do — go to dances with boys without a chaperone, and associate freely with girls and boys of the neighborhood or school. For a good Hispanic father to permit his daughter to go out unprotected is a serious moral failure. In traditional Hispanic towns, when a father has brought his daughters as virgins to marriage, he can hold up his head before his community; he enjoys the esteem and prestige of a good father. To ask the same father to allow his daughters to go free in New York is to ask him to do something that the men of his family have considered immoral. It is psychologically almost impossible for him to do this. This tension between parents and daughters is one of the most difficult for Hispanic parents to manage. It is frequently complicated because Americans, including schoolteachers and counselors, who are not aware of the significance of this, advise the parents to allow the girls to go out freely.

Finally, the classic tension between the generations takes place. The parents are living in the Hispanic culture in their homes. The children are being brought up in an American school, where American values are being presented. The parents will never really understand their children; the children will never really understand their parents.

Weakening of Extended Kinship

Apart from the conflict between generations, the experience of migration tends to weaken the family bonds that created a supporting network on which the family could always rely. To a growing extent, the family finds itself alone. This is partly the result of moving from place to place. It is also due to the fact that the way of life in mainland cities is not a convenient environment for the perpetuation of family virtues and values. The Department of Social Services provides assistance in time of need, but not with the familiar, informal sense of personal and family respect. Regulations in housing, consumer loans, schools, and courts create a requirement for professional help, and the family is less and less effective.

Replacement of Personalist Values

Closely related to all the above difficulties, and creating difficulties of its own, is the slow and steady substitution of impersonal norms — norms of the system rather than norms of personal relationships. The need to adjust to the dominant patterns of American society requires a preparation to seek employment and advancement on the basis of merit or ability. To people for whom the world is an extensive pattern of personal relationships, this is a difficult adjustment.

Individualism:
Hispanic Versus U.S. Style

Basic to this problem is the fact that the central value of both cultures, namely, individualism, is institutionalized differently in each culture. Individualism in the United States is institutionalized in an open class system in which, ideally, all persons will have equal access to opportunities to compete for self-fulfillment and self-advancement. In other words, individualism is really *equality,* conceived as a right of each person to develop himself or herself, and to rise to that social and economic level to which natural gifts and personal efforts entitle him or her. This is a basic principle on which the nation was founded. The founding fathers wanted to get away from the rigid class restrictions of Europe; they wanted a society in which each person would be *free* and have equal access to opportunities for development and in which it would be possible for each individual to advance to the level of society appropriate to his or her abilities.

In an extraordinary number of cases, this has been the experience of American citizens. We could all reflect on our own histories and, like myself, be aware that our predecessors came from humble backgrounds, and that our status and position is the consequence of a society that made advancement possible. We are also aware that there have been serious deviations from this ideal in the discrimination that has marred our history.

Like all social institutions, this pattern of equal opportunity and upward mobility has its dysfunctions. We have a tendency to value a person not by his or her qualities, but by the level he or she has attained in the society. He is the president of a bank; she is principal of a school, or director of a social agency; the less fortunate are building custodians, kitchen help, unskilled labor in factories. We tend to value the person not for what he or she *is,* but in terms of his or her position in society, and the wealth that is generally associated with that position. This is a materialistic norm, and motivation and appreciation tend to become associated with the materialistic rewards rather than with the quality of the person.

In the Hispanic world, individualism is institutionalized differently. As indicated above, the Hispanic world was a rigidly stratified society in which a small number of persons owned the land, possessed the wealth, and held political power. Everyone else was a peon. Within that framework, the value of the person, as it emerged from the Judeo-Christian tradition, expressed itself in a keen sense of the worth of individual persons, independently of the positions they held in society. Equality was not equality to compete for self-development and social advancement; equality was the equality of each creature before the Lord, the inner worth of the person, created by God and destined for eternal life. The focus of attention and awareness in this culture became the inner value of the person (dignidad), and the respect (respeto) with which that dignity was acknowledged. This does not mean that there was not exploitation or oppression; there was. But within that system, the value of the individual was perceived as being a quality of the person, regardless of social position. *Personalismo* became the basic value of the culture.

It is obvious that when a person moves out of a world of personalismo into a world where individualism is institutionalized in the form of equal access to opportunities for self-development, and where upward mobility is not only a social ideal, but is often expressed as a moral requirement, the shock of the change is radically upsetting.

This process of uprooting has been described before in the extensive literature about immigrants. It leads to three kinds of adjustments. The first involves escape from the immigrant or migrant group and an effort to become as much like the established community as possible in as short a time as possible. These people seek to disassociate themselves from their past. They sometimes change their names, change their reference groups, and seek to be accepted by the larger society. They are in great danger of becoming marginal. Having abandoned the way of life of their own people, in which they had a sense of "who they were," there is no assurance that they will be accepted by the larger community. They may find themselves in a "no man's land." In this stage, the danger of personal frustration is acute.

A second reaction is withdrawal into the old culture, a resistance to the new way of life. These people seek to retain the older identities by locking themselves into their old way of life.

The third reaction is the effort to build a cultural bridge between the culture of the migrants and that of the mainland. These are the people who have confidence and security in their own way of life, but who realize that it cannot continue. Therefore, they seek to establish themselves in the new society, but continue to identify themselves with the people from whom they come. These are the people through whom the process of assimilation moves forward.

In all these reactions to the process of adjustment, the family remains the major psychosocial support for its members. In many cases it is a broken family; in others it is hampered by poverty, unemployment, illness; but it remains the source of strength for most Hispanics in the presence of the impact of the culture of the United

States. This is reflected, for example, in the literature of the Puerto Ricans. In the turbulent action of the musical *West Side Story,* when Bernardo, leader of the Puerto Rican gang, sees Tony, a youth of another ethnic group, approaching his sister Maria, Bernardo pulls Maria away from Tony to take her home. He then turns to Tony in anger and shouts: "You keep away from my sister. Don't you know we are a family people!"

During 1966 the first presentation in New York of *The Ox Cart* took place. This is a play by a Puerto Rican playwright, René Marqués, that presents a picture of a simple farm family in the mountains of Puerto Rico, struggling to survive but reflecting the deep virtues of family loyalty and strength. Under the influence of the oldest son, the family moves to a slum section of San Juan in order to improve itself. But deterioration sets in as the slum environment begins to attack the solidarity and loyalty of the family members. The family then moves to New York, where the strain of the uprooting becomes worse, the gap between mother and children more painful, and the virtues of the old mountain family seem even more distant. After the violent death of the son, the play ends with the valiant mother setting out to go back to the mountains of Puerto Rico, where she hopes to regain the traditional values of Puerto Rican family life that were destroyed in San Juan and New York.

This is an ancient theme, and it may be as true for Puerto Ricans as it was for earlier newcomers. But if the Hispanics make it in the United States, it will be through the same source of strength that supported the immigrants of earlier times — the solidarity of the family.

THE ROLE OF RELIGION IN IMMIGRANT ADJUSTMENT

Studies of the adjustment of earlier immigrant groups have indicated clearly that religion, and a sense of identity based on religion, was a major element in the gradual adjustment of immigrants to the United States.[9] This was particularly true among Catholic groups in the role of the ethnic parish, or national parish, as it was sometimes called. Among the earlier immigrants, large numbers of priests and religious sisters and brothers accompanied the immigrants in their move to the new world. They established the ethnic or national parishes, German, French, Italian, Polish, and so on. These were the enclaves in which the culture of the old world was continued in the new. They were the little worlds in which the way of life was the same, the language, the style of life, the emphasis on traditional religious values, the emphasis on moral and religious practices. It was the stable, secure base in which the newcomers were "at home." This gave them a continuing sense of identity, psychosocial satisfaction of knowing where and who they were. This provided the secure base for a gradual adjustment to the new world to which they had come. One integrates from a position of strength, not from a position of weakness. The parish was the base for much of the strength and stability. Catholic schools were generally an integral part of the parish. This became an important institution for the maintenance of Catholic traditions and values, while the child was prepared for life in the new and strange world.

There are doubts that religion or the parish will play the same role for Hispanics. For the most part, they come without their clergy and they come at a time when American Bishops are choosing not to establish ethnic or national parishes for Hispanics. The pressure and influence of the immigrant clergy was important in the establishment of the national parishes. Very few of them are on the scene among Hispanics.[10] But the history of the national parishes in the third generation has left the bishops with serious problems (Fitzpatrick, 1971: ch. 8). Numerous national churches have lost their congregations to the suburbs; third-generation persons have lost their language and follow an American style of life. Therefore, bishops have chosen to staff existing parishes with American priests who speak Spanish, or clergy invited temporarily from Spain or South America. The consequence is that the strong, stable base for identity that the national parish gave to earlier immigrants is not available to any large extent for Hispanics. In many instances the existing territorial parish, or national parish, becomes a Hispanic parish as a neighborhood becomes completely Hispanic. But this is quite a different experience than that of the national parish, with priests and religious of the same ethnic background who constituted the transitional world of the Catholic parish.

RELIGIOUS HISTORY OF HISPANICS

A brief consideration of the religious history of Hispanic people makes clear the problem of religious adjustment to the United States. In the United States, the Catholic faith was brought by poor immigrant people who took advantage of the freedom and opportunity of the nation to develop a vigorous and influential body of American Catholic citizens.

In Latin America, religion came with conquest. The conquistadores were motivated strongly by "God, Gold, Glory." Emphasis on the conquest as a pursuit of gold and glory is sometimes exaggerated to a point that obscures the fact that the conquistadores also had God very much in mind. To a Spaniard, whether conquistador or not, the Catholic faith was the one true faith, the most important thing for which a man should live or die, and the most important gift he could give to another. The conquistadores had strange ideas about how the faith should be given to others, but they were determined to pass it on to the indigenous peoples they met in the New World. As a consequence, they created communities in which the Catholic faith was communicated, together with the Spanish language, colonial organization, and economy.

In order to develop this Spanish colonial culture and transfer it to the natives, the Spanish formed the *pueblo,* the town, and thus created a community. It was a positive principle of colonial policy that a person could not be a person without being a member of a community. Every community was formed in the same way. A plaza was designed that was to be the center of community life, the place where all members of the community could meet, celebrate fiestas, and participate in religious ceremonies. The main building on the plaza was the church; no community could exist unless God were a member of it. Thus all the members of the pueblo were conscious of being members of a community, and the community of necessity was Catholic. When a Latin American said he was *católico,* or, more commonly, *muy católico,* very Catholic, he did not necessarily mean he had been at mass or the sacraments; he simply meant that he was a member of a pueblo, which was Catholic. Periodically the pueblo, the community, worshipped God in great public demonstrations. In the United States, the pueblo in this sense (the community) never worships God. It guarantees to people the right to worship God according to their consciences. But practice of the faith in the United States is not a community manifestation; it is a matter of personal choice or commitment. The Latins, on the other hand, are "Catholic" because they belong to a Catholic people. This sense of identity, based on religion, which came to penetrate the life of Latin Americans very deeply, was related to a style of Catholicism with which they were familiar — the Catholicism of the pueblo, the community of which they were a part.

Two observations are helpful about this style of Catholicism. First, in Latin America, being religious is not perceived, as it is in the United States, in terms of adherence to the organized church. In the United States people are Catholic because they are affiliated with the church, belong to its associations, and identify themselves with its structures. In Latin America, religious practice is marked by the quality of *personalismo,* the pattern of close, intimate personal relationships that is characteristic of Spanish cultures everywhere. Thus people perceive their religious life as a network of personal relationships with the saints, the Blessed Virgin, or various manifestations of the Lord. They look on these as their compadres, their close friends. They pray to them, light candles to them, carry their images in procession, build shrines to them in their homes, make promises to them, and expect them to deliver the favors, help, or protection they need. Just as in their human relationships they need the padrino, the patron, or the compadre, so the *santo* is the counterpart in the realm of religion. But this personal relationship with the saints takes place quite outside the organized structure of the church. Indeed, if the organized church should be shut down, the relationship would go on as usual. Latins could be very anticlerical toward the hierarchy of the church without in any way thinking they were departing from the Catholicism that penetrates their lives.

Second, the effort to absorb all the natives into a Spanish colonial culture and a Catholic community was never entirely successful. Remnants of prediscovery religious rites have continued among many of the indigenous peoples, and African rites were brought by Negro slaves and intermingled with some of the practices of the Catholics. The result is a syncretism of cults and practices that is still very much alive in many parts of Latin America, for example, the *costumbre* of Central America, or the *macumba* or *candomblé* of Brazil. Although there is little evidence of this in Puerto Rico, there is widespread practice of spiritism. These practices are often called superstitions by the North Americans, and elements of superstition are no doubt intermingled with them. But actually they are a mixture, sometimes of pre-Columbian indigenous rites, a variety of Catholic devotion, and an elemental response to the sense of the presence of the sacred in everyday life.

Both of these features of Latin Catholicism — its traditional community character and its personalistic character in devotion to the saints — are very difficult for North Americans to grasp. It is equally difficult for Hispanics to adjust to American Catholicism. If the community character of their religious experience can be maintained during the early years of their presence in the United States, this will serve as a bridge to enable them to make a gradual adjustment in a religious environment that is familiar to them. However, we must not simply anticipate that the transition to American Catholicism will be the same for Hispanics as it was for European immigrants. The cultural background of Hispanics may involve some disadvantages as well as advantages in the transition. The style of "cultural" Catholicism or "folk" Catholicism may result in many of them being marginal to the church in the United States. They are not prepared for the kind of individual commitment and involvement required for active practice in the United States. This may explain the large percentage who are marginal to all religious groups in the United States. It may also explain the low rate of Catholic ceremonies in the marriages of Hispanics.

IS THERE A SUBSTITUTE?

Nevertheless, there has been evidence of great vitality among Hispanic Catholics in the United States. They introduced the *"Cursillo"* movement years ago and it has contributed a strong influence to Hispanic communities; the Christian Family Movement *(Movimiento Cristiano Familial)* and the Marriage Encounter *(Encuentro)* have contributed to the strength of Hispanic families; the Basic Christian Communities *(Comunidades de Base),* which have given such vitality to the church in Latin America, are becoming a more common feature of Hispanic religious experience; and the charismatic movement is strong among Hispanic people — the organization of Mexican workers under the banner of Our Lady of Guadalupe indicates a strong form of religious identity apart from the national parish. In 1969 Hispanic priests formed a national organization, Padres, to press for the religious, educational, and social rights of Hispanics; shortly after, Hispanic nuns organized Las Hermanas, a national organization of Hispanic sisters. In 1972, four years before the first national assembly of American Catholics at the "Call to Action" in Detroit, the Hispanics had held their first assembly (Encuentro) in Washington, D.C. A second Encuentro was held in 1977. Meantime, at the "Call to Action" meeting in Detroit, the Hispanics were the best organized caucus at the assembly.

All this vitality contributes to the strengthening of Hispanic families. The effort is focused on the preservation of the basic features of Hispanic culture, the emphasis on the primary importance of the family, on personalism, on a concern for spiritual values. If the predictions of Jaffee et al. (1980) are borne out, Hispanics will eventually absorb the dominant culture patterns of the United States. But a number of factors suggest that it may not happen rapidly. Hispanic culture is a strong and rugged culture. Hispanic homelands are very close to the United States mainland. Links to the old culture need not require periodic return. Furthermore, larger numbers of Hispanics will continue to arrive. The emphasis on bilingual and bicultural education may lead to a sharper perception among Americans of the importance of a lasting cultural pluralism. In any event, a new world is forming in the United States, and that new world may be profoundly influenced by the increasing number of Hispanics. The family values of Hispanics will be a major element in the process.

NOTES

1. The demographic data are taken from periodic reports of the U.S. Bureau of the Census as indicated in the references. The most exhaustive analysis of all available demographic data about Hispanics on the basis of the 1970 census is found in Jaffe et al. (1980).

2. There are numerous studies about the various Hispanic groups in the United States. The standard source for basic information is the *Harvard Encyclopedia of American Ethnic Groups* (Thurnstrom, 1980). See also the *Annals of the American Academy of Political and Social Science* (1981). For Mexicans, see Grebler et al. (1970); for Puerto Ricans, see Fitzpatrick (1971).

3. An important expression of the family as group is the system of *compadrazgo* or godparenthood. People who become godparents of a child at baptism or confirmation become like parents, and in the process become companions to the parents and protectors of the children. They may develop a network of ritual kinship, and come to depend on each other for economic assistance, support, encouragement, and even personal correction.

4. For references to machismo, see Stycos (1955).

5. For a clear insight into the phenomenon of consensual unions, see Mintz (1960).

6. For a background of slavery in Hispanic areas, see Diaz Soler (1965). Tannenbaum (1947) presents a very good treatment in English of the differences in slavery between Latin America and the United States.

7. One of the best analyses of the values of Hispanic peoples can be found in Gillin (1960).

8. For a lengthy discussion of this change of values and its relation to delinquency, see Fitzpatrick (1960).

9. One of the most helpful studies of the role of religion in the adjustment of immigrants can be found in Herberg (1955). See also Glazer and Moynihan (1970), Gordon (1964), and Tomasi (1975).

10. This again differs with the different Hispanic groups. Many Cuban clergy came with the Cuban refugees from Cuba, refugees themselves. The number of Chicano priests and bishops is slowly increasing. Puerto Ricans and Dominicans have very few. Central and South Americans have almost none.

REFERENCES

Annals of the American Academy of Political and Social Science (1981) " America as a multicultural society." Vol. 454 (March): whole issue.

Diaz Soler, L. M. (1965) Historia de la Esclavitud en Puerto Rico. Rio Piedras, Puerto Rico: Editorial Universitaria.

Fitzpatrick, J. P. (1971) Puerto Rican Americans: The Meaning of Migration to the Mainland. Englewood Cliffs, NJ: Prentice-Hall.

——— (1960) "Crime and our Puerto Ricans." Catholic Mind 58.

——— and D. Gurak (1979) Hispanic Intermarriage in New York City, 1975. Bronx, NY: Hispanic Research Center, Fordham University.

Gillin, J. (1960) "Some signposts for policy," in R. M. Adams (ed.) Social Change in Latin America Today. New York: Vintage.

Glazer, N. and D. Moynihan (1970) Beyond the Melting Pot. Cambridge: University of Massachusetts Press.

Gordon, M. (1964) Assimilation in American Life. New York: Oxford University Press.

Grebler, L., J. Moore, and R. Guzman (1970) The Mexican American People. New York: Macmillan.

Herberg, W. (1955) Protestant, Catholic, Jew. Garden City, NY: Doubleday.

Jaffe, A. J., R. M. Cullen, and T. D. Boswell (1980) The Changing Demography of Spanish Americans. New York: Academic.

Mintz, S. (1960) Worker in the Cane. New Haven, CT: Yale University Press.

Rogg, E. and R. Cooney (1980) The Adaptation and Adjustment of Cubans: West New York, New Jersey. Monograph 5. Bronx, NY: Hispanic Research Center, Fordham University.

Stycos, J. M. (1955) Family and Fertility in Puerto Rico. New York: Columbia University Press.

Tannenbaum, F. (1947) The Negro in America. New York: Knopf.

Thomas, P. (1967) Down These Mean Streets. New York: Knopf.

Thurnstrom, S. [ed.] (1980) The Harvard Encyclopedia of American Ethnic Groups. Cambridge, MA: Harvard University Press.

Tomasi, S. (1975) Piety and Power. Staten Island, NY: Center for Migration Studies.

U.S. Bureau of the Census (1981a) Age, Sex, Race, and Spanish Origin of the Population, Regions, Divisions, and States: 1980. 1980 Census of the Population, Supplementary Reports, PC80-S1-1. Washington, DC: Government Printing Office.

————— (1981b) Current Population Reports, Series P-60, No. 363. Washington, DC: Government Printing Office.

————— (1980a) Characteristics of the Population Below Poverty Level: 1978. Current Population Reports, Series P-60, No. 124. Washington, DC: Government Printing Office.

————— (1980b) Money Income and Poverty Status of Families and Persons in the United States: 1980. Current Population Reports, Series P-60, No. 127. Washington, DC: Government Printing Office.

————— (1980c) Persons of Spanish Origin in the United States: March 1979. Current Population Reports, Series P-20, No. 354. Washington, DC: Government Printing Office.

U.S. Bureau of Labor Statistics (1981) Employment and Earnings, Vol. 28, No. 1. Washington, DC: Government Printing Office.

Part III

Against the Tide:
Proselytizing Traditional Ways

There continue to be religious organizations that actively seek to reverse changes in family ways, and they are subject of this final set of chapters. In this section, Hadden analyzes the New Christian Right (the Moral Majority), Thomas describes the Church of Jesus Christ of Latter-day Saints (the Mormons), and Fichter writes about the Unification Church (the Moonies). The codes of ethics of these groups stress the patriarchal family with husband-fathers as heads of households and wife-mothers as housekeepers. Women's rights, divorce, singlehood, and childlessness are generally elements in the contemporary family scene that practitioners of these religions oppose. This opposition is also one of their bases of membership recruitment.

A concern for the traditional family type is combined in the New Christian Right, according to Hadden, with a conservative political policy emphasizing traditional free-enterprise policies and so less governmental regulation. The emphasis on social justice that has characterized pronouncements from the Catholic church and the main-line Protestant denominations is also less evident in the Church of Jesus Christ of Latter-day Saints and the Unification Church. The conflict between the communal values incorporated in families and religions and the individualist orientation of the broader society appears less problematic for these latter religions and the New Christian Right. What they cannot accept is the contemporary individualism that extends into the family and sees its members as having interests that may conflict with those of the husband-father.

Just as the religious organizations discussed in this section tend to view families as harmonious units whose well-being is represented by their male heads, so too does their concern for cooperation and self-sacrifice seem limited to their members. All religious organizations emphasize the division between members and nonmembers.

However, the familial nature of the Moonies' organizational ties described by Fichter and the heavy emphasis on family participation among the Mormons that Thomas discusses emphasize this division. Thomas and Fichter indicate how family imagery permeates the theology and practices of these two religions. The heavy effort the Mormons, Moonies, and the New Christian Right expend on proselytizing is their means for increasing the numbers who can receive the social support benefits not extended to outsiders. By gaining new members, the Mormons, Moonies, and New Christian Right can also justify their position against contemporary family diversity and reassure themselves of its correctness.

Because the Church of Jesus Christ of Latter-day Saints has existed longer than the other organizations discussed here, Thomas can show the social control that Mormon family doctrine exerts on members' behaviors in terms of age at marriage, fertility, divorce rates, and women's roles. Fichter, in his description of the role elder members play in mate selection, the occurrence of multiple wedding ceremonies, and the plan for members to provide services to neighborhood families, demonstrates how the Unification Church also will be able to maintain control over its members. The New Christian Right is a political movement characterized more by myriad competing media voices than by a body of religious organizations joined by a common set of beliefs. Television can be an effective means to reach large numbers of people, but Mormons' and Moonies' personal contacts are built into church activities in the interest of church doctrine. Such contacts are what make these religions so important to their members, both for social control and social support purposes.

Although the Moonies, the Mormons, and the New Christian Right are against much in the contemporary family scene, they remain distinctive groups. Consistent with the Reverend Sun Myung Moon's Asiatic background, the rationale for the Unification Church's family orientation stems from Confucius. As Fichter points out, the members favor intergenerational extended families and mate selection in which older persons play a role, and see the Unification church as a family, with the Reverend Moon and his wife as father and mother. Leadership roles generally fall to men.

Among Mormons this too is the case. The Mormon priesthood is one in which only male members participate. But the Mormon religion developed in the United States during the early part of the nineteenth century as part of a great upsurge in religious interest. Both Moonies and Mormons, however, stress the importance if not the necessity of marital ties for salvation. Among Mormons, this belief even extends to the "sealing" of those who have died unwed to others in wedlock to ensure their existence in the afterlife's "Celestial World." In contrast, the New Christian Right places heavy emphasis on the individual choosing to be saved, if need be at the expense of family ties.

Thomas and Fichter both address the issue of the continuance of the Mormons and Moonies, since their family beliefs, although not their economic predelictions, put them against the contemporary social tide. The outlook for the Mormons, Thomas concludes, appears to be generally bright, given their past success at gaining converts and retaining members. Fichter, however, argues that the very success of the Unification Church in gaining members threatens the familylike ties that have been one of its great attractions. Reverend Moon appears to be aware of the problem and some of the organizational changes he is initiating can be viewed as attempts to preserve the primary group atmosphere of the church.

Hadden's conclusion concerning the New Christian Right is that much more political power has been imputed to it than its actual strength in numbers warrants. "Televangelists," as opposed to persons in face-to-face contact, can provide limited social support to viewers and exercise little control over their behavior.

The main thing to remember about these groups, according to Hadden — and the same point holds true for the Mormons and the Moonies — is their existence. They appeal to a sizable number of people who are ill at ease with ongoing changes in the United States. These people receive religious support for maintaining conventional family behaviors and are sanctioned if they depart from them. Popular interest in the religions discussed in this section should keep their agendas in the public mind. Recognizing the legitimacy of their concerns can help us to avoid the polarization of opinion that closes off discussion and contributes to religious bigotry.

10

TELEVANGELISM AND THE MOBILIZATION OF A NEW CHRISTIAN RIGHT FAMILY POLICY

Jeffrey K. Hadden

In 1933, William F. Ogburn published a paper entitled "The Family and Its Functions" in a volume that resulted from the first presidentially commissioned social science investigation. Ogburn identified six primary functions of the family: economic, protective, religious, recreational, educational, and status conferring. The family's role in the performance of each of these functions, he argued, was eroding in modern industrial society.

By contemporary social science research standards, Ogburn's mustering of evidence to support his conclusion was seriously deficient (see, for example, Caplow et al., 1981). Nevertheless, for nearly fifty years, his forecast of the demise of the family has been part of the taken-for-granted stock of knowledge of scholars and popular writers alike.

Notwithstanding the considerable attention Ogburn's paper received at the time, it did not lead to governmental policy with respect to the family. The family has long been exalted by presidents and other politicians as the cornerstone of society, but, strangely, it has never been much of a political issue per se. In fact, Jimmy Carter was the first president ever to attempt to create an explicit family policy (Steiner, 1981). And his efforts to do so may well have been a significant factor in the mobilization of evangelical Christians who disagreed with his policies.

An evangelical Christian himself, Jimmy Carter believed American families were experiencing "steady erosion and weakening" (Steiner, 1981: 3). If elected, candidate Carter promised to "construct an administration that will reverse the trends we have seen toward the breakdown of family in our country" (Steiner, 1981: 3).

President Carter believed there was an inexorable relationship between government and the family. Strong families contribute to the strength of a good government; weak families add yet more burdens to the government. "If we want less government," Carter told a New Hampshire audience in 1976, "we must have stronger families, for government steps in by necessity when families have failed" (Steiner, 1981: 5). Carter was determined to create a family policy that would aid families in need of assistance and, at the same time, self-consciously seek to eliminate and avoid regulations and laws that might have deleterious effects on the family (for example, tax laws that tax a working couple at a higher rate than an unmarried couple or a couple with only one person in the labor force).

President Carter substantially failed to achieve his goal of creating a systematic government policy on the family, but he succeeded in making the family a highly obstreperous political issue. One important reason for his failure was the absence of consensus regarding what would constitute a sound profamily policy. Liberal philosophy would provide economic assistance and social services to families in need. Conservatives see such policies as creating dependence rather than self-reliance. Thus, conservatives see the good intentions of strengthening the family through economic assistance and social services as likely to have the exact opposite effect and weaken the family.

The White House Conference on the Family convened during the last year of the Carter administration, and the underlying ideological conflict regarding what measures might strengthen the family came to the fore. At that point, the "New Christian Right" emerged as a vocal dissident against the more liberal philosophies of the administration. Outmaneuvered in their bid for significant representation at the White House Conference, the New Christian Right went public and had considerable success in persuading a significant proportion of conservative Americans that the conference was dominated by voices dedicated to destroying rather than revitalizing the family.

In the waning days of the Carter administration, the White House Conference on the Family issued a report with a series of recommendations about what government could do to buoy up the presumed fast-fading fortunes of the American family. But the report was too late. The sweeping victories conservatives had scored in 1980 and the popular assumption of the effectiveness of the New Christian Right in those victories assured that the recommendations of the White House Conference would not be acted upon. At the same time, the issue of the family in American life would continue to demand attention.

In the first year of his administration, Ronald Reagan concentrated on putting his economic programs in place. Some of his New Christian Right supporters felt his failure to move simultaneously on social programs signaled a betrayal of their conservative goals.

Reagan continued to move cautiously on "pro-family" programs in 1982 precisely because they were even more controversial than his economic recovery measures. Still, his commitment to a social policy paralleling the goals of the New Christian Right is abundantly clear.

In his address before the National Affairs Briefing, sponsored by the Religious Roundtable in Dallas on August 22, 1980, Reagan told a wildly cheering crowd: "The office of the presidency must ensure that the awesome power of government respects the rights of parents and the integrity of the family" (Reagan, 1980: 4). Then, later in that address, he said that we should help families "to care for one another, rather than driving their members into impersonal dependence upon government programs and government institutions."

It was President Reagan's close friend and campaign manager in both 1976 and 1980, Senator Paul Laxalt, who introduced the Family Protection Act in 1980. An omnibus bill, the proposed legislation covered some 38 distinct measures dealing with education, welfare, First Amendment guarantees, taxation, and domestic relations. When Senator Laxalt first introduced the bill, it was not considered by most Washington analysts to be a serious piece of legislation. Not so when the Family Protection Act was reintroduced in 1981 with cosponsorship from Senator Roger Jepsen and Representative Albert Lee Smith.

President Reagan (1982) told the conservative National Religious Broadcasters that "rebuilding America begins with restoring family strength and preserving family values." In that same address, in a gesture of support to the New Christian Right leadership, he stated, "I do not agree with those who accuse you of trying to impose your views on others." The Family Protection Act, along with other legislation judged by conservatives to be profamily, received considerable attention in 1982, although it failed to be enacted into law.

TV PREACHERS AS THE VANGUARD OF THE NEW CHRISTIAN RIGHT

The New Christian Right is a coalescence of a range of diverse and previously only loosely connected groups. Many are single-issue groups fighting abortion and ERA, such as the Pro Family Forum, the Right to Life Commission, and the Eagle Forum. Some have been on the political scene for a long time, such as the Institute for Christian Economics. Others, such as the Moral Majority, Christian Voice, and the Christian Roundtable, are newcomers to the political process.

While they have diverse interests and goals, these groups share an anger about what is happening to America. American culture has moved significantly in directions that seriously affront their personal beliefs, which are grounded in evangelical faith. Explicit sex in print and broadcast media are morally wrong, they feel, and there is a clear causal relationship between this development and the soaring divorce rate, living together out of wedlock, casual sex, and so on. In their view, abortion is the taking of human life. To speak of the right of a woman to determine whether to carry a pregnancy is to hide the truth that millions of unborn babies have been murdered.

But these issues represent only the tip of the iceberg. Anger and moral indignation run deep, and resentment about what is happening in and to America has been growing for a long time. Perhaps what angers these groups most is that they do not believe that the rest of society and, particularly, the government have taken them seriously. They are tired of being treated as a lunatic fringe or just another interest group that is not strong enough to be factored into political decisions. Partly because their own values have held politics to be dirty and partly because the political process has discounted their importance, they have developed feelings of powerlessness and second-class citizenship.

From the vantage point of these groups, this nation has fallen from greatness because it has turned its back on God. "Getting right with God" requires repentance and cleaning up of a lot of individual and collective sin. Substantial segments of this belief system have been shared by evangelicals for many years. Billy Graham's crusades have not strayed very far from these themes in a quarter of a century.

However, two new ingredients make this emerging coalition important. The first is the belief that it is the *responsibility*, indeed the *duty*, of Christians to engage in the political process as a means to bring America back to God. While the notion that religion and politics do not mix is historically a myth, it has guided the consciousness of most evangelical Christians in recent history. The old beliefs had to be undone. Ironically, it was Jimmy Carter's public profession that he was a "born again" Christian that began to challenge conventional Bible Belt wisdom about the separation of church and state. By 1980 many evangelicals who supported Carter in 1976 were disillusioned with him, but not with the political process. Like the liberals of the 1950s and 1960s, they had come to believe that morality can be legislated; hence it is important to get the right people elected to office (see Vander Jagt, 1980).

The second factor that makes the emerging New Christian Right coalition important is involvement of the television preachers. These are the dynamos behind the thrust of born-again politics. While only a few of the "televangelists" have engaged in direct advocacy of political involvement, latent political messages are present in the messages of the large majority. They constantly remind their audiences of the collective sins of the nation and of the need to repent and bring America back to God.

There are now some 95 syndicated religious television programs being monitored by Arbitron. This does not include most of the programs that are telecast via satellite to a burgeoning cable system in America. There are approximately 600 commercial stations that offer exclusively religious programming, and a total of 1000 that offer at least 14 hours per week of religious content.

The reason the electronic church is important — the reason it has captured the concern of America — is not found in audience size or budgets or air time. It is found in the potential clout of these people to reshape American culture. Unlike the smorgasbord of religious pluralism that one can find in virtually every American community, the menu of spiritual messages on the airwaves is substantially limited to fundamentalist and evangelical offerings. While it would be naive and foolish to fail to see the diversity within the fundamentalist and evangelical camps, there is considerable homogeneity in the conservative theological emphasis. And, as repeated social science investigations have demonstrated, there are clear links between conservative theology and conservative political ideology. Only a few radio and television preachers have publicly pronounced the wedding of conservative theology and conservative politics. The latent link, however, is present in almost all of the conservative traditions.

From a long tradition of circuit riders, tent preachers, and Elmer Gantry-like revivalists, the evangelists — now the televangelists — have come a long way. No longer are they simply safeguarding the moral and spiritual character of their private constituency. No longer are they satisfied with Sister Lou or Brother Jim finding the Lord and being born again. For, while salvation may still be their goal, the sinner is not you and me anymore — it's America. And to save America takes a lot of believers, a lot of money, and a lot of power.

The power of the televangelists lies in their potential to mobilize large masses of everyday Christians. Various polls have estimated the number of evangelicals all the way from 30 to 85 million, depending on the defining criteria. What proportion of this group can be mobilized to support the political objectives of the New Christian Right depends on the political sophistication with which they develop their campaign.

Religious broadcasters represent a nascent social movement. One of the critical components of a successful social movement is access to media. Every important social movement since television has been waged via mass communications. Marches and demonstrations are means to gain the attention of the news media and thereby bring the causes of social movement leaders into America's living rooms on the evening news and in the morning newspapers.

The New Christian Right does not have to draw a crowd to attract the attention of the media. They have merely to turn on their television cameras. They already have access to large audiences, and they have developed proven methods to raise the money to retain access. The audiences they are reaching are not nearly as large as they claim, but they are sufficiently large to develop powerful social movement organizations. And when they want the rest of the country to pay attention, they can use their access to the airwaves to organize events such as "Washington for Jesus." Furthermore, as we have seen through the person of Jerry Falwell, they have considerable potential to capture the attention of even larger audiences via access to the secular media. Astutely mobilized, this potential power base will not be easily checked.

Yet another factor that gives this nascent social movement so much potential power is its mastery of the ancillary technology of television, which pivots around the computer. Direct mail, targeted to audiences likely to be sympathetic to a cause, is the foundation. It is a proven way to raise big money and mobilize people to a cause.

Still another component of a successful social movement is the cause or causes pursued. Virtually all social movements begin with no more than a small percentage of the general population in favor of the positions being advocated by social movement activists. To gain support they must eventually convince the general public of the legitimacy of their cause. There are a variety of ways to legitimize a cause, but all major social movements must ultimately legitimize their activities and goals at a cosmological level. The causes they advocate and the activities in which they engage are pursued because it is the will of the Almighty.

The civil rights movement owed its success in no small measure to its ability to identify brotherhood and justice as goals ordained by God. The leaders of the New Christian Right have carved out four basic issues they hope to define as God given and, therefore, self-evident: family, life, morality, and country. Of these four, the family is fast emerging as the *master* issue. Let us examine next how they have used the old prophecy of the death of the family to weave together their broad agenda to save America.

TELEVANGELIST MESSAGES ABOUT THE AILING AMERICAN FAMILY

Jerry Falwell is not the intellectual leader of the New Christian Right, but he is easily its most visible spokesperson. As the Moral

Majority has evolved, Falwell has elaborated the list of things for which the organization stands. Most of the issues that the Moral Majority addresses can be seen as elaborations on four initial issues. The Moral Majority is (1) traditional profamily, (2) prolife, (3) promorality, and (4) pro-America.

Affirmation of the "traditional" family is a rejection of all forms of family life other than the marriage of a man to a woman. Implicit in this affirmation is a rejection of divorce, because marriage is for life. Homosexual and common-law marriages are rejected explicitly. Rejection of the ERA can also be subsumed under the affirmation of the traditional family, for the ERA constitutes a threat to traditional sex roles and the division of labor between husband and wife.

A "prolife" stand is a stand in opposition to abortion under any circumstances. The Moral Majority rejects the 1973 Supreme Court decision that legalized abortion, and they are prepared to work for legislation and/or a constitutional amendment to outlaw abortion.

Promorality focuses mainly on opposition to pornography, although opposition to illegal drug traffic is also included. To date, the Moral Majority has devoted much more energy to fighting pornography than to fighting drugs.

All of these issues, in one way or another, deal with the Moral Majority's perception of the "traditional" family. Pornography, print and broadcast, destroys families by filling minds with lust, which leads to disobedience of God's commandments about sex. Even the affirmation of a strong America is rooted in the alleged demise of the family. As members of the Moral Majority see it, sinister forces are at work to topple America from greatness. The strategy America's enemies have chosen for the accomplishment of this goal is the destruction of the traditional family.

What is presented as a set of positive affirmations by the Moral Majority thus turns out to be a rejection of "nontraditional" lifestyles and values.

It is important to stress that while the New Christian Right is a loose coalition, there is rather considerable consensus about the centrality of the family in its agenda of social concerns. There is also the same strong negativism that is found in the writings and sermons of Falwell. Most of the members of the New Christian Right see enemies of the family everywhere, working to destroy this holy of holy institutions. The strong element of defensiveness can be gleaned from the titles of their books: *Attack on the Family, The Battle for the Family,* and *How to Protect the Family.*

But what do the New Christian Right leaders affirm about the family? Writes Falwell (1981: 110):

The family is the fundamental building block and basic unit of our society, and its continued health is a prerequisite for a healthy and prosperous nation.

James Robison (1980: 7) a fiery televangelist from Texas and vice-president of the Christian Roundtable, agrees:

> All that America has become — a strong, thriving nation, full of creativity, variety, and uniqueness — owes itself to the foundational influence of marriage and the family.

Charles Stanley, pastor of the First Baptist Church in Atlanta, the home base for his television ministry called "In Touch," also concurs. Speaking to the "Washington for Jesus" rally on April 20, 1980, Stanley said:

> [The] home is the most important institution in America today. No nation has ever survived the collapse of its home life. The home is established by God, and the home is to be the foundation of society.

Similar affirmations of the centrality of the family to the well-being of the country can be found in the sermons and tracts of virtually all of the televangelists — whether or not they cross over into the political arena with Falwell.

But what about the family itself? What about the positive roles of nurture, love, and support? One can infer from the sermons of the leaders of the New Christian Right, and from short passages in their books, that the family is a loving, supporting institution. But relatively little space or time is devoted to elaboration of these positive dimensions of the family. The overwhelming message that comes across in their printed and audiovisual messages is that the family is an institution for which the primary function is the exercise of social control over the base impulses of human beings. And, at this moment in history, it stands in perilous danger of losing the battle.

There is virtual consensus among the televangelists that the American family is under attack as never before in the nation's history. The attackers are diffuse, but evangelical theology allows that Satan is behind the onslaught. (In contrast to main-line Christian theology, demonic forces are very much alive in fundamentalist-evangelical theology). In the 1950s, Satan's instrument to destroy America was unabashedly the atheistic communists. They are still around. Falwell (1980: 82-96) has a chapter on "the threat of communism" in his book, *Listen America*. James Robison (1980: 9-11) writes about "the collectivists" in his book, *Attack on the Family,* and cites (inaccurately) content from *The Communist Manifesto* to identify their goals. But the scare tactics of a "commie in every closet" and "better dead than red," which characterized the era of Joseph McCarthy, are largely missing.

The communists who in the 1950s threatened to infiltrate and take over our government have been replaced by new enemies who have already infiltrated our government, media, and educational institutions. In many instances, the new enemies mean well, but their minds have been corrupted by the awesome arsenal of Satanic forces. If they are diverse in their motives, these enemies stand united in their intent to destroy the family. And what better way to destroy America than to erode the family — the foundation upon which this godly nation was built?

Tim LaHaye, pastor of one of the largest churches in the country, founder and president of Family Seminars, and one of the three members of the board of directors of the Moral Majority, gave the new enemies a name. In his best-selling book, *The Battle for the Mind*, LaHaye (1980) details how the *secular humanists* have plotted to take over America. Beginning with only a tiny cadre early in this century, they have profoundly influenced media, education, and public policy. Even today, according to LaHaye, there are only about a quarter of a million dedicated secular humanists. But they have so influenced how we think and what we think that they have impact far beyond their number.

Through the skillful use of the media, the secular humanists are said to promote world views that erode commitment to traditional family values. Abortion, adultery, premarital sex, free love, divorce and remarriage, and rebellion against authority, to name but a few issues, have become commonplace subjects in the media. To deal with these issues without moral protestation is to render them legitimate. In the name of fairness and openness to alternative viewpoints, thus, the media have sanctioned rebellion against God's commandments.

Falwell believes the media have been instrumental in promoting the "cult of the playboy." He sees this philosophy as the "most dangerous" factor in the "war against the family." "This . . . philosophy," writes Falwell (1980: 123-124), "tells men that they do not have to be committed to their wife and to their children. . . . It is more than just a revolution of dirty magazines. It represents a life style that ultimately corrupts the family." Kennedy (1981: 2) echoes Falwell on this point: "The 'playboy philosophy' promotes a life style that says 'up with lust, down with the family.'"

Education, too, has become a sanctuary for advocating rebellion against God's word. "Creation versus evolution" has become another rallying cry of the fundamentalists. But the heart of the issue is not what the public schools teach about how the world was created. The problem is that public schools socialize young people to all sorts of values that run contrary to fundamentalist doctrine, not the least of which is the legitimacy of developing independent thought and the questioning of authority.

The Christian school movement may once have received support from persons whose primary motive was the avoidance of desegregation. Today the issue is not racial segregation, but segregation of children from public school systems that threaten the values of these fundamentalist Christians. Let it be noted that this movement is not without precedent. Virtually every sectarian school movement in the history of this nation has been motivated by the desire to socialize children to a particular group's world view.

According to the New Christian Right, the media and our public education system have molded a cultural value system that is anchored in secular humanism rather than godly principles. Secular humanism has penetrated the halls of Congress, the courts, and the executive office. The goal of the New Christian Right is to change the composition of all branches of government, replacing those who willfully or unwittingly have fallen prey to the secular humanist philosophy.

The armies of the New Christian Right, like the loyal supporters of Senator McCarthy, know that their enemies are everywhere. The true believers among their troops, like the dedicated forces in any social movement, know that the world can be divided between those who are for them and those who serve the pernicious secular humanists. This reasoning is captured in a fundamentalist bumper sticker that reads: "God said it. I believe it. That settles it." Either you are for them in every painstaking detail or you serve secular humanism.

Alarm about the rise of the New Christian Right has generated a predictable countermobilization of persons who stand in opposition to the group's beliefs. In fact, there is something approaching a state of hysteria about the implications of fundamentalist Christians becoming as zealous about their politics as they are about their faith. Those who believe that the New Christian Right constitutes a threat to our pluralistic culture are busy creating organizations and putting new life into old organizations in an effort to combat its influence.

In the final section of this chapter, I examine the potential of the New Christian Right to exert significant political influence and thereby impose on America its viewpoints about the family.

ASSESSING THE POWER
OF THE NEW CHRISTIAN RIGHT

The single most important fact in assessing the rise of the New Christian Right is that its power has been grossly exaggerated.[1] Prior to the 1980 National Republican Convention in Detroit, the New Christian Right was virtually unknown to the media and, hence, America. When Jerry Falwell and his Moral Majority showed up in force, the media took note. When they learned a few weeks later that Ronald Reagan was to address a gathering of born-again politicians in Dallas, the press showed up in force — more than 250 strong.

From that date forward, the involvement of right-wing Christians in the election was one of the big campaign stories. By election time, the country was braced for the election of a former second-rate cowboy movie star to the White House, but the stunning defeat of many liberal senators and house members required explanation.

Jerry Falwell, whose name became practically a household word during the campaign, wasted no time in stepping forward to claim responsibility for the political upsets in the name of the Moral Majority and other New Christian Right organizations. Pollster Louis Harris agreed with Falwell's assessment. So did several of the defeated senators and members of Congress. It seemed — and the media played up the idea — that the televangelists had created a force to be reckoned with.

Skeptics thought that Jerry Falwell and the Moral Majority would go away after the election. They were wrong. Not everybody bought Falwell's claims about being a central figure in the outcome of the elections, but neither were his claims seriously challenged. At age 47, with nearly 25 years of experience in front of television cameras, Falwell proved to be very adept at gaining media attention.

Much of what was written about Falwell and his followers was not very favorable, but people kept writing. A year after the elections, Falwell was in the news more than he was during the 1980 campaign. Through a combination of luck and skillful media manipulation, Falwell kept himself in the limelight in the role of emerging power broker.

Shortly after the national elections, the Moral Majority joined forces with a little group called the Coalition for Better Television. They threatened to boycott sponsors of programs that "promote sex, violence and profanity." They called off the boycott during the summer of 1981, claiming a major victory, when Procter and Gamble announced withdrawal of sponsorship of network programs that did not meet its program guidelines. This was hailed as a great victory and evidence of the group's political power. No one challenged the ability of the Moral Majority and its allies to stage a successful boycott.

Liberals did a lot to help Falwell's cause. Even before the elections, Norman Lear (1980), creator of several of the most successful television situation comedies of the 1970s, organized People for the American Way to combat the "pernicious danger" of "fascism masquerading as Christianity." After his defeat, former Senator George McGovern organized another group called Americans for Common Sense. The ACLU wasted little time in sounding an alert about the assault on civil liberties being orchestrated by the Moral Majority. Common Cause (1981) also joined the campaign, claiming that Falwell and other New Christian Right leaders were trying to "radically change our Constitutional system of checks and balances."

Many individuals joined in sounding the alarm. Yale University President A. Bartlett Giamatti sent a letter to the entering freshman class in the fall of 1981 warning against the radical assault on freedom coming from the Moral Majority and other New Christian Right organizations. Wrote Giamatti (1981: 28):

> Angry at change, rigid in the application of chauvinistic slogans, absolutistic in morality, they threaten through political pressure or public denunciation whoever dares to disagree with their authoritarian positions. Using television, direct mail and economic boycott, they would sweep before them anyone who holds a different opinion.

Several other college presidents quickly followed suit, publicly denouncing Falwell and his followers. For months there was an almost never-ending outpouring of attacks on Falwell. Each public outcry resulted in at least two news stories: one an account of the criticism and another a report of a rebuttal from Falwell or his spokesman.

Falwell's friends also helped to keep him visible. When Israeli Prime Minister Menachem Begin bombed the Saudi nuclear power plant, he called Falwell and asked him to rally Americans in support of this act. And later that year, when Begin visited Washington, he warmly received Falwell and a group of the Moral Majority leader's friends at Blair House. President Reagan also gave credence to the image of Falwell as an important spokesman for conservatives when he called Falwell to ask for his support when he nominated Sandra O'Connor to be the first woman Supreme Court justice. And Falwell's initial feisty defiance made him seem all the stronger.

The only problem with the unfolding political drama portraying Jerry Falwell as the powerful leader of many emerging New Christian Right organizations was that the press and the politicians did not bother to check the facts.

Jerry Falwell is not alone when it comes to exaggerating the size of his television audience. Virtually all the televangelists do, just as itinerant evangelists are prone to exaggerate the number of souls that were saved in their last crusade down the road. It is an accepted part of fundamentalist folk culture.

In June 1981, two independently published reports, one using Arbitron data, the other Nielson data, reported Jerry Falwell's audience to be about 1.5 million, not the 25 or 50 million variously claimed by Falwell (Hadden and Swann, 1981; Martin, 1981). The false claims about audience size proved to be a popular news item around the country for several months. Still, there seemed to be a reluctance to accept the implications of this datum: If Falwell had lied about his TV following, is it not possible that he had also uttered misleading statements about both his Moral Majority following and its political accomplishments?

The answer is an emphatic yes. The first significant evidence pointing to the conclusion that America had overestimated the power of the evangelical involvement in the elections was presented in an article by Lipset and Raab published in *Commentary* in March 1981. Having examined a mass of polling and election data, Lipset and Raab (1981: 30) conclude: "What all these findings seem to indicate is that the efforts to mobilize a religious constituency for political purposes in America had *no measurable effect* on the 1980 elections" (emphasis added). Lipset and Raab (1981: 30) continue:

> Instead, the available evidence appears to sustain the thesis that the electoral swing toward conservatism and the emergence of a political evangelical movement will parallel developments which have been mutually reinforcing rather than related to one another as cause and effect.

Lipset and Raab (1980: 30) further warn that the danger of giving groups such as the Moral Majority "more credit than they deserve [is] to run the risk of self-fulfilling prophecy. . . . If politicians become convinced that the Moral Majority is a decisive force in American life, they are likely to treat it as such, just to be on the safe side."

In *Prime Time Preachers* (1981), Charles Swann and I wrote about the great *potential* evangelicals have to amass political power, but we cautioned against interpreting the 1980 election outcomes as evidence of power achieved. And we presented substantial data to support our caution. Some of our data paralleled evidence presented by Lipset and Raab, but we used independent data sources.

Evidence challenging the assumption of the great power and influence of Jerry Falwell and the Moral Majority continues to mount. A *Washington Post* ABC News poll conducted in June 1981 found that only 49 percent of the American public had heard or read about the Moral Majority (Peterson and Sussman, 1981). This, even after the enormous amount of publicity Falwell and the organization had received over the previous ten months. Of those who had heard of the Moral Majority, 37 percent said they generally approved of the group's positions. But this figure is very misleading. Almost half who said they generally approved of Moral Majority positions also favored the Equal Rights Amendment. And 40 percent approving Moral Majority positions agreed with the proposition that "homosexuals and lesbians should be allowed to teach in public schools, and that homosexual relations between consenting adults should be legal" (Peterson and Sussman, 1981). The Moral Majority stands in strong opposition to the ERA and the homosexual propositions. The 37 percent approval of Moral Majority positions thus must be interpreted as a very soft number. The truth is that a lot of people do not know where the Moral Majority stands on a lot of issues.

One might assume that Falwell would have both greater recognition and a greater following close to home. These assumptions are not supported by two independent polls conducted during the Virginia gubernatorial race during the fall of 1981. A *Richmond Times-Dispatch* (1981: 1) poll revealed that only 13 percent of Virginians approved of the Moral Majority's goals, while 49 percent said they disapproved. Right in his home state, thus, almost 4 out of 10 citizens did not know or had no opinion about Falwell's Moral Majority. An even more telling indicator of Falwell's political strength in Virginia is revealed by the *Times-Dispatch* poll: Only 4 percent of those surveyed said they would be more inclined to vote for a candidate endorsed by Falwell, while 24 percent said they would be less likely to do so (Richmond Times-Dispatch, 1981: 1).

The second Virginia poll, conducted for the *Virginia Pilot* (1981: 27) in Norfolk, found that only 10 percent of those surveyed had positive evaluations of Falwell, while 54 percent had negative evaluations.

A survey conducted in the Dallas-Fort Worth metropolitan area during the same time span affirms other evidence of the limited influence of the New Christian Right (Shupe and Stacey, 1981). Only 14 percent of those surveyed in the metropolis supported the Moral Majority. And, as in the *Washington Post* poll, many who said they supported the Moral Majority did not support Moral Majority positions: 34 percent disagreed with the proposition "Abortion is a sin against God's law," and 41 percent supported the ERA to guarantee women equal rights.[2]

An examination of the social and demographic characteristics of the supporters of the Moral Majority leads sociologists Shupe and Stacey (1981: 28) to conclude that the New Christian Right "is a social movement whose membership/support base is preponderantly composed of fundamentalist Christians rather than some interdenominational or ecumenical population."

If the preponderance of data runs counter to the widely held assumption that the evangelical Christians have already amassed enormous power and are now positioned to take over America, extreme caution should be exercised in shifting to the opposite conclusion that they are totally lacking in a power base. There are several reasons this is so.

The first reason is the group's unique access to mass media. No other social movement has ever had the kind of access to media that they do. Even after we discount Falwell's exaggerated audience claims, he is still talking to approximately 1.5 million persons each week. And there are a lot of other televangelists reaching significant audiences with messages that, though not blatantly political, are generally supportive of the proposition that America must return to godly principles. Furthermore, the televangelists have command of the ancillary technology of the electronic church that is so critical to the raising of large sums of money. Media access and money are clearly two of the most important ingredients of a successful social movement.

A second important reason that the New Christian Right is not to be dismissed is that their potential constituency is very large. To date, no more than one-third to one-half of the religiously conservative Protestants in America could be counted as sympathetic to the Moral Majority or some other New Christian Right organization. If mobilized, they would represent a significant political minority in America.

A recently released study of American values found that 26 percent of those over age 14 are "highly religious" (Pollock, 1981: 43). That amounts to 45 million adults. While it is theoretically possible to score "high" on the study's eight-item scale of religiosity without being theologically conservative, it is unlikely. Of those aged 65 or over, 46 percent were "highly religious." This fact has long-range implications as our nation gradually ages.

In addition to the potential to mobilize evangelicals and fundamentalists, there are a lot of conservative persons who are only marginally religious. While not institutionally involved in religion, they stand ready to "vote" for religion. A 1978 George Gallup survey estimated the number of unchurched Americans at 61 million. What most impressed Gallup in his examination of the characteristics of the unchurched was their similarity to the churched. They pray. They believe in Jesus Christ. They believe in the resurrection. "With a few distinct variations . . . the unchurched claim the church as the churched — except they are *not* attending, supporting, or belonging to a congregation of the visible church" (Gallup and Poling, 1980: 89). Furthermore, the unchurched, like the churched, affirm traditional family values (Gallup and Poling, 1980: 82).

The Shupe and Stacey (1981) study also demonstrates the potential for support among the nominally religious. Of the persons they surveyed in the Dallas-Fort Worth area, 44 percent reported church attendance of only "now and then" or less.[3] Still, 87 percent of their sample believed that prayer should be allowed in the schools, and 73 percent favored teaching the Biblical account of creation in public schools.[4]

Social movements are first and foremost in the business of shaping public opinion. Almost always they begin from minority positions and gradually develop support for their causes. To sustain a movement, they need a solid core of supporters. The mass of public support can be soft so long as it constitutes a majority and responds affirmatively to the questions posed by the pollsters. How people respond to questions depends on how the questions are raised. This means that the success of a social movement depends, in part, on shaping the questions so that it is easy for people to agree with them.

By selecting the family as one of its central concerns, the New Christian Right has aligned itself with a plurality issue. No one is against the family — or hardly anyone. The strategic issue is *how* the group aligns itself with the family. To date, the moral absolutism of the New Christian Right has deprived it of a lot of potential support. The abortion issue illustrates the matter well. Even the most liberal Protestant leaders in America have difficulty supporting unrestricted abortion. It is an agonizing issue that defies a satisfactory moral position. By taking an absolute and uncompromising position on abortion as murder, the New Christian Right deprives itself of many potential supporters. The same can be said of almost every other issue that troubles the New Christian Right.

All social movements are caught between holding on to a hard core of "true believers" and reaching out to build larger constituencies. It can be a precarious and dangerous line to walk. What we have learned thus far about the New Christian Right is that it has not strayed very far from the old issues of personal morality that have bothered and periodically rallied conservative Christians for a long time. And as a result, it has not broadened the base of its constituency.

As long as the New Christian Right defines issues *only* in absolutist principles, it will be perceived as an extremist element in society and will not significantly increase its following. The Moral Majority may become a very vocal minority in America, but it is not likely to build a significant following until it succeeds in presenting its concerns in ways that can be *perceived* as reasonable by much larger sectors of society.

TOWARD UNDERSTANDING THE REAL PROBLEMS OF THE FAMILY

The American family is a troubled institution. Few will deny this proposition. Ogburn's (1933) analysis of the demise of the family a half-century ago was not based on speculation alone. The critical flaw in his analysis, however, was not very different from the error in reasoning of the modern-day "family fixers." Both Ogburn and the New Christian Right leadership confuse change with demise. Certainly change produces disruption in processes that over time come to be defined as "normal." But this is not necessarily synonymous with demise.

The disruptions that are occurring in the American family result from both *changing social structures* and *changing values*. The changing size and composition of the nuclear family is an example of structural change. One of the most important comparisons that can be made between the mid-nineteenth- and mid-twentieth-century American family is that the former had an average of six children, in contrast to only two for the latter (U.S. Bureau of the Census, 1974). The mid-nineteenth-century mother spent virtually her entire adult life in a nuclear family with children present; on the average, there was a period of only 1.8 years between the marriage of the last child and the mother's death. By contrast, the mid-twentieth-century mother can expect an empty nest for fully three decades, and can expect to survive her spouse by nearly a decade.

Choosing to have fewer children or the female's choice to pursue a career are examples of changing patterns. Whether husband and wife pursue dual careers, or the female enters the labor force out of boredom, the need for a second paycheck, or the desire for extra earnings to enhance leisure lifestyle activities, the movement of women into the labor force alters the division of labor and the mutual expectations husbands and wives have one for another. This is very likely to create tension.

The New Christian Right leadership would interpret this tension as resulting from a violation of the fundamental and God-ordained division of labor between the husband and wife. In their view, although there may be exceptions, in the final analysis the woman's place is in the home as mother, wife, and homemaker. To assert that women have the right to pursue a career is to utter the heresy of feminism, a godless ideology grounded in secular humanism.

The New Christian Right is seriously lacking in any systematic analysis or appreciation of structural and value changes that are taking place in American society. They seek scapegoats that can explain complex phenomena with simple labels. A case in point is LaHaye's (1982) treatment of the phenomenon of women in the labor force. LaHaye, executive committee member of the Moral Majority and one of the "intellectual" leaders of the New Christian Right, offers several reasons, including economic necessity, for the presence of women in the labor force. Then he proceeds to chip away at the legitimacy of each of these reasons and concludes, in the final analysis, that is is "the feminist movement, which has agitated careerism, . . . based on humanist commitment to self actualization" that is responsible for women in the labor force (LaHaye, 1982: 176).

LaHaye's book *The Battle for the Family* (1982), like his earlier best seller, *The Battle for the Mind* (1980), is a diatribe about what is wrong with American society from the fundamentalist's perspective. Only tangentially does the book deal with the family. His laundry list of things that ail America closely parallels Jerry Falwell's. How these ills are related to the family is often not clear. We are told that social ills are destroying the family, while, in almost the same breath, we are told that the breakdown of traditional Christian values is what has permitted the social ills to flourish. Careful reading of the books and sermons of these men fails to reveal any systematic cause-and-effect analysis.

So long as Jerry Falwell, Tim LaHaye, Pat Robertson, James Robison, and the other New Christian Right leaders possess the "truth" about what ails the family, we are probably safe from the most pernicious acts they might commit in the name of fixing the family. This is not to say they will not be mischievous. They will. But their views are simply too far afield from the mainstream of American values to garner sufficient political strength to impose their family policy package on this nation.

In his 1933 assessment of the status of the family, Ogburn identifies a seventh function, which he calls, a bit awkwardly, "personality." Somewhat timidly, Ogburn argues that the decline in the other functions, especially the economic functions, of the family is shifting the central role of the family toward personal development and socioemotional fulfillment. Had Ogburn been bold enough to pursue this, he might have analyzed how love, rather than economic necessity, functions as the glue that holds the family together.

If the New Christian Right were to grasp this important fact about the modern American family, much of its contrived rhetoric against feminists and secular humanists could be eschewed and replaced with a gospel of love. A theology that emphasizes how love can overcome the tensions and contradictions of modern life could establish a much firmer foundation to build a *real* moral majority.

Jerry Falwell and his New Christian Right friends appear to be engaging in pugnacious resistance to compromise their social agenda. While chiding unrelenting fundamentalists like Bob Jones III, Falwell seems more preoccupied with looking over his shoulder to see if the likes of Jones are following him than with charting a course of accommodation that would permit him to build a broader constituency.

If and when the Moral Majority sets its mind on becoming a real majority, America will be faced with a great opportunity as well as great peril. The danger is that the group will enhance its political skills and abilities to manipulate the media without altering its agenda. This possibility must be taken seriously. If groups such as Norman Lear's People for the American Way have overreacted to any real and immediate danger, they nevertheless serve an important role in guarding against political excesses from the right.

On the other hand, there is nothing to fear from a Moral Majority that can learn to temper its rhetoric and change its mind in the face of evidence. To date, the members of the New Christian Right appear to have treated the family as a symbol of all that troubles them about American society. But the family is the locus of real problems that are crying for understanding and solutions. Opportunity rests in the prospect of liberals and conservatives joining in the honest pursuit of real solutions to real problems.

NOTES

1. For arguments regarding the exaggerated strength of the New Christian Right, see Hadden and Swann (1981) and Lipset and Raab (1981).
2. The figures cited here were computed from Shupe and Stacey (1981: 19, Table 3).
3. See note 2.
4. See note 2.

REFERENCES

Caplow, T. E. et al. (1981) Middletown Families: 50 Years of Change and Continuity. Minneapolis: University of Minnesota Press.

Common Cause (1981) Advertisement in the New York Times, October 11.

Falwell, J. (1981) The Fundamentalist Phenomenon: The Resurgence of Conservative Christianity. (Edited with E. Dobson and E. Hindson.) Garden City, NY: Doubleday.

———— (1980) Listen America. Garden City, NY: Doubleday.

Gallup, G., Jr., and D. Poling (1980) The Search for America's Faith. Nashville: Abingdon.

Gallup Opinion Index (1978) Survey of the Unchurched American. Princeton, NJ: American Institute of Public Opinion.

Giamatti, A. B. (1981) "Liberal education and the new coercion." Yale Alumni Magazine (October): 27-29.

Hadden, J. K. and C. E. Swann (1981) Prime Time Preachers. Reading, MA: Addison-Wesley.

Kennedy, D. J. (1981) "Assault on the family." Messenger 3 (September): 1981.

LaHaye, T. (1982) The Battle for the Family. Old Tappan, NJ: Fleming H. Revell.

———— (1980) The Battle for the Mind. Old Tappan, NJ: Fleming H. Revell.

Lear, N. (1980) People for the American Way direct mail letter, October.

Lipset, S. M. and E. Raab (1981) "The election and the evangelicals." Commentary 71 (March): 25-31.

Martin, W. C. (1981) "The birth of a media myth." Atlantic (June): 9-11, 16.

Ogburn, W. F. with the assistance of C. Tibbits (1933) "The family and its functions," pp. 661-708 in Recent Social Trends in the United States. New York: McGraw-Hill.

Peterson, B. and B. Sussman (1981) "Moral Majority is growing in recognition, but it remains unknown to half the public." Washington Post (June 13).

Pollock, J. C. (1981) The Connecticut Mutual Life Report on American Values in the '80s: The Impact of Belief. Hartford: Connecticut Mutual Life Insurance.

Reagan, R. (1982) Address to the National Religious Broadcasters, Washington, D.C., February 9.

———— (1980) Address to the Roundtable National Affairs Briefing, Dallas, August 22.

Richmond Times-Dispatch (1981) September 27: 1.

Robison, J. (1980) Attack on the Family. Wheaton, IL: Tyndale House.

Shupe, A. D:, Jr., and W. A. Stacey (1981) "An assessment of grass roots support for the new religious right." Department of Sociology, University of Texas — Arlington. (unpublished)

Stanley, C. (1980) Address to Washington for Jesus rally, Washington, D.C., April 29.

Steiner, G. Y. (1981) The Futility of Family Policy. Washington, DC: Brookings.

U.S. Bureau of the Census (1974) Fertility Histories and Birth Expectations of American Women: June 1971. Current Population Reports, Series P-20, No. 263. Washington, DC: Government Printing Office.

Vander Jagt, G. (1980) Address to the Roundtable National Affairs Briefing, Dallas, August 21.

Virginia Pilot (1981) October 4: 27.

11

FAMILY IN THE MORMON EXPERIENCE

Darwin L. Thomas

Formidable challenges face any observer of religious phenomena, but the challenges seem especially acute for the observer of the Mormon scene. O'Dea (1957: 115) the sociological analyst and describer of Mormonism,[1] is at times not sure whether Mormonism is best seen as a "near-sect" or a "near-nation." *The Harvard Encyclopedia of American Ethnic Groups* categorizes the Mormons as ethnic and notes they are "perhaps the only American ethnic group whose principal migration began as an effort to move out of the United States" (May, 1980: 720). Ahlstrom (1972: 508), in his history of American religions, observes that the historian is ill equipped to deal with Mormonism since no one is sure whether it is a "sect, a mystery cult, a new religion, a church, a people, a nation or an American subculture."

With Ralph Waldo Emerson's categorization of Mormonism as "an afterclap of puritanism" (Michaelsen, 1977: 149), cultural explanations have been offered for many of the distinctive characteristics of Mormon thought and practice. Bushman[2] refers to such cultural context explanations as "sponge theory," meaning that the founder of Mormonism, Joseph Smith, simply soaked up what was in the culture around him, squeezed the filled-up sponge and out gushed Mormonism (Madsen, 1978: xi; Bushman, 1976). O'Dea (1957: 32) to the contrary, Bushman (1976: 4) argues that the dominant political themes of the Book of Mormon, namely, deliverance through fleeing, opposition to monarchy through righteous living, and rule by judges,

Author's Note: Appreciation is expressed to the editors of this volume as well as to the following people for helpful suggestions on earlier drafts of this chapter: Wes Burr, Kim Hawkins, Dave Kline, John Putvin, Boyd Rollins, Jim Smith, Phil Kunz, John Sorenson, and Don Herrin. This chapter is a condensed and revised version of a paper presented at the University of Notre Dame, July 1981. Copies of the more detailed manuscript are available from the author.

are all very "un-American" but are understandable when placed in Old World cultural contexts. Bushman (1976: 20) concludes: "The innermost structure of Book of Mormon politics and history are biblical, while American forms are conspicuously absent."

Nibley, in a series of publications, has argued that much of Mormonism can only be understood in light of cultural patterns of the ancient world rather than as a product of nineteenth-century Americana: the significance of the temple (1975), the Book of Mormon as a product of ancient Jewish, Egyptian, and Bedouin cultures (1952, 1957, 1967), and Book of Mormon family patterns having more in common with ancient Hebrew and Bedouin family patterns than with nineteenth-century America (1957: 77-83).[3] According to the above historians, ancient Old World cultures are the seed beds of many distinctive patterns of Mormon writings, belief, and practices, and not nineteenth-century New England.

Given the bewildering array of conflicting opinion about the nature of Mormonism and its relationship to the American experience, I recognize, along with others (for example, see Michaelsen, 1977), the existence of many enigmas in interpreting Mormonism and the impossibility of any single treatment on Mormonism holding the promise of resolving the controversies. Therefore, I have chosen what I hope is a more manageable approach. My first purpose is to present briefly the view of the family as it is embedded in basic Mormon teachings. This is an effort at exposition from an insider's[4] point of view, with an emphasis on theological underpinnings of the institution of the family. My second purpose is to discuss what some of the likely consequences are and will be for the Mormon family given its distinctive value structure in the context of the larger American value system. The second phase of this chapter looks at social science research on various characteristics of the Mormon family. It is hoped that these two thrusts of this treatment of the Mormon family will provide greater insight into the central place of the family as a religious and social institution in Mormonism and the nature of the encounter between the Mormon family and the larger American society.

FAMILY IN MORMON TEACHINGS

For the Mormon, this world's history can only be understood in connection with God's dealings with his children. And God's dealings with his children in this world can only be fully understood in connection with (1) life as it was lived before this world was created, (2) life in this mortal existence, and (3) life as it will be lived in the postmortal sphere.

In Mormon theology, the essence of the human being is coeternal with God himself. Eternal progression is the central purpose of each individual. The family becomes the central institution in each sphere of existence for the purpose of assisting the individual's eternal progress. The pre-earth life was lived as a spiritual offspring of God, our Heavenly Father, and Heavenly Mother.

While there is not scriptural support for the teaching of a heavenly mother, the concept has been important in Mormon theology from its very early history. The various leaders of Mormonism have repeatedly called attention to the central place of the concepts of heavenly parents and have taught that mortal men and women could become like their heavenly parents (O'Dea, 1957: 126-127).

Mormonism, with its anthropomorphic view of God (see Cherbonnier, 1978) and its view of eternal progress leading to the status of godhood, sees humankind as offspring of the races of the gods.[5] Its emphasis is not on "humanizing God but of deifying man, not as he is but as he may become" (Arrington and Bitton, 1980: 35).

Many of the central experiences in the processes of becoming more like God are those directly related to the family. With the purpose of this earth defined as the place where spiritual children would dwell in physical tabernacles, mortal parents become cocreators with God in his divine plan. To bear and properly teach children is one of the most important dimensions of earth life. If parents fail to teach their children of Christ, the sin will then be "upon the heads of the parents" (Doctrine and Covenants 68:25). A recent president of the church said, "Now, you husbands remember that the most important of the Lord's work that you will ever do will be the work you do within the walls of your own home" (Lee, 1973: 7).

The parent's role is not only to teach but to perform sacred ordinances. The father is expected to baptize his children, ordain them deacons, teachers, and priests in the Aaronic priesthood, and confer upon his children the Melchizedek priesthood. With the restoration of the gifts of the spirit as a basic part of the LDS church, the father is authorized to lay his hands upon the heads of his family members and heal them when ill and give them a variety of other special blessings at important times in their lives.

Parents are charged to form families, teach their children, and perform the sealing work in temples as preparatory work for the millennial reign of Christ.[6] But in a more profound way, the family is given central place in Mormonism above the functions of teaching children, giving them priesthood authority and blessings of the spirit, and preparing them for missions and spreading the gospel of Christ. This is the function of performing sacred ordinances in the temple. No man will be exalted in the celestial kingdom without a wife and no woman without a husband. Men and women can only become gods together (Doctrine and Covenants 131). Eternal family units are created by "sealing" the husband and wife together then "sealing" children to that union. Thus, as a social institution in this world, the eternal family unit is the only one with the promise of continuing into life after death. The organization of the church with apostles, prophets, and so on is seen as a this-world organization, whereas the family is a celestial social order.

If revelation is the dominant theme of Mormonism, the temple is the dominant symbol, pointing toward a man and a woman sealed for eternity entering into the presence of God. The highest and most sacred priesthood ordinances performed in the temple can only be performed by a man and a woman together. This togetherness is symbolic of the unity between Heavenly Father and Heavenly Mother.

MORMON FAMILIES IN
THE LARGER SOCIAL CONTEXT

Attempts at describing Mormonism in general lead to many enigmas, and the social scientist wishing to describe the Mormon family is likewise forced to acknowledge an acute lack of hard data and an overabundance of soft opinion. This is so because most of the standard census forms and national surveys do not include religious affiliation items such that Mormons, for example, could be pulled out and analyzed separately. The records of the Mormon church are not open to everyone's use, do not have a lot of family-related information in them, and have an unknown margin of error.[7] Neither Mormon nor non-Mormon social scientists have found the Mormon family to be an area of sustained research inquiry (Thomas, 1979).

Most of the information about Mormon families comes from a variety of relatively small, nonrepresentative samples and from census data for the state of Utah compared to national averages. The comparison of Utah with national data has to be treated with extreme caution, because no one is sure what percentage of the state of Utah is Mormon. The best guesses tend to place the non-Mormon population of the state at about 25 percent (plus or minus 10 percent; see Bahr, 1981a, for the best collection of Utah and national comparisons). With these necessary caveats, I now proceed to an analysis of available data.

Family Size

Assuming that religious beliefs affect behavior, one would expect Mormons to have higher fertility rates than Americans in general.

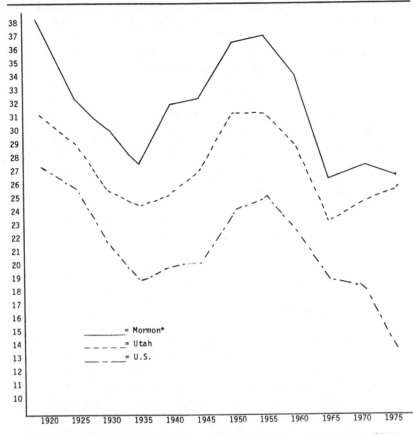

SOURCE: Adapted from Thornton (1979) and Spicer and Gustavus (1974).
Used by permission.
*This is the birthrate from Mormon church records and includes Mormons
from all parts of the world.

Figure 11.1: Crude Birthrate for Mormons, Utah, and United States, 1920-1975

Virtually all comparisons show this to be so. Figure 11.1 shows the
crude birthrate[8] for Mormons, Utah, and the United States from 1920
to 1975. In 1975, Mormons had about twice as many children born per
1000 population as the United States in general.

Fluctuations in Mormon fertility patterns appear to follow those
in the United States, suggesting that the forces existing in the larger
society have an impact on Mormon patterns also. However,
Mormons continue to have considerably higher fertility rates than the
general population. There is a hint at a beginning of a different pattern
from 1965 to 1975. Up to 1965, fertility for both the United States and

Mormons was declining. The United States continued its rather steep decline through 1975, whereas the Mormons increased or at least leveled off. Thus, since 1965, the crude birthrates for Mormons and the United States have diverged more than previously.

When Mormons are analyzed separately and family size is related to religious commitment, it is apparent that the more religious Mormons have larger families. In a study of families in Salt Lake City, Thomas (1979) reports that relatively inactive Mormons who were not married in the temple had an average of 4.2 children, while active Mormons who were married in the temple averaged 6.4 children. While this is a sample in which larger families having two children of junior high or high school age are overrepresented, it still shows the effect of religious belief and practice on family size. A difference of 2 children is a sizable difference in family size research.

The above finding becomes even more important when it is realized that the more highly committed Mormon families are also the ones with higher educational and occupational levels. Traditionally, higher educational and occupational attainment has been characterized by smaller family size. The reverse of this is true for Mormons (Thomas, 1979; Nelson, 1952). The Mormon pattern of a positive relationship between educational and occupational attainment and family size is similar to the pattern that has been reported for Catholics (Clausen, 1966). However, there is some available evidence on a number of religious dimensions that seems to show that Catholics in the United States are becoming much more like American Protestants (McIntosh and Alston, forthcoming). It may be that Catholics will no longer show the positive relationship between educational/occupational attainment and fertility rates.

Given the larger society's acceptance of a small family ethic, it can be predicted that the Mormon family, at least the committed Mormon family with a larger number of children, will experience increased strain in its encounters with institutions in the larger social settings. One consequence of the increased strain will likely be that Mormon families will seek each other out for mutual support. There is some evidence that the church and intergenerational family structure is relatively successful in giving large families enough community support that negative consequences of family size found in other families — such as increased coercive discipline and decreased affectional relations — may not characterize large Mormon families (Wilkinson and Tanner, 1980; Thomas 1979).

For those Mormons not finding sufficient support for their large family ethic in their immediate social environs, it seems reasonable to predict that they will opt for fewer children. Thus, with respect to family size, the expectation is that the polarization phenomena will continue, in that inactive Mormons will become more like families in the larger society, while active Mormons will become less like them.

Sexual Attitudes and Behavior

A religion that sees parents as partners with God in the divine plan of creation and defines sexual intercourse outside of marriage, both premarital and extramarital, as a sin ranking next to murder in seriousness (Book of Mormon, Alma 39:5) will see itself as different from the society that has just gone through the sexual revolution of the 1960s and 1970s. Some questions remain in this area of obvious strain between Mormonism's values and those of the larger society. What are contemporary sexual ethics in the Mormon family? How are Mormon values and behavior changing?

As expected, Christensen's (1962, 1976; Christensen and Gregg, 1970) research documents the conservative nature of Mormon sexual values. Respondents in the intermountain (Mormon) area were clearly more conservative than midwestern (non-Mormon) respondents, and both American samples were more conservative than Scandinavian respondents. Mauss's (1976) research showed that within Mormonism, youths' sexual attitudes varied by place of residence. A Salt Lake City sample was more orthodox in sexual attitudes and behavior than were respondents in a West Coast city. Smith's (1974, 1976) research gives further evidence about the nature of Mormon sexual values and allows for some preliminary assessment of changing attitudes and behavior.

Smith (1974) surveyed students enrolled in sociology classes at five large universities and two small colleges in the northwestern part of the United States in 1950, 1961, and 1971 (N = 8584). Thus his research covers the years of the most dramatic changes in sexual attitudes and behavior in the United States. His findings show that after controlling for age and religious activity levels, the responses of Mormon students at Brigham Young University (BYU) compared to the other universities did not differ significantly. Thus active Mormons of the same age held similar values in both Utah and the Northwest.

The most important findings, for our purposes, reported by Smith (1976) are presented in Table 11.1. As can be seen, the shift to a more liberal pattern occurred in three groups: the non-Mormon frequent and infrequent church attenders and the Mormon infrequent attenders. In these groups the change to a more liberal behavior holds for both males and females in each group. No significant change occurred from 1950 to 1961, while major attitude shifts occurred in the groups from 1961 to 1972. These data, like other research, show that the most striking liberalization occurred for females, especially the infrequent church attenders, where 87 percent reported no present participation in coitus in 1967. By 1972 this had dropped almost 40 percent to 49 percent.

TABLE 11.1   Respondents Reporting No Present Participation in Coitus Out
              of Wedlock

| | Mormons | | Non-Mormons | |
Do Not Now Participate	Frequent Church Attenders %	Infrequent Church Attenders %	Frequent Church Attenders %	Infrequent Church Attenders %
Males				
1950	91.8	62.5	66.6	55.4
1961	94.5	62.3	74.2	60.6
1972	96.2	52.1	63.0	36.8
Females				
1950	95.6	85.0	90.4	87.8
1961	96.7	78.0	93.9	87.1
1972	97.0	62.2	70.8	48.8

SOURCE: Adapted from Smith (1976). Used by permission.

Contrary to the liberal shift discussed above, the active Mormons reveal a slight trend toward a more orthodox sexual behavior. This is true for both active Mormon males and females. The trend observed in the general population, namely, the sexual behavior of females becoming more liberal and more similar to that of males, is apparently not true for active Mormon college students. With active Mormons, any change for males seems to be in the direction of a more conservative behavior similar to that of females. As Smith (1976) notes, the fact that active Mormons are becoming more conservative is remarkable, given the opposite shift in behavior for inactive Mormons as well as non-Mormons in the larger society. Christensen (1962, 1976) reports a similar finding and concludes that "the Mormon faith is more influential than most other faiths in limiting premarital sexual activity; inactive Mormons are not more restrained than non-Mormons." This polarization of values between active and inactive Mormons is best documented in research on sexual attitudes and behavior, but it appears in other findings also.

A related concern for social scientists looking at sexual behavior is the incidence of premarital pregnancies and births to teenage mothers. Some have noted with concern that since the mid-1970s, the Utah birthrate for women ages 15 to 19 has been above the national average. Figure 11.2 presents the comparison. Some have wondered what such a high teenage pregnancy rate for Utah would mean for the quality of life of mother and child involved, and have wondered how Mormon values might be related to the "unusually" high teenage pregnancy rate (Chadwick, 1981).

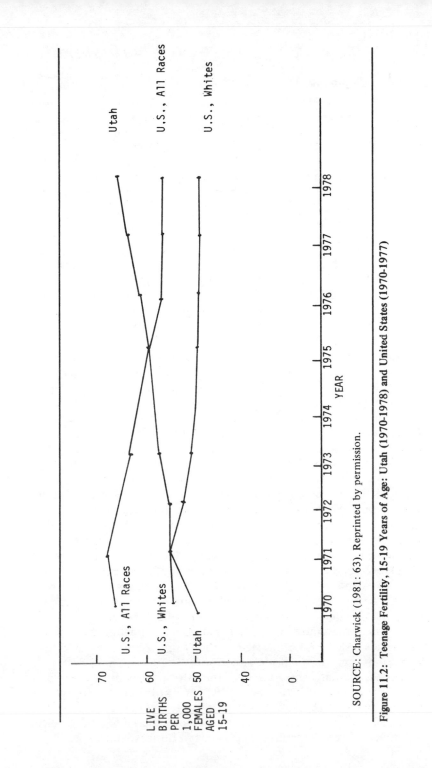

SOURCE: Charwick (1981: 63). Reprinted by permission.

Figure 11.2: Teenage Fertility, 15-19 Years of Age: Utah (1970-1978) and United States (1970-1977)

In a more detailed analysis, Chadwick (1981) shows that most of the teenage pregnancies in Utah occur in the 18-to-19-year-old range (67 percent) and that those ages have the lowest out-of-wedlock birthrate. Thus to lump all teenage pregnancies into one category obscures the real issue, namely, births out of wedlock. In that category, Utah has consistently been the lowest or next to lowest state reporting illegitimacy statistics. In 1977, "Utah had 48 out-of-wedlock births for every 1,000 live births while the national average was 155" (Chadwick, 1981: 72).

Age at Marriage

Utah has had one rather consistent trend in comparison to national statistics, namely, a younger age at marriage for both bride and groom. While age at marriage has been rising slightly since 1972 for both Utah and the United States in general, the U.S. age has been rising faster than the Utah age, so that the gap between the two has been widening.

Since young marriages seem problem prone, if Mormons are marrying young, it could portend difficulties for such marriages. Unfortunately, good data are not currently available to provide insight into how young marriages fare in the Mormon culture. the only data available that hint toward some possible conclusions are reported by Cannon and Steed (1969). They sampled from the marriages performed in four Utah counties in 1955 and then contacted the couples in 1968 to determine the present status of their marriages. Their analysis by age at marriage showed the typical negative relationship between age at marriage and divorce. For the low religious commitment couples, there was a negative relationship between the age at marriage and divorce. For example, 50 percent of those with low religious commitment (were not married in the LDS temple) who were 15 or younger when they married were divorced; 33 percent of those 16 years old at marriage were divorced; 20 percent of those 17 years old at marriage; and 11 percent of those 18 years old at marriage. There were so few divorces for the temple-married group that no patterns were discernible. Those divorces that did occur did not seem to be related in any particular pattern to the age at marriage categories. Also, those married in the temple tended to have fewer very young ages of the bride and groom.

If the promarriage values of the Mormon culture and values against premarital sex combine, as some have suggested (Christensen, 1976: 68), to encourage early marriage and these marriages are performed outside the temple, then it logically follows that those Mormon families face a dismal future as far as stability is

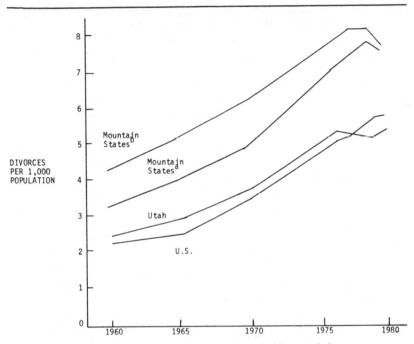

SOURCE: Bahr and Goodman (1981: 33). Reprinted by permission.
a. This profile is the median of divorce rates for the eight mountain states considered individually, and therefore is not as affected by Neveda's inordinately high divorce rate as the profile based on total divorces in the region.
b. Arizona, Colorado, Idaho, Montana, Nevada, New Mexico, Utah, and Wyoming.

Figure 11.3: Divorce Rates (per 1000 population) in the United States, Utah, and the Mountain States, 1960, 1965, 1970, and 1975-1978

concerned. It is probably safe to assume that many of the young, nontemple marriages are performed because the bride is pregnant, thus having the problems of this additional stigma. More study is needed to better understand the problems of early marriages in the Mormon subculture.

Divorce

Given that Mormonism places such a premium on family life and emphasizes marital commitment into the eternities, and that Utah is about 75 percent Mormon, one would logically conclude that Utah should have a low divorce rate compared to the national average. Such is not the case. Figure 11.3 presents the comparison for the United States, Utah, and mountain states regional divorce rates. For most of the past two decades, Utah's divorce rate has been above the national average.

However, when compared to states in the mountain region, Utah is considerably lower. A state-by-state comparison by Bahr and Goodman (1981: 36) shows that Utah consistently ranks lowest. These researchers discuss some of the possible reasons that the Utah rate is as high as it is. Chief among the suspected causes is the number of young marriages discussed above, relatively lenient divorce laws, and migrant divorce (Bahr and Goodman, 1981: 39-44). Even with the above speculations, questions still remain as to what the divorce rates are in Mormon families and how Mormon rates compare to those for non-Mormons.

Good research evidence to answer these questions is not available currently. The only data come from a variety of studies of Mormon families using different samples and methodologies over the last three decades. Thus conclusions drawn across these studies must remain very tenuous. Table 11.2 presents a summary of the findings.

Two general patterns are discernible. The first is that Mormons have a lower divorce rate than non-Mormons. The second is the familiar one that the more religiously committed families have the lowest divorce rates. The temple-married Mormons have an unusually low divorce rate. They are about six times less likely to divorce than are Mormons married in civil ceremonies (see Table 11.2). If the temple-married Mormons have an unusually low divorce rate, then it logically follows that inactive or noncommitted Mormons must have an unusually high divorce rate.

Recent research comparing interfaith marriages for Mormon and non-Mormon marriages adds additional information about the influence of religion on divorce (Bahr, 1981b). The research replicates an obvious finding of the lower divorce rate for Catholics, Protestants, and Mormons who marry within their own faiths. Of the three, Mormons have the lowest divorce rate, but the differences are small.

A second pattern is that couples in which the husband has no preference about religion while the wife does have a relatively low divorce rate. Those groups of couples with wives of Catholic, Protestant, or Mormon religions with the husband having no religious preference have divorce rates only slightly higher than intrafaith marriages. This pattern probably means that in these marriages religious beliefs are not a source of conflict, since the wife traditionally makes the major decisions about family and religious concerns, for example, taking children to church and having them taught in religious settings.

TABLE 11.2 Divorces by Type of Marriage for Mormon and Non-Mormon Marriages

Researchers	Sample	Data	Mormons Temple	Mormons Church	Mormons Civil	Non-Mormons Church	Non-Mormons Civil
Widstoe (1948, 1952)	LDS marriages performed in SLC, St. George, and Arizona in 1936	LDS church records	6.4	15.6	19.4		
Kunz (1964)	451 students from 2 western universities	questionnaire	2.2		12.3	19.3	23.7
Cannon (1966)	Utah population	Utah vital statistics	1:8			10.2	
Cannon and Steed (1969)	548 LDS persons from various counties in Utah	interview	2.8	12.3			
Goodman and Bahr (1978)	population of Utah	vital statistics divorce records		9.7		19.4	
Bahr (1978)	3 samples at different times from Washington, Montana, Idaho, Utah, Wyoming, Colorado, Nevada, Arizona, and New Mexico	questionnaire	5		33		

NOTE: Those values appearing with arrows on either side are for all groups contained within the arrows, since the original research did not present values for the respective subgroups.

279

A third pattern is also evident. As Bahr (1981b) observes, "Divorce rates for Mormon husbands are lowest if their wives have no religious preference, higher if they are Protestant, and highest if they are Catholic. The same order appears for Mormon wives in interfaith marriages: they are least likely to divorce husbands having no religious preference and most apt to divorce Catholic husbands." The same relationship holds for Catholic husbands and wives and for mixed marriages among the Protestants where the wife is the Protestant. This pattern in the data suggested to Bahr (1981b: 257) that there is a "direct relationship between divorce-proneness and the conservative/traditional/authoritarian nature of the religion with which the spouse is identified." Thus Mormons marrying Catholics (at least in Utah) have a relatively high divorce rate.

These findings underscore the importance of religious commitment as it relates to marital stability. When husband and wife are of the same religion the divorce rate is low, but when they are of religiously mixed marriages where the religions stress the importance of high religious commitment to marriage within their own faith, these mixed marriages will experience relative instability.

From the above it seems logical to conclude that highly committed Mormons are again different from inactive Mormons, who are more likely to marry outside their faith. The divorce data, when combined with the fertility data and the sexual values data, give further evidence of the polarization of lifestyles and values between active and inactive Mormons.

Sex Roles

Research evidence is virtually nonexistent that compares the extent to which children reared in Mormon families either accept or reject traditional sex roles. It seems logical to conclude that acceptance of traditional sex roles would be relatively high for active Mormon families. This follows from the theological position discussed earlier, which sees men and women as different and their differences complementing each other as they create a unity through marriage. Each is a help*meet* (Genesis 2:18) for the other. The Old English word "meet" means a "suitable helper." It does not mean a "helpmate." Thus man and woman are suitable for one another and their highest potential can only be attained as they create a oneness through temple marriage leading to eventual godhood. In addition to the theological underpinnings, research shows that children will tend to model the gender-linked behavior of the same-sex parent (Rollins and Thomas, 1979). It seems reasonable to assume that Mormon parents would more frequently engage in gender-linked behaviors. Research is needed, however, to test these assumptions.

Some research does exist that compares husband-wife power in conjugal decision making for Mormons and non-Mormons as well as for subgroups within Mormonism. Beginning with Strodbeck's (1950) research, the evidence generally supports the conclusion that husbands in Mormon families have more decision-making power than do non-Mormon husbands. However, those who have reviewed available research conclude that the evidence is "somewhat contradictory" (Campbell and Campbell, 1977: 399). Some findings seem to indicate that Mormon families are democratic, with egalitarian husband-wife relations (Christopherson, 1963; McBride, 1963), while other research presents evidence for the more traditional husband dominance pattern (Christopherson, 1956; Wise and Carter, 1965).

Thomas (1979) measured conjugal decision making across religious, child-raising, economic, and home-related areas and analyzed it in five different levels of religiously committed Mormon families. In general, the higher the religious commitment, the more influence the husband had in conjugal decision making, with the exception of one of the five groups of families. The other clear finding is that the Mormon families with high religious commitment report egalitarian decision-making patterns, with the score only slightly above the point at which husbands and wives share equally in decision-making power. The low religious commitment families tend to be characterized by a pattern of the wife making most of the decisions. In these families, the husband's low score may more accurately reflect his relative absence from family-related issues, since these families tend to come from the lower educational and occupational social class strata. The emphasis on family in Mormonism may tend to involve the father more in decisions related to family affairs that have traditionally been seen as the domain of the wife, namely, religious, child-rearing, and home-related decision areas. The available evidence probably warrants the hypothesis that Mormon conjugal relations are not characterized by husband-dominant relations.

While Mormon theology emphasizes the importance of the woman's role in the home, the expectations for the woman's role outside the home are not as well defined or understood. There is evidence from research on educational attainment that seems to indicate that Utah women are underrepresented in advanced degrees compared to the rest of the United States (McDonald, 1981a, 1981b). This is in sharp contrast to the overall high educational attainment by citizens of Utah in general. In addition, women college graduates are overrepresented in such "traditionally female-dominated fields as interior decorating, education, and home economics" (McDonald, 1981a: 184). Thus it appears that Utah women, and, therefore, Mormons, are not encouraged to pursue nontraditional careers. This has obvious implications for some concerns of the women's rights movement and is an issue that will undoubtedly be highlighted in the coming decades whenever sex roles are discussed in Mormonism.

Socialization

Not a great deal of research evidence exists on parent-child relations in Mormon and non-Mormon comparisons. The conclusion that Mormons are very similar to non-Mormons in child-rearing practices seems to be supported by the limited available research. Kunz (1963) found the Mormons were not given to more discipline than non-Mormons and were quite willing to accept child-rearing advice from both Mormon and non-Mormon sources. Some research (Thomas and Weigert, 1971; Weigert and Thomas, 1972, 1979) has found similar patterns in Mormon adolescents' relations with their parents as predictive of the adolescents' religiosity. For both Catholics and Mormons, emotional support and acceptance from parents was positively related to adolescent religiosity. The parental control dimension for Mormons seemed to better predict, in a positive direction, adolescents' religious activity than it did for Catholics. In short, children raised in supportive family environments will be less likely to turn to alternative values in peer or other social contexts (Thomas et al., 1974).

Mormon parents may be described as affectionate, inclined to establish and enforce rules, and very concerned about their children's welfare. There is some suggestive evidence, however, that for some highly committed fathers, there is a tendency to express less emotional support towards sons (Thomas, 1979). If this decreased support from highly religious fathers toward their sons is replicated in additional research and shown to be characteristic of the more religious Mormon families, it could be seen as a possible forerunner for social-emotional problems for some Mormon sons. Past research (Rollins and Thomas, 1979) has shown that in the absence of emotional support from parents, children have more difficulty developing social competence skills. They exhibit a proneness for a variety of social-emotional problems along the lines of aggression, drug abuse, and learning disabilities.

Since Mormons place great importance on missionary work and encourage young men over 19 years of age to fill a 2-year mission at their own expense, a central question is how well do the socialization processes work in encouraging the young men to fill missions? Preliminary analysis of church data from the United States and Canada by the LDS church evaluation studies show that of children born to Mormon parents, 40 percent go on church missions. Considering the commitment of 2 years out of their lives at a time when formal schooling and occupational training become important, along with the cost of thousands of dollars over the 2-year period, 40 percent seems remarkably high. There is some indication that the percentage of young men filling missions for the church has generally increased over the past 60 years. This pattern of increased commitment generally among active church members appears to be occurring across a number of different indicators of religious commitment.

CONCLUSION

The strength of Mormonism does not appear to be waning. Within the last three decades, observers (O'Dea, 1957, 1972; Bellah, 1978; Benz, 1978) have commented on Mormonism's staying power. In the 1950s and 1960s no one predicted the upsurge in Mormon activity or conversions that occurred during the 1960s and 1970s (Stark and Bainbridge, 1980). While many churches were struggling to maintain membership, the Mormons were wondering how they were going to accommodate the growth (Duke and Johnson, 1981). Many of those converts were families who saw new meaning in their lives together as husbands, wives, and children.

As these many converts enter the church, they will continue to add vitality as well as bring new challenges. Social control will be maintained to the extent that the church, in the form of its many organizations, can marshal its energies to offer emotional support systems to these convert families. Since Mormonism is relatively high on the control dimension required of its members, it will need to provide sufficient emotional support. There is some research showing that social institutions such as the family that attempt to exercise control in the absence of sufficient social support systems may generate behavioral problems in the form of rebellion, deviance, rejection of values, or the like. Conversely, institutions that are high on the social support dimension are characterized by internalization of values, development of social competence skills, low incidences of nonconforming rebellious or deviant behavior, and relatively high feelings of self-esteem and happiness (Thomas et al., 1974, Rollins and Thomas, 1979).

Mormonism will probably succeed in the decades ahead to the degree the church becomes a supportive system to the family rather than a competing institution for the family members' time and energies. Given the emphasis on family observed over the past years in Mormonism, and Mormonism's past record of creative response to challenges, it is likely that it will be successful in meeting the challenge of growth by increasing the amount of social support given to the institution of the family.

A religion with a large family ethic, a sexual ethic that approves sexual relations only in marriage and that, as Christensen (1976: 68) says, is "among the strictest in the world," and an ethic that says that men and women can only achieve their greatest potentials together will encounter and generate strain in contemporary society. This strain will likely increase in a society that, among other things, generally accepts a small family ethic, believes that sex is potentially good as long as it is between consenting persons, and sees many aspects of domestic life as millstones around the neck of the wife, preventing her from reaching her real potential for a full and meaningful life.

The tendency in Mormonism to emphasize the family organization over priesthood or other church-related organizations (Shipps, 1978) contrasts markedly with those tendencies in the larger society to devalue family forms and functions. As lifestyles outside the family become the more dominant forms, especially for women, those Mormons not embedded in family relations, such as single adult men and women, divorcees, the widowed, and the orphaned, will feel increasingly more estranged and isolated in Mormonism. As polarization in lifestyles increases between active and inactive Mormons, the greater the probability for those not enmeshed in family relations to define themselves, and be defined by others, as peripheral to the hub of Mormonism. The mesh of family and nonfamily roles for Mormon men and women, especially the latter, will be one of those areas in which Mormon creativity and resourcefulness will be tested in coming decades.

As Mormon women carve out meaningful roles for themselves both in and out of the family in a society that is seriously questioning past division of labor arrangements, we see two symbolic presentations of women's activities as being especially helpful. The first of these is the description of Eve encountered in Mormon scripture and the second is the role of the woman in temple ordinances.

Adam, in Mormon theology, never really does much until he wakes from his deep sleep and finds woman, Eve, on the scene. It is then that important things begin to happen, and Eve figures centrally in most of these. When the two must earn their bread by the sweat of their brows, eve "labors" with Adam. The two of them are repeatedly taught by God, and Eve in turn instructs Adam about some of the more important teachings. The two offer sacrifices and Eve, along with her husband, teaches their children and mourns over their wickedness, and seeks the Lord in prayer (Pearl of Great Price, Moses 5). The image is of a very capable and active Eve.

Likewise, the image of woman portrayed in temple ceremonies and ordinances is one of great capability with much important work to do. Without women performing sacred preparatory ordinances in the temple, the highest ordinances performed on this earth by men and women could not be completed. Thus the temple ceremonies are in that sense symbolic of men's and women's highest potential: alone the necessary ordinances cannot be done, while together and in unity man and woman develop their highest divine potential.

NOTES

1. O'Dea's works undoubtedly constitute the best set of works on Mormonism written by a non-Mormon social scientist. As a sociologist, O'Dea lived among the Mormons and devoted much of his professional writing to an analysis of Mormonism. His articles and books appeared from the 1950s to the 1970s. Arrington (1966: 22), a leading contemporary Mormon historian, says that O'Dea's works "offer unquestionably the best 'outside' view of Mormon thought and practice now available." See the references for some of O'Dea's works on Mormonism.

2. Bushman, a Mormon, is a professor of history at Boston University.

3. Among Mormon intellectuals, Hugh W. Nibley is without peer. He is Professor Emeritus of Ancient Scripture at Brigham Young University. For an annotated and selected list of over 90 of his articles and books published from 1926 to 1977, see the bibliography in *Nibley on the Timely and the Timeless* (1978: 307-323).

4. I am currently a practicing Mormon and a professor of sociology at Brigham Young University; I am married, with 6 children. From 1975 to 1981, I served as a bishop, which is a lay priesthood calling in the church with the responsibility of directing the ecclesiastical and temporal affairs of a ward (congregation) of about 600 members. I am currently a member of a Stake High Council, which is an ecclesiastical governing body of 12 men responsible for the church programs in a stake. A stake is an ecclesiastical organization in the LDS church similar to a diocese. Each stake consists of 6 to 10 wards and is presided over by a stake president, who is assisted by two counselors, an executive secretary, and the Stake High Council.

The advantage of an "insider's" treatment of such a topic is the possibility that greater understanding of Mormonism can be given. As Arrington and Bitton (1980: xiii) note, some things "can never be understood adequately except from within." I think this is especially true of Mormons' views of the family as it pertains to the premortal existence, this world's experience, and the family in the postmortal existence. The problem with the insider's exposition is that the zeal for that being described and analyzed may create something less than an objective assessment as judged by "outsiders." The debate between the relative merits of insiders' versus outsiders' evaluations will obviously never be settled once and for all since there are advantages and disadvantages to each. My hope is that by giving a description of Mormonism from an insiders' view, I will give the reader a more adequate feel for basic Mormon values as they relate to the family. I am hopeful that the reader will also better see possible points of tension between the Mormon family and the larger society.

Thus the first part of this chapter is written from an insider's point of view. It conveys an absolutistic tone of belief in the tenets of Mormonism, and does not present a historical analysis of the development of Mormon beliefs. I recognize that Mormons of differing historical times would vary as to the degree of their acceptance of the views expressed in the first section of this chapter. I have tried, however, to present the contemporary mainstream position in as simple and straightforward a manner as possible. This allows me to highlight the central role of family in Mormon theology and to call attention to the leap of faith that Mormonism asks of its believing and practicing members. The second part of the chapter addresses more traditional social science research and is therefore more tentative and qualified, since analysis in the social sciences is always historically bound.

5. The general outline of Mormon theology emphasizes creation out of eternally existing matter, spiritual birth to celestial parents, family units consisting of "sealed" linkages between generations, and attainment of Godhood with the attendant work of creating and peopling worlds. However, the consequences and interrelationships of such beliefs have not been carefully worked out by Mormon philosophers and theologians. Non-Mormon observers such as O'Dea, Shipps, and Woodward have pointed to this pressing need for more careful analysis. Woodward (1980) wishes Mormons would give more careful thought to some of the theological problems inherent in a religion that does not address the qualities of what a godlike life would entail. O'Dea (1972) sees a need for Mormons to become more committed to the benefit of a contemplative life rather than be committed to activity for activity's sake. Shipps (1978) observes that the essence of Mormonism's theology has not yet "distilled," but will do so as the central ideas are tested in the process of acculturation as Mormonism meets its international church.

6. For a discussion of the dominance of these themes in Mormon thought, see O'Dea (1957) or Arrington and Bitton (1980).

7. While no one is sure about the margin of error in Mormon membership records, some informal attempts at estimation have suggested that the rate may be as high as 20 percent. Each ward is the basic record-keeping unit of membership records and lay clerks are called to process all the information. Such clerks will work for an average of about two to three years and then will be replaced by others. This changeover in personnel, as well as the never-ending changes in family composition, creates accuracy problems. The church is continually trying to improve, and, with the advent of computerized systems, the error margin should be significantly reduced.

8. The crude birthrate is not a good index of fertility because anything that changes the population structure will change the crude birthrate, even though the actual number of children being born to women of childbearing age may not have changed.

REFERENCES

Ahlstrom, S. E. (1972) A Religious History of the American People. New Haven, CT: Yale University Press.

Arrington, L. J. (1966) "Scholarly studies of Mormonism in the twentieth century." Dialogue 1: 52-53.

———— and D. Bitton (1980) The Mormon Experience: A History of the Latter-day Saints. New York: Random House.

Bahr, H. M. [ed.] (1981a) Utah in Demographic Perspective: Regional and National Contrasts. Provo, UT: Family and Demographic Research Institute, Brigham Young University.

———— (1981b) "Religious intermarriage and divorce in Utah and the mountain states." Journal for the Scientific Study of Religion 20, 3: 251-261.

———— (1978) Mormon Families in Comparative Perspective: Denominational Contrasts in Divorce, Marital Satisfaction, and Other Characteristics. Provo, UT: Family Research Institute, Brigham Young University.

———— and K. Goodman (1981) "Divorce," pp. 31-46 in H. M. Bahr (ed.) Utah in Demographic Perspective: Regional and National Contrasts. Provo, UT: Family and Demographic Research Institute, Brigham Young University.

Bellah, R. N. (1978) "American society and the Mormon community," pp. 1-12 in T. G. Madsen (ed.) Reflections on Mormonism: Judaeo-Christian Parallels. Salt Lake City: Bookcraft.

Benz, E. (1978) "Mormonism and the secularizations of religions in the modern world," pp. 282-293 in F. L. Tullis (ed.) Mormonism: A Faith for All Cultures.... Provo, UT: Brigham Young University Press.

Bushman, R. L. (1976) "The Book of Mormon and the American Revolution."
    Brigham Young University Studies 17 (Autumn): 3-20.
Campbell, B. L. and E. E. Campbell (1977) "The Mormon family," pp. 379-412 in
    C. H. Mindel and R. W. Haberstein (eds.) Ethnic Families in America. New
    York: Elsevier.
Cannon, K. L. (1966) "Utah's divorce situation." Family Perspective 1, 1: 10-16.
——— and S. D. Steed (1969) "Religious commitment and family stability for LDS
    marriage." Family Perspective 4, 2: 43-48.
Chadwick, B. A. (1981) "Teenage pregnancy," pp. 61-78 in H. M. Bahr (ed.) Utah in
    Demographic Perspective: Regional and National Contrasts. Provo, UT:
    Family and Demographic Research Institute. Brigham Young University.
Cherbonnier, E. L. (1978) "In defense of anthropomorphism," pp. 155-174 in T. G.
    Madsen (ed.) Reflections on Mormonism: Judaeo-Christian Parallels. Salt Lake
    City: Bookcraft.
Christensen, H. T. (1976) "Mormon sexuality in cross-cultural perspective."
    Dialogue 10, 2: 62-75.
——— (1962) "A cross-cultural comparison of attitudes toward marital infidelity."
    International Journal of Comparative Sociology 3: 124-137.
——— and C. F. Gregg (1970) "Changing sex norms in America and Scandinavia."
    Journal of Marriage and the Family 32, 4: 616-627.
Christopherson, V. A. (1963) "Is the Mormon family becoming more democratic?"
    pp. 317-328 in B. Porter (ed.) The Latter-day Saint Family. Salt Lake City:
    Deseret.
——— (1956) "An investigation of patriarchal authority in the Mormon family."
    Marriage and Family Living 18 (November): 328-333.
Clausen, J. A. (1966) "Family structure, socialization and personality," pp. 1-53 in
    M. L. Hoffman and L. W. Hoffman (eds.) Review of Child Development Re-
    search, Vol. 2. New York: Russell Sage.
Duke, J. T. and B. L. Johnson (1981) "The saints go marching on: learning to live with
    success." Utah Holiday 10 (June): 33-35, 37-42, 44-48.
Goodman, K. L. and H. M. Bahr (1978) Utah Divorce in National and Regional
    Perspective. Provo, UT: Family Research Institute, Brigham Young
    University.
Kunz, P. R. (1964) "Mormon and non-Mormon divorce patterns." Journal of
    Marriage and the Family 26 (May): 211-213.
——— (1963) "Religious influences on parental discipline and achievement
    demands." Marriage and Family Living 24 (May): 224-225.
Lee, H. B. (1973) "Strengthening the home." Church of Jesus Christ of Latter-day
    Saints, Salt Lake City. (pamphlet)
McBride, G. P. (1963) "Marriage role expectations of Latter-day Saint adolescents in
    Utah County." Brigham Young University (unpublished)
McDonald, L. B. (1981a) "Educational attainment," pp. 157-184 in H. M. Bahr (ed.)
    Utah in Demographic Perspective: Regional and National Contrasts. Provo,
    UT: Family and Demographic Research Institute, Brigham Young University.
——— (1981b) "Quality of education," pp. 185-203 in H. M. Bahr (ed.) Utah in
    Demographic Perspective: Regional and National Contrasts. Provo, UT:
    Family and Demographic Research Institute, Brigham Young University.
McIntosh, W. A. and J. P. Alston (forthcoming) "Lenski revisited: the linkage role of
    religion in primary and secondary groups." American Journal of Sociology.
Madsen, T. G. [ed.] (1978) Reflections on Mormonism: Judaeo-Christian Parallels.
    Salt Lake City: Bookcraft.
Mauss, A. L. (1976) "Shall the youth of Zion falter? Mormon youth and sex: a two
    city comparison." Dialogue 10, 2: 82-84.
May, D. L. (1980) "Mormons," pp. 720-731 in S. Thurnstrom (ed.) The Harvard
    Encyclopedia of American Ethnic Groups. Cambridge, MA: Harvard
    University Press.
Michaelsen, R. S. (1977) "Enigmas in interpreting Mormonism." Sociological
    Analysis 38, 2: 145-153.

Nelson, L. (1952) "Education and the changing size of Mormon families." Rural
    Sociology 17, 4: 335-342.
Nibley, H.W. (1978) Nibley on the Timely and the Timeless. Salt Lake City:
    Bookcraft.
——— (1975) The Message of the Joseph Smith Papyri: An Egyptian Endowment.
    Salt Lake City: Deseret.
——— (1967) Since Cumorah: The Book of Mormon in the Modern World. Salt Lake
    City: Deseret.
——— (1957) An Approach to the Book of Mormon. Salt Lake City: Council of the
    Twelve Apostles, Church of Jesus Christ of Latter-day Saints.
——— (1952) Lehi in the Desert and the World of the Jaredites. Salt Lake City:
    Bookcraft.
O'Dea, T. F. (1972) "Sources of strain in Mormon history reconsidered," pp. 147-167
    in M.S. Hill and J.B. Allen (eds.) Mormonism and American Culture. New
    York: Harper & Row.
——— (1957) The Mormons. Chicago: University of Chicago Press.
Rollins, B.C. and D.l. Thomas (1979) "Parental support, power and control tech-
    niques in the socialization of children," in W.R. Burr et al. (eds.) Contemporary
    Theories About the Family. New York: Macmillan.
Shipps, J. (1978) "The Mormons: looking forward and outward." Christian Century
    (August16-23): 482-487.
Smith, W.E. (1976) "Mormon sex standards on college campuses, or deal us out of
    the sexual revolution." Dialogue 10, 2: 76-81.
——— (1974) "The constancy of Mormon chastity," pp. 624-641 in G.M. Vernon
    (ed.) Research on Mormonism. Salt Lake City: Association for the Study of
    Religion.
Spicer, J.C. and S.O. Gustavus (1974) "Mormon fertility through half a century:
    another test of the Americanization hypothesis." Social Biology 21 (Spring):
    70-71.
Stark, R. and W.S. Bainbridge (1980) "Networks of faith: interpersonal bonds and
    recruitment to cults and sects." American Journal of Sociology 85/86: 1376-1395.
Strodtbeck, F.L. (1950) "A study of husband-wife interaction in three cultures."
    Ph.D. dissertation, Harvard University.
Thomas, D.L. (1979) "Correlates of religious commitment in Mormon families:
    some preliminary findings and a challenge." Presented at the Fourteenth Annual
    Virginia F. Cutler Lecture, Brigham Young University.
——— and A.J. Weigert (1971) "Socialization and adolescent conformity to
    significant others: a cross-national analysis." American Sociological Review 36
    (October): 835-847.
Thomas, D.L., V. Gecas, A.J. Weigert, and E.A. Rooney (1974) Family
    Socialization and the Adolescent. Lexington, MA: D.C. Heath.
Thornton, A. (1979) "Religion and fertility: the case of Mormonism." Journal of
    Marriage and the Family 41: 131-142.
Weigert, A.J. and D.L. Thomas (1979) "Family socialization and adolescent
    conformity and religiosity: an extension to Germany and Spain." Journal of
    Comparative Family Studies.
——— (1972) "Socialization and religiosity: an extension of previous research."
    Journal for the Scientific Study of Religion 11 (December): 389-394.
Widtsoe, J.A. (1952) "Does temple marriage reduce divorce?" Improvement Era 55
    (January): 14-15.
——— (1948) "Does temple marriage diminish divorce?" Improvement Era 51
    (January): 641-656.
Wilkinson, M.L. and W.C. Tanner III (1980) "The influence of family size,
    interaction and religiosity on family affection in a Mormon sample." Journal of
    Marriage and the Family 42, 2: 297-303.
Wise, G.M. and D.C. Carter (1965) "A definition of the role of homemaker by two
    generations of women." Journal of Marriage and the Family 27 (November):
    531-532.
Woodward, K.L. (1980) "What Mormons believe." Newsweek (September 1): 68-71.

12

FAMILY AND RELIGION AMONG THE MOONIES
A Descriptive Analysis

Joseph H. Fichter, S. J.

The members of the Holy Spirit Association for the Unification of World Christianity are commonly known as "Moonies." They are brothers and sisters of the Unification Church and like to call themselves the United Family. The whole church is perceived as a "True Family" in which the Reverend Sun Myung Moon and his wife are the "True Parents" of all members who are their spiritual children. One of the basic tenets of their revealed scripture, *Divine Principle,* is the "four-position foundation," which is manifested as "God, husband and wife and their offspring" (Holy Spirit Association, 1977: 32). The essential point to comprehend here is that religion is for them the most important ingredient in marital and familial love. This is not quite the same as saying with D'Antonio (1980) that "love is the most important ingredient in religion," although Unificationists are full ready to agree. These concepts require clarification as we propose to analyze the familial-ecclesial relation in the Holy Spirit Association.

THE FAMILY OF GOD

Who are the members of this familial-ecclesial system, and where do they come from? The original core membership consisted of Koreans who soon made converts in Japan. These Orientals came as missionaries to the United States and began to convert young Americans of practically all ethnic backgrounds, with names that are English, German, Irish, Italian, Polish, and French, but among the American minorities, more Orientals than blacks and Hispanics. The goal of Unification is aimed not only at believers of different religious orientation but also at families that grow out of interracial and international marriages. The United Family is meant to bring together all God's children regardless of their present creeds, races, or nationalities.

The church is growing so rapidly that demographic statistics have not been carefully gathered, and the available figures tend to shift. In the early years of my acquaintance with the church, I could write that "by some odd coincidence the majority of young Moonies with whom I have spoken used to be Roman Catholics" (Fichter, 1979). This is no longer the case, but it is commonly said within the movement that Catholics and Jews are disproportionate to their numbers in the American population. Some of the younger and less knowledgeable members say the Unification Church embraces all religions, "you don't have to give up your own religion when you join."

In most instances, however, these young people were disillusioned with their previous church organizations even while they maintained a strong personal belief in God. They did not come from a position of religious ignorance; most of them had been reading about religion and searching for an acceptable affiliation. Nor did they come from disadvantaged or broken homes. Barker (1980), who has researched Moonies in England and America, finds that their new religion "is not in compensation for material deprivation but rather is an *escape* from materialism." The young Moonies are in their mid-twenties when they join the church, have had more than average years of schooling, and have not suffered the psychic, social, or economic deprivations that are said to drive people into "deviant" religious sects.

Since the Unification Church is reputedly a "caring" community in which a familial spirit of love is expressed among the members, the assumption is sometimes made that young people are seeking a refuge from unloving homes, hateful parents, and families rife with hostility. As a matter of fact, most of them report that their families of origin are friendly, with fairly pleasant relations between parents and children and among the siblings. Obviously, the fully committed Moonies leave their homes and dedicate themselves to the service of the church. In most instances they maintain good relations with their parents. "The hypothesis that people become Moonies because they are seeking the family atmosphere they never had does not fit the facts nearly so well as the hypothesis that they wish to continue or repeat the experience of a close and loving family" (Barker, 1980: 396). Even those families that feel a "sense of outrage" to the point of kidnapping their children away from the church seem to be demonstrating strong parental love for them (Stoner and Parke, 1977: 216).

THE FAMILIAL-ECCLESIAL THESIS

Do we have here a church that acts like a family, or a family that acts like a church? While there is no evidence to support Sommerfeld's (1968) hypothesis that all trinitarian belief systems lead to a familial-type religious organization, or that all people who worship God the father build a patriarchal kind of church, the fact is that the Unification Church deliberately models itself on a family system and focuses its worship on God, the father of all creation. Jesus is not God, but is a "true" spiritual father. The Holy Spirit is not God, but is a "true" spiritual mother. The love between these two infuses a new life, a spiritual "rebirth," for the believer in Christ (Divine Principle, 1977: 216). All the Moonie members deliberately cultivate a religious family solidarity, although they were physically born into a variety of racial, ethnic, and religious backgrounds.

The religious beliefs and practices of the Unification Church are intentionally centered on family relations: wife and husband, parents and children, sisters and brothers. In studying the church itself we focus on the manner in which this religion promotes fidelity and family solidarity. Although the Moonies were refused corporate membership in the National Council of Churches, there can be no doubt that they constitute an authentic religion in terms of Durkheim's (1965: 62) widely quoted definition: "a unified system of beliefs and practices relative to sacred things, that is to say, things set apart and forbidden — beliefs and practices which unite into one single moral community called a Church, all those who adhere to them."

The church of Reverend Moon is still in its infancy, with aspirations to become a universal religion that "desires to cover the whole life of humanity." It is already well organized and tends to approach the "ideal" church type envisioned by Max Weber and elaborated by Ernst Troeltsch. It is overwhelmingly conservative and reaches out to the masses. Apparently, the Unification Church aims to utilize the state and the ruling classes and to weave these elements into its own life. As Troeltsch (1960: 331) remarks, "She then becomes an integral part of the existing social order; from this standpoint, then, the Church both stabilizes and determines the social order." Students of sociology will recognize this description of the universal *ecclesia* that is said to have been approximated by medieval Catholicism. This is no less than the Moonie ambition to unify world Christianity.

It is true that the Unificationists do not have a sacramentally ordained clergy, but they are led by a ministry of full-time functionaries. They are inspired by the divine revelation of the Old and New Testaments, but their central scripture is the volume called *Divine Principle*. Besides a full-time ministry and a holy book, the Unification Church possesses the four elements that sociologists find essential to every organized religion. This chapter shall investigate the manner in which the principles of marriage and family are found in each of them: (a) the theological creed, (b) the code of moral behavior, (c) the system of worship services, and (d) the structure of social relations.

The conceptual framework of this analysis is obviously that of the sociology of religion rather than the sociology of the family. Employing the familial construct would have required research of the Moonie system of family relations and examination of how it is influenced in practice by the Moonie religious system. The fact is that insufficient research data are available on the family life of American members to allow this approach, mainly because these Moonie families have not existed for even one generation. We have some preliminary information about institutionalized mate selection, which differs from typical American courtship procedures. We have much less research data about the marital institution among the Moonie couples, although we know the moral and religious principles governing this relationship.

The functional perspective seemed a useful tool of sociological research at a time when the family provided multiple activities: economic, educational, recreational, and religious. Murdock's (1949) classic anthropological research did not include religion among the four universal and essential functions of the family. The research report on sociocultural trends, however, done by Ogburn (1934) in the early 1930s, included a discussion of the religious functions of the American family. The Unification Church is determined to restore religion as an essential function of the family. While the religious principles are well known, and while family and religion are intertwined among the Moonies, the sociologist of the family does not yet have enough research data to make this functional analysis.

THEOLOGICAL BELIEFS

The nature of God and the doctrine of salvation are among the Moonie theological beliefs that are obviously familistic. The Unificationist sees God as a loving father who actually suffers because his heart has been wounded by the sins of his children. "Unification theology underscores the fact that the Almighty God is not only the source of energy, the origin and preserver of life, but also Father of Heart, Subject Being of Limitless Love" (Kim, 1976: 38).

God had intended from all eternity that human beings should form an intimate relationship with the Creator, a relationship of father and child, of lover and beloved, and thus be a reflection of God's perfect image and likeness. The God of the Moonies is not the unmoved mover, "the timeless Absolute of Greek philosophy." The nature of God in the Unification faith is similar to that of process philosophers such as Alfred Whitehead (1971), and of process theologians who see God as "concerned with the world; he is involved in its suffering and its tragedy."

The deeply personal encounter between the divine father and his individual child is the important first blessing, but it is only the initial step to eternal salvation. The second and essential step to salvation is marriage and family. The ideal divine-human relationship must be multiplied in human-human bonds, which have to be essentially in familial relations.

> Unification theology takes into account man's relatedness and responsibility by using the family as a model. For *Divine Principle* the God-centered family represents the best example of how God works in history. God creates men and women to seek togetherness. Their union leads to biological regeneration, personal fulfillment and social progress. As a base of four positions, to use the Unification theology term, the family ties which bind together God, husband, wife and children prove the fundamental pattern for all worthwhile forms of human relatedness. Hence, *Divine Principle* shows the family-centered foundation for the coming divine kingdom. An ideal society can be erected once a truly God-centered family comes into being [Kim, 1980: 76].

Quite aside from its relation to the larger society, the God-centered family appears to be a Confucian ideal that gives dignity to marriage and procreation because the child is born in collaboration of husband, wife, *and heaven,* so that "any one may be called the son of his mother or the son of Heaven" (Dawson, 1915: 145).

The establishment of God-centered families is not merely for the salvation of the individual involved, nor is it simply a foundation upon which the larger community, nation, and world can be built. It is the essential salvific link between the sinful past and the prophetic millennium. Without the first blessing, Adam and Eve were never able to realize God's "second blessing," which would have been achieved when they became husband and wife, forming one unity, and with their children establishing the four-position foundation. Without the "second blessing" or perfect parents who produce large numbers of perfect children, the human race could not be in readiness for the Second Advent. "The goal of history has been to prepare the foundation for the messiah, first at the family level, then the national level, and finally the worldwide level" (Bryant, 1980: 166).

Orthodox Christian doctrine holds that redemption for sinful human creatures comes through the suffering and death of Jesus Christ. The Unification interpretation of the *Heilsgeschichte* is that the adultery (fornication) of the first parents caused the spiritual death that has been visited on all their descendants and that the sacrifice of Jesus was sufficient only for spiritual redemption. Moon himself said:

> One of my most important revelations is that Jesus Christ did not come to die. He came to this world to consummate his messianic mission given by God, which was the establishment of the kingdom of God here on earth. Through his crucifixion, however, Jesus gave himself as a sacrifice for the faithlessness of the world, and by his resurrection, he established spiritual salvation [Sontag, 1977: 134].

The full restoration of the human race, therefore, had to require both spiritual and physical redemption. The Lord of the First Advent (Jesus) was killed before he could marry and originate the true family of God-centered persons, from whom there would emerge the promised Kingdom of God.

THE MORAL CODE

The second essential element in any organized religion consists of the system of morality, the code of behavior, that the members of the church promise to observe. The Moonies, like others in the Judeo-Christian tradition, accept the Decalogue as a generalization of the kinds of behavior that people in Western society should embrace. It is by following the law of God that they do the will of the father and creator who loves them and in this way constitute their first blessing of perfection in union with God. The "fallen nature" of man, however, derives from characteristics inherited from Lucifer by Eve and Adam and transmitted to their descendants. Satan is very real for the Moonies, and so is sin. The first sin of Eve was adultery (fornication), later shared with Adam. Theologian Kim (1976) observes that "adultery in the Talmud is considered such a serious sin that it can only be compared with idolatry and murder."

While the Unification code of conduct includes all the patterns of Judeo-Christian morality, both personal and social, the focus is on the "eschatological final sin," the sin of fornication. The Moonie leaders and members deplore this historical basic source of every other kind of immorality. They are saddened by the contemporary relaxation of sexual mores as evidenced in pornography, widespread venereal disease, teenage pregnancies, and premarital and extramarital affairs. In striking contrast, the Unification Church emphasizes celibacy before marriage and chastity within marriage. The *Divine Principle* explicitly states that

> the principal cause of the downfall of numerous nations, national heroes and patriots, was adultery, because the urge to commit adultery, the root of sin, was always at work in the mind of man without his being conscious of it. We may be able to eradicate all other sins by elevating the ethics and morality of man through religion, education, and improvement of the economic and social system. But in present conditions no one can prevent the crime of adultery, which has become increasingly prevalent as the development of civilization makes human life easier and more indolent. Therefore we can never expect the ideal world to be established unless we can eradicate the source of this crime [Divine Principle, 1977: 75].

Turning from the proscription of sin to the prescription of virtue, Unification theology promotes the God-centered family as the model and source of all moral conduct. We are assured that "Reverend Moon did not consciously set out to create a syncretistic combination of Confucianism and Christianity," yet we are also assured that "there are obvious resemblances between Unification theology's family-centered ethic and Confucian morality" (Kim, 1980: 77). Filial piety is the first of all Confucian virtues, and family relations provide the model for social behavior. As among the Confucians, the Unificationists insist on the intimate relationship between family and religion. "The family has always been the center of Confucian life and ethics, and family life itself has demonstrated the nature of Confucianism itself, not only as a system of ethics, but also as a philosophy of religion" (Ching, 1977: 97).

The minimal and essential purpose of the family insitution, as viewed by sociologists, is to provide for the regulation of sexual relations and for the introduction of children into society and their education. It is probably correct to say that in all human societies "marriage defines the responsibilities of the partners in terms of sexual behavior, childrearing, inheritance and the provision of food and other necessities" (DeFleur et al., 1981: 443). The Moonies are impatient with casual talk of "open marriage," "alternative life-styles," and "creative divorce" in America, just as they are hostile to the communist system, which destroyed the extended family among the Chinese. The Unificationists are on the side of those experts who, as Lasch (1977) writes, "seek to rescue domesticity by reviving the extended family." They are unhappy about the "opposite solution, a futher shrinkage of the family," and about the contemporary "renewed insistence that companionship, not child rearing, is the essence of married life."

The Unificationists not only favor the multiple functioning and intergenerational extended family, but they think of their own religious fellowship itself as a large family. They see the "breakdown of the family" as a social and ethical calamity, an immoral handicap for both the society and the individual. There is, therefore, a logical relationship between the preservation of the total society, which depends on the preservation of marriage, and the restoration of the family, which in turn depends on the proper regulation of sexual conduct between the spouses. Adam and Eve failed in marriage because they were immature, and they failed therefore in constituting a God-centered family. As a result, all subsequent generations suffered. "Thus the restoration of marriage is understood by Reverend Moon to be the beginning of the restoration of mankind in the last days" (Flinn, 1978).

The virtue of chastity is in practice a personal pattern of behavior, but, because of its consequences for other human beings, it must also be recognized as a social virtue. While the central concept of sexual morality is intimately aligned with behavioral patterns of relations between male and female, the Moonies interpret its broader and deeper implications, and thus the full scope of morality. The principles of Unification moral conduct are based in the Judeo-Christian tradition of the Ten Commandments, and in the corporal and spiritual works of mercy as spelled out in the Beatitudes. Reverend Moon observed with some pessimism that "the degradation of the moral standard through drug problems, moral crises, and family problems is bringing American youth into a helpless position." In the larger view of society, he declared that he wanted to "revive the Christian spirit by igniting a new spiritual fervor with new spiritual truth" (Sontag, 1977: 156-157).

When the Unification Church is termed a "world-transforming movement" (Shupe and Bromley, 1979), the connotation shifts it clearly beyond the question of the personal purity and spirituality of the family. The ideology is geared to a complete social reformation of all socio-cultural institutions: education, politics, economics, and recreation. The collective concern for the whole of society is demonstrated in the varieties of "social works" in which the church has been involved. Critics tend to focus on fund-raising techniques and refuse to believe that the funds are widely used in social service to the underprivileged. As Sontag (1977: 21) remarks, "This church raises the issues of the deterioration of our family structure, the lethargy of many traditional religious institutions, the problem of religions intruding their goals into politics, and the religious control of money and power."

CULTIC PRACTICES

The third basic dimension of every organized religion is that of shared ritual and public worship, patterns of piety and spirituality, which the members practice in common to manifest their relationship with God. One of the most regular devotional patterns among the Moonies is Bible study and the discussion of scriptural texts. Most of them had received earlier instruction in the Bible, both Old and New Testaments, which they now view as "an imperfect record written down by people, many of whom didn't understand what God was trying to say. Obviously, we have to interpret it, and the *Divine Principle* is the outcome of that" (Bryant and Foster, 1980: 56, 63-77). The members believe that divine inspiration and revelation allowed their revered Father Founder to systematize God's whole scheme of creation and salvation. This belief is essential to an understanding of their system of prayer and worship, how it resembles and how it differs from conventional Christian spirituality.

The most solemn repetitive ritual among the Unificationists is the Pledge, a prayer recited in unison at five o'clock in the morning on every Sunday, on the first day of each month, and on the four annual holy days. The familistic significance of the holy days reflects the fact that the annual Parents' Day commemorates the wedding of Moon and his wife in Korea in 1960. Children's Day annually celebrates the birth of the Moons' first child the following year. The Pledge is recited on two other annual festivals, the Day of All Things, and God's Day. The latter emphasizes the members' rededication to God, to each other, and to the church's mission, and serves as a reminder of why they joined the church and what they hope to accomplish.

The less formal worship service is held twice a day wherever a group is living in community or in close proximity. Leadership of the service rotates among all the center members, and includes song, scripture reading, prayer, and an interpretative message. The evening service consists of song and prayer, but includes and is followed by spiritual conversation and religious sharing. Sunday services are more formal and are open to the public. Rice (1978) describes a sunrise service at the Belvedere estate in Tarrytown, attended by about 500 members who had come up from New York City. They listened, "seemingly captivated," to Reverend Moon's sermon. After the sermon "an associate led the audience in a fifteen minute prayer in which he asked repeatedly if they were willing to sacrifice themselves for the church." With the rising sun they sang a church hymn, after which Reverend Moon concluded the worship service with a ten-minute prayer in Korean.

Evangelizing and recruiting are essential spiritual tasks in which all members participate, individually and collectively. They are constantly seeking "spiritual children," newcomers who are welcomed joyously to affiliation with the Unified Family. The enactment of the spiritualized parental role is seen as practical experience in socializing converts and raising them in spiritual kinship. It is also a preliminary learning process in preparation for the physical and spiritual parental role with their own future children after marriage.

The emphasis for the recruit is on joining the spiritual Unified Family, rather than on just taking out membership in a church. The disordering of family relations came about through the infidelity of Adam and Eve, and the *Divine Principle* teaches that the rebirth of fidelity to God requires membership in the restored Unified Family. Lewis (1978) explains that

> this spiritual-social family is seeking to be that group of people whose relationships are being perfected. Consistent with this view the sacramental life of Unification Church members is focused entirely upon the process of unifying with the family of the Lord of the Second Advent. For Unificationists, the traditional sacraments of Baptism, Eucharist and Holy Matrimony happen all at once, one time only, on the glorious occasion of their "Blessing," when they are married within their Church and they are united permanently with their new family.

There is no formal baptismal ceremony to symbolize entrance into the Unified Family. The usual American pattern has been to invite the recruit to live in the local community until the personal decision is made to affiliate. Everyone has the "marital vocation," and is intended by God and by destiny for marriage and parenthood. The period of waiting for this real and special blessing is like that of a novitiate training in the many spiritual and material tasks of the ongoing church. Living like, and with, the Moonies, achieving the first blessing of a salvific spiritual union with God, and the maintenance of a celibate style of life are all preparatory to the well-documented "matching" of prospective spouses.

The prayerful preparation for the engagement ceremony precludes teenage marriages, or mixed religious marriages with non-Moonies, or any other rash and thoughtless spouse selection. An informal committee of already "Blessed Wives," women who have been married within the Unification Church, gathers information about the prospective marriage partners, whom they interview about their expectations and preferences in a mate. Those who are eligible for the blessing of marriage (24 years of age and 3 years of membership in the Unification Church) and who wish to be con-sidered at the next matching are required to fill out an application. With this background information, Reverend Moon has a rational basis for the assignment of members to their future mates, but the prospective marriage partners believe also that he is inspired by divine guidance in his decisions. Before accepting the decision, each couple retires from the public meeting to talk about the prospect, with the option of changing their minds.

The religious ceremony that publicly witnesses this "engagement" is a simple declaration of intention and not a solemn binding betrothal. The prospective spouses exchange a cup of "holy wine," with the expectation that the marriage will be solemnized when Reverend Moon so decides. Since the founder of the Unification Church is accepted as a "True Parent" of all the members, he is modifying the Oriental Confucian matching procedure by enacting a kind of "double paternity." Under the ancient rules of family discipline, the father of the young man makes arrangements with the father of the prospective wife, but Reverend Moon acts as "True Father" of both. This parental guidance in the choice of a mate among the Moonies is quite different from the traditional services rendered by the professional Jewish *shadchan,* an "outsider," who is paid a fee.

The public liturgy of the "Second Blessing" is the spectacular mass wedding ceremony that is conducted from time to time under the auspices of the "True Parents," Reverend and Mrs. Sun Myung Moon. Multiple weddings were inaugurated in 1961 for the 36 blessed couples who still form the main Advisory Council for the church. The numbers increased to 72 couples in 1962, 430 couples in 1967, 777 couples in 1970, 1800 in 1975, and 2075 in 1982. "The most prevalent feeling was that God had been arranging the whole thing all along, that their mates had been created just for them. Master, knowing God's heart and will for each of them, had brought them together" (Sontag, 1977: 167). The prospective spouses have their expenses paid by the church, including international air transportation to the city chosen for the ceremony.

The important symbolism of large multiple wedding ceremonies reflects the belief that a marriage must be much more than a private contract between two people. The mass wedding demonstrates to the world that these couples are part of a large religious family, a Unified Church of all Christians under the fatherhood of God. The members have been spiritually prepared for this central liturgical event that is said to have "elements of the traditional Christian sacraments, as well as much that is new or different. For instance, during the wedding ceremony, holy water is used in a baptismal fashion and holy wine is employed like the Eucharist . . . and the blessing has a soteriological meaning because through it we believe we obtain salvation. During the blessing ceremony, Unification theology declares, we are forgiven of our sins and freed from the accusations from Satan."

STRUCTURE AND POLITY

The fourth essential element of an authentic organized religion is its group formation, the permanent association of members under some kind of polity. In ecclesiastical language, the polity may range from a loosely organized congregational system, with emphasis on the autonomy of lower-echelon members, to a tightly structured episcopal system, with functional control residing in the top leadership. The Unification Church exemplifies a bureaucratic hierarchy, with authority emanating from the top leadership in the person of God's messenger and prophet. The well-known "Five Relationships" of Confucius, which are applicable to the extended Oriental family, have been modified in the contemporary Unification Church. Even in this modernized familial-ecclesial system, it should probably be said that "the relationships continue to require reciprocal duties and responsibilities, but the superior partners have more rights, and the inferior more duties" (Ching, 1977: 99).

From the perspective of organizational polity, the church may best be called a paternalistic episcopal system with the benign ruler occupying the seat of authority by "divine right." The earthly head of the church is obviously Reverend Moon, who acts in the capacity of vicar for God the father of all humanity while preparing for the Second Advent. He and Mrs. Moon are the "True Parents" representing the third chance that God has provided for the restoration of the world. Adam and Eve failed. Jesus, the second Adam, had no Eve. The third Adam and (the second) Eve are the Moon couple. This is not the role of messiah, but that of a precursor to the Lord of the Second Advent. "I had to start with the role of John the Baptist," said Reverend Moon, "in order to lay the initial foundation upon which I could construct my own mission," to proclaim the coming of the messianic age (Sontag, 1977: 131, 134).

Reverend Moon is not an ordained, or enthroned, or crowned and mitred head of the church, but he is the acknowledged earthly leader to whom his followers bow as to their true paternal and spiritual mentor. There are no ordained clergy in their church, no monsignors, archbishops, or eparchs. There is no sacred congregation of cardinals, but the "True Father" is assisted in governance by the members of the 36 blessed families, who trace back to the first mass public wedding of 1961 and who "represent the immediate personal foundation for the mission of Rev. Moon." His paternity depends also on the advice of informal counselors, and he has appointed a president for the church in America, Dr. Mose Durst, who had previously been director of the church in Northern California.

While some of the women members have done excellent missionary work and have exhibited fine leadership qualities, the state leaders are selected from among the experienced males. The local urban centers and communities are also generally under the charge of male leaders. Some feminists are likely to attribute the gender inequality among the Unification leadership to the patriarchal and Confucian structure of this ecclesial family. The ancient Korean kinship system had the female always subject to the male, the maiden to her father and elder brother, the wife to her husband, the widow to her son (Dawson, 1915). It should be noted, however, that the first Moonie missionary to America was a woman, so is the church's leading theologian, as well as the academic dean of the Unification Theological Seminary at Barrytown.

The development of the home church movement, which was instituted by Reverend Moon in the summer of 1978, promises to engage the energy and talent of Moonie sisters to a greater extent than the males (Fichter, 1982). In its initial phases the home church was known in some places as "Project Volunteer," because it obliged each Unificationist to give unpaid personal service to 360 households in the immediate neighborhood. As the experienced members move out of the community centers and settle down to their roles in family and occupation, they continue their missionary influence in the home church. It is also at the grassroots level of membership that room can be made for bachelors and single women who have not fulfilled the blessed vocation to marriage and family. Aside from the category of full-time committed Unificationists, there are increasing numbers of converts, laypersons with jobs and families willing to promote the doctrines of *Divine Principle* by ministry to their non-Moonie neighbors.

FAMILISTIC RELATIONS

The Unificationist dream that a religious collectivity can function as a large happy family is not a new one. The autonomous Benedictine Abbey is a celibate brotherhood that maintains a kind of family spirit as long as its members remain relatively few. A typical contemporary example is the Charismatic Renewal Movement, which tried to remain spontaneous, informal, and unstructured, but inevitably succumbed to routinization and institutionalization (Fichter, 1975). The evolution of the religious body from a small sect to a large *ecclesia* has been frequently described by sociologists who recognize the initial family model ultimately expands into the model of bureaucracy (Brewer, 1952).

Like other small religious groups with aspirations for intimate personal relationships based on family patterns, the Unification Church has had to respond to the demands of expansion, Sorokin (1947) described the evolution from familistic relations in the small community to contractual relations in the large association, and indicated that even relations within the family — husband and wife, parents and children — were becoming contractual. Reverend Moon believes that it is possible under religious inspiration to offset this development by insisting on a familial social structure for the church. This ideal is inculcated in the membership, as expressed by one American member: "I believe that he is my spiritual father. He is trying to bless us and bring us into perfection as individuals and as families. The idea of True Parents is a necessary symbol to bring mankind to the consciousness of being one family" (Sontag, 1977: 62).

At the lower echelons of the church, the members are siblings by spiritual adoption, sisters and brothers who are spiritual children of their "Father in the Faith," as the Catholic seminarian may think of the bishop as his spiritual father, or as the Catholic laity everywhere look with filial devotion to the Holy Father in the Vatican. The spiritual childhood of Moonies is a temporary status that changes with the passage of years. Practically all of the young Americans who are attracted to the Unification Church are unmarried, and their status of spiritual childhood endures while they are being socialized into the Unified Family. The concept of the church as a kinship group, and the vision of the total world society as an enormous extended family, must necessarily have places for the elderly as well as the young, for the poor as well as the middle class and wealthy.

People grow away from their families of origin and sometimes also leave their churches, but they cannot completely opt out of society. It seems quite clear that Reverend Moon's background was influenced by the fact that "the Confucian society regards itself as a large family" (Ching, 1977: 96). He seems intent on binding family, church, and society in an unbreakable web of personal relationships. Confucian philosophy blends with Unification ecclesiology. The pivotal role of the family is not only a source of socialization for young people in the virtues of respect, generosity, and compassion; it is also the continuing model of altruistic social relations in the larger community. "It personalizes and deepens the ties which bind men together to advance the common good. Thus, filial piety undergirds a stable, just and peaceful social order" (Kim, 1980: 78).

The filial piety of the spiritual child in the Moonie family translates to the humble obedience of the newest recruits to the church. From the perspective of social status, the hardworking fund raisers are mainly in the lower ranks, doing what are often considered disagreeable tasks. Motivation for soliciting money and for persuading newcomers to visit the local center is seen also as fulfilling the conditions of "indemnity," a form of penitential restitution to God for the sins of the world. "Life is organized around the center leader, whose closest counterpart is the abbot of a monastic community now made coed" (Sontag, 1977: 163). When a group is "on the road" together the mission leader often becomes the model, or "significant other," for younger members. Gradually, with experience, the evangelistic tasks meld into philanthropic tasks as the younger people become "middle" members and then assume more responsibility as "senior" members. As a matter of principle there are no salaried members at any level of the church organization, and everybody lives and works under a missionary system.

One need not be a prophet to suggest that while familistic relations may continue among smaller, primary, face-to-face groups in the church, and at the local level of the home church that limits itself to 360 households in the immediate neighborhood, the larger and more complex the Unification Church becomes, the more it will develop contractual relations in a bureaucratic organization. Sontag (1977: 201) also makes this prediction: "I see the movement inevitably evolving into another established church, and I am not sure that this can be prevented, although constant reform and renewal can keep the original spirit alive." If the church does not evolve into a bureaucratic structure, it is likely to collapse. Indeed, realistic evidence on this point is provided by Harrison's (1971) study of the American Baptist Convention, which sees itself as an informal congenial fellowship. Harrison concludes that if the convention had not built a bureaucratic structure, "the result would have been no effective leadership, complete separation of the local congregations, an absence of common symbols, limited inter-church communication, no denominational unity, and no evangelical program."

Whatever else may be said about the paternalistic and patriarchal polity of the Unification Church at the higher administrative levels, the brothers and sisters who live in communal centers and who work together on team tasks continue to demonstrate primary, personal, and familistic relations. Growing experience in the home church movement is extending this loving relation of service to non-Moonie strangers. Interviews with the Moonies and casual observation of their expressions of group solidarity indicate that they put a higher value on human relations than on social structures. They seem determined to focus on family life in the home church rather than on a parochial house of worship.

Gazing into the future, Reverend Moon says: "Gradually we will be moving into family settlements. We will have our enterprises and businesses. In the future we will have many, many places where families can be productive, raise their children, and build schools to educate the children." He has no intention to organize parishes, dioceses, judicatories, or vicariates. "I emphasize that our movement has always been centered upon families as the basic unit of the heavenly society. The family emphasis is always the same. This means that more blessings in marriage will be given, more children will be born, more families will be created. Then we will become elevated from the present communal type of centers to family-oriented homes. The family will always be the basic unit of happiness and cornerstone of the kingdom of god on earth and thereafter in heaven" (Sontag, 1977: 156-157).

REFERENCES

Barker, E. (1980) "Free to choose? Some thoughts on the Unification Church and other religious movements." Clergy Review 65: 365-368, 392-398.
Brewer, E. D. (1952) "Sect and church in Methodism." Social Forces 30: 400-408.
Bryant, D. [ed.] (1980) Proceedings of Virgin Islands' Seminar on Unification Theology. New York: Rose of Sharon.
——— and D. Foster [eds.] (1980) Hermeneutics and Unification Theology. New York: Rose of Sharon.
Ching, J, (1977) Confucianism and Christianity. New York: Harper & Row.
D'Antonio, W. V. 1980) "The family and religion: exploring a changing relationship." Journal for the Scientific Study of Religion 19: 89-104.
Dawson, M. M. (1915) The Basic Teaching of Confucius. New York: Home Library.
DeFleur, M., W. V. D'Antonio, and L. DeFleur (1981) Sociology: Human Society. Glenview, IL: Scott Foresman.
Divine Principle (1977) New York: Holy Spirit Association.
Durkheim, E. (1965) The Elementary Forms of the Religious Life. New York: Macmillan.
Fichter, J. H. (1982) "Home church: alternative parish," in J. H. Fichter (ed.) Alternatives to American Mainline Churches. New York: Rose of Sharon.
——— (1979) "Marriage, family and Sun Myung Moon." America 141: 226-228.
——— (1975) The Catholic Cult of the Paraclete. New York: Sheed & Ward.
Flinn, F. K. (1978) "Christian hermeneutics and Unfication theology," pp. 141-166 in D. Bryant and H. Richardson (eds.) A Time for Consideration. New York: Mellen.
Harrison, P., (1971) Authority and Power in the Free Church Tradition. Carbondale: Southern Illinois University Press.
Kim, Y. O. (1980) Unification Theology. New York: Holy Spirit Association.
——— (1976) Unification Theology and Christian Thought. New York: Golden Gate.
Lasch, C. (1977) Haven in a Heartless World: The Family Besieged. New York: Basic Books.
Lewis, W. (1978) "Is the Reverend Sun Myung Moon a heretic?" pp. 167-219 in D. Bryant and H. Richardson (eds.) A Time for Consideration. New York: Mellen.
Murdock, G. P. (1949) Social Structure. New York: Macmillan.
Ogburn, W. F. (1934) "The family and its functions," in Recent Social Trends in the United States. New York: McGraw-Hill.
Rice, B. (1978) "The pull of Sun Moon," pp. 226-241 in I. L. Horowitz (ed.) Science, Sin and Scholarship. Cambridge: MIT Press.
Shupe, A. and D. Bromley (1979) "Characteristics of world-transforming movements." Sociological Analysis 40: 326-328.
Sommerfeld, R. (1968) "Conceptions of the ultimate and the social organization of religious bodies." Journal for the Scientific Study of Religion 7: 178-196.
Sontag, F. (1977) Sun Myung Moon and the Unification Church. Nashville: Abingdon.
Sorokin, P. (1947) Society, Culture and Personality. New York: Harper & Row.
Stoner, C and J. A. Parke (1977) All God's Children: The Cult Experience. Radnor, PA: Chilton.
Troeltsch, E. (1960) The Social Teaching of the Christian Churches. New York: Harper & Row.
Whitehead, A. N. (1971) "God and the world," pp. 85-99 in E. Cousins (ed.) Process Theology. New York: Newman.

Epilogue

In this epilogue, we will delineate some of the enduring issues affecting religions and families in the United States, including their relations with the broader society in which they exist. These issues include: (1) the similarities the two institutions share, similarities that can place them in conflict with the values of other societal institutions; (2) the ambivalence of people in relations with these institutions; (3) the way in which religions attempt to deal with families that are in the process of rejecting traditional religious norms and values about family life; and (4) the consequences for all of us of the existing variety of religions and families.

With regard to the first issue, the authors of the several chapters make clear that families and religions share a number of characteristics. Their mutual advocacy of the values of love, compassion, and self-sacrifice, along with acceptance of others on the basis of their intrinsic worth sets the two institutions apart from the individualistic values emphasized in U.S. schools, workplaces, and governments. Families and religions also take a variety of forms in the United States, although this has only recently been recognized as being true of families. To varying degrees, Mormons, Catholics, and those lumped together under the rubric "fundamentalist" continue to see this variety as a phenomenon to be rigorously discouraged.

Families and religions are also linked by the changes they are undergoing, changes reflected in the increasing numbers of families no longer conforming to the husband-wife-children form, and the appearance of new religious sects such as the Unification Church, described in this book by Fichter. It is the state of the family that people inquire anxiously about, but Dashevsky and Levine, Hargrove, and D'Antonio and Cavanaugh have analyzed membership changes and clergy-congregation disagreements that suggest that religions, too, are experiencing discontinuity with the past. Finally, families and religions tend to see themselves as dealing with private matters rather than public concerns. Their purview is the complexities of interpersonal relations rather than the intricacies of societal arrangements, a point Hargrove discusses in her chapter on churches and modernization. This perception, of course, ignores the societal consequences of couples' family size decisions, abortion decisions, and the like.

But, too, much can be made of the characteristics religions and families share. Other institutions can be categorized with them. After all, to take just two examples, families and religions are not alone in being wracked by change, as witness the economy or, in their variety of forms, the levels and types of governing bodies. Moreover, one can question how much families and religions are really against the tide of values an individualistic society espouses. In fact, one issue affecting religions and families is their ambivalence toward these values. Hargrove, in her chapter on modernization, describes how the Protestant Reformation shattered the solidarity of a world of ascribed statuses legitimated and presided over by the Roman Catholic church. By creating alternatives to the universal Church, Protestants joined Jews as persons outside the established order. To the feudal Church's emphasis on salvation, Protestantism added other individualistic values, including the right of the individual to forswear group loyalty in the interest of duty to self and to the greater glory of God. Success in this world along with salvation in the next became a religious concern. The individual was the focus in both instances.

Families also hold individualistic values. Traditionally, men have mediated between the private world of the family and the public world of the economy, government, and community. Men's occupational activities have not only involved them in societal affairs, but have pointed up the individualistic values that men stand for in the socialization of children (Kohn, 1969). There was a gender split inside the family, with men representing individualistic values and women collective values. But women, too, encouraged individualism, if only for their menfolk. This situation is currently changing. The foregoing chapters reveal how this change is occurring differentially within and across religious groupings, and including the two major ethnic/racial minorities, the blacks and the Hispanics. There is some pressure on men from women to participate more within the home, and much greater pressure on women to move out into the broader society.[1] Here, as Aldous notes, they are more often placing their own welfare on a par with that of their families, as men have customarily done. Income, education, and length of time in urban centers further affect rates of change for men and women.

Individualistic values of achievement and activity, with their links to material comfort, are seductive, according to D'Antonio. At the same time, they have often been destructive of traditional family patterns. The fragility of intimate family ties today contrasts with the sense of duty and obligation of women's and men's relations to the traditional family. These relations were sustained and sanctioned by all major religions just a century ago, and continue to find varying degrees of support. But religions also have something to say about the

tangle of interpersonal relationships created by the variety of contemporary family forms, as the chapters in this volume indicate. How
they are dealing with this array of families is another issue that runs
throughout this book.

The Protestant churches are an interesting case since their
predecessors helped to create this individualistic society. Their so-
called main-line representatives appear to have made their peace with
families and their problems as they exist today. It is true that they and
all other religious groupings discussed here have not yet brought
women into their organizations on a basis of equality with men as
church functionaries, although their doctrines have been supportive
of women's rights. The patriarchal tradition has been ingrained in
Judaism and Christianity and continues to be influential despite calls
from men and women alike for greater gender equality in families and
religions as well as other social institutions.

Although main-line Protestant leaders appear to be ahead of
their members on this and other controversial issues, according
to Hargrove, the situation is different among Catholics. Here,
D'Antonio and Cavanaugh believe, lay members are ahead of church
leaders in their acceptance, if not approval, of divorce and
remarriage. Jewish leaders, too, may have lost touch with potential
members. As Dashefsky and Levine point out, Judaism's distinctive
values and ways of living, which set it apart from the surrounding
Christian society, seem to be losing influence. Assimilation into the
broader society, as measured by intermarriage, divorce, and low
fertility, nullifies the appeal of Jewish religious organizations.

From the chapters of Jackson and Fitzpatrick, we are able to gain
some understanding of the place of religions in the lives of blacks and
Hispanics in the process of transition to modernization. It is not at all
clear how much hold organized religion has on these groups. We are
hampered by a lack of evidence, but it appears that the functions that
religion has performed for blacks of providing comfort, group identity,
and a meaning to life in a grindingly racist society may be diminishing
in importance. Blacks have had some success in taking legislative
avenues to equality, although political leaders continue to come from
churches. More educated blacks also are enjoying middle-class levels
of living in recent years, which has weakened the attraction of religion
as a compensation for lack of worldly success. For these blacks,
religion may be serving the same function it does for middle-class
whites.

Hispanic families come from a number of different countries and
backgrounds, a point that is well worth the emphasis Fitzpatrick gives
it. Although they have shared an ostensible Catholic background,
these new arrivals to the United States have not centered their family

life about the church as did earlier immigrant groups. The absence of national parishes, reports Fitzpatrick, has led Hispanics to form their own Catholic religious groups and to be active in the charismatic movement. This appears to be another instance of laypersons and priests taking the initiative when church leaders are inactive. Fitzpatrick also points out that a large percentage are either unchurched or drawn to fundamentalist Protestantism.

But if there is a discrepancy between the views of leaders and communicants in some denominations, in others the two groups appear to be in agreement. The religious bodies analyzed in this volume by Hadden, Thomas, and Fichter take clear stands on family issues, and the Unification Church, Latter-day Saints, and fundamentalist church leaders try to enforce these doctrines. Members who disagree face the alternatives of becoming inactive or leaving the church. The difference between them and the main-line Protestants and Catholics is that for the latter the social control sanctions of excommunication just do not carry the weight they used to.

The churches discussed by Hadden, Thomas, and Fichter tend to be against the tide of individualistic values insofar as those values imply support for the Equal Rights Amendment and what that stands for. However, the Mormons and fundamentalists are supportive of individualism in macroeconomic matters. The mainstream Protestants, in their rhetoric at least, appear to reverse these positions. They tend to favor giving women more opportunities within the family and in the broader society, while they question individualism as traditionally conceived in the economy. Thus religious bodies as well as families vary in the individualistic values they support or deplore.

In dealing with issues of the variety of families and religions and the ways religions are facing the array of existing families, the issue of the consequences of this variety arises. Paradoxically, herein lies the strength as well as the weakness of religious bodies in the United States. Those that appeal to a broad constituency have difficulty enforcing positions on controversial issues. Their social control function is limited in large part to group pressure, because, as Sullivan details in her chapter, people no longer see this life as only a preface to what occurs after death. In the large congregations that tend to characterize the urban parishes (synagogues and churches), intimate ties between leaders and communicants and among the latter are more difficult to maintain. Persons who disapprove of widely publicized religious positions and who are not emotionally caught up in religious activities can "drop out" or join other bodies. Thus families can "shop around" for the religions they find consistent with their views and needs. They are less apt to tailor their views and needs to the doctrines of the religions into which they were born.

But the cacophony of voices with which organized religion speaks means that no one agenda of issues, whether that of the Moral Majority or some other organized body, becomes the focus of all religious concern. Families seeking certitude, support, or meaning can find comfort somewhere, regardless of their characteristics. The varying emphases of religious bodies also provide a constant source of criticism for the excesses of individualism in society.

Foreigners often remark about the seeming importance of religion in the United States, despite this country's unrelenting secularism. Because it is characterized by no one position, religion serves neither as a constant apologist nor as an adversary of the society. Thus it can work with all families to temper the uncomfortable coexistence both institutions experience in a society with antithetical values. Relegated to the private sphere by the power of economic and political institutions and by their plurality of voices, both maintain some sense of caring for their members. It is little wonder then that Americans give at least lip service to the importance of both institutions. Their very variety invites a search for understanding, just as that variety guarantees some sort of response to the search. And in a restless society, the emotional ties both institutions symbolize give some sense of stability.

In the end, then, both religions and families have adapted in varying degrees to the pressures for change created by a dynamic, individualistically oriented economic system that is sustained by a political system in which the focus also has been strongly individualistic. The values that undergird the macro systems also allow and encourage the plurality of family and religious forms that now dot the American landscape. The wide range of families and religions that have resulted reveal, for example, that some families that call themselves Catholic are closer in lifestyle and religious practice to some Protestants and Jews than they are to other Catholics. And so the patterns go. There is something for just about everybody in the supermarket of family and religious patterns. This may be one reason that such a large majority of Americans continue to say in annual polls, stretching over more than 20 years, that they are satisfied with their lives, their families, and their religions. But it may also help to explain why they think other people are not doing so well.

Religions will continue to act as mediating structures between families and the larger society. The evidence suggests that they will offer a variety of controlling and supporting features that many families will find helpful. Indeed, as religious leaders engage political and economic leaders in debate over the morality of nuclear war, there may be far-reaching consequences at the family level that we can only now glimpse through a glass darkly.

NOTE

1. Some of the reasons for this pressure, in addition to the high cost of living, are the greater education women are receiving and the fewer children they are bearing (Smith, 1979).

REFERENCES

Kohn, M. L. (1969) Class and Conformity: A Study in Values. Chicago: University of Chicago Press.

Smith, R. E. (1979) "The movement of women into the labor force," pp. 1-20 in R. E. Smith (ed.) The Subtle Revolution: Women at Work. Washington, DC: Urban Institute.

Author Index

Subject Index

About the Authors

JOAN ALDOUS is William R. Kenan Professor of Sociology at the University of Notre Dame. She is the author of *Family Careers: Developmental Change in Families,* coeditor (with Wilfried Dumon) of *The Politics and Programs of Family Policy: United States and European Perspectives,* and editor of *Two Paychecks: Life in Dual-Earner Families.* Currently, she is conducting research with David Klein concerning the effect of parent-child relations during the child-rearing years and the effect of family size on intergenerational relations of preretirement couples.

MARK J. CAVANAUGH is a member of the Congregation of Christian Brothers (C.F.C.). Currently, he is a member of the Brothers' community at Iona College in New Rochelle, New York, and is completing graduate studies at the University of Notre Dame, where he has taught courses in social psychology. His areas of interest include philosophy of the social sciences, social psychology, the work of the Institute for Social Research (Frankfurt School), and the sociology of George Simmel, as well as the sociology of religion.

WILLIAM V. D'ANTONIO is Professor of Sociology, on leave from the University of Connecticut, and Executive Officer of the American Sociological Association. He is Past President of the North Central Sociological Association, the Society for the Scientific Study of Religion, and the University of Connecticut and University of Notre Dame chapters of the American Association of University Professors. His research interests include the family, religion, ethnicity, and politics. He has published numerous articles in major journals, and is coauthor of *Sociology: Human Society* (with M. DeFleur and L. DeFleur) and *Female and Male: Dimensions of Human Sexuality* (with Elaine M. Pierson).

ARNOLD DASHEFSKY is Associate Professor of Sociology and Director of the Center for Judaic Studies and Contemporary Jewish Life at the University of Connecticut in Storrs. He earned his B.A. and M.A. degrees at Temple University and a Ph.D. in Sociology at the University of Minnesota; he also earned a bachelor of Hebrew literature degree at Gratz College. He studied at the Hebrew University and Hayim Greenberg College in Jerusalem. He is the author of *Ethnic Identification Among American Jews* (with H. M. Shapiro) and editor of *Ethnic Identity in Society*. Currently, he serves as consultant to the Hartford Jewish Federation and the national United Jewish Appeal, for which he is codirecting a study on nongivers (with Bernard Lazerwitz).

JOSEPH H. FICHTER, S.J., is Emeritus Professor of Sociology, Loyola University of New Orleans. He is a past member of the Council of the American Sociological Association, and President of the Southern Sociological Society. His current research projects include the study of family relations in cultic religions and work concerning the National Health Survey of Catholic Clergy. His recent books include *Rehabilitation of Clergy Alcoholics* and *Religion and Pain*, and he is the editor of *Alternatives to American Mainline Churches*.

JOSEPH P. FITZPATRICK, S.J., is Professor of Sociology at Fordham University. Father Fitzpatrick is well known for his studies of the Puerto Rican community, such as *Puerto Rican Americans: The Meaning of Migration to the Mainland* and (with D. Gurak) *Hispanic Intermarriage in New York City, 1975* (1979). He has been active in the Puerto Rican community. He is Vice-President of the Puerto Rican Family Institute, a member of the Board of the Puerto Rican Legal Defense and Education Fund, and a member of the Board of the Centro de Orientación y Servicios, a delinquency prevention program in Ponce Playa, Puerto Rico.

JEFFREY K. HADDEN is Professor of Sociology at the University of Virginia and Past President of the Association for the Sociology of Religion. He is the author of several books, including *The Gathering Storm in the Churches* and *Prime Time Preachers: The Rising Power of Televangelism* (with Charles Swann). He has also written several other books and many articles dealing with religion and society, including "The Private Generation," which appeared in *Psychology Today* and has been translated into seventeen languages.

BARBARA HARGROVE is Professor of the Sociology of Religion at the Iliff School of Theology in Denver. She is the author of *Reformation of the Holy, Sociology of Religion: Classical and Contemporary Approaches, Religion for a Dislocated Generation,* and (with Jackson Carroll and Adair Lummis) *Women of the Cloth*. She has taught previously at Hollins College, the University of North Florida at Jacksonville, and Yale University Divinity School. She also spent a year as a research associate at the University of California at Berkeley, working with a team studying "the new religious consciousness." She plans to spend an upcoming leave investigating the relationship of religion to the so-called new class.

JACQUELYNE JOHNSON JACKSON (Ph. D., Sociology, Ohio State University, 1960) was the first black female faculty member at Duke University. A pioneer in ethnogerontology, her research interests have focused on Negro civil rights movements, changes in the socioeconomic and health statuses of Negro women and of Negro aged, and factors affecting the stability and functioning of Negro families. In addition to her books, *These Rights They Seek* (1962) and *Minorities and Aging* (1980), she has written numerous articles and chapters for professional and popular publications. A founder of the National Caucus on the Black Aged and a former editor of the *Journal of Health and Social Behavior* of the American Sociological Association, she has also been active in many professional organizations.

IRVING M. LEVINE is Director of the Institute on Pluralism and Group Identity and Director of Program Planning for the American Jewish Committee. He currently teaches at Fordham University. He has previously served as a member of the National Equity Committee of the American Civil Liberties Union and of the Commission on Jewish Studies of the American Association for Jewish Education, and as Chairman of the Annual Convention of the National Association of Intergroup Relations Officials. He consults widely with government and private groups on urban and ethnic affairs.

TERESA A. SULLIVAN is Associate Professor of Sociology and Training Director of the Population Research Center at the University of Texas at Austin. A demographer with broad intellectual interests, she is coauthor, with Andrew M. Greeley, of *Young Catholics in the United States and Canada* (1981) and has contributed articles to *America* and *Concilium* as well as to many scholarly journals. She is currently conducting research on the mortality of Hispanics, using the Catholic parish death records from three southwestern states.

DARWIN L. THOMAS is Professor of Sociology and Past Director of the Family and Demographic Research Institute at Brigham Young University. Among his publications are *Population Resources and the Future: Non-Mathusian Perspectives* (1972), *Family Socializations and the Adolescent: Determinants of Self-Concept, Conformity, Religiosity, and Countercultural Values* (1974), *Social Psychology* (1980), and numerous journal articles. His research interests have focused on social psychological dimensions of family interaction. He is Program Chairperson for the Twelfth Annual Family and Demographic Research Conference to be held March 1984 at Brigham Young University on the theme "Religion and the Family."